The **LITTLE,** **BROWN** COMPACT **HANDBOOK**

Custom Fourth Edition

Jane E. Aaron

Additional Contributions by Kathy Sole
University of Phoenix

Taken from:

The Little, Brown Compact Handbook, Fourth Edition,
by Jane E. Aaron
Copyright © 2001 by Addison Wesley Educational Publishers, Inc.
A Pearson Education Company
Reading, Massachusetts 02494

This special edition published in cooperation with Pearson Custom Publishing.

Printed in the United States of America

10 9 8 7 6 5 4

Please visit our web site at www.pearsoncustom.com

ISBN 0–536–62854–8

BA 992986

PEARSON CUSTOM PUBLISHING
75 Arlington Street, Suite 300, Boston, MA 02116
A Pearson Education Company

Copyright Acknowledgments

FREQUENTLY ASKED QUESTIONS

The chapter titles on the left list the book's main topics. Across from the titles are questions commonly asked about the topics. Follow either a chapter title or a question to the appropriate page in the book. Or follow a blue-green bar to the appropriate tabbed divider, which contains a more detailed outline of that part of the book. For a complete detailed contents, see page 552.

VIII. SPECIAL WRITING SITUATIONS

Preface for Students

The University of Phoenix has produced this custom edition of *The Little, Brown Compact Handbook,* Fourth Edition, exclusively for its students. This edition is designed to meet the specific needs of University of Phoenix students and includes resources available only to University of Phoenix students, faculty, and alumni. This edition is the approved style guide for all University of Phoenix undergraduate and graduate business courses.

University of Phoenix students taking courses in the College of Undergraduate and Graduate Business, the College of Information Systems & Technology, and the College of General and Professional Studies may use either the MLA or the APA format in *The Little, Brown Compact Handbook* depending upon their personal or campus preferences.

For courses in the College of Nursing & Health Sciences, the College of Counseling & Human Services, and the College of Education, University of Phoenix campuses may elect to have students use the expanded coverage of APA documentation and format in this custom edition of *The Little, Brown Compact Handbook*, or, for full coverage of APA requirements, they may require students to purchase the *Publication Manual of the American Psychological Association*, Fourth Edition.

The Little, Brown Compact Handbook contains the basic information you'll need for writing in and out of school. Here you can find out how to get ideas, use commas, search the Internet, cite sources, craft an argument, and write a résumé—all in a convenient, accessible package.

This book is mainly a reference for you to dip into as needs arise. You probably won't read the book all the way through, nor will you use everything it contains: you already know much of the content anyway, whether consciously or not. The trick is to figure out what you *don't* know—taking cues from your own writing experiences and the comments of others—and then to find the answers to your questions in these pages.

Page ix details the many ways you can find information in the handbook. You'll want to be familiar with three symbols that highlight special information appearing throughout the book:

- The computer shown here signals tips for using computers productively for all kinds of writing activity, from discovering ideas through citing sources.

- The web shown here marks lists of helpful Web sites that can supplement the handbook. The Web addresses are as up to date as possible, but inevitably some sites will move or disappear. For more current links, see this book's own site at *http://www.awlonline.com/littlebrown.*

- The symbol **ESL** flags material for students using English as a second language, which is integrated throughout the handbook. A guide to all the ESL topics appears on page 551.

Before you begin using this book, you may need to clear your mind of a very common misconception: that writing is only, or even mainly, a matter of correctness. True, any written message will find a more receptive audience if it is correct in word choice, grammar, punctuation, and similar matters. But these concerns should come late in the writing process, after you've allowed yourself to discover what you have to say, freeing yourself to make mistakes along the way. As one writer put it, you need to get the clay on the potter's wheel before you can shape it into a bowl, and you need to shape it into a bowl before you can perfect it. So get your clay on the wheel and work with it until it looks like a bowl. Then worry about correctness.

Use a directory.

- "Frequently Asked Questions" (pages iv–vi) provides questions in everyday language that are commonly asked about the book's main topics.
- The "Contents" (page 552–555) provides an overview of the entire book.
- Detailed outlines on the tabbed dividers direct you to the material covered in each part of the book.

Use the index.

An alphabetical list of all topics, terms, and problem words and expressions appears on pages 509–550.

Use the elements of the page.

❶ Running head (header) showing the topic being discussed on this page.

❷ Chapter number and title.

❸ Web links in blue-green boxes: helpful sites on the chapter's topic.

❹ Key term for this discussion.

❺ Examples, always indented. Underlining highlights sentence elements and revisions.

❻ Page tab, containing the code of the nearest section heading (**27a**) and the symbol or abbreviation for the topic being discussed (**pn agr**).

❼ Computer symbol: tip for using computers effectively.

❽ ESL pointer for students using English as a second language.

❶ Agreement of pronoun and antecedent **205**

27 Agreement of Pronoun and Antecedent

Information on the pronoun-antecedent agreement:
http://webster.commnet.edu/HP/pages/darling/grammar/pronouns.htm From the Guide to Grammar and Writing.
http://owl.english.purdue.edu/Files/79.html From the Purdue Online Writing Lab.

The ANTECEDENT of a pronoun is the noun or other pronoun to which the pronoun refers:

Homeowners fret over their tax bills.
antecedent   pronoun

Its constant increases make the tax bill a dreaded document.
pronoun   antecedent

For clarity, a pronoun should agree with its antecedent in person, number, and gender.

Note A computerized grammar and style checker cannot help you with agreement between pronoun and antecedent. You'll need to check for errors on your own.

ESL The gender of a pronoun should match its antecedent, not a noun that the pronoun may modify: *Sara Young invited her* [not *his*] *son to join the company's staff.* Also, nouns in English have only neuter gender unless they specifically refer to males or females. Thus nouns such as *book, table, sun,* and *earth* take the pronoun *it.*

27a Antecedents joined by *and* usually take plural pronouns.

Mr. Bartos and I cannot settle our dispute.

KEY TERMS

PERSON	NUMBER	
	SINGULAR	PLURAL
FIRST	*I*	*we*
SECOND	*you*	*you*
THIRD	*he, she, it,* indefinite pronouns, singular nouns	*they,* plural nouns
GENDER		
MASCULINE	*he,* nouns naming males	
FEMININE	*she,* nouns naming females	
NEUTER	*it,* all other nouns	

pn agr
27a

❾ Section heading, a main convention or topic labeled with the section code, **27a:** the chapter number (**27**) and the section letter (**a**).

❿ Box defining secondary terms used on the page. Refer to these white boxes whenever a term is unclear. Otherwise, ignore them.

Preface for Instructors

For three editions now, *The Little, Brown Compact Handbook* has provided writers with an accessible reference, one that helps them find what they need and then use what they find. Combining the authority of its parent, *The Little, Brown Handbook*, with a briefer and more convenient format, the *Compact Handbook* addresses writers of varying experience, in varying fields, answering the questions they ask about the writing process, grammar and style, research writing, and more.

The fourth edition improves on the handbook's strengths as a clear, concise, and accessible reference, but it also takes on two subjects that are central to writing today: thinking critically and using computers efficiently and wisely. In the context of the handbook's many reference functions, the following pages highlight the most significant additions and changes.

A reference for writing with computers

The handbook offers practical advice for using computers in all phases and kinds of writing:

- Sixty-five new COMPUTER TIPS, for a total of ninety, integrate computer use with writing and research. The tips explain when computers can help and also when they cannot.
- Nearly two hundred new WEB LINKS in chapter-opening boxes give addresses of helpful sites that supplement the handbook.
- A new Part II, "COMPUTERS IN WRITING," includes three new chapters that encourage students to use the machines effectively for their writing situations:

  "ESSENTIAL COMPUTER SKILLS" covers file management, formatting, spelling and grammar/style checkers, e-mail, online collaboration, and Web basics.

  "DOCUMENT DESIGN" connects the principles and elements of design to academic, business, and publicity writing.

  "WEB COMPOSITION" covers principles of writing and designing for the Web.

A reference for researching with computers

New or expanded discussions of research with computers bring the handbook up to the minute.

- A new discussion and screen shot show how to find BIBLIOGRAPHIC INFORMATION FOR ONLINE SOURCES.
- An expanded discussion of WEB RESEARCH includes appropriate cautions and a detailed case study.

- An expanded discussion of EVALUATING ONLINE SOURCES includes a detailed checklist.
- A new section on ACKNOWLEDGING ONLINE SOURCES addresses issues of copyright and fair use.
- New ELECTRONIC DOCUMENTATION MODELS illustrate all styles: MLA, APA, Chicago, and CBE.
- A new chapter details COLUMBIA STYLE FOR ONLINE SOURCES in the humanities and the sciences and shows how Columbia can supplement the other styles.
- New lists give specific WEB RESOURCES for the academic disciplines.

A reference for research writing

The handbook already provided strong support for research writers: specific tips for planning, finding sources, working with sources, and writing the paper; detailed guidelines for MLA, APA, Chicago, and CBE documentation; and sample MLA and APA papers. Now, in addition to the material on electronic research, several changes have strengthened these chapters:

- Key concerns of research writers receive added attention: FORMULATING A RESEARCH QUESTION; DEVELOPING A RESEARCH STRATEGY, including tapping into one's own knowledge and balancing print and online sources; AVOIDING PLAGIARISM; INTEGRATING QUOTATIONS, including introducing, altering, and interpreting them; and DOCUMENTING SOURCES, a conceptual discussion addressing why disciplines' styles vary.
- A NEW SAMPLE MLA PAPER—"Who Pays the Bill for Internet Shopping?"—includes many marginal annotations on content and format.

A reference for critical thinking and argument

The handbook's concise coverage of argument is more useful and more prominent:

- A NEW CHAPTER, placed early in the book, links argument with critical thinking.
- A new discussion of CRITICAL THINKING AND READING includes a sample annotated reading and an extended example of analyzing a Web site.
- FALLACIES and ORGANIZATION OF ARGUMENTS receive expanded coverage.

A reference for grammar, usage, and punctuation

The handbook's core reference material continues to feature concise explanations and annotated examples from across the curriculum. The changes here are small but significant:

- Frequent computer tips spell out the uses and limitations of GRAMMAR/STYLE AND SPELLING CHECKERS.
- A new foregrounded CHAPTER ON EMPHASIS focuses on strong subjects and verbs and movement from old to new information.
- The new MLA STYLE FOR BRACKETS WITH ELLIPSIS MARKS receives detailed coverage and is clearly distinguished from other disciplines' styles.
- CHANGES IN EXAMPLES are now more visible, highlighted with color underlining instead of italics.

A reference for ESL students

The handbook continues to provide rhetorical and grammatical help for ESL students, all integrated into the rest of the book so that students do not have to distinguish between ESL problems and those they share with native speakers. The symbol **ESL** signals ESL notes and sections, and an ESL guide just before the back endpapers pulls all the coverage together in one place.

- TWELVE NEW ESL NOTES cover writing and research as well as grammar, bringing the total to fifty-nine notes and thirteen sections.

A reference for the writing process

In well-focused, practical chapters, the handbook provides tips on invention, the thesis, revision, and more.

- The opening chapter now includes a detailed CHECKLIST FOR ASSESSING THE WRITING SITUATION and an expanded discussion of PURPOSE.
- A new student work-in-progress on Internet communication provides examples at every stage, including first, revised, and final drafts.

An accessible reference

The Little, Brown Compact Handbook is an open book for students. As before, it features not only the convenient format of comb binding and tabbed dividers but also an unusually accessible organization, "Frequently Asked Questions" on the front endpapers, more than fifty summary and checklist boxes, a self-teaching text with minimal terminology and cross-references, and unique "Key Terms" boxes for essential definitions.

- The new COLOR DESIGN is more inviting for students but preserves the clean page format. Screen shots and other illustrations are now reproduced in color.
- COLORED TABBED DIVIDERS clearly distinguish the handbook's rhetorical, editing, research, and reference sections.

Supplements

Accompanying *The Little, Brown Compact Handbook* is a large array of supplements for both instructors and students, such as two books of exercises; a CD-ROM with both visual and audio explanations and other multimedia features; a companion Web site at *http://www.awlonline/littlebrown;* and the Daedalus Online writing environment. For more on these or any other supplements, contact your Addison Wesley Longman sales representative.

Acknowledgments

The Little, Brown Compact Handbook benefits from the generous and thoughtful comments of instructors who speak to sales representatives and editors, send me personal notes, and write detailed reviews. For this edition, I am especially grateful to the many teachers who communicated with me directly or through reviews: Michael E. Barrett, Moberly Area Community College; Michael S. Bodek, Bergen Community College; Terry Bowman, Southern Illinois University; Denise Coulter, Atlantic Cape Community College; David M. Cratty, Cuyahoga Community College; Juan F. Flores, Del Mar College; Jill Dix Ghnassia, University of Hartford, Hillyer College; Susan Halter, Delgado Community College; Candy Henry, Seton Hill College; Pamela R. Howell, Midland College; Shirley Kahlert, Merced College; Bill Lamb, Johnson County Community College; Faye G. O'Neal, Del Mar College; Nelljean M. Rice, Coastal Carolina University; Nancy J. Schneider, University of Maine, Augusta; Todd Slover, Hesser College; Vicky L. Trussel, Blue River Community College; Mary E. Vandiver, Henderson State University; Jenny Williams, Hazard Community College.

In developing this revision, I had the help of many creative people. Daniel Anderson, University of North Carolina, Chapel Hill, was the handbook's astute and unflappable technology consultant, a pleasure to work with. Sylvan Barnet, Tufts University, continued to lend his expertise in the chapter "Reading and Writing About Literature," which is adapted from his *Short Guide to Writing About Literature* and *Introduction to Literature* (with Morton Berman, William Burto, and William E. Cain). And Kathy Sole, University of Phoenix, provided invaluable help with the material on documentation and format.

Colleagues at and around Longman contributed intelligence, enthusiasm, support, and more: on the editorial side, Arlene Bessenoff, Donna Campion, Linda Stern, and David Munger; in marketing, Carlise Paulson and Nicole Rund; and on the production side, Robert Ginsberg, Kathryn Graehl, Nancy Bell Scott, Judy Kiviat, Wendy Fredericks, and Carole Desnoes. I am grateful to all of these collaborators.

I

The Writing Process

1

The Writing Process

1 Overview

 http://www.awlonline.com/littlebrown   Links to Web resources on the writing process and the writing situation.

http://www.powa.org/   The Paradigm Online Writing Assistant, featuring writing models and strategies.

http://owl.english.purdue.edu/   The Purdue Online Writing Lab, featuring a searchable collection of more than 130 handouts on writing.

http://webster.commnet.edu/HP/pages/darling/original.htm   The Guide to Grammar and Writing, featuring advice on writing at every level, from the essay through grammar.

Like most writers (even very experienced ones), you may find writing sometimes easy but more often difficult, sometimes smooth but more often halting. Writing involves creation, and creation requires freedom, experimentation, and, yes, missteps. You might start writing without knowing what you have to say, circle back to explore a new idea, or keep going even though you're sure you'll have to rewrite later.

Although writing might seem unstructured, most good writers follow a step-by-step process to create a finished document. This process helps ensure that the written work is complete, accurate, clear, and concise. And, as uncertain as the writing task may be, viewing it as a process also helps give the task some order and helps you determine how to proceed.

The steps of the writing process can be described as follows:

- Assessing the writing situation
- Discovering ideas
- Developing a thesis and organizing your material
- Creating the first draft
- Refining the draft

Note that you cannot hope to produce an excellent paper with your first draft. Your draft must be refined, and, often, much rewriting is necessary to create an effective and well-written finished product. Refining the draft involves revising, editing, and proofreading to ensure that your writing is accurate, brief, clear, and well organized. Your paper must also be formatted before it is ready for submission. Begin your assignments as early as possible to make certain you have enough time to complete all steps in the writing process necessary to create an effective finished document.

Let's look at each step in more detail.

3

2   The Writing Situation

Any writing you do for others occurs in a context that both limits and clarifies your choices. You are communicating something about a particular subject to a particular audience of readers for a specific reason. You may need to conduct research. You'll probably be up against a length requirement and a deadline. And you may be expected to present your work in a certain format.

These are the elements of the WRITING SITUATION, and analyzing them at the very start of a project can tell you much about how to proceed.

2a   Choosing and narrowing your subject

Subject

- What does your writing assignment instruct you to write about? If you don't have a specific assignment, what do you want to write about?
- What interests you about the subject? What do you already have ideas about or want to know more about?
- What does the assignment require you to do with the subject?

A subject for writing has several basic requirements:

- It should be suitable for the assignment.
- It should be neither too general nor too limited for the length of paper and deadline assigned.
- It should be something you care about.

When you receive an assignment, study its wording and its implications about your writing situation to guide your choice of subject:

- *What's wanted from you?* Many writing assignments contain words such as *discuss, describe, analyze, report, interpret, explain, define, argue,* or *evaluate.* These words specify the way you are to approach your subject, what kind of thinking is expected of you, and what your general purpose is. (See pp. 8–10.)

- *For whom are you writing?* Some assignments will specify your readers, but usually you will have to figure out for yourself whether your audience is the general reading public, your classmates, your boss, the college community, your instructor, or some other group or individual. (For more on analyzing your audience, see pp. 5–8.)
- *What kind of research is required?* Sometimes an assignment specifies the kinds of sources you are expected to consult, and you can use such information to choose your subject. (If you are unsure whether research is required, check with your instructor.)
- *Does the subject need to be narrowed?* To do the subject justice in the length and time required, you'll often need to limit it. (See below.)

Answering questions about your assignment will help set some boundaries for your choice of subject. Then you can explore your own interests and experiences to narrow the subject so that you can cover it adequately within the space and time assigned. Federal aid to college students could be the subject of a book; the kinds of aid available or why the government should increase aid would be a more appropriate subject for a four-page paper due in a week. Here are some guidelines for narrowing broad subjects:

- Break your broad subject into a6s many specific topics as you can think of. Make a list.
- For each topic that interests you and fits the assignment, roughly sketch out the main ideas and consider how many paragraphs or pages of specific facts, examples, and other details you would need to pin those ideas down. This thinking should give you at least a vague idea of how much work you'd have to do and how long the resulting paper might be.
- If an interesting and appropriate topic is still too broad, break it down further and repeat the previous step.
- Remember that it is usually better to discuss a few aspects of a subject in detail than it is to touch lightly on many different aspects.

2b Considering your audience

The readers likely to see your work—your audience—may influence your choice of subject and your definition of purpose. Your audience certainly will influence what you say about your subject and how you say it—for instance, how much background information you give and whether you adopt a serious or a friendly tone. Consider, for instance, these two memos written by a student who worked part-time at a small company and wanted to persuade the company to recycle paper:

Addressed to coworkers

Ever notice how much paper collects in your trash basket every day? Well, most of it can be recycled with little effort, I promise. Basically, all you need to do is set a bag or box near your desk and deposit wastepaper in it. I know, space is cramped in these little cubicles. But what's a little more crowding when the earth's at stake? . . .

Information: how employees could handle recycling; no mention of costs

Role: cheerful, equally harried colleague

Tone: informal, personal (*Ever notice; you; what's; Well; I know, space is cramped*)

Addressed to management

In my four months here, I have observed that all of us throw out baskets of potentially recyclable paper every day. Considering the drain on our forest resources and the pressure on landfills that paper causes, we could make a valuable contribution to the environmental movement by helping to recycle the paper we use. At the company where I worked before, the employees separate clean wastepaper from other trash at their desks. The maintenance staff collects trash in two receptacles, and the trash hauler (the same one we use here) makes separate pickups. I do not know what the hauler charges for handling recyclable material. . . .

Information: specific reasons; view of company as a whole; reference to another company; problem of cost

Role: serious, thoughtful, responsible employee

Tone: formal, serious (*Considering the drain; forest resources; valuable contribution;* no *you* or contractions)

For academic papers, your instructor will read your work. However, you may also make an oral presentation of your paper to the class. Therefore, you should consider your instructor and your classmates to be your audience.

The box on the next page contains questions that can help you analyze and address your audience. Depending on your writing situation, some questions will be more helpful than others. For instance, your readers' knowledge of your topic will be important to consider if you are trying to explain how a particular computer program works, whereas readers' beliefs and values may be important if you are trying to gather support for a change in education policy.

Questions about audience

- Who *are* my readers?
- Why are readers going to read my writing? What will they expect?
- What do I want readers to know, think, or do after reading my work, and how should I make that clear to them?
- How will readers' characteristics, such as those below, influence their attitudes toward my topic?

   Age or sex
   Occupation: students, professional colleagues, etc.
   Social or economic role: adult children, car buyers, potential employers, etc.
   Economic or educational background
   Ethnic background
   Political, religious, or moral beliefs and values
   Hobbies or activities

- What do readers already know and *not* know about my topic? How much do I have to tell them?
- If my topic involves specialized language, how much should I use and define?
- What ideas, arguments, or information might surprise readers? excite them? offend them? How should I handle these points?
- What misconceptions might readers have of my topic and/or my approach to the topic? How can I dispel these misconceptions?
- What is my relationship to my readers? How formal or informal will they expect me to be? What role and tone should I assume? What role do I want readers to play?
- What will readers do with my writing? Should I expect them to read every word from the top, to scan for information, or to look for conclusions? Can I help them with a summary, headings, illustrations, or other special features? (See pp. 72–89 on document design.)

You can download the audience questions from this book's Web site: *http://www.awlonline.com/littlebrown.* Store them in a file of their own, and duplicate the file for each writing project. Insert appropriate answers for that project between the questions, save the answers, and print a copy for reference while you develop your paper.

ESL If English is not your native language, you may not be accustomed to appealing to your readers when you write. In some cultures, for instance, readers may accept a writer's statements with little or no questioning. In English, however, readers expect the writer to reach out to them by being accurate, fair, interesting, and clear.

2c   Defining your purpose

Your purpose in writing is your chief reason for communicating something about your subject to a particular audience of readers. When defining yor purpose, ask yourself the following questions:

- What aim does your assignment specify? For instance, does it ask you to explain something or argue a point?
- Why are you writing? What do you want to accomplish?
- How can you best achieve your purpose?

You will be asked to write many different types of papers in your University of Phoenix courses. These papers may include essays, position papers, case studies, business documents, short and long reports, and research papers.

Some assignments may ask you to relate a personal experience or to explore your feelings about an issue; others will require that you conduct research to determine what other people have observed or experienced.

Some assignments may require that you test your opinions against published material; still others require you to suspend judgment and to investigate and report the findings of researchers, without considering your own ideas or opinions at all.

In some academic papers, you may be assigned an issue to analyze and propose alternative courses of action; in still others, you may be asked to recommend a course of action and to support it with evidence.

When you are assigned a paper in a University of Phoenix class, be sure you clearly understand what the assignment requires. The guidelines below may assist you in assessing the writing purpose and determining the approach to take with your writing. However, be sure to clarify with your instructor what he or she is looking for in the finished paper.

Most academic writing can be classified into three types: expressive (or interpretive), analytical (or referential), and persuasive (or argumentative).

- ***Expressive (or interpretive) writing*** involves stating personal opinions; relating experiences; providing personal viewpoints, judgments, or information; or examining feelings. Expressive papers are usually written in first person (I, we) and employ narration to tell a story or to describe events from your own perspective. This type of writing is usually read from start to finish sequentially and allows for more freedom of expression than other types of writing. Essays and personal opinion papers fall into this category. (See additional information in Part VIII, Special Writing Situations, p. 449)

- *Analytical (or referential) writing* involves analysis of issues or subjects. It employs factual data, statistics, and/or findings from research. The purpose of analytical writing is to describe situations, to explain mechanisms or processes, or to report the findings of research. Analytical papers are usually written in the third person, *(he, she, it, they)* from an objective point of view.

    Analytical papers often require you to synthesize information from a number of different sources, and the reader must be able to quickly find data in the document. Thus, this type of writing requires greater structure and organization of ideas than expressive writing. Analytical writing is usually organized into discrete sections, and it often includes headings and subheadings to facilitate random access to information. More complex papers may include a table of contents, a table of figures, or other aids to organize the information. Case studies, research papers, business documents or projects, and many reports fall into this category. Technical writing can also be considered in this category. (See additional information in Part VIII, Research and Documentation, p. 279)

- *Persuasive (or argumentative) writing* may involve both factual data and personal opinion designed to support a personal opinion, judgment, attitude, or argument. Persuasive writing attempts to appeal to the reader's reasoning and to his or her emotions. The purpose of persuasive writing is to convince readers to accept a particular point of view or to move them to take some action. Persuasive papers may be written in first, second *(you)*, or third person, and they often use language that is subjective and partial to a particular viewpoint. Position papers, proposals, sales messages, and persuasive or recommendation reports fall into this category. (See additional information in Part VIII, Special Writing Situations, p. 449)

These purposes often overlap in a single paper, but usually one predominates. And the dominant purpose will influence your particular slant on your subject, the details you choose, and even the words you use.

Many writing assignments narrow the purpose by using a signal word, such as the following:

- *Report:* survey, organize, and objectively present the available evidence on the subject.

- *Summarize:* concisely state the main points in a text, argument, theory, or other work.
- *Discuss:* examine the main points, competing views, or implications of the subject.
- *Compare and contrast:* explain the similarities and differences between two subjects. (See also p. 479.)
- *Define:* specify the meaning of a term or a concept—distinctive characteristics, boundaries, and so on. (See also p. 477–478.)
- *Analyze:* identify the elements of the subject, and discuss how they work together. (See also p. 478.)
- *Interpret:* infer the subject's meaning or implications.
- *Evaluate:* judge the quality or significance of the subject, considering pros and cons. (See also p. 286–287.)
- *Argue:* take a position on the subject, and support your position with evidence. (See also pp. 481–492.)

You can conceive of your purpose more specifically, too, in a way that incorporates your particular topic and the outcome you intend:

To explain how Annie Dillard's "Total Eclipse" builds to its climax so that readers appreciate the author's skill.

To explain the steps in a new office procedure so that staffers will be able to follow it without difficulty.

To persuade readers to support the college administration's plan for more required courses.

To argue against additional regulation of health-maintenance organizations so that readers will perceive the disadvantages for themselves.

2d   Conducting research

If your assignment requires you to conduct research, the following questions may help you determine how to proceed:

Research

- What kinds of evidence—such as facts, examples, and the opinions of experts—best suit your topic, audience, and purpose?
- Does your assignment require you to consult sources of information or conduct other research, such as interviews, surveys, or experiments?
- Besides the requirements of the assignment, what additional information do you need to develop your topic? How will you obtain it?

- What style should you use to cite your sources? (See pp. 337–339 on source documentation in the academic disciplines.)

2e Determining document deadline and length

Be sure to look at your assignment early and ask yourself the following questions:

Deadline and length

- When is the assignment due? How will you apportion the work you have to do in the available time?
- How long should your writing be? If no length is assigned, what seems appropriate for your topic, audience, and purpose?

Many University of Phoenix assignments indicate an expected word count or range. Some instructors will expect your paper to conform exactly to the word count specified. Other instructors use the word count merely as a guideline. Check with your instructor about the expected length of your assignments. If your instructor uses the word count as a guideline, consider that 250–350 words equal one page of text, double-spaced. The exact number of words on a page depends upon the margins, the typeface used, and the font size. The word count refers to the number of words in the text and does not include any preliminary pages or the "Works Cited" or "References" page. Most computer word-processing programs calculate word count for you. Under the File menu, view the document properties to obtain this information.

2f Determining document design and format

Depending upon the academic program in which you are enrolled, the University of Phoenix requires that your assignments follow one of the following formats:

- The MLA format specified in Chapter 52 of this book,
- The APA format specified in Chapter 53 of this book, or
- The APA format specified in the *Publication Manual of the American Psychological Association*, Fourth Edition.

Proper format is an important component of the grading criteria for your academic papers.

3 Discovery

http://webware.princeton.edu/Writing/wc4b.htm   Exploring ideas, from Princeton University.

http://www.powa.org/whtfrms.htm   Discovery techniques, from the Paradigm Online Writing Assistant.

http://207.158.243.119/html/journals___diaries.html   Information and resources on journal keeping, from the Journals and Diaries site. (In the address, type three underscores between *journals* and *diaries*.)

Before you write, you must discover ideas and information to write about. If your assignment is to do some expressive writing about a topic of personal interest, you must generate some ideas to write about. If your assignment requires research, you must determine the subjects or keywords you will use in your search for data.

Writers use a host of techniques to help invent or discover ideas and information about their subjects. *Whichever of the following techniques you use, do your work in writing, not just in your head.* Your ideas will be retrievable, and the very act of writing will lead you to fresh insights.

 Several innovative computer software programs on the market today provide tools to aid you in generating ideas and organizing your thinking. These tools include flow-charting software, concept and idea maps, and diagramming and outlining tools. Using this software, you can rearrange ideas and prioritize them to help develop your ideas.

ESL The discovery process encouraged here rewards rapid writing; you won't need to do a lot of thinking beforehand about what you will write or how. Some ESL writers find it helpful initially to do this exploratory writing in their native language and then to translate the worthwhile material for use in their drafts. However, this practice does require the extra work of translating not only sentences but thought patterns, and it merely postpones the need to think and create in English.

3a   Keeping a journal

A JOURNAL is a diary of ideas kept on paper or on a computer. It gives you a place to record your thoughts and can provide ideas for writing. Because you write for yourself, you can work out your ideas without the pressure of an audience "out there" who will evaluate logic or organization or correctness. If you write every day, even just for a few minutes, the routine will loosen your writing muscles and improve your confidence.

You can use a journal for varied purposes: perhaps to confide your feelings, explore your responses to movies and other media, practice certain kinds of writing (such as poems or news stories), think critically about what you read (see p. 281), or pursue ideas from your courses. In both examples following, the students planted the seeds for essays they later wrote. Megan Polanyis pondered something she learned from her biology textbook:

> *Ecology and economics* have the same root—Greek word for house. Economy = management of the house. Ecology = study of the house. In ecology the house is all of nature, ourselves, the other animals, the plants, the earth, the air, the whole environment. Ecology has a lot to do with economy: study the house in order to manage it.

Sara Ling responded to an experience:

> Had an exchange today with a man who just joined the snowboarding forum—only he turns out to be a woman! She says she's been afraid to write to the forum as a woman because the guys there might shout her down. (When she figured out I was a woman, she decided to fess up to me.) She asked about my experiences. Had to admit I'd had problems of the what-does-a-girl-know sort—advised her to keep her gender a secret to see what happens. Wish I'd thought of it myself. Maybe I'll start over with a new screen name.

(Further examples of Ling's writing appear on p. 15 and in the next three chapters.)

ESL A journal can be especially helpful if you're writing in English as a second language. You can practice writing to improve your fluency, try out sentence patterns, and experiment with vocabulary words. Equally important, you can experiment with applying what you know from experience to what you read and observe.

3b   Observing your surroundings

Sometimes you can find a good subject or good ideas by looking around you, not in the half-conscious way most of us move from place to place in our daily lives but deliberately, all senses alert. On a bus, for instance, are there certain types of passengers? What seems to be on the driver's mind? To get the most from observation, you should have a tablet and pen or pencil handy for notes and sketches. Back at your desk, study your notes and sketches for oddities or patterns that you'd like to explore further.

3c

3c   Freewriting

Writing into a subject

Many writers find subjects or discover ideas by FREEWRITING: writing without stopping for a certain amount of time (say, ten minutes) or to a certain length (say, one page). The goal of freewriting is to generate ideas and information from *within* yourself by going around the part of your mind that doesn't want to write or can't think of anything to write. You let words themselves suggest other words. *What* you write is not important; that you *keep* writing is. Don't stop, even if that means repeating the same words until new words come. Don't go back to reread, don't censor ideas that seem dumb or repetitious, and above all don't stop to edit: grammar, punctuation, spelling, and the like are irrelevant at this stage.

The physical act of freewriting may give you access to ideas you were unaware of. For example, the following freewriting by a student, Robert Benday, gave him the subject of writing as a disguise:

> Write to write. Seems pretty obvious, also weird. What to gain by writing? never anything before. Writing seems always—always—Getting corrected for trying too hard to please the teacher, getting corrected for not trying hard enuf. Frustration, nail biting, sometimes getting carried away making sentences to tell stories, not even true stories, *esp.* not true stories, *that* feels like creating something. Writing just pulls the story out of me. The story lets me be someone else, gives me a disguise.

(A later phase of Benday's writing appears on p. 17.)

If you write on a computer, you can ensure that your freewriting keeps moving forward by turning off your computer's monitor or turning its brightness control all the way down so that the screen is dark. The computer will record what you type but keep it from you and thus prevent you from tinkering with your prose. This INVISIBLE WRITING may feel uncomfortable at first, but it can free the mind for very creative results. When you've finished freewriting, simply turn the monitor on or turn up the brightness control to read what you've written, and then save or revise it as appropriate. Later, you may be able to transfer some of your freewriting into your draft.

ESL   Invisible writing can be especially helpful if English is not your first language and you tend to worry about errors while writing: the blank computer screen leaves you no choice but to explore ideas without regard for their expression. If you choose to write with the monitor on, concentrate on *what* you want to say, not *how* you're saying it.

Focused freewriting

FOCUSED FREEWRITING is more concentrated: you start with your topic and write about it without stopping for, say, fifteen minutes or one full page. As in all freewriting, you push to bypass mental blocks and self-consciousness, not debating what to say or editing what you've written. With focused freewriting, though, you let the physical act of writing take you into and around your subject.

An example of focused freewriting can be found in the work of Sara Ling, whose journal entry appears on page 13. In a composition course Ling's instructor had distributed "Welcome to Cyberbia," an essay by M. Kadi about communication on the Internet. The instructor then gave the following assignment:

> M. Kadi's "Welcome to Cyberbia" holds that the Internet will do little to bridge differences among people because its users gravitate toward other users who are like themselves in most respects. In an essay of 500–700 words, respond to Kadi's essay with a limited and well-supported opinion of your own: Can the Internet serve as a medium for positive change in the way people of diverse backgrounds relate to each other? If so, how? If not, why not? The first draft is due Monday, April 4, for class discussion.

On first reading Kadi's essay, Ling had been impressed with its tight logic but had found unconvincing its pessimistic view of the Internet's potential. She reread the essay and realized that some of Kadi's assertions did not correspond to her own Internet experiences. This discovery prompted the following focused freewriting:

> Kadi says we only meet people like ourselves on the Internet, but I've met lots with very different backgrounds and interests. Actually, "turned out to have" is more like it, since I didn't know anything about them at first. There's the anonymity thing, but Kadi ignores it. You can be anyone or no one. I can pose as a man if I want (probably should have, to avoid rejection on the snowboarding forum). No one has to know I'm female or Asian American or a student. We're not stuck in our identities. Not hampered by them in expressing our views and getting those views accepted. Communication without set identity, especially physical appearance. This could make for more tolerance of others, of difference.

(An outline and drafts of Ling's paper appear on pp. 25–27, 30–31, and 48–50.)

3d Brainstorming

A method similar to freewriting is BRAINSTORMING—focusing intently on a subject for a fixed period (say, fifteen minutes), pushing

3e

yourself to list every idea and detail that comes to mind. Like free-writing, brainstorming requires turning off your internal editor so that you keep moving ahead. (The technique of invisible writing on a computer, described on p. 14, can help you move forward.)

Here is an example of brainstorming by a student, Johanna Abrams, on what a summer job can teach:

> summer work teaches—
>> how to look busy while doing nothing
>> how to avoid the sun in summer
>> seriously: discipline, budgeting money, value of money
> which job? Burger King cashier? baby sitter? mail-room clerk?
> mail room: how to sort mail into boxes: this is learning??
> how to survive getting fired—humiliation, outrage
> Mrs. King! the mail-room queen as learning experience
> the shock of getting fired: what to tell parents, friends?
> Mrs. K was so rigid—dumb procedures
> initials instead of names on the mail boxes—confusion!
> Mrs. K's anger, resentment: the disadvantages of being smarter
>> than your boss
> The odd thing about working in an office: a world with its own
>> rules for how to act
> what Mr. D said about the pecking order—big chick (Mrs. K) pecks
>> on little chick (me)
> a job can beat you down—make you be mean to other people

(A later phase of Abrams's writing process appears on pp. 25–26.)

 Working on a computer makes it fairly easy to edit and shape a brainstorming list into a preliminary outline of your paper (see p. 23). With a few keystrokes, you can delete weak ideas, expand strong ones, and rearrange items. You can also freewrite from the list if you think some ideas are especially promising and deserve more thought.

3e   Clustering

Like freewriting and brainstorming, CLUSTERING (also known as MIND-MAPPING) also draws on free association and rapid, unedited work. But it emphasizes the relations between ideas by combining writing and nonlinear drawing. When clustering, you radiate outward from a center point—your topic. When an idea occurs, you pursue related ideas in a branching structure until they seem exhausted. Then you do the same with other ideas, staying open to connections, continuously branching out or drawing arrows.

The example of clustering on the next page shows how Robert Benday used the technique for ten minutes to expand on the topic of writing as a means of disguise, an idea he arrived at through freewriting (see p. 14).

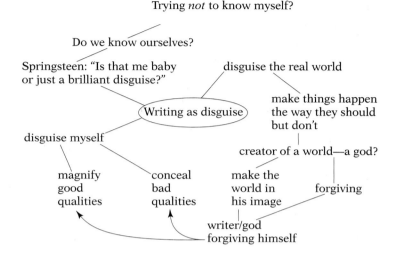

Trying *not* to know myself?

Do we know ourselves?

Springsteen: "Is that me baby   disguise the real world
or just a brilliant disguise?"

make things happen
the way they should
but don't

Writing as disguise

disguise myself

creator of a world—a god?

magnify   conceal   make the
good   bad   world in   forgiving
qualities   qualities   his image

writer/god
forgiving himself

3f   Conducting preliminary research

When you write a research paper, you will usually gather most of your information from studies conducted by others, rather than performing your own original research. One way to generate ideas for your research paper is to examine what aspects of your subject have been studied by other researchers.

Begin by creating a list of terms that relate to your subject. These terms can be single words that are synonyms of one another or phrases that relate to your subject. Then, using the University of Phoenix Library Online Collection and the World Wide Web, conduct searches of these terms and phrases. Try to determine which areas of the subject are controversial, which aspects have been studied extensively, and which have not been examined in much detail.

This preliminary examination will help you determine the amount of information available on your subject and help you decide if you will need to broaden or narrow the scope of your inquiry.

3g Asking questions

Asking yourself a set of questions about your subject—and writing out the answers—can help you look at the topic objectively and see fresh possibilities in it.

 You can download either of the following sets of questions from this book's Web site *http://www.awlonline.com/littlebrown.* Save the list in a file of its own, duplicate it for each writing project, and insert appropriate answers between the questions. Print your answers so they're handy while you develop your paper. You can also move passages from the answers directly into your draft.

1 Journalist's questions

A journalist with a story to report poses a set of questions:

Who was involved?
What happened, and what were the results?
When did it happen?
Where did it happen?
Why did it happen?
How did it happen?

These questions can also be useful in probing an essay subject, especially when you are telling a story or examining causes and effects.

2 Questions about patterns

We think about and understand a vast range of subjects through patterns such as narration, classification, and comparison and contrast. Asking questions based on the patterns can help you view your topic from many angles. Sometimes you may want to develop an entire essay using just one pattern.

How did it happen? (Narration)
How does it look, sound, feel, smell, taste? (Description)
What are examples of it or reasons for it? (Illustration or support)
What is it? What does it encompass, and what does it exclude? (Definition)
What are its parts or characteristics? (Division or analysis)
What groups or categories can it be sorted into? (Classification)
How is it like, or different from, other things? (Comparison and contrast)
Why did it happen? What results did or could it have? (Cause-and-effect analysis)
How do you do it, or how does it work? (Process analysis)

For more on these patterns, including paragraph-length examples, see pages 475–480.

3h   Reading

Many assignments require reading. To respond to M. Kadi's essay about the Internet, for instance, Sara Ling had to digest Kadi's work. Essays on literary works as well as research papers also demand reading. But even when reading is not required by an assignment, it can help you locate or develop your topic by introducing you to ideas you didn't know or expanding on what you do know.

Say you were writing in favor of amateur athletics, a subject to which you had given a lot of thought. You might be inclined to proceed entirely on your own, drawing on facts, examples, and opinions already in your head. But a little digging in sources might open up more. For instance, an article in *Time* magazine could introduce you to an old rule for amateur status, or a posting to an online newsgroup could suggest a pro-amateurism argument that hadn't occurred to you. (See pp. 299–318 for techniques of library and computer research that you can use to locate sources on a topic.)

People often read passively, absorbing content like blotters, not interacting with it. To read for ideas, you need to be more active, probing text and illustrations with your mind, nurturing any sparks they set off. Always write while you read so that you can keep notes on content and—just as important—on what the content makes you *think*. See pages 281–287 for specific guidelines on the process of active reading.

Note Whenever you use the information or ideas of others in your writing, you must acknowledge your sources in order to avoid the serious offense of plagiarism. (See p. 329.)

3i   Thinking critically

Even if you do not read for information and ideas on your topic, you can still think critically about it. Critical thinking (discussed on pp. 281–287) can produce creative ideas by leading you to see what is not obvious. It can also lead you systematically to conclusions about your topic.

Sara Ling, writing about communication on the Internet, used the operations of critical thinking to explore her topic:

- ANALYSIS: What are the subject's elements or characteristics? Ling looked at the ways Internet users can communicate because of their anonymity.
- INTERPRETATION: What is the meaning or significance of the elements? Ling saw that the anonymity of Internet users could help them transcend their physical differences.

- SYNTHESIS: How do the elements relate to each other, or how does this subject relate to another one? Ling perceived important and hopeful differences between anonymous Internet communication and face-to-face interaction.
- EVALUATION: What is the value or significance of the subject? Ling concluded that by making people more tolerant of each other, the Internet could help build community out of diversity.

4 Thesis and Organization

Guidance on writing and revising thesis statements:

http://webster.commnet.edu/HP/pages/darling/grammar/composition/thesis.htm From the Guide to Grammar and Writing.

http://www.english.uiuc.edu/cws/wworkshop/tips/thesisstmt.htm From the University of Illinois, Urbana-Champaign.

Resources for organizing papers:

http://www.powa.org/orgnfrms.htm From the Paradigm Online Writing Assistant.

http://wuacc.edu/services/zzcwwctr/orgdev_menu.html From Washburn University.

Shaping your raw material helps you clear away unneeded ideas, spot possible gaps, and energize your topic. The two main operations in shaping material are focusing on a thesis (below) and organizing ideas (p. 23).

4a Conceiving a thesis statement

Your readers will expect your paper to be focused on and controlled by a main idea, or THESIS. To focus your paper, try to summarize the main idea in a single, declarative sentence of twenty-five words or less. If someone asked you to state the main idea or point of your paper, what would it be? In your final draft you may express this idea in a THESIS STATEMENT, often at the end of your introduction.

The thesis statement

- It narrows your subject to a single, central idea that you want readers to gain from your essay.
- It names the topic and asserts something specific and significant about it.
- It conveys your reason for writing, your purpose.
- It often provides a concise preview of how you will arrange your ideas in the essay.

All of the following thesis statements fulfill the first three functions listed in the box (the nature of the assertion is highlighted in brackets). Examples 4 and 5 also fulfill the fourth function, previewing organization.

Subject	Thesis statement
1. The pecking order in an office	Two months working in a large agency taught me that an office's pecking order should be respected. [*Topic:* office's pecking order. *Assertion:* should be respected.]
2. The direct distribution of music to consumers via the World Wide Web	Because artists can now publish their music directly via the Web, consumers have many more choices than traditional distribution allows. [*Topic:* consumers. *Assertion:* have many more choices.]
3. Federal aid to college students	To compete well in the global economy, the United States must make higher education affordable for any student who qualifies academically. [*Topic:* a competitive United States. *Assertion:* must make higher education affordable.]
4. Preventing juvenile crime	Juveniles can be diverted from crime by active learning programs, full-time sports, and intervention by mentors and role models. [*Topic:* juveniles. *Assertion:* can be diverted from crime in three ways.]

4a

Subject	Thesis statement
5. The effects of strip-mining	Strip-mining should be tightly controlled in this region to reduce its pollution of water resources, its destruction of the land, and its devastating effects on people's lives. [*Topic:* strip-mining. *Assertion:* should be tightly controlled for three reasons.]

ESL In some cultures it is considered unnecessary or impolite for a writer to have an opinion or to state his or her main idea outright. But readers of English usually expect a clear and early idea of what a writer thinks.

2 Development of the thesis statement

A thesis will not usually leap fully formed into your head: you will have to develop and shape the idea as you develop and shape your paper. Still, trying to draft a thesis statement early can give you a point of reference when changes inevitably occur. In a research paper, instead of a thesis, writers usually formulate a research question or a hypothesis. (See additional information on p. 289–291)

You will probably go back and revise your thesis statement, your research question, or your hypothesis as you refine your paper.

While you are developing your thesis statement, ask questions about each attempt:

Checklist for revising the thesis statement

- Does the statement make a concise *assertion* about your topic?
- Is the assertion *limited* to only one idea?
- Is the assertion *specific* and *significant?*
- Does the statement at least imply your *purpose?*
- Is the statement *unified* so that the parts relate to each other?
- Is the thesis statement one single sentence?

Here are examples of thesis statements revised to meet these requirements:

Original	Revised
This new product brought in over $300,000 last year. [A statement of fact, not an assertion: what is significant about the product's success?]	This new product succeeded because of its innovative marketing campaign, including widespread press coverage, in-store entertainment, and a consumer newsletter.

Original	Revised
People should not go on fad diets. [A vague statement that needs limiting with one or more reasons: what's wrong with fad diets?]	Fad diets can be dangerous when they deprive the body of essential nutrients or rely on excessive quantities of potentially harmful foods.
Televised sports are different from live sports. [A general statement that needs to be made more specific: how are they different, and why is the difference significant?]	Although television cannot transmit all the excitement of being in a crowd during a game, its close-ups and slow-motion replays more than compensate.
Seat belts can save lives, but now carmakers are installing air bags. [Not unified: how do the two parts of the sentence relate to each other?]	If drivers had used lifesaving seat belts more often, carmakers might not have needed to install air bags.

4b   Organizing your ideas

Most papers share a basic pattern of introduction (states the subject), body (develops the subject), and conclusion (pulls the paper's ideas together). Introductions and conclusions are discussed on pages 471–475. Within the body, every paragraph develops some aspect of the paper's main idea, or thesis. See pages 48–50 for Sara Ling's essay, with annotations highlighting the body's pattern of support for the thesis statement.

ESL If English is not your native language, the pattern of introduction-body-conclusion and the particular schemes discussed here may differ from what you are used to. For instance, instead of focusing the introduction quickly on the topic and thesis, writers in your native culture may take an indirect approach. (See also p. 472–473.) And instead of arranging body paragraphs to emphasize general points and then support those points with specific details, examples, or reasons, writers in your native culture may leave the general points unsupported (assuming that readers will supply the evidence themselves) or may give only the specifics (assuming that readers will infer the general points). (See also p. 36.) When writing in English, you need to address readers' expectations for directness and for the statement and support of general points.

1 The general and the specific

To organize material for a paper, you need to distinguish general and specific ideas and see the relations between ideas. GENERAL and SPECIFIC refer to the number of instances or objects included in a group signified by a word. The following "ladder" illustrates a general-to-specific hierarchy:

Most general

> life form
> plant
> rose
> Uncle Dan's prize-winning American Beauty rose

Most specific

As you arrange your material, pick out the general ideas and then the specific points that support them. Set aside points that seem irrelevant to your key ideas. On a computer, you can easily experiment with various arrangements of general ideas and supporting information: save the master list, duplicate it, and then use the Cut and Paste functions to move material around or (a little quicker) drag selected text to where you want it.

2 Schemes for organizing papers

A paper's body paragraphs may be arranged in many ways that are familiar to readers. The choice depends on your subject, purpose, and audience.

- *Spatial:* In describing a person, place, or thing, move through space systematically from a starting point to other features— for instance, top to bottom, near to far, left to right.
- *Chronological:* In recounting a sequence of events, arrange the events as they actually occurred in time, first to last.
- *General to specific:* Begin with an overall discussion of the subject; then fill in details, facts, examples, and other support.
- *Specific to general:* First provide the support; then draw a conclusion from it.
- *Climactic:* Arrange ideas in order of increasing importance to your thesis or increasing interest to the reader.
- *Problem-solution:* First outline a problem that needs solving; then propose a solution. (See pp. 489–492 for an example.)

3 Outlines

It's not essential to craft a detailed outline before you begin drafting a paper; in fact, too detailed a plan could prevent you from discovering ideas while you draft. Still, even a rough scheme can show you patterns of general and specific, suggest proportions, and highlight gaps or overlaps in coverage.

There are several different kinds of outlines, some more flexible than others.

Scratch or informal outline

A scratch or informal outline includes key general points in the order they will be covered. It may also suggest the specific evidence for them.

Here is Sara Ling's scratch outline for her essay on Internet communication:

Thesis statement

By lowering the barriers of physical appearance in communication, the Internet's uniquely anonymous form of interaction could build diversity into community.

Scratch outline

No fear of prejudgment
    Physical attributes unknown—age, race, gender, etc.
    We won't be shut out because of appearance
Inability to prejudge others
    Assumptions based on appearance
    Meeting of minds only
    Finding shared interests and concerns

A scratch or informal outline may be all you need to begin drafting. Sometimes, though, it may prove too skimpy a guide, and you may want to use it as a preliminary to a more detailed outline. Indeed, Sara Ling used her scratch outline as a base for a detailed formal outline that gave her an even more definite sense of direction (see the next page).

Tree diagram

In a tree diagram, ideas and details branch out in increasing specificity. Unlike more linear outlines, this diagram can be supplemented and extended indefinitely, so it is easy to alter. Johanna Abrams developed the following example from her brainstorming about a summer job (p. 16):

Thesis statement

Two months working in a large agency taught me that an office's pecking order should be respected.

4b

Tree diagram

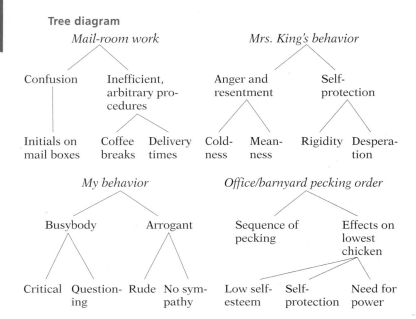

 A tree diagram can be especially useful for planning a project for the World Wide Web. The diagram can help you lay out the organization of your project and its links and then later can serve as a site map for your readers. (For more on composing for the Web, see pp. 88–95.)

Formal outline

A formal outline not only lays out main ideas and their support but also shows the relative importance of all the paper's elements. On the basis of her scratch outline (previous page), Sara Ling prepared this formal outline for the body of her essay on the Internet:

Thesis statement

By lowering the barriers of physical appearance in communication, the Internet's uniquely anonymous form of interaction could build diversity into community.

Formal outline

I. No fear of being prejudged
   A. Unknown physical attributes
      1. Gender
      2. Age
      3. Race
      4. Style

      B. Freer communication
      C. No automatic rejection
  II. Inability to prejudge others
      A. No assumptions based on appearance
        1. Body type
        2. Physical disability
        3. Race
      B. Discovery of shared interests and concerns
        1. Sports and other activities
        2. Family values
        3. Political views
      C. Reduction of physical bias

This example illustrates several principles of outlining that can ensure completeness, balance, and clear relationships:

- All parts are systematically indented and labeled: Roman numerals (I, II) for primary divisions; indented capital letters (A, B) for secondary divisions; further indented Arabic numerals (1, 2) for supporting examples. (The next level down would be indented further still and labeled with small letters: a, b.)
- The outline divides the material into several groups. A long list of points at the same level—more than six or seven—should be broken up into groups.
- Topics of equal generality appear in parallel headings (with the same indention and numbering or lettering).
- All subdivided headings break into at least two parts because a topic cannot logically be divided into only one part.
- All headings are expressed in parallel grammatical form—in the example, as phrases using a noun plus modifiers. This is a topic outline; in a sentence outline all headings are expressed as full sentences (see p. 382).
- All headings are independent and do not overlap one another.

Note Because of its structure, a formal outline can be an excellent tool for analyzing a draft before revising it. See page 32.

4 Unity and coherence

Two qualities of effective writing relate to organization: unity and coherence. When you perceive that someone's writing "flows well," you are probably appreciating these qualities.

To check an outline or draft for UNITY, ask these questions:

- Is each section relevant to the main idea (thesis) of the essay?
- Within main sections, does each example or detail support the principal idea of that section?

5a

To check your outline or draft for COHERENCE, ask the following questions:

- Do the ideas follow a clear sequence?
- Are the parts of the paper logically connected?
- Are the connections clear and smooth?

See also pages 37–43 on unity and coherence in paragraphs.

5 Drafting

 Advice on overcoming writer's block and drafting:

http://webster.commnet.edu/HP/pages/darling/grammar/composition/ brainstorm.htm   From the Guide to Grammar and Writing.
http://owl.english.purdue.edu/Files/132/7-draft.html   From the Purdue Online Writing Lab.
http://webware.princeton.edu/Writing/wc4a.htm   From Princeton University.

Drafting is an occasion for exploration. Don't expect to transcribe solid thoughts into polished prose: solidity and polish will come with revision and editing. Instead, while drafting let the very act of writing help you find and form your meaning.

5a   Starting to draft

Beginning a draft sometimes takes courage, even for seasoned professionals. Procrastination may actually help if you let ideas for writing simmer at the same time. At some point, though, you'll have to face the blank paper or computer screen. The following techniques can help you begin:

- Read over what you've already written—notes, outlines, and so on—and immediately start your draft with whatever comes to mind.
- Freewrite (see p. 14).
- Write scribbles or type nonsense until usable words start coming.
- Pretend you're writing to a friend about your topic.
- Conjure up an image that represents your topic—a physical object, a facial expression, two people arguing over something, a

giant machine gouging the earth for a mine, whatever. Describe that image.

- Skip the opening and start in the middle. Or write the conclusion. Write wherever the ideas begin to flow.
- Write a paragraph on what you think your paper will be about when you finish it.
- Using your outline, divide your paper into chunks—say, one for the introduction, another for the first point, and so on. Start writing the chunk that seems most eager to be written, the one you understand best or feel most strongly about. See pages 470–475 for specific information on writing introductions, body paragraphs, and conclusions.

5b Keeping momentum

Drafting requires momentum: the forward movement opens you to fresh ideas and connections. To keep moving while drafting, try one or more of these techniques:

- Set aside enough time for yourself. (For a brief paper, a first draft is likely to take at least an hour or two.)
- Work in a place where you won't be interrupted, and make yourself comfortable.
- If you must stop working, leave a note with the draft about what you expect to do next. Then you can pick up where you stopped with minimal disruption.
- Be as fluid as possible, and don't worry about mistakes. Spontaneity will allow your attitudes toward your subject to surface naturally in your sentences, and it will also make you receptive to ideas and relations you haven't seen before. Mistakes will be easier to find and correct later, when you're not also trying to create.
- Keep going. Skip over sticky spots; leave a blank if you can't find the right word; put alternative ideas or phrasings in brackets so that you can consider them later without bogging down. If an idea pops out of nowhere but doesn't seem to fit in, quickly jot it down on a separate sheet, or write it into the draft and bracket or boldface it for later attention. You can use an asterisk (*) or some other symbol to mark places where you feel blocked or uncertain. On a computer you can find these places later by using the Search command to locate the symbol.
- Resist self-criticism. Don't worry about your style, grammar, spelling, punctuation, and the like. Don't worry about what your readers will think. These are very important matters, but save them for revision. If you're writing on a computer, help yourself resist self-criticism by turning off automatic spelling

or grammar checkers (see p. 59) or by trying invisible writing as described on page 14.

- Use your thesis statement and outline to remind you of your planned purpose, organization, and content.
- But don't feel constrained by your thesis and outline. If your writing leads you in a more interesting direction, follow. Then, go back and revise your thesis statement and outline to reflect the new direction your writing has taken.
- In a research paper, make sure to include research material where appropriate. (See information beginning on p. 289 on conducting research.) If you incorporate information from an outside source, make sure to note in the text where this material was obtained. You do not have to worry about proper citation format at this stage, but make sure you can identify the source so you can complete the citation when you refine your paper.

 If you write on a computer, frequently save or file the text you're drafting—at least every fifteen minutes or every couple of pages and every time you leave the computer. In addition, back up your drafts on a separate disk, and perhaps even print paper copies (so-called hard copy) in case anything happens to your disks.

5c Examining a sample first draft

Sara Ling's first draft on Internet communication appears below. (Her earlier work appears on pp. 15, 19, and 25–27.) The draft also appears on this book's Web site at *http://www.awlonline. com/littlebrown.*

Title?

In "Welcome to Cyberbia," M. Kadi says that the Internet will lead to more fragmentation in society because people just seek out others like themselves. But Kadi ignores the Internet's uniquely anonymous form of interaction could actually build diversity into community by lowering the barriers of physical appearance in communication.

Anonymity on the Internet. It's one of the best things about technology. No one knows your age or gender or race. Whether your fat or thin or neat or sloppy. What kind of clothes you wear. (Maybe your not wearing clothes at all). People who know you personally don't even know who you are with an invented screen name.

We can communicate freely without being prejudged because of our appearance. For example, I participate in a snowboarding forum that has mostly men. I didn't realize what I was getting into when I used my full name as my screen name. Before long, I was often being shouted down with such insults as "What does a girl know?" and "Why don't you go back to knitting?" Then a nice man I had been exchanging messages with wrote me a private e-mail, and he turned out to be a she! This woman had been wiser than me and hidden her gender with her screen name. She hadn't received any of the hostile responses I had, just because no one knew she was a woman. As this example shows, posing as people different from who they really are can enable people to make themselves heard in situations where normally (in the real world) they would be shut out.

We cannot prejudge others because of their appearance. Often in face-to-face interaction we assume we know things about people just because of the way they look. Assumptions prevent people from discovering their shared interests and concerns, and this is particularly true where race is concerned. The anonymity of the Internet makes physical barriers irrelevant, and only people's minds meet. Because of this, the Internet could create a world free of physical bias.

Logged on to the Internet we can become more tolerant of others. We can become a community.

6 Refining

http://owl.english.purdue.edu/Files/132/8-revise.html Revising papers, with examples and links to additional resources, from the Purdue Online Writing Lab.

http://webster.commnet.edu/HP/pages/darling/grammar/composition/editing.htm Editing and proofreading tips, from the Guide to Grammar and Writing.

http://www.gmu.edu/departments/writingcenter/handouts/eiphand.html "A Guide to Gracious Criticism," from George Mason University.

http://www.nau.edu/~comp/Portfolio_System.html Information about developing a writing portfolio, intended for students at Northern Arizona University but useful for others as well.

6a

Good writing involves rewriting. Once you have created a first draft, that draft must be refined. Refining means polishing the draft to make sure you have created an effective document. It consists of three separate activities: revising, editing, and proofreading. These activities are explained in detail below.

6a Revising

Revising means, literally, "re-seeing." When you revise, you step back from your writing and view it from the standpoint of your readers. You also look at the draft as a whole and ensure that you have expressed your ideas and organized your material in the most effective manner. Additionally, revising involves reading your draft for coherence—to determine how easily your writing flows and how well your ideas are tied together.

To revise your writing, you have to read it critically (see p. 281), and that means you have to create some distance between your draft and yourself. One of the following techniques may help you see your work objectively:

- Take a break after finishing the draft to pursue some other activity. A few hours may be enough; a whole night or day is preferable.
- Ask someone to read and react to your draft. If your instructor encourages collaboration among students, by all means take advantage of the opportunity to hear the responses of others. (See pp. 50–52 and 66–67 for more on collaboration.)
- If you compose your draft in handwriting, type it before revising it. The act of transcription can reveal gaps in content or problems in structure.
- Outline your draft. While reading it, highlight the main points supporting the thesis. Write these sentences down separately in outline form. (If you're working on a computer, you can copy and paste these sentences.) Then examine the outline you've made for logical order, gaps, and digressions. A formal outline can be especially illuminating because of its careful structure (see pp. 24–27).
- Listen to your draft: read it out loud to yourself or a friend or classmate, read it into a tape recorder and play the tape, or have someone read the draft to you.

 Computerized word processing has removed the mechanical drudgery of revision, but writers disagree over whether it's better to consider revisions on a paper printout or on screen.

- Paper copy allows you to see the whole draft at once and may be easier to read accurately, but if your work is stored on a computer you then have to key in your changes.
- Working on a computer allows you to see changes as you make them and to experiment with different versions of the same passage, but it can prevent you from seeing your work as a whole.

Whatever your own preference, do take a couple of precautions. First, work on a duplicate of any draft you're revising so that the original remains intact until you're truly finished with it. (You may be able to do without the duplicate if your word processor has a function that shows, or "tracks," changes alongside the original text, allowing you later to accept or reject alterations. See p. 62.) And second, save successive drafts under their own file names in case you need to consult them for ideas or phrasings. (See p. 57.)

Checklist for revision

- *Purpose:* What is the paper's purpose? Does it conform to the assignment? Is it consistent throughout the paper? (See pp. 8–10.)
- *Thesis:* What is the thesis of the paper? Where does it become clear? How well do thesis and paper match: Does the paper stray from the thesis? Does it fulfill the commitment of the thesis? (See pp. 20–23.)
- *Structure:* What are the main points of the paper? (List them.) How well does each support the thesis? How effective is their arrangement for the paper's purpose? (See pp. 20–21.)
- *Development:* How well do details, examples, and other evidence support each main point? Where, if at all, might readers find support skimpy or have trouble understanding the content? (See pp. 5–8, 475–479.)
- *Tone:* What is the tone of the paper? How do particular words and sentence structures create the tone? How appropriate is it for the purpose, topic, and intended readers? Where is it most and least successful? (See pp. 6–7.)
- *Unity:* What does each sentence and paragraph contribute to the thesis? Where, if at all, do digressions occur? Should these be cut, or can they be rewritten to support the thesis? (See pp. 23, 36–37.)
- *Coherence:* How clearly and smoothly does the paper flow? Where does it seem rough or awkward? Can any transitions be improved? (See pp. 23–24, 37–43.)
- *Title, introduction, conclusion:* How accurately and interestingly does the title reflect the paper's content? (See page 34.) How well does the introduction engage and focus readers' attention? (See pp. 471–474.) How effective is the conclusion in providing a sense of completion? (See pp. 474–475.)

6a

Set aside at least as much time to revise your paper as you took to draft it. Plan on going through the draft several times to answer the questions in the checklist on the previous page and to resolve any problems you uncover.

If you work on a computer, you can download the revision checklist from the Web site for this book: *http://www.awlonline.com/ littlebrown*. Save the list in a file, and duplicate it for each writing project. Then insert your answers to the questions along with ideas for changes. Print the expanded list so it's handy while you revise.

A note on titling your paper

The revision stage is a good time to consider a title because attempting to sum up your paper in a phrase can focus your attention sharply on your topic, purpose, and audience.

Here are some suggestions for titling a paper:

- A DESCRIPTIVE TITLE is almost always appropriate and is usually expected for academic writing. It announces the topic clearly, accurately, and as briefly as possible. Sara Ling's final title— "The Internet: Fragmentation or Community?"—is an example. Other examples are "Images of Lost Identity in *North by Northwest*"; "An Experiment in Small-Group Dynamics"; "Why Lincoln Delayed Emancipating the Slaves"; "Food Poisoning Involving *E. coli* Bacteria: A Review of the Literature."
- A SUGGESTIVE TITLE—the kind often found in popular magazines—may be appropriate for more informal writing. Examples include "Making Peace" (for an essay on the Peace Corps) and "Anyone for Soup?" (for an essay on working in a soup kitchen). For a more suggestive title, Ling might have chosen something like "What We Don't Know Can Help Us" or "Secrets of the Internet." Such a title conveys the writer's attitudes and hints at the topic, thereby pulling readers into the essay to learn more. A source for such a title may be a familiar phrase, a fresh image, or a significant expression from the essay itself.
- A title tells readers how big the topic is. For Ling's essay, the title "The Internet" or "Anonymity" would have been too broad, whereas "Lose Your Body" or "Discovering Common Ground" would have been too narrow because each deals with only part of the paper's content.
- A title should not restate the assignment or the thesis statement, as in "The Trouble with M. Kadi's Picture of the Internet" or "What I Think About Diversity on the Internet."

For more information on titles, see pages 378 (the format of a title in the final paper) and 269–270 (capitalizing words in a title).

6b   Revising paragraphs

A PARAGRAPH is a group of related sentences set off by a beginning indention or, sometimes, by extra space. Paragraphs give you and your readers a breather from long stretches of text, and they indicate key steps in the development of your thesis.

In the body of your paper, you may use paragraphs for any of these purposes:

- To introduce one of the main points supporting your paper's central idea (its thesis) and to develop the point with examples, facts, or other supporting evidence. (See pp. 20–23 for a discussion of an paper's thesis.)
- Within a group of paragraphs centering on one main point, to introduce and develop a key example or other important evidence.
- To shift approach—for instance, from pros to cons, from problem to solution, from questions to answers.
- To mark movement in a sequence, such as from one reason or step to another.

This chapter discusses two qualities of an effective body paragraph: unity (next page) and coherence (p. 37). See pages 471 and 474 for discussion of two special kinds of paragraphs: introductions and conclusions.

ESL   Not all languages share the conventions of English paragraphs. In some languages, for instance, writing moves differently from English—not from left to right, but from right to left or down

---

Checklist for revising paragraphs

- Is the paragraph UNIFIED? Does it adhere to one general idea that is either stated in a TOPIC SENTENCE or otherwise apparent? (See next page.)
- Is the paragraph COHERENT? Do the sentences follow a clear sequence (p. 38)? Are the sentences linked as needed by parallelism (p. 38), repetition or restatement (p. 39), pronouns (p. 39), consistency (p. 40), and transitional expressions (p. 41)?
- Is the paragraph DEVELOPED? Is the general idea of the paragraph well supported with specific evidence such as details, facts, examples, and reasons? An effective, well-developed paragraph always provides the specific information that readers need and expect in order to understand you and to stay interested in what you say. Paragraph length can be a rough gauge of development: anything much shorter than 100 to 150 words may leave readers with a sense of incompleteness.

6b

rows from top to bottom. Even in languages that move as English does, writers may not use paragraphs at all. Or they may use paragraphs but not state the central ideas or provide transitional expressions to show readers how sentences relate. If your native language is not English and you have difficulty with paragraphs, don't worry about paragraphing during drafting. Instead, during a separate step of revision, divide your text into parts that develop your main points. Mark those parts with indentions.

1 Maintaining paragraph unity

An effective paragraph develops one central idea—in other words, it is UNIFIED. For example:

> <u>Some people really like chili, apparently, but nobody can agree how the stuff should be made.</u> C. V. Wood, twice winner at Terlingua, uses flank steak, pork chops, chicken, and green chilis. My friend Hughes Rudd of CBS News, who imported five hundred pounds of chili powder into Russia as a condition of accepting employment as Moscow correspondent, favors coarse-ground beef. Isadore Bleckman, the cameraman I must live with on the road, insists upon one-inch cubes of stew beef and puts garlic in his chili, an Illinois affectation. An Indian of my acquaintance, Mr. Fulton Batisse, who eats chili for breakfast when he can, uses buffalo meat and plays an Indian drum while it's cooking. I ask you.
> —CHARLES KURALT, *Dateline America*

Kuralt's paragraph works because it follows through on its central idea, which is stated in the underlined first sentence, the TOPIC SENTENCE. After the topic sentence, each of the next four sentences offers an example of a chili concoction. (In the final sentence Kuralt comments on the examples.)

What if instead Kuralt had written his paragraph as follows? Here the topic of chili preparation is forgotten mid-paragraph, as the sentences digress to describe life in Moscow:

> Some people really like chili, apparently, but nobody can agree how the stuff should be made. C. V. Wood, twice winner at Terlingua, uses flank steak, pork chops, chicken, and green chilis. My friend Hughes Rudd, who imported five hundred pounds of chili powder into Russia as a condition of accepting employment as Moscow correspondent, favors coarse-ground beef. He had some trouble finding the beef in Moscow, though. He sometimes had to scour all the markets and wait in long lines. For any American used to overstocked supermarkets and department stores, Russia can be quite a shock.

Instead of following through on its topic sentence, the paragraph loses its way. It is not unified.

A topic sentence need not always come first in the paragraph. For instance, it may come last, presenting your idea only after you have provided the evidence for it. Or it may not be stated at all, especially in narrative or descriptive writing in which the point becomes clear in the details. But always the idea should govern the paragraph's content as if it were standing guard at the opening.

2 Achieving paragraph coherence

When a paragraph is COHERENT, readers can see how it holds together: the sentences seem to flow logically and smoothly into one another. Exactly the opposite happens with this paragraph:

> The ancient Egyptians were masters of preserving dead people's bodies by making mummies of them. Mummies several thousand years old have been discovered nearly intact. The skin, hair, teeth, finger- and toenails, and facial features of the mummies were evident. It is possible to diagnose the diseases they suffered in life, such as smallpox, arthritis, and nutritional deficiencies. The process was remarkably effective. Sometimes apparent were the fatal afflictions of the dead people: a middle-aged king died from a blow on the head, and polio killed a child king. Mummification consisted of removing the internal organs, applying natural preservatives inside and out, and then wrapping the body in layers of bandages.

The paragraph is hard to read. The sentences lurch instead of gliding from point to point.

As it was actually written, the paragraph is much clearer (next page). Not only did the writer arrange information differently; he also built links into his sentences so that they would flow smoothly. The highlighting on the actual paragraph emphasizes the techniques:

- After stating the central idea in a topic sentence, the writer moves to two more specific explanations and illustrates the second with four sentences of examples.
- Circled words repeat or restate key terms or concepts.
- Boxed words link sentences and clarify relationships.
- Underlined phrases are in parallel grammatical form to reflect their parallel content.

6b

6b

Central idea
The ancient Egyptians were masters of preserving dead peo-
Explanation
ple's bodies by making mummies of them. Basically, mummifica-
tion consisted of removing the internal organs, applying natural
preservatives inside and out, and then wrapping the body in layers
Explanation
of bandages. And the process was remarkably effective. Indeed,
mummies several thousand years old have been discovered nearly
Specific examples
intact. Their skin, hair, teeth, finger- and toenails, and facial features are still evident. Their diseases in life, such as smallpox,
arthritis, and nutritional deficiencies, are still diagnosable. Even
their fatal afflictions are still apparent: a middle-aged king died
from a blow on the head; a child king died from polio.

—MITCHELL ROSENBAUM (student), "Lost Arts of the Egyptians"

Paragraph organization

A coherent paragraph organizes information so that readers
can easily follow along. These are common paragraph schemes:

- *General to specific:* Sentences downshift from more general statements to more specific ones. (See the paragraph above by Rosenbaum.)
- *Climactic:* Sentences increase in drama or interest, ending in a climax. (See the paragraph by Lawrence Mayer opposite.)
- *Spatial:* Sentences scan a person, place, or object from top to bottom, from side to side, or in some other way that approximates the way people actually look at things. (See the paragraph by Virginia Woolf on p. 475.)
- *Chronological:* Sentences present events as they occurred in time, earlier to later. (See the paragraph by Kathleen LaFrank on p. 41.)

Parallelism

Parallelism helps tie sentences together. In the following paragraph the underlined parallel structures of *She* and a verb link all

KEY TERM

PARALLELISM   The use of similar grammatical structures for similar elements of meaning within or among sentences: *The book caused a stir in the media* and *aroused debate in Congress.* (See also Chapter 12.)

sentences after the first one. Parallelism also appears *within* many of the sentences. Aphra Behn (1640–89) was the first English-woman to write professionally.

> In addition to her busy career as a writer, Aphra Behn also found time to briefly marry and spend a little while in debtor's prison. She found time to take up a career as a spy for the English in their war against the Dutch. She made the long and difficult voyage to Suriname [in South America] and became involved in a slave rebellion there. She plunged into political debate at Will's Coffee House and defended her position from the stage of the Drury Lane Theater. She actively argued for women's rights to be educated and to marry whom they pleased, or not at all. She defied the seventeenth-century dictum that ladies must be "modest" and wrote freely about sex.   —ANGELINE GOREAU, "Aphra Behn"

Repetition and restatement

Repeating or restating key words helps make a paragraph coherent and also reminds readers what the topic is. In the following paragraph note the underlined repetition of *sleep* and restatement of *adults:*

> Perhaps the simplest fact about sleep is that individual needs for it vary widely. Most adults sleep between seven and nine hours, but occasionally people turn up who need twelve hours or so, while some rare types can get by on three or four. Rarest of all are those legendary types who require almost no sleep at all; respected researchers have recently studied three such people. One of them—a healthy, happy woman in her seventies—sleeps about an hour every two or three days. The other two are men in early middle age, who get by on a few minutes a night. One of them complains about the daily fifteen minutes or so he's forced to "waste" in sleeping.
> —LAWRENCE A. MAYER, "The Confounding Enemy of Sleep"

Pronouns

Because pronouns refer to nouns, they can help relate sentences to each other. In the paragraph above by Angeline Goreau, *she* works just this way by substituting for *Aphra Behn* in every sentence after the first.

┌─ KEY TERM ───

PRONOUN   A word that refers to and functions as a noun, such as *I, you, he, she, it, we, they: The patient could not raise her arm.* (See p. 139.)

6b

Consistency

Consistency (or the lack of it) occurs primarily in the person and number of nouns and pronouns and in the tense of verbs. Any inconsistencies not required by meaning will interfere with a reader's ability to follow the development of ideas.

Note the underlined inconsistencies in the next paragraphs:

Shifts in tense

In the Hopi religion, water <u>is</u> the driving force. Since the Hopi <u>lived</u> in the Arizona desert, they <u>needed</u> water urgently for drinking, cooking, and irrigating crops. Their complex beliefs <u>are</u> focused in part on gaining the assistance of supernatural forces in obtaining water. Many of the Hopi kachinas, or spirit essences, <u>were</u> directly concerned with clouds, rain, and snow.

Shifts in number

<u>Kachinas</u> represent spiritually the things and events of the real world, such as cumulus clouds, mischief, cornmeal, and even death. A <u>kachina</u> is not worshipped as a god but regarded as an interested friend. <u>They</u> visit the Hopi from December through July in the form of men who dress in kachina costumes and perform dances and other rituals.

Shifts in person

Unlike the man, the Hopi <u>woman</u> does not keep contact with kachinas through costumes and dancing. Instead, <u>one</u> receives a tihu, or small effigy, of a kachina from the man impersonating the kachina. <u>You</u> are more likely to receive a tihu as a girl approaching marriage, though a child or older woman may receive one, too.

 The grammar checker on a word processor cannot help you locate shifts in tense, number, or person among sentences. Shifts are sometimes necessary (as when tenses change to reflect actual differences in time), and even a passage with needless shifts may still consist of sentences that are grammatically correct (as all the sentences are in the above examples). The only way to achieve con-

---

KEY TERMS

TENSE   The form of a verb that indicates the time of its action, such as present (*I run*), past (*I ran*), or future (*I will run*). (See p. 167.)

NUMBER   The form of a noun, pronoun, or verb that indicates whether it is singular (one) or plural (more than one): *boy, boys.*

PERSON   The form of a pronoun that indicates whether the subject is speaking (first person: *I, we*), spoken to (second person: *you*), or spoken about (third person: *he, she, it, they*). All nouns are in the third person.

sistency in your writing is to review it yourself. (See pp. 60–61 for more on grammar checkers.)

Transitional expressions

Transitional expressions such as *therefore, in contrast,* or *meanwhile* can forge specific connections between sentences, as do the underlined expressions in this paragraph:

> Medical science has thus succeeded in identifying the hundreds of viruses that can cause the common cold. It has also discovered the most effective means of prevention. One person transmits the cold viruses to another most often by hand. For instance, an infected person covers his mouth to cough. He then picks up the telephone. Half an hour later, his daughter picks up the same telephone. Immediately afterward, she rubs her eyes. Within a few days, she, too, has a cold. And thus it spreads. To avoid colds, therefore, people should wash their hands often and keep their hands away from their faces.
>
> —KATHLEEN LAFRANK (student), "Colds: Myth and Science"

Note that you can use transitional expressions to link paragraphs as well as sentences. In the first sentence of LaFrank's paragraph, the word *thus* signals that the sentence refers to an effect discussed in the preceding paragraph.

The following box lists many transitional expressions by the functions they perform:

Transitional expressions

To add or show sequence
again, also, and, and then, besides, equally important, finally, first, further, furthermore, in addition, in the first place, last, moreover, next, second, still, too

To compare
also, in the same way, likewise, similarly

To contrast
although, and yet, but, but at the same time, despite, even so, even though, for all that, however, in contrast, in spite of, nevertheless, notwithstanding, on the contrary, on the other hand, regardless, still, though, yet

To give examples or intensify
after all, an illustration of, even, for example, for instance, indeed, in fact, it is true, of course, specifically, that is, to illustrate, truly

(continued)

Transitional expressions
(continued)

To indicate place
above, adjacent to, below, elsewhere, farther on, here, near, nearby, on the other side, opposite to, there, to the east, to the left

To indicate time
after a while, afterward, as long as, as soon as, at last, at length, at that time, before, earlier, formerly, immediately, in the meantime, in the past, lately, later, meanwhile, now, presently, shortly, simultaneously, since, so far, soon, subsequently, then, thereafter, until, until now, when

To repeat, summarize, or conclude
all in all, altogether, as has been said, in brief, in conclusion, in other words, in particular, in short, in simpler terms, in summary, on the whole, that is, therefore, to put it differently, to summarize

To show cause or effect
accordingly, as a result, because, consequently, for this purpose, hence, otherwise, since, then, therefore, thereupon, thus, to this end, with this object

Note Draw carefully on this list of transitional expressions because the ones in each group are not interchangeable. For instance, *besides, finally,* and *second* may all be used to add information, but each has its own distinct meaning.

ESL If transitional expressions are not common in your native language, you may be tempted to compensate when writing in English by adding them to the beginnings of most sentences. But such explicit transitions aren't needed everywhere, and in fact too many can be intrusive and awkward. When inserting transitional expressions, consider the reader's need for a signal: often the connection from sentence to sentence is already clear from the context or can be made clear by relating the content of sentences more closely (see pp. 38–40). When you do need transitional expressions, try varying their positions in your sentences, as illustrated in the sample paragraph on page 41.

6c   Examining a sample revision

In revising her first draft, Sara Ling had the help of her instructor and several of her classmates, to whom she showed the draft as part of her assignment. (See p. 50 for more on this kind of collaboration.) She revised thoroughly in response to others' comments and her own evaluation of the draft's strengths and weaknesses. The first half of the revision begins on the next page. The main changes are explained below and keyed to the revision by numbers (some numbers are used more than once).

1. With a descriptive title, Ling named her topic and forecast how she would approach it.
2. Ling rewrote and expanded the previous abrupt introduction to draw readers into the question she would explore and to give a fuller summary of Kadi's essay.
3. Ling rewrote the transitions between paragraphs to make each paragraph relate clearly to her thesis statement and to make the essay flow more smoothly.
4. Ling added examples to support her general statements. This and the following two categories of changes occupied most of Ling's attention during revision.
5. Ling condensed the example from her experience. Some readers commented that it overwhelmed the paragraph, and Ling realized that she had given more background than needed.
6. In response to her classmates, Ling qualified her ideas to acknowledge complexities she had previously ignored. (The qualification created an overlong paragraph, so Ling broke the paragraph in two.)

You can also view Ling's revision on this book's Web site: *http://www.awlonline.com/littlebrown.*

6d

1

The Internet: Fragmentation or Community?
~~Title?~~

2

We hear all sorts of predictions about how the Internet will enrich our lives and promote equality, tolerance, and thus community in our society. But are these promises realistic? In her essay "Welcome to Cyberbia," M. Kadi argues that they are not. Instead, she maintains,

~~In "Welcome to Cyberbia," M. Kadi says that~~ the Internet will lead
not community,   *users merely*
to more fragmentation in society because ~~people just~~ seek out others
with the same biases, needs, and concerns as their own. The
point is an interesting one, but Kadi overlooks
~~like themselves. But Kadi ignores~~ the Internet's uniquely anonymous
which
form of interaction could actually build diversity into community by

lowering the barriers of physical appearance in communication.
Writing on the Internet, you can be as anonymous as you like. Unless   3
~~Anonymity on the Internet. It's one of the best things about tech-~~
you tell them, the people you communicate with do not   *you're*
~~nology. No one knows~~ your age or gender or race. Whether ~~your~~ fat or
you're
thin or neat or sloppy. What kind of clothes you wear. (Maybe ~~your~~ not
Even p
wearing clothes at all). ~~P~~eople who know you personally don't even
if you conceal your identity
know who you are with an invented screen name.
Because of this anonymity, we
~~We~~ can communicate freely without being prejudged because of   3

our appearance. For example, *a high school student can participate in a*   4
*physics discussion group, and not be dismissed by professional physicists
in the group just because of her age. An adult man can chat about music
with teenagers, who might otherwise ignore or laugh at him.*
A woman I know posed as a man on   *and received none of the hostile*   5
I participate in a snowboarding forum ~~that has mostly men. I didn't re-~~
responses such as "What does a girl know?" that I got when I revealed my
~~alize what I was getting into when I used my full name as my screen~~
gender on the same forum.
~~name. Before long, I was often being shouted down with such insults~~

~~as "What does a girl know?" and "Why don't you go back to knitting?"~~

~~Then a nice man I had been exchanging messages with wrote me a pri-~~

~~vate e-mail, and he turned out to be a she! This woman had been wiser~~

~~than me and hidden her gender with her screen name. She hadn't re-~~

~~ceived any of the hostile responses I had, just because no one knew she~~

~~was a woman.~~

Granted, concealing or altering identities on the Internet can be a problem, as when adults pose as children to seduce or harm them. These well-publicized occurrences say a great deal about the need to monitor the use of the Internet by children, and being cautious about getting together with Internet correspondents. However, they do not undermine the value of

As this example shows, posing as people different from who they really

being able

are can onable people to make themselves heard in situations where

normally (in the real world) they would be shut out.

6d Editing

After you have revised your paper so that all the content is in place, you should turn to the important work of editing the draft for style, sense, and correctness. When you edit, you read your paper to make sure your ideas are stated as clearly and concisely as possible. Editing also involves checking for errors in spelling, punctuation, grammar, and word usage and verifying facts and in-text citation of sources.

Try these approaches to discover what needs editing:

- Take a break, even fifteen or twenty minutes, to clear your head.
- Read the draft *slowly,* and read what you *actually see.* Otherwise, you're likely to read what you intended to write but didn't.
- As you read the draft, imagine yourself encountering it for the first time, as a reader will.
- Have a friend or relative read your work. (If your native language is not English, you may find it especially helpful to have a native speaker read your revised drafts.) When you share your work in class, listen to the responses of your classmates or instructor. (See p. 50.)
- As when revising, read the draft aloud, preferably into a tape recorder, listening for awkward rhythms, repetitive sentence patterns, and missing or clumsy transitions.
- Learn from your own experience. Keep a record of the problems that others have pointed out in your writing. When editing, check your work against this record.

 If you write on a computer, consider these additional approaches to editing:

- Don't rely on your word processor's spelling, grammar, and style checkers to find what needs editing. See the discussion of these checkers on pages 59–61.

6d

Checklist for editing

- *Clarity:* How well do words and sentences convey their intended meanings? Which if any words and sentences are confusing? Check the paper especially for these:

  Exact words (pp. 121–127)
  Parallelism (pp. 107–110)
  Clear modifiers (pp. 206–211)
  Clear reference of pronouns (pp. 193–196)
  Complete sentences (pp. 212–215)
  Sentences separated correctly (pp. 216–219)

- *Effectiveness:* How well do words and sentences engage and direct readers' attention? Where, if at all, does the writing seem wordy, choppy, or dull? Check the paper especially for these:

  Emphasis of main ideas (pp. 99–107)
  Smooth and informative transitions (pp. 41–43)
  Variety in sentence length and structure (pp. 111–114)
  Appropriate words (pp. 115–121)
  Concise sentences (pp. 129–134)

- *Correctness:* How little or how much do surface errors interfere with clarity and effectiveness? Check the paper especially for these:

  Spelling (pp. 261–265)
  Verb forms, especially *-s* and *-ed* endings and correct forms of irregular verbs (pp. 154–158)
  Verb tenses, especially consistency (pp. 167–174)
  Agreement between subjects and verbs, especially when words come between them or the subject is *each, everyone,* or a similar word (pp. 178–183)
  Pronoun forms (pp. 184–189)
  Agreement between pronouns and antecedents, especially when the antecedent contains *or* or it is *everyone, person,* or a similar word (pp. 189–193)
  Sentence fragments (pp. 212–215)
  Commas, especially with comma splices (pp. 216–219), with *and* or *but* (227–229), with introductory elements (229–230), with nonessential elements (230–234), and with series (234)
  Apostrophes in possessives but not plural nouns (*Dave's/witches,* pp. 244–246) and in contractions but not possessive personal pronouns (*it's/its,* p. 247)
  Compounding, especially correct use of hyphens (p. 265)
  Capitalization (p. 267)

6e

- If possible, work on a double-spaced paper copy. Most people find it much harder to spot errors on a computer screen than on paper.
- Use the Find command to locate and correct mistakes or stylistic problems that tend to crop up in your writing—certain misspellings, overuse of *there is,* wordy phrases such as *the fact that,* and so on.
- The ease of editing on a computer can lead to overediting and steal the life from your prose. Resist any temptation to rewrite sentences over and over. (If your computer's grammar and style checker contributes to the temptation, consider turning it off.)
- Inserting or deleting text on a computer requires special care not to omit needed words or leave in unneeded words.

In your editing, work first for clarity and a smooth movement among sentences and then for correctness. Use the questions in the checklist on the next page to guide your editing, referring to the page numbers in parentheses as needed. If you work on a computer, you can download the editing checklist from this book's Web site: *http://www.awlonline.com/littlebrown.* Save the list in a file, and duplicate it for each writing project. Then insert your answers to the questions along with notes on specific changes you need or want to make. Print the expanded list so it's handy while you edit.

6e Proofreading

After editing your essay, retype or print it one last time. Be sure to proofread the final essay several times to spot and correct errors. To increase the accuracy of your proofreading, you may need to experiment with ways to keep yourself from relaxing into the rhythm and the content of your prose. Here are a few tricks, including some used by professional proofreaders:

- Read printed copy, even if you will eventually submit the paper electronically. Most people proofread more accurately when reading type on paper than when reading it on a computer screen. (At the same time, don't view the printed copy as necessarily error-free just because it's clean. Clean-looking copy may still harbor errors.)
- Read the paper aloud, very slowly, and distinctly pronounce exactly what you see.
- Place a ruler under each line as you read it.

6f

- Read "against copy," comparing your final draft one sentence at a time against the edited draft.
- Take steps to keep the content of your writing from distracting you while you proofread. Read the paper backward, end to beginning, examining each sentence as a separate unit. Or, taking advantage of a computer, isolate each paragraph from its context by printing it on a separate page. (Of course, reassemble the paragraphs before submitting the paper.)

6f   Examining a sample editing and final draft

The second paragraph of Sara Ling's edited draft appears below. One change Ling made throughout the essay shows up here: she resolved an inconsistency in references to *you, people,* and *we,* settling on a consistent *we.* In addition, Ling corrected several sentence fragments in the middle of the paragraph.

Writing on the Internet, ~~you~~ *we* can be as anonymous as ~~you~~ *we* like. Unless ~~you~~ *we* tell them, the people ~~you~~ *we* communicate with do not know ~~your~~ *our* age or gender or race~~.~~ ~~W~~ *w*hether ~~you're~~ *we're* fat or thin or neat or sloppy~~.~~ ~~W~~ *w*hat kind of clothes ~~you~~ *we* wear~~.~~ ~~(Maybe you're not~~ *if we're* wearing clothes at all). Even people who know ~~you~~ personally don't know who ~~you~~ *we* are if ~~you~~ *we* conceal ~~your~~ *our* identit*ies* with ~~an~~ invented screen name*s*.

Sara Ling's final essay appears below, typed in MLA format except for page breaks. (See pp. 376–381.) Comments in the margins point out key features of the essay's content. (You can also view Ling's final draft and the marginal comments on this book's Web site: *http://www.awlonline.com/littlebrown.*)

Sara Ling

Professor Nelson

English 120A

14 April 2000

The Internet:

Fragmentation or Community?

We hear all sorts of predictions about how the
Internet will enrich our individual lives and promote
communication, tolerance, and thus community in our

Descriptive title

Introduction

society. But are these promises realistic? In her essay "Welcome to Cyberbia," M. Kadi argues that they are not. Instead, she maintains, the Internet will lead to more fragmentation, not community, because users merely seek out others with the same biases, concerns, and needs as their own. The point is an interesting one, but Kadi seems to overlook that the Internet's uniquely anonymous form of interaction could actually build diversity into community by lowering the barriers of physical appearance in communication.

1. Question to be addressed

2. Summary of Kadi's essay

3. Thesis statement

Writing on the Internet, we can be as anonymous as we like. Unless we tell them, the people we communicate with do not know our age or gender or race, whether we're fat or thin or neat or sloppy, or what kind of clothes we wear (if we're wearing clothes at all). Even people who know us personally don't know who we are if we conceal our identities with invented screen names.

Explanation of Internet's anonymity

Because of this anonymity, we can communicate freely on the Internet without being prejudged because of our physical attributes. For example, a high school student can participate in a physics discussion group without fear of being dismissed by the group's professional physicists just because of her age. Similarly, an adult man can chat about music with teenagers who might otherwise ignore or laugh at him. A woman I know posed as a man on a snowboarding forum and received none of the hostile responses--such as "What does a girl know?"--that I got when I innocently revealed my gender on the same forum.

First main point: We are not prejudged by others.

1. Examples

Granted, concealing or altering identities on the Internet can be a problem, as when adults pose as children to seduce or harm them. These well-publicized occurrences say much about the need to monitor children's use of the Internet and be cautious about

2. Qualification of first main point

6g

meeting Internet correspondents. However, they do not undermine the value of being able to make ourselves heard in situations where normally (in the real world) we would be shut out.

3. Conclusion of first main point

The Internet's anonymity has a flip side, too: just as we cannot be prejudged, so we cannot prejudge others because of their appearance. Often in face-to-face interaction, we assume we know things about people just because of the way they look. People with athletic builds must be unintelligent. Heavy people must be uninteresting. People in wheelchairs must be unapproachable or pathetic. Perhaps most significant, people of other races must have fixed and contrary views about all kinds of issues, from family values to crime to affirmative action. Assumptions like these prevent us from discovering the interests and concerns we share with people who merely look different. But with the anonymity of the Internet, such physical barriers to understanding are irrelevant.

Second main point: We cannot prejudge others.

1. Clarification of second main point

2. Examples

3. Effects

4. Conclusion of second main point

A world without physical bias may be an unreachable ideal, but the more we communicate with just our minds, the more likely it is that our minds will find common ground. Logged on, we can become more accepted and more accepting, more tolerated and more tolerant. We can become a community.

Conclusion, summarizing essay

Work Cited

Kadi, M. "Welcome to Cyberbia." Utne Reader Mar.-Apr. 1995: 57-59.

Work cited in MLA style (see p. 357)

6g   Revising collaboratively

In many writing courses students work together on writing, most often commenting on each other's work to help with revision. This collaborative writing gives experience in reading written work critically and in reaching others through writing. Collaboration may occur face to face in small groups, via drafts and comments on paper, or on computers.

Whether you collaborate in person, on paper, or on a computer, you will be more comfortable and helpful and will benefit more from others' comments if you follow a few guidelines.

Commenting on others' writing

- Be sure you know what the writer is saying. If necessary, summarize the paper to understand its content. (See p. 283–284.)
- Unless you have other instructions, address only your most significant concerns with the work. (Use the revision checklist on p. 33 as a guide to what is significant.) Remember that you are the reader, not the writer. Resist the temptation to edit sentences, add details, or otherwise assume responsibility for the paper.
- Be specific. If something confuses you, say *why*. If you disagree with a conclusion, say *why*.
- Be supportive as well as honest. Tell the writer what you like about the paper. Word comments positively: instead of *This paragraph doesn't interest me,* say *You have an interesting detail here that I almost missed.* Question the writer in a way that emphasizes the effect of the work on you, the reader: *This paragraph confuses me because. . . .* And avoid measuring the work against a set of external standards: *This essay is poorly organized. Your thesis statement is inadequate.*
- While reading, make your comments in writing, even if you will be delivering them in person later on. Then you'll be able to recall what you thought.

- If you are reading the paper on a computer, not on paper, then be sure to specify what part of the paper each of your comments relates to. When you review papers using e-mail, you can embed your comments directly into the paper. You can do the same when you review papers in word-processor files, or you may be able to use your word processor's Comment function to insert your comments as annotations on the paper. (See pp. 66–67 and 68–69 for more about collaborating with computers.)
- If you are responding on paper or online, not face to face with the writer, remember that the writer won't be able to ask for immediate clarification or infer additional information from your gestures, facial expressions, and tone of voice. In these situations, word your comments carefully to avoid misunderstandings.

6h

Benefiting from comments on your writing

- Think of your readers as counselors or coaches who will help you see the virtues and flaws in your work and sharpen your awareness of readers' needs.
- Read or listen to comments closely.
- Make sure you know what the critic is saying. If you need more information, ask for it, or consult the appropriate section of this handbook.
- Don't become defensive. Letting comments offend you will only erect a barrier to improvement in your writing. As one writing teacher advises, "Leave your ego at the door."
- When comments seem appropriate, revise your work in response to them. You will learn more from the act of revision than from just thinking about changes.
- Though you should be open to suggestions, you are the final authority on your paper. You are free to decline advice when you think it is inappropriate.
- Keep track of both the strengths and weaknesses others identify. Then in following assignments you can build on your successes and give special attention to problem areas.

ESL In some cultures writers do not expect criticism from readers, or readers do not expect to think and speak critically about what they read. If critical responses are uncommon in your native culture, collaboration may at first be uncomfortable for you. Consider that many writers in English think of a draft or even a final paper as more an exploration of ideas than the last word on a subject, and they are interested in their readers' questions and suggestions. Readers of English, in turn, often approach a text in a skeptical frame of mind. Their tactful questions and suggestions are usually considered appropriate.

6h   Preparing a writing portfolio

Your writing instructor may ask you to assemble samples of your writing into a portfolio, or folder, once or more during the course. Such a portfolio gives you a chance to consider all your writing over a period and showcase your best work.

Although the requirements for portfolios vary, most instructors are looking for a range of writing that demonstrates your progress and strengths as a writer. You, in turn, see how you have advanced from one assignment to the next, as you've had time for new knowledge to sink in and time for practice. Instructors often allow students to revise papers before placing them in the portfolio, even if the papers have already been submitted earlier. In that case, every paper in the portfolio can benefit from all your learning.

An assignment to assemble a writing portfolio will probably also provide guidelines for what to include, how the portfolio will be evaluated, and how (or whether) it will be weighted for a grade. Be sure you understand the purpose of the portfolio and who will read it. For instance, if your instructor will be the only reader and his or her guidelines encourage you to show evidence of progress, you might include a paper that took big risks but never entirely succeeded. In contrast, if a committee of instructors will read your work and the guidelines urge you to demonstrate your competence as a writer, you might include only papers that did succeed.

Unless the guidelines specify otherwise, provide error-free copies of your final drafts, label all your samples with your name, and assemble them all in a folder. Add a cover letter or memo that lists the samples, explains why you've included each one, and evaluates your progress as a writer. The self-evaluation involved should be a learning experience for you and will help your readers assess your development as a writer.

7 Formatting

Formatting is the last step in the writing process. It requires that you focus on two aspects of your paper: its form and appearance and the documentation of sources. Chapter 9 of this book provides some general principles and elements of document design, form, and appearance.

To ensure that written documents are clear and consistent, most organizations, academic institutions, and fields of study adopt a specific STYLE GUIDE. A style guide contains essential information and standards that writers in a specific organization, institution, or field of study use to ensure clarity and consistency of written documents. A style guide provides four types of guidance for writers:

- Prescribes the layout, form, and appearance of your paper.
- States preferences for rules of grammar and word usage that are in dispute.
- Prescribes the format for citing sources in the body of the paper.
- Prescribes the format for citing sources at the end of the paper.

7

   The University of Phoenix has three approved style guides, depending upon your campus and your field of study. Two of the approved style guides for the university are *The Little, Brown Compact Handbook's* guidelines for MLA format and documentation (p. 343) and its guidelines for APA format and documentation (p. 391). Some campuses do not use the APA guidelines in *The Little, Brown Compact Handbook*. Instead, they require students to use the *Publication Manual of the American Psychological Association*, Fourth Edition. Be sure to check with your instructor to confirm that you have the current edition of the approved style guide for your program.

II

Computers in Writing

II

Computers in Writing

http://help.unc.edu/documentation Computer basics, from the University of North Carolina.

http://microsoft.com/education/tutorial/classroom Word-processing tutorials for use in and out of the classroom, from Microsoft.

http://www.corel.com/support/options/tips.htm Tips and tricks for the word processor WordPerfect and other programs, from Corel.

http://www.pbs.org/uti Internet basics, from the Public Broadcasting Service.

http://www.learnthenet.com/english/section/e-mail.html E-mail basics, from Learn the Net.

http://www.fau.edu/netiquette/net/index.html A guide to Internet etiquette, from Florida Atlantic University.

8a

 This and the following two chapters introduce techniques that can help you achieve your purpose when you work with a computer. This chapter treats the range of computer skills that are especially relevant to writers: word processing, using spelling checkers and other tools, writing electronic mail, and using the World Wide Web. Chapter 9 discusses and illustrates the principles of document design. And Chapter 10 explains the basics of composing for the Web.

Note The examples in these chapters illustrate functions and concepts that are common to most computer systems and software. However, the system or software that you use may rely on slightly different terms and operations. If you need assistance, use the Help menu built into most software programs, consult your instructor, or see the technology advisers at your school.

8a   Using a word processor

If you have used a computer at all, you are probably familiar with Cut, Copy, Paste, and other basic word-processing functions. Many tips for using a word processor appear in Chapters 1–6 opposite the marginal computer symbol. Here, you'll find more advice for managing files and formatting documents.

1   Working with files

On many word processors you create, save, and open documents using the File menu: click New to create a new document, Save to save the document as a file, and Open to retrieve and read a saved document. To organize files, you can store one or more related document files in a folder. You can also go beyond these basics to try out revisions and make comments on a draft while keeping the original intact. The following screen shots and explanations (keyed to each other by number) show how you can work with different versions of a paper by saving files under different names.

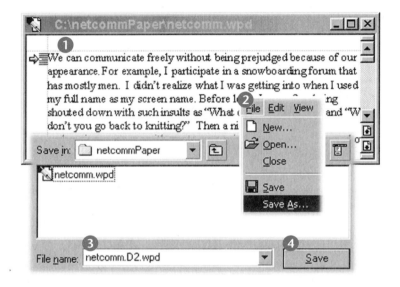

1. Save the original draft with a file name you'll be able to recognize later. The illustrated document's name is *netcomm.wpd*. Place the file in a folder of its own—you'll add later versions to the same folder. (The folder name for the illustrated document is *netcommPaper*.)
2. Create a duplicate version of the original by selecting Save As from the File menu.
3. Give the duplicate a new file name. Use a simple system for naming files—for instance, adding *D2* to the original name for the second draft, *D3* for the third draft, and so on.
4. Save the new version. The original remains intact.

Besides creating duplicates to retrieve ideas and track the development of your papers, you can also save the same file with an alternative name when you need to match the file-naming conventions of a class—for instance, renaming *netcomm* as *Assignment 1*. In addition, creating duplicates of files makes it easy to provide comments on others' documents (see p. 61).

2 Formatting documents

A few essential word-processor functions will help you format many of your academic papers. For more on using these functions on your word processor, consult its Help menu. For more on document design, see the following chapter.

- Set margins by selecting Page Setup in the File menu. Page Setup also controls paper size, paper source, the orientation of the page, and other features.
- Unless you also plan to use headers or footers (see below), add page numbers by selecting Page Numbers in the Format or Insert menu.
- Add your name, the paper title, the date, or other information as headers (tops of pages) or footers (bottoms of pages) by selecting Headers and Footers in the View or Insert menu. You can add page numbers at the same time.
- Use the Format menu to create bulleted or numbered lists (select Bullets and Numbering) or to create text in more than one column (select Columns).
- Use the Insert menu for many functions, such as creating a new page (select Break or New Page), adding an illustration to a document (select Graphics or Picture), or adding footnotes or endnotes to a document (select Footnote/Endnote).
- Preview the way your final document will appear when it is printed by selecting Print Preview from the File menu.

8b

8b Working with spelling checkers and other word-processing tools

Most word processors include a Tools menu with functions such as a spelling checker, a grammar and style checker, a thesaurus, and a program for tracking revisions. However, these tools will help you only if you approach them critically. Used uncritically, they can cause you considerable problems.

Note The first two tools discussed on the following pages—spelling checkers and grammar and style checkers—can usually be set to flag possible errors as soon as you type them. But many writers find this function distracting when they are trying to generate ideas or do in-depth revision. If you are attending too much to the flagged surface problems in your writing, use the Tools menu to turn off the checker. You can always instruct the computer to check for errors when you are ready to do so.

1 Using a spelling checker

Your word processor's spelling checker can be a great ally: it will flag words that are spelled incorrectly and usually suggest alternative spellings that resemble what you've typed. However, this ally also has the potential to undermine you because of its limitations:

- The checker flags all words that don't match entries in its dictionary. Thus it may flag a word that you've spelled correctly just because it doesn't recognize the word.
- In providing a list of alternative spellings for your word, the checker may highlight the one it considers most likely to be correct. You need to verify that this alternative is actually what you intend before selecting it. Keep in mind, too, that the checker's list may not provide a correct alternative at all. Consult an online or printed dictionary when you aren't sure of the checker's recommendations (see pp. 121–122).
- Most important, a spelling checker will not flag words that appear in its dictionary but are misused by you. It cannot recognize typos such as *of* for *or*, *form* for *from*, or *now* for *not*. Nor can it spot misuses of commonly confused words such as *their/there*, *its/it's*, and *affect/effect*.

You can supplement a spelling checker by maintaining a file of your frequent misspellings and selecting Find under the Edit menu to check for them. But in the end *the only way to rid your papers of spelling errors is to proofread your papers yourself.* (See pp. 47–48 for proofreading tips.)

For more advice on spelling, see Chapter 41.

2 Using a grammar and style checker

Word processors' grammar and style checkers can flag incorrect grammar or punctuation and wordy or awkward sentences. However, these programs can call your attention only to passages that *may* be faulty. They miss many errors because they are not yet capable of analyzing language in all its complexity (for instance, they can't accurately distinguish a word's part of speech when there are different possibilities, as *light* can be a noun, a verb, or an adjective). And they often question passages that don't need editing, such as an appropriate passive verb or a deliberate and emphatic use of repetition.

In the screen shot opposite, the checker has flagged a direct repetition of *light* in the first sentence but left unflagged the other intrusive repetitions of the word. And the checker has flagged the entire second sentence because it is long, but in fact the sentence is grammatically correct and clear.

8b

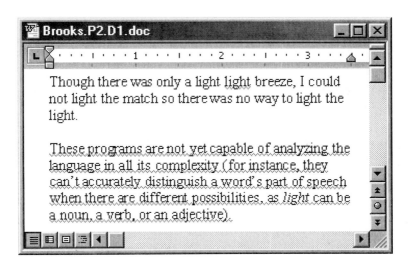

To make a grammar and style checker most useful, you can customize it to suit your needs and habits as a writer. On most word processors, for instance, you can select Options under the Tools menu and then specify certain features to look for, such as possessives and plurals, subject-verb agreement, passive voice, and clichés. If you have little problem with agreement, you can instruct the checker to ignore that error. But if you overuse the passive voice or mistakenly add apostrophes to plural nouns, you can set the checker to find possible problems.

As with a spelling checker, so with a grammar and style checker: it will not do your editing for you. Each time it questions something, you must determine whether a change is needed at all and what change will be most effective, and you must read your papers carefully on your own to find any errors the program missed.

3 Using other word-processing tools

Word processors either come with or are compatible with a number of optional programs. Some of these programs, too, can help or hurt your writing depending on how critically you use them.

- A *comment program* enables you to provide feedback on others' writing or to annotate your own work. Select Comment from the Insert menu and then compose your commentary. An icon or highlight in the text will indicate that a comment has been added, and readers can view the commentary by selecting the icon or highlighted item.

- A *change-tracking program*, found in the Tools or File menu, records the revisions you make in documents—for instance, highlighting additions and inserting cross-out lines through deletions. Using this program, you may feel freer to revise because you can always revert to your original text. You can also weigh the effectiveness of the original and revised versions because you can see them side by side (and easily accept or reject changes). And you can evaluate the kinds of changes you are making. For instance, if you see only minor surface alterations (like word substitutions and added punctuation), you might consider whether you need to make more fundamental changes.

8b

- A *thesaurus program* helps with word choices by responding to your word with a display of several synonyms (words that have similar meanings). A single keystroke allows you to replace your word with a displayed word. Thesaurus programs are limited, however, because they display only some synonyms, not all, and even a narrow list may contain words that do not suit your meaning. Neither an electronic nor a printed thesaurus will be any help if it leads you to misuse words whose meanings you don't know. Before you use a word suggested by a thesaurus, always check its meaning in a dictionary. (See p. 122 for more on thesauruses.)

- An *invention or discovery program* helps you develop a topic by prompting you with a structured set of questions or by providing creative analogies that help you think imaginatively. These programs can help you get started, develop new insights, and conceive a purpose for your writing. But they can also be limited because many employ all-purpose prompts. Use such programs critically, thinking of additional ways to explore the elements of your topic.

- An *outlining program* helps you organize your work by providing automatic indentions, easy resequencing, and other features. However, some writers consider these programs straitjackets because they allow little leeway in outline structure. To experiment with whether an outlining program can help you, select Bullets and Numbering or Outline/Bullets and Numbering from the Format or Insert menu of your word processor.

- A *graphics program* allows you to create charts and graphs or images to be inserted into your documents. You can also use the programs to resize and crop images that you wish to add to your documents. (See pp. 79–83 for more on illustrations.)

- A *documentation program* helps you format your source citations in various disciplines' styles. (See pp. 329–330 for more on these programs.)

- A *readability program* can help you determine the degree to which your work is clear and easy to read. A readability program provides statistics about average word, sentence, and paragraph length and the average number of syllables per word. Some readability programs also rate the reading ease or the grade level of the document.

8c   Using electronic mail

If you work on a computer, you'll probably be using electronic mail, or e-mail, for a host of reasons, from conversing with friends to conducting serious research. This section covers e-mail basics: composing and sending messages, responding to messages, observing Internet etiquette, and using e-mail to interact with the other students in a course. For more on using e-mail as a research tool, see page 315.

1   Composing and sending messages

The screen shot below illustrates the essential features of an e-mail message.

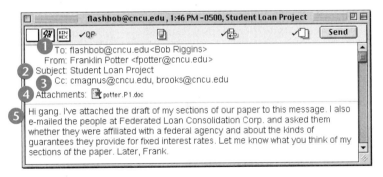

1. Enter the e-mail address of the person you are contacting in the To or Recipient field. Type the address exactly: an incorrect letter will send the message astray.
2. Give the message a subject heading that describes its content. Then your reader knows what priority to assign the message— a particular help for readers who receive many messages a day.
3. Include in the Cc field the e-mail addresses of others to whom you want to send copies of the message. In the screen shot above, the author was asking for feedback on a group project, and he sent his message to the other members of his group, too.

4. You can attach a file—such as a document from your word processor—to be sent with the e-mail message to all the message's recipients. Be aware, though, that attachments are not always readable because of incompatible file formats or translation problems. If you and your partners use different word processors (such as WordPerfect and Microsoft Word), you may not be able to read each other's files. And documents sent over the Internet are sometimes encoded in special formats (such as MIME) that may need to be decoded at the recipients' end. You can usually solve the problem of incompatible word processors by saving the files in a generic format such as rich text format (RTF). To learn how to decode attachments, consult with your school's technology advisers.

5. Compose a suitable message that is concise and relevant to your recipients' concerns. Adjust the formality of your message to your writing situation: for instance, you might use slang and be casual about spelling and grammar in a quick reply to a friend, but you'd want to be more formal (and scrupulously correct) in addressing a potential employer. In the message shown on the preceding page, the writer knows the recipients well and yet has serious information to convey to them, so he writes informally and yet states his points carefully. (See the next page for more on composing e-mail messages.)

Note Only some e-mail programs allow underlining, italics, and boldface. Even if you can use such highlighting, you should assume that your recipients will not be able to see it in your messages. For alternatives, use underscores to indicate _underlining_ or asterisks to provide *emphasis*.

2 Responding to messages

To respond to an e-mail message, use the Reply or Respond feature of your e-mail program, keeping the following in mind:

- Check that the response addresses the appropriate person or people. Using the Reply or Respond feature generally prompts the e-mail program to provide a message screen with the original sender's address inserted in the To field, your address inserted in the From field, and the addresses of the original copy recipients inserted in the Cc field. If a message is relevant to a single person only, delete any additional addresses.

- Check that the reply still has an appropriate subject heading. Most e-mail programs label a response with the same subject heading as the original, preceded by *Re:* (from Latin, meaning "In reference to"). If your response indeed continues the same subject, then *Re:* indicates as much. However, if you raise a new issue, you should rewrite the subject heading to say so.

- Use quoted material from earlier messages critically. Most e-mail programs can copy the original message into your response, setting off the quoted material with angle brackets (>) or some other device. By weaving your replies into the quoted material, you can respond to the author point by point, as you would in conversation. However, delete from the original anything you are not responding to so that your recipient can focus on what you have to say without wading through his or her own words.

3 Observing netiquette

To communicate effectively online, you'll need to abide by some rules of behavior and simple courtesies. You won't always see others observing this NETIQUETTE, or Internet etiquette, but you will see that those who do observe it receive the more thoughtful and considerate replies.

Composing messages

- In the body of your message, address your reader(s) by name if possible and sign off with your own name and information on how to contact you. Your own name is especially important if your e-mail address does not spell it out.
- Take the time to read and revise your message before sending it, looking for ways to condense and clarify your ideas and moderate your tone. Use short paragraphs with blank lines between them. For long messages—which recipients can review only one screen at a time—a tight structure, a clear forecast of the content, and a clear division into parts (using headings if necessary) not only improve effectiveness but also show courtesy. Proofread all but the most informal messages for errors in grammar, punctuation, and spelling.
- Pay careful attention to tone in online messages. Refrain from FLAMING, or attacking, correspondents. Don't use all-capital letters, which SHOUT. And use irony or sarcasm only cautiously: in the absence of facial expressions, they can lead to misunderstandings. To indicate irony and emotions, you can use EMOTICONS, such as the smiley :-). These sideways faces made up of punctuation can easily be overused, though, and should not substitute for thoughtfully worded opinions.
- Avoid saying anything in e-mail that you would not say in a printed document such as a letter or memo. E-mail can usually be retrieved from the server, and in business and academic

settings it may well be retrieved in disputes over contracts, grades, and other matters.

Reading and responding to messages

- Be a forgiving reader. Avoid nitpicking over spelling or other surface errors. And because attitudes are sometimes difficult to convey, give authors an initial benefit of the doubt: a writer who at first seems hostile may simply have tried too hard to be concise; a writer who at first seems unserious may simply have failed at injecting humor into a worthwhile message.
- You may want to forward a message you've received to someone else, but do so only if you know that the author of the message won't mind.
- Avoid participating in flame "wars," overheated dialogues that contribute little or no information or understanding. If a war breaks out in a discussion, ignore it: don't rush to defend someone who is being attacked, and don't respond even if you are under attack yourself.

4   Collaborating using e-mail

Many instructors integrate e-mail collaboration into their courses, encouraging students to use it for exchanging and commenting on drafts of projects and also for discussing class readings, ideas for writing, and other topics. Your instructor may provide instructions in addition to those below for the activities in his or her course.

Working on drafts

If you use e-mail to exchange and comment on drafts, following a few guidelines can help the work proceed smoothly and productively:

- Your instructor may suggest how often you should check incoming e-mail or how quickly you should respond to messages. If not, work with your group or partner to establish a procedure: for instance, checking messages every day, responding immediately to urgent messages, and responding to other messages within one or two days.
- To share drafts and comments by e-mail, you can copy and paste text into your e-mail messages or send word-processor files as attachments. (See pp. 63–64 on attachments.) Your group may need to experiment a bit to see which option works better, and you can then agree on procedures.

- When you are responding to others' drafts, especially early drafts, concentrate on deep issues such as thesis, purpose, audience, organization, and support for the thesis. (See p. 33 for a revision checklist that can guide your reading.) Since it's often difficult to take in an entire paper when you're reading it one screen at a time, consider printing out the draft for review. Hold comments on style, grammar, punctuation, and other surface matters until you're reviewing late drafts, if indeed you are expected to comment on them at all.

Participating in class discussions

8c

In addition to exchanging drafts and comments by e-mail, you may have access to a class discussion list through which you can communicate with classmates for gathering information, generating and testing ideas for assignments, or responding to readings. Once you subscribe to the class list (your instructor will tell you how), you will receive other list members' messages in your incoming e-mail. Messages addressing the same topic form a THREAD. Your message may start a new thread or may join a thread already in progress.

When participating in an e-mail discussion list, consider these guidelines:

- Your discussion list will need to establish a code of conduct for participation—for instance, what topics will be appropriate, how frequently postings are required, and how formal or informal the conversations should be. Your instructor may offer suggestions, or the group may make such a code the topic of an early exchange.
- The class e-mail list is a public space. It can be easy (and embarrassing) to send a message that you intended for one person to the entire class instead. Always double-check the addresses on your messages before sending them.
- Participating in a discussion list can serve social as well as academic purposes, helping to cement the list's members into a cohesive group. Messages that do not contribute information or ideas for class work may still be worthwhile if they give the members a social foundation for collaborating. However, such messages should not overwhelm the threads devoted to writing. To keep the conversation on track, your instructor may ask list members to submit messages for checking or grading. Or you and your classmates may take it upon yourselves to channel the conversation productively.

8d Going places and working on the Web

Using the World Wide Web both efficiently and critically is fast becoming a requirement for college and work. This section explains the basics of Web addresses, describes Web-based student collaboration, and directs you to resources on a range of Web activities.

1 Using Web addresses

Every file on the Web has a unique location, called a UNIFORM RESOURCE LOCATOR, or URL. A URL has three parts and a fixed form: *protocol://domain/path.* Here is a translation of the address *http:// www.nyu.edu/urban/leaders.html:*

- The Internet uses specific standards or PROTOCOLS to transfer files. It transfers most Web files using the hypertext transfer protocol (HTTP). The abbreviation is typed in small letters at the beginning of a URL and followed by a colon and two slashes.
- Immediately after the two slashes, the DOMAIN names the computer, or SERVER, that houses the document you seek. Each server has a unique name, usually referring to the organization that owns it. In *www.nyu.edu,* for instance, *nyu* stands for New York University and *edu* indicates an educational institution. (Domain names can be useful in evaluating Internet sources; see p. 322.)
- The PATH specifies the location and name of the document you seek. For instance, */urban/leaders.html* identifies a directory (*urban*) and a file inside it (*leaders.html*).

Note *A URL must be typed exactly as you find it:* same capital and small letters, same punctuation, same spacing. Even a tiny error will keep you from reaching your destination.

To reach a Web site and its files, you need a program called a BROWSER: Netscape Communicator and Microsoft Internet Explorer are the most common, and one of them is probably in use at your school. Enter the URL in the Address or Location field at the top of the browser window, and then press the Enter or Return key.

2 Collaborating using Web class tools

Increasingly, the Web serves as a medium for online collaboration among students in a course. Your class may have access to a Web site where you can check assignments, find resources, post messages, and share files, among other activities. Such a Web site can be the primary work space for the class, requiring the same investment that you would bring to class meetings. The advice given earlier about online etiquette (pp. 65–66) and collaborating by e-mail (pp. 66–67) applies to Web collaboration, too.

Note If the class Web site is password protected, you'll need to enter an account name and password every time you access the site. Whether the account name and password are assigned to you or chosen by you, *remember them*. Write them down if you have a secure place to do so, or else etch them in your memory.

3 Consulting Web resources

Both in this book and on the Web itself, you can find resources that will help you become a proficient Web user:

- Information about the workings and possibilities of the Internet appears on many Web sites, including the following:
  Learn the Net
    http://www.learnthenet.com/english/section/intbas.html
  Newbie Net
    http://www.newbie.net/CyberCourse
  Public Broadcasting Service
    http://www.pbs.org/uti
- Information about composing for the Web, with links to helpful Web sites, appears on pages 87–95.
- Information about conducting research on the Web, including using search engines, appears on pages 310–315.
- Guidelines for evaluating Web and other online sources appear on pages 320–325.
- Web sites for specific disciplines appear on pages 301–305.
- Documentation models for electronic sources appear on pages 364–72 (MLA style), 403–405 (APA style), 426–428 (Chicago style), 435–436 (CBE style), and 439–448 (Columbia online style).

8e

8e University of Phoenix electronic resources

Writing skills are critical to your success at the University of Phoenix and in your professional career. To help you improve these skills, the university makes a number of electronic resources available to all students, faculty, and alumni. All these resources can be accessed from your home page on the University of Phoenix Student Web Site. Most services are free of charge, and we encourage you to make use of these valuable tools.

1   Online Library Collection

The University of Phoenix Library Online Collection is a fully functional digital library where you can search and retrieve millions of articles from thousands of publications, using a desktop or laptop computer. The Online Collection includes numerous general and specialized databases and a wide range of reference materials including:

- General and specialized encyclopedias, dictionaries, and biographical data.
- Directories to locate public companies and key personnel.
- Financial data from publicly held companies in the US and around the world and statistics about the economy and foreign trade.
- Access to over 1200 classic books, specialized texts in information systems and technology, and downloads of Microsoft Reader® and future electronic books.
- Articles, many of them full-text, from over twenty academic and general interest indexes and databases.

2   Selected links

The selected links section of the University of Phoenix library contains many helpful Web sites for research that were selected and recommended by library staff. These sites are organized into the following categories for quick access by library users:

- General reference (including numerous writing guides)
- Business
- Counseling
- Education
- Health sciences
- Information technology
- Legal issues
- Web sites relating to Canadian business, statistics, and law

3   Other UOP library services

In addition to the resources discussed above, the University of Phoenix Digital Library also offers User Guides to assist you in accessing and understanding the library system, and the "Ask a Librarian" service, where you can request guidance and obtain recommendations for effective research about specific topics. These services can be accessed by telephoning the library at 800-366-9693 or by e-mail at library@uophx.edu.

8e

4 Virtual Writing Lab

The Virtual Writing Lab is an e-mail address where students can send their written materials (papers, projects, etc.) to be reviewed by a qualified University of Phoenix faculty member. You can send your materials to the lab twenty-four hours a day and receive a reply within a couple of days. The faculty member will assess the writing and provide detailed feedback on how it could be improved. You can access this service by selecting the Writing Lab from the menu on your University of Phoenix Student Web Site home page.

5 Other UOP electronic writing resources

8e

The University strives continually to enhance its student services and currently provides a number of other electronic resources to assist you in improving your writing skills. These resources are all available from your University of Phoenix Student Web Site, and they include multimedia and Web-based computer software tutorials; the online Student Proficiency Assessment System (PAS); and the Skills Enhancement Center on the PAS, which contains English tutorials and practice exams to help students prepare for the university's proficiency examinations.

9 Document Design

http://www.graphic-design.com General design resources, from the Internet Design and Publishing Center.

http://www.pomona.edu/Academics/courserelated/classprojects/ Visual-lit/intro/intro.html Conceptual discussion of shape, color, scale, and visual elements, from the On-Line Visual Literacy Project.

http://www.fontsite.com Information about typography and fonts, from the FontSite.

http://www.colostate.edu/Depts/WritingCenter/references/graphics.htm In-depth information about using tables, figures, and images, from Colorado State University.

des

9a

Imaginehowharditwouldbetoreadandwriteiftextlookedlikethis. To make reading and writing easier, we place spaces between words. This convention and many others—such as page margins, paragraph breaks, and headings—have evolved over time to help writers communicate clearly with readers.

This chapter looks at the principles and elements of design that can help you present any document effectively. Guidelines for specific kinds of documents appear elsewhere in this book:

- Designing pages for the World Wide Web, Chapter 10, page 87.
- Formatting academic papers in MLA style, Chapter 52, page 376.
- Formatting academic papers in APA style, Chapter 53, page 407.
- Designing documents for business, Chapter 58, page 461.

9a Considering principles of design

Most of the principles of design respond to the ways we read. White space, for instance, relieves our eyes and helps to lead us through a document. Groupings or lists help to show relationships. Type sizes, images, and color add variety and help to emphasize important elements.

As you begin to design your own documents, think about your purpose, the expectations of your readers, and how readers will move through your document. Also consider the general principles of design discussed below, noting how they overlap and support each other. The flyer on the next page illustrates some of these principles. An advertisement intended both to attract attention and to convey information, the flyer is at first glance visually appealing, but it also effectively organizes information and directs our attention.

Literacy Volunteers

ANNUAL

AWARDS

DINNER

**Friday Night
February 25th
7:30-9:30
Suite 42
Springfield
VA Hospital**

 **Enjoy food and beverages provided by
some of Springfield's finest restaurants.**

 **Celebrate the efforts and special
accomplishments of our students.**

 **Congratulate our tutors
for their wonderful service.**

For information, contact VA Literacy Volunteers at (962) 555-9191.

Creating flow

Many of the other design principles work in concert with the larger goal of conducting the reader through a document by establishing flow, a pattern for the eye to follow. In some documents, such as reports, flow may be achieved mainly with headings, lists, and illustrations (see pp. 78–80). In other documents, such as the flyer opposite, flow will come from the arrangement and spacing of information as well as from headings.

Spacing

The white space on a page eases crowding and focuses readers' attention. On an otherwise full page, just the space indicating paragraphs (an indention or a line of extra space) gives readers a break and reassures them that ideas are divided into manageable chunks.

In papers, reports, and other formal documents, spacing appears mainly in paragraph breaks, in margins, and around headings and lists. In publicity documents, such as flyers and brochures, spacing is usually more generous between elements, helping boxes, headings, and the like pop off the page.

des

9a

Grouping

Grouping information shows relationships visually, reinforcing the sense of the text itself. Here in this discussion, we group the various principles of design under visually identical headings to emphasize them and their similar importance. In the flyer on the previous page, a list set off with check marks itemizes the activities planned for the advertised event. The list covers *all* the activities and *only* the activities: details of date, time, and place, for instance, appear elsewhere on the page. Thinking of likely groups as you write can help you organize your material so that it makes sense to you and your readers.

Emphasizing

Part of a critical reader's task is to analyze and interpret the meaning of a document, and design helps the reader by stressing what's important. Type fonts and sizes, headings, indentions, color, boxes, white space—all of these guide the reader's eye and establish hierarchies of information, so that the reader almost instinctively grasps what is crucial, what is less so, and what is merely supplementary. In the flyer on the previous page, for instance, color and a box emphasize crucial information about the event being advertised. In this book, color, size, and indention establish the relative importance of various headings: for instance, the colored rule above heading 9b, opposite, indicates that it is a primary heading, more important than the numbered headings following it. As you design a document, considering where and how you want to emphasize elements can actually help you determine your document's priorities.

Standardizing

As we read a document, the design of its elements quickly creates expectations in us. We assume, for instance, that headings in the same size and color signal information of the same importance or that a list contains items of parallel content. Just as the design creates expectations, so it should fulfill them, treating similar elements similarly. Anticipating design standards as you write a document can help you develop a consistent approach to its elements and then convey that approach to readers.

Standardizing also creates clear, uncluttered documents. Even if they are used consistently, too many variations in type fonts and sizes, colors, indentions, and the like overwhelm readers as they try to determine the significance of the parts. Many formal documents, such as papers and reports, need no more than a single type font for text and headings, with type size and highlighting (such as CAPITAL LETTERS, **boldface,** or *italics*) distinguishing the levels of headings. Publicity documents, such as flyers and brochures, generally employ more variation to arrest readers' attention. The flyer on page 73, for example, uses three type fonts: one for the organization's name, another for the event's title, and a third for everything else. Variations in the third font distinguish the box, the list, and the information along the bottom.

9b   Using the elements of design

Applying the preceding design principles involves seven main elements of document design: print quality (below), margins (p. 76), text (p. 76); lists (p. 78); headings (p. 78); tables, figures, and images (p. 79); and color (p. 83). You won't use all these elements for every project, however, and in many academic- and business-writing situations you will be required to follow a prescribed format. See pages 343 and 391 for specific guidelines for MLA and APA style.

Note Your word processor may provide wizards or templates for many kinds of documents, such as letters, memos, reports, agendas, résumés, and brochures. WIZARDS guide you through setting up and writing complicated documents. TEMPLATES are preset forms to which you add your own text, headings, and other elements. Wizards and templates can be helpful, but not if they lead you to create cookie-cutter documents no matter what the writing situation. Always keep in mind that a document should be appropriate for your subject, audience, and purpose.

1   Print quality

The cartridge on your printer should be fresh enough to produce a dark impression. A printer that forms characters out of tiny dots may be acceptable for your academic papers, but make sure the tails on letters such as *j*, *p*, and *y* fall below the line of type, as they do here. For documents that are complex or that will be distributed to the public, use an inkjet or laser printer, which creates characters more like the ones you see here. If you require color, varied type fonts, or illustrations and your printer is not up to the job, you may be able to use more advanced equipment in your school's computer lab.

2   Margins

Margins at the top, bottom, and sides of a page help to prevent the page from overwhelming readers with unpleasant crowding. Most academic and business documents use a minimum one-inch margin on all sides. Publicity documents, such as the flyer on page 73, often use narrower margins, compensating with white space between elements. For setting margins on a word processor, see page 59.

3   Text

A document must be readable. You can make text readable by attending to line spacing, type fonts and sizes, highlighting, word spacing, and line breaks.

Line spacing

Most academic documents are double-spaced, with an initial indention for paragraphs, while most business documents are single-spaced, with an extra line of space between paragraphs. Double or triple spacing sets off headings in both. Publicity documents, such as flyers and brochures, tend to use more line spacing to separate and group distinct parts of the content.

Type fonts and sizes

The readability of text also derives from the type fonts (or faces) and their sizes. For academic and business documents, choose a type size of 10 or 12 points, as in these samples:

10-point Courier   10-point Times New Roman
12-point Courier   12-point Times New Roman

For text, generally use a font with SERIFS—the small lines finishing the letters in the samples above and in the font you're reading now. SANS SERIF fonts (*sans* means "without" in French) include this one found on many word processors:

10-point Arial   12-point Arial

Though fine for headings, sans serif type can be more difficult than serif type to read in extended text.

Your word processor probably offers many decorative fonts as well:

10-POINT COPPERPLATE   **10-point Dom Casual**

10-point Corvallis Sans   **10-point Eras Demi**

10-POINT STENCIL   *10-point Park Avenue*

10-point Lubalin Graph   10-POINT TRAJAN

Such fonts often appear in publicity documents like the flyer on page 73, where they can attract attention, create motion, and reinforce a theme. (In publicity documents, too, font sizes are often much larger than 10 or 12 points, even for passages of text.) In academic and business writing, however, many decorative fonts are inappropriate: letter forms should be conventional and regular.

Note The point size of a type font is often an unreliable guide to its actual size, as the decorative fonts above illustrate: all the samples are 10 points, but they vary considerably. Before you use a font, print out a sample to be sure it is the size you want.

des

9b

Highlighting

Within a document's text, underlined, *italic,* **boldface,** or even color type can emphasize key words or sentences. Underlining is most common in academic writing situations, where instructors often prefer it to italics for titles in source citations. (See p. 271.) Other than for this purpose, avoid any highlighting for emphasis in academic papers. Italics are more common in business writing and publicity documents. Business writing sometimes uses boldface to give strong emphasis—for instance, to a term being defined—and publicity documents often rely extensively on boldface to draw the reader's eye. Neither academic nor business writing generally uses color within passages of text. In publicity documents, however, color may be effective if the color is dark enough to be readable. (See p. 83 for more on color in document design.)

No matter what your writing situation, use highlighting selectively to complement your meaning, not merely to decorate your work. Many readers consider type embellishments to be distracting.

des
9b

Line breaks

Your word processor will generally insert appropriate breaks between lines of continuous text: it will not, for instance, automatically begin a line with a comma or period, and it will not end a line with an opening parenthesis or bracket. When you instruct it to do so (usually under the Tools menu), it will also automatically hyphenate words to prevent very short lines. However, you will have to prevent it from breaking a two-hyphen dash or a three-dot ellipsis mark by spacing to push the beginning of each mark to the next line.

4   Lists

Lists give visual reinforcement to the relations between like items—for example, the steps in a process or the elements of a proposal. A list is easier to read than a paragraph and adds white space to the page.

When wording a list, work for parallelism among items—for instance, all complete sentences or all phrases (see also p. 110). Set the list with space above and below and with numbering or bullets (centered dots or other devices, used in the list below about headings). Most word processors can format a numbered or bulleted list automatically (see p. 59).

5   Headings

Headings are signposts: they direct the reader's attention by focusing the eye on a document's most significant content. Most publicity documents, such as flyers and brochures, use headings both functionally, to direct readers' attention, and decoratively, to capture readers' attention. In contrast, most academic and business documents use headings only functionally, to divide text, orient readers, and create emphasis. Short academic and business documents, such as a three-page paper or a one-page letter, may not need headings at all. But for longer documents follow these guidelines:

- Use one, two, or three levels of headings depending on the needs of your material and the length of your document. Some level of heading every two or so pages will help keep readers on track.
- Create an outline of your document to plan where headings should go. Reserve the first level of heading for the main points (and sections) of your document. Use a second and perhaps a third level of heading to mark subsections of supporting information.

- Keep headings as short as possible while making them specific about the material that follows.
- Word headings consistently—for instance, all questions (*What Is the Scientific Method?*), all phrases with *-ing* words (*Understanding the Scientific Method*), or all phrases with nouns (*The Scientific Method*).
- Indicate the relative importance of headings with type size, positioning, and highlighting, such as capital letters, underlining, or boldface.

des

9b

FIRST-LEVEL HEADING

<u>Second-Level Heading</u>

Third-Level Heading

First-Level Heading

Second-Level Heading

Third-Level Heading

Generally, you can use the same type font and size for headings as for the text. For variety you may want to increase the heading size a bit and try a sans serif font like the one in the second example above. Avoid very decorative fonts like the Corvallis Sans or Stencil shown on page 77.

- Don't break a page immediately after a heading. Push the heading to the next page.

Note Document format in psychology and some other disciplines requires a particular treatment of headings. See pages 409–413 for specific guidelines on APA style.

6   Tables, figures, and images

Tables, figures, and images can often make a point for you more efficiently than words can. Tables present data. Figures (such as graphs and charts) usually recast data in visual form. Images (such as diagrams, drawings, photographs, and clip art) can explain processes, represent what something looks like, add emphasis, or convey a theme.

Academic and many business documents tend to use tables, figures, and images differently from publicity documents. In the latter, illustrations are generally intended to attract readers' attention, enliven the piece, or emphasize a point, and they may not be linked directly to the document's text. In academic and business writing, however, illustrations directly reinforce and amplify the text. Follow these guidelines when using tables, figures, or images in academic and most business writing:

des
9b

- Focus on a purpose for your illustration—a reason for including it and a point you want it to make. Otherwise, readers may find it irrelevant or confusing.
- Provide a source note whenever the data or the entire illustration is someone else's independent material (see p. 329). Each discipline has a slightly different style for such source notes: those in the table and figures on pages 80–81 reflect the style of the social sciences. See also Chapters 52–55.
- Number figures and images together, and label them as figures: Figure 1, Figure 2, and so on. Number and label tables separately from figures: Table 1, Table 2, and so on.
- Refer to each illustration (for instance, "See Figure 2") at the point(s) in the text where readers will benefit by consulting it.
- Unless your document includes many illustrations, place each one on a page by itself immediately after the page that refers to it.

Note Many businesses and academic disciplines have preferred styles for illustrations that differ from those given here. When in doubt about how to prepare and place tables and figures, ask your instructor or supervisor.

Tables

Tables usually summarize raw data, displaying the data concisely and clearly.

- Above the table, provide a self-explanatory title. Readers should see what the table shows without having to refer to your text.
- Provide self-explanatory headings for horizontal rows and vertical columns. Use abbreviations only if you are certain readers will understand them.
- Lay out rows and columns for maximum clarity. In the sample below, lines divide the table into parts, headings align with their data, and numbers align vertically down columns.

Table 1

Computers, Telephones, and Televisions per 1000 People (1998)

Location	Computers	Telephones	Televisions
Worldwide	41	156	184
United States	429	966	916
Europe	108	521	429
Japan	131	651	632
Former Soviet republics	18	148	347

Note: From 12th Annual Computer Industry Almanac (p. 47), by
K. P. Juliussen and E. Juliussen, 1999, Incline Village, NV:
Computer Industry Almanac.

des
9b

Figures

Figures represent data graphically. They include the three kinds
presented on the next page: pie charts (showing percentages making up a whole), bar graphs (showing comparative data), and line
graphs (showing change).

- Below the figure, provide a self-explanatory caption or legend.
  Readers should see what the figure shows without having to
  refer to the body of your document.
- Provide self-explanatory labels for all parts of the figure.
- Draw the figure to reflect its purpose and the visual effect you
  want it to have. For instance, shortening the horizontal date
  axis in Figure 3 on the next page emphasizes the dramatic
  upward movement of the line over time.
- When preparing a graph, generally make the width greater than
  the height. All graphs should have a zero point so that the values are clear.

Photographs, clip art, and other images

Images can either add substance to a document or simply enliven it. In a psychology paper, for instance, a photograph may illustrate a key experiment, while in a brochure a photograph may add
the visual interest of, say, people working together. In academic and
most business documents, images may include not only photographs but also diagrams and drawings. They cannot represent
your ideas by themselves: you need to consider carefully how they

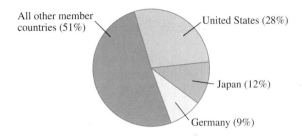

des
9b

Figure 1. Member countries' assessments to United Nations budget of $1.1 billion in 1994. From "The U.N. at 50," by R. Mylan, 1995, October 18, Newsweek, p. 17.

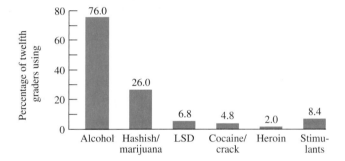

Figure 2. Use of alcohol, compared with other drugs, among twelfth graders (1997). Data from Monitoring the Future Study, 1998, Ann Arbor, MI: University of Michigan Press.

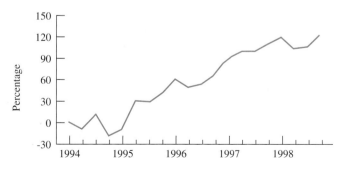

Figure 3. Five-year cumulative return for equities in Standard & Poor's 500 Index, 1994–1998.

relate and add to your text, you need to explain their significance, and you need to label, number, and caption them (see p. 81–82).

One kind of image rarely appears in academic and business writing: CLIP ART, icons and drawings such as the writing hand used in the flyer on page 73. Many word processors provide files of clip art, and they are also available from CD-ROMs and Web sites. But even in publicity documents you should be selective in using these resources: clip art is mostly decorative, and an overdecorated document is not only cluttered but unemphatic.

Note When using an image prepared by someone else—for instance, a photograph downloaded from the Web or an item of clip art from a CD-ROM—you must verify that the source permits reproduction of the image before you use it. In most documents but especially academic papers, you must also cite the source. See pages 332–333 on copyright issues with Internet sources.

des

9b

7 Color

With a color printer, many word processors and most desktop publishers can produce documents that use color for bullets, headings, borders, boxes, illustrations, and other elements. Publicity documents generally use color, whereas academic and business documents consisting only of text and headings may not need color. (Ask your instructor or supervisor for his or her preferences.) If you do use color, follow these guidelines:

- Employ color to clarify and highlight your content. Too much color or too many colors on a page will distract rather than focus readers' attention.
- If you use color for type, make sure the type is readable. For text, where type is likely to be relatively small, use only dark colors. For headings, lighter colors may be readable if the type is large and boldfaced.
- Stick to the same color for all headings at the same level (for instance, red for main headings, black for secondary headings).
- For bullets, box backgrounds, lines, and other nontext elements, color can be used more decoratively to enliven the page. Still, stick to no more than a few colors to keep pages clean.
- For illustrations, use color to distinguish the segments of charts, the lines of graphs, and the parts of diagrams. Use only as many colors as you need to make your illustration clear.

9c   Examining a sample report and newsletter

You can use the design principles and elements discussed on pages 72–84 to good effect in reports and in documents such as flyers and newsletters. A sample flyer appears on page 73. Parts of a report and a newsletter are shown on the next two pages.

A report

The illustration on the next page shows the opening of a business report intended to outline a problem and propose a solution. In keeping with a formal business-writing situation, the document is single-spaced (with double spacing between paragraphs and around the list), and the overall appearance is restrained. Color appears only in headings and the figure. The document uses two type fonts, one for the text and headings and one for the figure. Headings clearly delineate the structure of the page: first a summary, then an outline of the problem, and then a discussion of the solution. The figure is visually pleasing and clear, with a caption and labels that explain its content. A bulleted list emphasizes a group of solutions.

Note In many academic disciplines and business organizations, reports have specific formatting requirements: in psychology, for instance, a report should include an abstract (see pp. 407–409). If you are unsure about the format expectations for your reports, ask your instructor or supervisor.

A newsletter

The sample on page 86 comes from a newsletter that is designed to engage, motivate, and inform volunteer tutors who work with military veterans. Typically for newsletters, this one is formatted in columns, which create more room for text and headings and allow variations in the length and emphasis of sections. To suit its purpose, the newsletter is lively in appearance, using extra-large type for title and headings, devices such as lines and borders to separate sections, and color to catch readers' eyes and focus their attention on distinct sections. The most important article on the page, the report on the awards dinner, spreads across two columns. A colored box in the first column provides information readers can use to work through the rest of the document. And a bulleted list (with decorative bullets) highlights and groups related items.

Canada Geese at ABC Institute:
An Environmental Problem

Summary

The flock of Canada geese on and around ABC Institute's grounds has grown dramatically in recent years. What was once a source of pleasure for institute employees and others using the grounds has become a nuisance and an environmental problem. This report reviews the problem, considers the options for reducing the flock, and proposes as a solution the cooperation of ABC Institute, the municipalities around Taylor Lake, and the US Fish and Wildlife Service to reduce the flock by humane means.

The Problem

Canada geese began living at Taylor Lake, adjacent to ABC Institute, when they were relocated there in 1980 by the state game department. As a nonmigratory flock, the geese are present year-round, with the highest population each year occurring in fall, winter, and early spring, after the young have fledged.

In recent years the flock of geese at Taylor Lake has grown dramatically. The Audubon Society's annual Christmas bird census shows a thirty-fold increase from the 37 geese counted in 1982 to the 1125 counted in 1998 (see Figure 1).

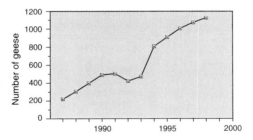

Figure 1. Goose population of Taylor Lake, 1987–1998.

The principal environmental problem caused by the geese is pollution of grass and water by defecation. During high-population months, geese droppings cover the ABC Institute's grounds as well as the park's athletic fields and picnicking areas. The runoff from these droppings into Taylor Lake has substantially affected the quality of the lake's water, so that local authorities have twice (1997 and 1998) issued warnings against swimming.

The Solution

Several possible solutions to the goose overpopulation and resulting environmental problems are *not viable alternatives:*

- Harass the geese with dogs, light, and noise so that the geese choose to leave. This solution is inhumane to the geese and unpleasant for human neighbors.
- Feed the geese a chemical that will weaken the shells of their eggs and thus reduce growth of the flock. This solution is inhumane to the geese and also impractical, because geese are long–lived.
- Kill adult geese. This solution is, obviously, inhumane to the geese.

The most appropriate and humane solution is to thin the goose population by trapping and removing many geese (perhaps 600) to areas less populated by humans, such as wildlife preserves and wilderness areas. Though costly (see figures below), this solution would be efficient and harmless to the geese, provided that sizable netted enclosures are used for traps. [Discussion of solution continues, followed by "Recommendations."]

des

9c

des
9c

Literacy Volunteers

Springfield Veterans Administration Hospital   **SPRING 2000**

From the director

Can you help us? With more and more learners in the VA's literacy program, we need more and more tutors. You may know people who would be interested in participating in the program, if only they knew about it.

Those of you who have been tutoring VA patients in reading and writing know both the great need you fulfill and the great benefits you bring to your students. New tutors need no special skills (we'll provide the training), only patience and an interest in helping others.

We've scheduled an orientation meeting for Friday, June 6, at 6:30 PM. Please come and bring a friend who is willing to contribute a couple of hours a week to our work.

Thanks,
Nancy Thomas

IN THIS ISSUE

AWARDS FOR STUDENTS AND TUTORS AT ANNUAL DINNER

The annual SVAH literacy awards dinner on February 25 was a great success. George Bello obtained food and beverage contributions from area restaurants and suppliers, and the students decorated the dining room on the theme of books and reading. In all, eighty-six people attended.

The highlight of the night was the awards ceremony. Ten students, recommended by their tutors, received certificates recognizing their efforts and special accomplishments in learning to read and write:

Ramon Berva
Edward Byar
David Dunbar
Tony Garnier
Chris Giugni
Akili Haynes
Pat Laird
Jim Livingston
Paul Obeid
B.J. Resnansky

In addition, nine tutors received certificates commemorating five years of service at SVAH:

Anita Crumpton
Felix Cruz-Rivera
Bette Eigen
Kelly Bortoluzzi
Harriotte Henderson
Andy Obiso
Carla Puente
Robert Smith
Sara Villante

Congratulations to all!

New Guidelines on PTSD

Most of us are working with veterans who have been diagnosed with post-traumatic stress disorder. Because this disorder is often complicated by alcoholism, depression, anxiety, and other problems, the National Center for PTSD has issued some guidelines for helping PTSD patients in a way that reduces their stress:

- The hospital must know your tutoring schedule, and you need to sign in and out before and after each tutoring session.

- Cancellations are stressful for patients. Stick to your schedule.

- To protect patients' privacy, meet them only in designated visiting and tutoring areas, never in their rooms.

- Treat patients with dignity and respect, even when (as sometimes happens) they grow frustrated and angry. Seek help from a nurse or orderly if you need it.

With many elements in play, standardizing a newsletter design is crucial: similar elements should be treated similarly, and the overall appearance should be eye-catching but not so cluttered that it confuses the reader.

10 Web Composition

http://www.webcom.com/webcom/html   Resources for Web publishing, including guides and links to other sources, from WebCom.

http://www.gettingstarted.net   Beginning, intermediate, and advanced design advice, from Project Cool.

http://developer.netscape.com   Information about Web building and design using Netscape software, from Netscape.

http://msdn.microsoft.com/workshop/default.asp   Information about Web building and design using Internet Explorer software, from Microsoft.

This chapter provides advice for composing your own Web pages—whether for family and friends, a group you belong to, or projects for courses. The chapter notes some key differences between Web compositions and printed documents (below); gives sources for HTML editors, the software used to create Web compositions (p. 89); and discusses content and design issues for posting papers on the Web (p. 90) and creating original sites (p. 91).

10a   Distinguishing Web compositions from printed documents

We generally read printed documents LINEARLY—that is, straight through from first page to last. Reference aids such as indexes and cross-references can help us find material out of the linear order, but the text is usually intended to be read in sequence, as shown on the next page:

10a

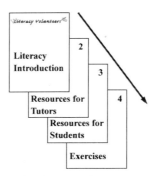

In contrast, a HYPERTEXT such as a Web site is intended to be examined in the order readers choose as they follow electronic links among the pages of the site and often to related sites.

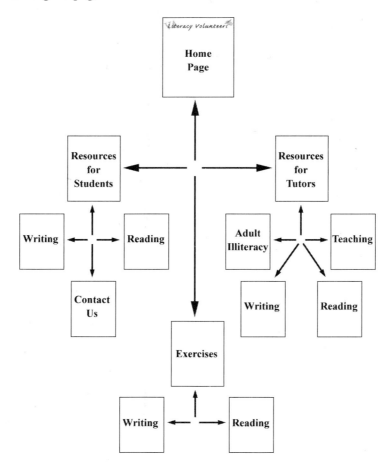

The preceding illustration shows the structure of a fairly simple Web site: readers can move in any direction signaled by arrows or back to the home page with a single click of the mouse.

The main disadvantage of a hypertext is that it can disorient readers as they explore the various links. A Web site requires careful planning of the links between pages and thoughtful cues to help readers keep track of their location in the site.

Note It's easy to incorporate material from other sources into a Web site, but you have the same obligation to cite your sources as you do in a printed document (see pp. 329–332). Further, you may need to seek the copyright holder's permission before publishing the material on the Web. See pages 332–333 for more on copyright.

10b

10b   Using HTML

Most Web pages are created using hypertext markup language, or HTML, and an HTML editor. The HTML editing program inserts command codes into your document that achieve the effects you want when the material appears on the Web.

From the user's point of view, most HTML editors work much as word processors do, with similar options for sizing, formatting, and highlighting copy and with a display that shows what you will see in the final version. Indeed, you can compose a Web page without bothering at all about the behind-the-scenes HTML coding. As you gain experience with Web building, however, you may want to create more sophisticated pages by editing the codes themselves, using the HTML editor or a basic text editor such as Notepad or SimpleText.

There are many HTML editors on the market. Four with advanced features are FrontPage, PageMill, HomePage, and Dreamweaver. But your computer may already have a good HTML editor if it is fairly new or includes a popular Web browser: Composer comes with Netscape Communicator, and FrontPage Express comes with Microsoft Internet Explorer. Students can also download these and other free or low-cost editors from a number of Web sites, including the following:

Microsoft
http://www.microsoft.com/downloads
Netscape
http://www.netscape.com/download
TechWeb
http://www.filemine.com/showDig?id=34
University of Toronto
http://www.utoronto.ca/webdocs/HTMLdocs/tools_home.html

10c   Creating online papers

When you create a composition for the Web, it will likely fall into one of two categories: pages such as class papers that resemble printed documents in being linear and text-heavy and that call for familiar ways of writing and reading (discussed below); or "native" hypertext documents that you build from scratch, which call for screen-oriented writing and reading (pp. 91–95).

If an instructor asks you to post a paper to a Web site, you can compose it on your word processor and then use the Save As HTML function available on most word processors to translate it into a Web page. After translating the paper, your word processor should allow you to modify some of the elements on the page, or you can open the translated document in an HTML editor.

The illustration below shows the opening screen of a student's project for a composition course. The project incorporates many of the design features that make any text-heavy document more accessible to Web readers:

- Use a simple white or cream-colored background for your pages. It is more difficult to read text on a computer screen than on paper, and bright or dark background colors compound the problem.

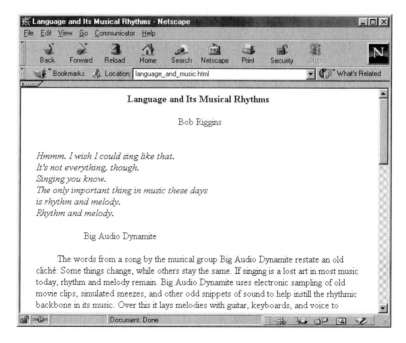

- Use a standard type font for text (see p. 76–77), and use a type size that will be readable on various systems. With standard fonts, a size of at least 12 points should ensure that pages are readable on most systems.
- Web pages automatically run text the full width of the screen unless you give other instructions. To make reading easier, increase the margins so that lines run no more than seventy to eighty characters (including spaces).
- Use headings as signposts in documents that require scrolling through several screens. Otherwise, readers may lose their sense of the document's overall organization.

10d

10d   Creating original sites

When you create an original Web site, you need to be aware that Web readers generally alternate between skimming pages for highlights and focusing intently on sections of text. To facilitate this kind of reading, you'll want to consider the guidelines above for handling text and also your site's structure and content, flow, ease of navigation, and use of images, video, and sound.

1   Structure and content

Your site's organization should be easy to grasp so that it does not disorient readers.

- Sketch possible site plans before getting started. (See p. 88 for an example.) Your aim is to develop a sense of the major components of your project and to create a logical space for each component. As you conceive the organization of your site, consider how menus on the site's pages can provide overviews of the organization as well as direct access to the pages (see pp. 93–94).
- Treat the first few sentences on any page as a crucial get-acquainted space for you and your readers. In this opening, try to hook readers with an interesting question or a central concern, and help to orient them by clarifying the relation of this page to the others on the site.
- Create links among the pages of your own site to help readers move around easily. Create links to other sites that are strictly relevant to your own ideas: too many links or unrelated links will confuse and frustrate readers. For every link, indicate what's at the other location. Instead of just *Click here*, for instance, say *Click here for writing exercises* or *Further information about snowboarding*. When you provide a list of links to related sites, annotate each one with information about its contents.

- Distill your text so that it includes only essential information. Of course, concise prose is essential in any writing situation, but Web readers expect to scan text quickly and, in any event, have difficulty following long text passages on a computer screen. (See pp. 129–134 for advice on writing concisely.)

2 Flow

Beginning Web authors sometimes start at the top of the page and then add element upon element until information proceeds down the screen much as it would in a printed document. However, by thinking about how information will flow on a page, you can take better advantage of the Web's visual nature.

The screen shot below shows part of the opening page of the site mapped on page 88. Though simple in content and design, the page illustrates how the arrangement of elements can invite readers in and direct their attention. A large banner headline contains the sponsoring organization's logo. The opening text is set in a readable font, is written to engage readers' interest, and is broken into short paragraphs. A text box to the right adds variety to the page and provides a menu of the site so that readers can quickly move to the information they seek.

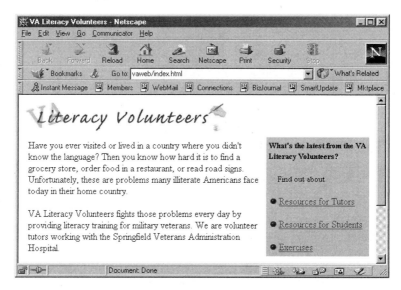

To achieve flow on your Web pages, follow these guidelines:

- Standardize elements of your design to create expectations in readers and to fulfill those expectations. For instance, develop a uniform style for the main headings of pages, for headings within pages, and for menus. (For more on standardizing, see p. 74–75.)

- Make scanning easy for readers. Focus them on crucial text by adding space around it. Use icons and other images to emphasize text. (See next page.) Add headings to break up text and to highlight content. Use lists to reinforce the parallel importance of items. (See pp. 78–79 for more on headings and lists.)
- Position boxes, illustrations, and other elements to help conduct readers through a page. Such elements can align in the center or on the left or right of the page. Use space around the elements to keep them from interfering with text and to highlight them.

10d

3 Ease of navigation

A Web site of more than a couple of pages requires a menu on every page that lists the features of the site, giving its plan at a glance. By clicking on any item in the menu, readers can go directly to a page that interests them. The menu can use just text to indicate links, as in the screen shot on the previous page, or it can include icons to catch the reader's eye, as in the following illustration. (Always supplement icons with verbal descriptions of the links to be sure readers understand where each link leads.)

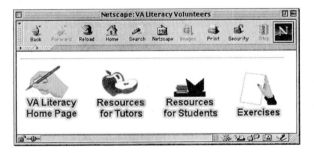

You can embed a menu at the top, side, or bottom of a page. Menus at the top or side are best on short pages because they will not scroll off the screen as readers move down the page. On longer pages menus at the bottom prevent readers from reaching a dead end, a point where they can't easily move forward or backward. You can also use a combination of menus—for instance, one near the top of a page and another at the bottom.

In designing a menu, keep it simple: many different type fonts and colors will overwhelm readers instead of orienting them. And make the menus look the same from one page to the next so that readers recognize them easily.

4 Images, video, and sound

The Web makes it possible to incorporate multimedia elements such as icons, graphics, photographs, artwork, animation, video clips, and sound clips. Exploring the Web, you'll see that site designers have taken advantage of these capabilities—so much so that Web readers often expect at least some visual enhancement of text.

Images

Several guidelines can help you use images effectively in your Web compositions:

10d

- Visual elements should supplement or replace text, highlight important features, and direct the flow of information. Don't use them for their own sake, as mere decoration.
- Make the size of your files a central concern so that readers don't have to wait forever for your site to download. As a rule, don't use images with a file size of more than thirty kilobytes (30k).
- A graphics program can reduce the size of images and thus the time it takes to download them. The JPEG format works best for color photographs; the GIF format works well for black-and-white images or for images with just a few colors.
- Compose descriptions of images that relate them to your text. Don't ask the elements to convey your meaning by themselves.
- Provide alternative descriptions of images to give a sense of them to readers with disabilities or readers whose Web browsers can't display them.

Video and sound

Video and sound files can provide information that is simply unavailable in printed documents. For instance, as part of a film review you could place a short clip from the film on your Web page and then provide a close reading of the clip. Or as part of a project on a controversial issue you could provide links to sound files containing political speeches.

However, the advantages of video and sound in Web compositions are offset by at least two complications: the files are generally large and difficult to work with, and both you and your readers need the right computer equipment (readers' systems must have programs that can read video and sound files).

For information on working with video and sound, see the technology advisers at your school. You can also consult one of the Web sites devoted to multimedia, such as Webmonkey's at *http://www.hotwired.com/webmonkey/multimedia/index.html.*

Sources for images, video, and sound

For the multimedia elements in a Web composition, you can use your own or obtain them from other sources:

- Create your own graphs, diagrams, and other illustrations with your word processor's graphics program or a freestanding program such as Photoshop, CorelDraw, FreeHand, or Canvas. Any graphics program requires learning and practice to be used efficiently, but the investment pays off in professional-looking illustrations.
- Incorporate your own artwork, photographs, video clips, and sound recordings. You need special equipment and software, but you may be able to find them (and technical advice) at your campus computer lab.
- Obtain icons, drawings, photographs, video, and sound from CD-ROMs or from the Web itself. Be sure that you have enough space on your hard drive or a diskette to hold the file. Many sound and video files will not fit on a diskette.

10d

Note Sometimes CD-ROM and Web multimedia are not restricted by copyright, and you can use them freely as long as you acknowledge your sources. Often, however, these resources are restricted, and you must seek the copyright holders' permission before using them. See pages 332–333 for more on copyright.

III

Clarity and Style

Clarity and Style

11 Emphasis

Advice on achieving emphasis:

http://owl.english.purdue.edu/Files/89.html   From the Purdue Online Writing Lab.

http://researchpaper.com/writing_center/89.html   From Research-paper.com.

http://www.rpi.edu/dept/llc/writecenter/web/text/proseman.html   From Rensselaer Polytechnic Institute.

http://www.wisc.edu/writing/Handbook/ClearConciseSentences.html From the University of Wisconsin at Madison.

Emphatic writing leads readers to see your main ideas both within and among sentences. You can achieve emphasis by attending to your subjects and verbs (below), using sentence beginnings and endings (p. 101), coordinating equally important ideas (p. 103), and subordinating less important ideas (p. 105). In addition, emphatic writing is concise writing, the subject of Chapter 16.

Note Many computerized grammar and style checkers can spot some problems with emphasis, such as nouns made from verbs, passive voice, wordy phrases, and long sentences that may also be flabby and unemphatic. However, the checkers cannot help you identify the important ideas in your sentences or whether those ideas receive appropriate emphasis.

emph
11a

11a   Using subjects and verbs effectively

The heart of every sentence is its subject, which usually names the actor, and its verb, which usually specifies the subject's action: *Children* [subject] *grow* [verb]. When these elements do not identify the key actor and action in the sentence, readers must find that information elsewhere and the sentence may be wordy and unemphatic.

In the following sentences, the subjects and verbs are underlined.

KEY TERMS

SUBJECT   Who or what a sentence is about: *Biologists often study animals.* (See p. 145.)

VERB   The part of a sentence that asserts something about the subject: *Biologists often study animals.* (See p. 140.)

99

Unemphatic   The intention of the company was to expand its workforce. A proposal was also made to diversify the backgrounds and abilities of employees.

These sentences are unemphatic because their key ideas (the company's intending and proposing) do not appear in their subjects and verbs. Revised, the sentences are not only clearer but more concise:

Revised   The company intended to expand its workforce. It also proposed to diversify the backgrounds and abilities of employees.

Several constructions can drain meaning from a sentence's subject and verb:

- Nouns made from verbs can obscure the key actions of sentences and add words. These nouns include *intention* (from *intend*), *proposal* (from *propose*), *decision* (from *decide*), *expectation* (from *expect*), *persistence* (from *persist*), *argument* (from *argue*), and *inclusion* (from *include*).

Unemphatic   After the company made a decision to hire more disabled workers, its next step was the construction of wheelchair ramps and other facilities.

Revised   After the company decided to hire more disabled workers, it next constructed wheelchair ramps and other facilities.

- Weak verbs, such as *made* and *was* in the unemphatic sentence above, tend to stall sentences just where they should be moving and often bury key actions:

Unemphatic   The company is now the leader among businesses in complying with the 1990 disabilities act. Its officers make frequent speeches on the act to business groups.

Revised   The company now leads other businesses in complying with the 1990 disabilities act. Its officers frequently speak on the act to business groups.

Don't try to eliminate every use of *be, have,* or *make: be* and *have* are essential as helping verbs (*is going, has written*); *be* links sub-

emph

11a

KEY TERMS

NOUN   A word that names a person, thing, quality, place, or idea: *student, desk, happiness, city, democracy.* (See p. 138.)

HELPING VERB   A verb used with another verb to convey time, obligation, and other meanings: *was drilling, would have been drilling.* (See p. 141.)

jects and words describing them (*Planes are noisy*); and *have* and *make* have independent meanings (among them "possess" and "force," respectively). But do consider replacing forms of *be*, *have*, and *make* when one of the words following the verb could be made into a strong verb itself, as in these examples:

Unemphatic	Emphatic
was influential	influenced
is a glorification	glorifies
have a preference	prefer
had the appearance	appeared, seemed
made a claim	claimed

- Verbs in the passive voice state actions received by, not performed by, their subjects. Thus the passive de-emphasizes the true actor of the sentence, sometimes omitting it entirely. Generally, prefer the active voice, in which the subject performs the verb's action. (See also p. 176.)

Unemphatic   The 1990 <u>law</u> <u>is seen</u> by most businesses as fair, but the <u>costs</u> of complying <u>have</u> sometimes <u>been exaggerated</u>.

Revised   Most <u>businesses</u> <u>see</u> the 1990 law as fair, but some <u>opponents</u> <u>have exaggerated</u> the costs of complying.

emph

11b

11b Using sentence beginnings and endings

Readers automatically seek a writer's principal meaning in the main clause of a sentence—essentially, in the subject that names the actor and the verb that usually specifies the action (see p. 99). Thus you can help readers understand your intended meaning by controlling the information in your subjects and the relation of the main clause to any modifiers attached to it.

 KEY TERMS

PASSIVE VOICE   The verb form when the subject names the *receiver* of the verb's action: *The house <u>was destroyed</u> by the tornado.*

ACTIVE VOICE   The verb form when the subject names the *performer* of the verb's action: *The tornado <u>destroyed</u> the house.*

MAIN CLAUSE   A word group that can stand alone as a sentence, containing a subject and a verb and not beginning with a subordinating word: *The books were expensive.* (See p. 150.)

MODIFIER   A word or word group that describes another word or word group—for example, *sweet candy, running in the park.* (See pp. 142 and 148.)

Old and new information

Generally, readers expect the beginning of a sentence to contain information that they already know or that you have already introduced. They then look to the ending for new information. In the unemphatic passage below, the subjects of the second and third sentences both begin with new topics (underlined) while the old topics (the controversy and education) appear at the ends of the sentences:

> Unemphatic   Education almost means controversy these days, with rising costs and constant complaints about its inadequacies. But the <u>value of schooling</u> should not be obscured by the controversy. The <u>single best means of economic advancement</u>, despite its shortcomings, remains education.

In the more emphatic revision, the underlined old information begins each sentence and new information ends the sentence. The passage follows the pattern A→B. B→C. C→D.

> Revised   Education almost means controversy these days, with rising costs and constant complaints about its inadequacies. But <u>the controversy</u> should not obscure the value of schooling. <u>Education</u> remains, despite its shortcomings, the single best means of economic advancement.

Cumulative and periodic sentences

You can call attention to information by placing it first or last in a sentence, reserving the middle for incidentals:

> Unemphatic   Education remains the single best means of economic advancement, despite its shortcomings. [Emphasizes shortcomings.]
>
> Revised   Despite its shortcomings, education remains the single best means of economic advancement. [Emphasizes advancement more than shortcomings.]
>
> Revised   Education remains, despite its shortcomings, the single best means of economic advancement. [De-emphasizes shortcomings.]

A sentence that begins with the main clause and then adds modifiers is called CUMULATIVE because it accumulates information as it proceeds:

> Cumulative   Education has no equal in opening minds, instilling values, and creating opportunities.
>
> Cumulative   Most of the Great American Desert is made up of bare rock, rugged cliffs, mesas, canyons, moun-

tains, separated from one another by broad flat basins covered with sun-baked mud and alkali, supporting a sparse and measured growth of sagebrush or creosote or saltbush, depending on location and elevation. —EDWARD ABBEY

The opposite kind of sentence, called PERIODIC, saves the main clause until just before the end (the period) of the sentence. Everything before the main clause points toward it:

Periodic   In opening minds, instilling values, and creating opportunities, education has no equal.

Periodic   With people from all over the world—Korean grocers, Jamaican cricket players, Vietnamese fishers, Haitian cabdrivers, Chinese doctors—the American mosaic is continually changing.

The periodic sentence creates suspense for readers by reserving important information for the end. But readers should already have an idea of the sentence's subject—because it was discussed or introduced in the preceding sentence—so that they know what the opening modifiers describe.

coord

11c

11c Using coordination

Use COORDINATION to show that two or more elements in a sentence are equally important in meaning and thus to clarify the relation between them:

- Link two main clauses with a comma and a coordinating conjunction, such as *and* or *but*.

  equally important
  Independence Hall in Philadelphia is now restored, but fifty years ago it was in bad shape.

- Link two main clauses with a semicolon alone or with a semicolon and a conjunctive adverb, such as *however*.

  equally important
  The building was standing; however, it suffered from decay.

KEY TERMS

COORDINATING CONJUNCTIONS *And, but, or, nor,* and sometimes *for, so, yet.* (See p. 144.)

CONJUNCTIVE ADVERBS Modifiers that describe the relation of the ideas in two clauses, such as *hence, however, indeed,* and *thus.* (See p. 219.)

- Within clauses, link words and phrases with a coordinating conjunction, such as *and* or *or*.

> equally
> ⟵—important—⟶
> The people and officials of the nation were indifferent to Indepen-
> ⟵—equally important—⟶
> dence Hall or took it for granted.

- Link main clauses, words, or phrases with a correlative conjunction such as *not only . . . but also.*

> ⟵—equally important—⟶
> People not only took the building for granted but also neglected it.

 Note Computerized grammar and style checkers may spot some errors in punctuating coordinated elements, and they can flag long sentences that may contain excessive coordination. But otherwise they provide little help with coordination because they cannot recognize the relations among ideas in sentences. You'll need to weigh and clarify those relations yourself.

1 Coordinating to relate equal ideas

Coordination shows the equality between elements, as illustrated above. At the same time as it clarifies meaning, it can also help smooth choppy sentences:

| Choppy sentences | We should not rely so heavily on oil. Coal and uranium are also overused. We have a substantial energy resource in the moving waters of our rivers. Smaller streams add to the total volume of water. The resource renews itself. Coal and oil are irreplaceable. Uranium is also irreplaceable. The cost of water does not increase much over time. The costs of coal, oil, and uranium rise dramatically. |

The revision groups coal, oil, and uranium and clearly opposes them to water (the connecting words are underlined):

| Ideas coordinated | We should not rely so heavily on coal, oil, and uranium, for we have a substantial energy resource in the moving waters of our rivers and streams. Coal, oil, and uranium are irreplaceable and thus subject to dramatic cost increases; water, however, is self-renewing and more stable in cost. |

┌─ KEY TERM ───
│
│ CORRELATIVE CONJUNCTIONS   Pairs of connecting words, such as *both . . . and, either . . . or, not only . . . but also.* (See p. 144.)
└──

2 Coordinating effectively

Use coordination only to express the *equality* of ideas or details. A string of coordinated elements—especially main clauses—implies that all points are equally important:

Excessive coordination	The weeks leading up to the resignation of President Nixon were eventful, and the Supreme Court and the Congress closed in on him, and the Senate Judiciary Committee voted to begin impeachment proceedings, and finally the President resigned on August 9, 1974.

Such a passage needs editing to stress the important points (underlined below) and to de-emphasize the less important information:

Revised	<u>The weeks leading up to the resignation of President Nixon were eventful</u>, as the Supreme Court and the Congress closed in on him and the Senate Judiciary Committee voted to begin impeachment proceedings. Finally, <u>the President resigned on August 9, 1974.</u>

Even within a single sentence, coordination should express a logical equality between ideas:

Faulty	John Stuart Mill was a nineteenth-century utilitarian, and he believed that actions should be judged by their usefulness or by the happiness they cause. [The two clauses are not separate and equal: the second expands on the first by explaining what a utilitarian such as Mill believed.]
Revised	John Stuart Mill, <u>a nineteenth-century utilitarian</u>, believed that actions should be judged by their usefulness or by the happiness they cause.

sub

11d

11d Using subordination

Use SUBORDINATION to indicate that some elements in a sentence are less important than others for your meaning. Usually, the main idea appears in the main clause, and supporting details appear in subordinate structures:

- Use a subordinate clause beginning with *although, because, if, who (whom), that, which,* or another subordinating word:

more important

┌────less important (subordinate clause)────┐ ┌───(main clause)───┐
Although production costs have declined, they are still high.

less important
(subordinate clause)
Costs, which include labor and facilities, are difficult to control.
more important (main clause)

- Use a phrase:

less important   more important
(phrase)   (main clause)
Despite some decline, production costs are still high.

less important (phrase)
Costs, including labor and facilities, are difficult to control.
more important (main clause)

- Use a single word:

Declining costs have not matched prices.
Labor costs are difficult to control.

 Note Computerized grammar and style checkers may spot some errors in punctuating subordinated elements, and they can flag long sentences that may contain excessive subordination. But otherwise they provide little help with subordination because they cannot recognize the relations among ideas in sentences. You'll need to weigh and clarify those relations yourself.

sub

11d

1 Subordinating to emphasize main ideas

A string of main clauses can make everything in a passage seem equally important:

**String of
main clauses**   In recent years computer prices have dropped, and production costs have dropped more slowly, and computer manufacturers have had to struggle, for their profits have been shrinking.

Emphasis comes from keeping the truly important information in the main clause (underlined) and subordinating the less important details:

Revised   Because production costs have dropped more slowly than prices in recent years, computer manu-facturers have had to struggle with shrinking profits.

┌─ KEY TERMS ──────────────────────────────────────

SUBORDINATE CLAUSE   A word group that contains a subject and a verb, begins with a subordinating word such as *because* or *who*, and is not a question: *Words can do damage when they hurt feelings.* (See p. 151.)

PHRASE   A word group that lacks a subject or verb or both: *Words can do damage by hurting feelings.* (See p. 148.)

2 Subordinating effectively

Use subordination only for the less important information in a sentence.

> **Faulty** Ms. Angelo was in her first year of teaching, although she was a better instructor than others with many years of experience.

The sentence above suggests that Angelo's inexperience is the main idea, whereas the writer intended to stress her skill *despite* her inexperience. Subordinating the inexperience and elevating the skill to the main clause (underlined) gives appropriate emphasis:

> **Revised** Although Ms. Angelo was in her first year of teaching, <u>she was a better instructor than others with many years of experience</u>.

Subordination loses its power to organize and emphasize when too much loosely related detail crowds into one long sentence:

> **Overloaded** The boats that were moored at the dock when the hurricane, which was one of the worst in three decades, struck were ripped from their moorings, because the owners had not been adequately prepared, since the weather service had predicted the storm would blow out to sea, which they do at this time of year.

The revision stresses important information in the main clauses (underlined):

> **Revised** Struck by one of the worst hurricanes in three decades, <u>the boats at the dock were ripped from their moorings</u>. <u>The owners were unprepared</u> because the weather service had said that hurricanes at this time of year blow out to sea.

//
12

12 Parallelism

Information on parallelism:

http://webster.commnet.edu/HP/pages/darling/grammar/parallelism.htm From the Guide to Grammar and Writing.

http://owl.english.purdue.edu/Files/68.html From the Purdue Online Writing Lab.

http://leo.stcloudstate.edu/grammar/parallelism.html From St. Cloud State University.

PARALLELISM is a similarity of grammatical form for similar elements of meaning within a sentence or among sentences.

The air is dirtied by <u>factories belching smoke</u>
　　　　　　　　　　and
　　　　　　　　　　<u>cars spewing exhaust</u>.

In this example the two underlined phrases have the same function and importance (both specify sources of air pollution), so they also have the same grammatical construction. Parallelism makes form follow meaning.

   Note   A computerized grammar and style checker cannot recognize faulty parallelism because it cannot recognize the relations among ideas. You will need to find and revise problems with parallelism on your own.

//

12a

12a   Using parallelism with *and, but, or, nor, yet*

The coordinating conjunctions *and, but, or, nor,* and *yet* always signal a need for parallelism:

The industrial base was <u>shifting</u> and <u>shrinking</u>. [Parallel words.]

Politicians rarely <u>acknowledged the problem</u> or <u>proposed alternatives</u>. [Parallel phrases.]

Industrial workers were understandably disturbed <u>that they were losing their jobs</u> and <u>that no one seemed to care</u>. [Parallel clauses.]

When sentence elements linked by coordinating conjunctions are not parallel in structure, the sentence is awkward and distracting:

Nonparallel	Three reasons why steel companies kept losing money were that their plants were inefficient, high labor costs, and foreign competition was increasing.
Revised	Three reasons why steel companies kept losing money were <u>inefficient plants</u>, high labor costs, and <u>increasing foreign competition</u>.
Nonparallel	Success was difficult even for efficient companies because of the shift away from all manufacturing in the United States and the fact that steel production was shifting toward emerging nations.

┌─ KEY TERM ──────────────────────────────────────

COORDINATING CONJUNCTIONS   Words that connect elements of the same kind and importance: *and, but, or, nor,* and sometimes *for, so, yet*. (See p. 144.)

Revised   Success was difficult even for efficient companies
                 because of the shift away from all manufacturing in
                 the United States and <u>toward steel production in
                 emerging nations</u>.

All the words required by idiom or grammar must be stated in
compound constructions (see also p. 128):

Faulty   Given training, workers can acquire the skills and
                 interest in other jobs. [Idiom dictates different
                 prepositions with *skills* and *interest.*]

Revised   Given training, workers can acquire the skills <u>for</u>
                 and interest in other jobs.

12b   Using parallelism with *both . . . and, not . . . but,* or another correlative conjunction

Correlative conjunctions stress equality and balance between
elements. Parallelism confirms the equality.

> It is not <u>a tax bill</u> but <u>a tax relief bill</u>, providing relief not <u>for the
> needy</u> but <u>for the greedy</u>.   —Franklin Delano Roosevelt

With correlative conjunctions, the element after the second connector must match the element after the first connector:

Nonparallel   Huck Finn learns not only that human beings have
                 an enormous capacity for folly but also enormous
                 dignity. [The first element includes *that human
                 beings have;* the second element does not.]

Revised   Huck Finn learns <u>that human beings have</u> not only
                 an enormous capacity for folly but also enormous
                 dignity. [Repositioning *that human beings have*
                 makes the two elements parallel.]

12c   Using parallelism in comparisons

Parallelism confirms the likeness or difference between two elements being compared using *than* or *as:*

Nonparallel   Huck Finn proves less a bad boy than to be an
                 independent spirit. In the end he is every bit as

┌─ KEY TERM ───
│ CORRELATIVE CONJUNCTIONS   Pairs of words that connect elements of
│ the same kind and importance, such as *both . . . and, either . . . or,*
│ *neither . . . nor, not . . . but, not only . . . but also.* (See p. 144.)
└──

//
12c

determined in rejecting help as he is to leave for "the territory."

Revised   Huck Finn proves less a bad boy than <u>an indepen-dent spirit</u>. In the end he is every bit as <u>determined to reject help</u> as he is to leave for "the territory."

(See also p. 200 on making comparisons logical.)

12d Using parallelism with lists, headings, and outlines

The items in a list or outline are coordinate and should be parallel. Parallelism is essential in the headings that divide a paper into sections (see pp. 78–79) and in a formal topic outline (p. 25).

Nonparallel	Revised
Changes in Renaissance England	Changes in Renaissance England
1. Extension of trade routes	1. Extension of trade routes
2. Merchant class became more powerful	2. <u>Increased power</u> of the merchant class
3. The death of feudalism	3. <u>Death</u> of feudalism
4. Upsurging of the arts	4. <u>Upsurge</u> of the arts
5. Religious quarrels began	5. <u>Rise</u> of religious quarrels

13 Variety and Details

Information on achieving sentence variety:

http://webster.commnet.edu/HP/pages/darling/grammar/sentences.htm From the Guide to Grammar and Writing.

http://owl.english.purdue.edu/Files/113.html   From the Purdue Online Writing Lab.

http://leo.stcloudstate.edu/style/sentencev.html   From St. Cloud State University.

Writing that's interesting as well as clear has at least two features: the sentences vary in length and structure, and they are well textured with details.

Note Some computerized grammar and style checkers will flag long sentences, and you can check for appropriate variety in a series of such sentences. But generally these programs cannot help you see where variety may be needed because they cannot recognize the relative importance and complexity of your ideas. Nor can they suggest where you should add details. To edit for variety and detail, you need to listen to your sentences and determine whether they clarify your meaning.

13a   Varying sentence length

In most contemporary writing, sentences tend to vary from about ten to about forty words, with an average of between fifteen and twenty-five words. If your sentences are all at one extreme or the other, your readers may have difficulty focusing on main ideas and seeing the relations among them:

- If most of your sentences contain thirty-five words or more, your main ideas may not stand out from the details that support them. Break some of the long sentences into shorter, simpler ones.
- If most of your sentences contain fewer than ten or fifteen words, all your ideas may seem equally important and the links between them may not be clear. Try combining them with coordination (p. 103) and subordination (p. 105) to show relationships and stress main ideas over supporting information.

var
13b

13b   Varying sentence structure

A passage will be monotonous if all its sentences follow the same pattern, like soldiers marching in a parade. Try these techniques for varying structure.

1   Subordination

A string of main clauses in simple or compound sentences can be especially plodding:

Monotonous   The moon is now drifting away from the earth. It moves away at the rate of about one inch a year.

┌─ KEY TERM ──

MAIN CLAUSE   A word group that contains a subject and a verb and does not begin with a subordinating word: *Tourism is an industry. It brings in over $2 billion a year.* (See p. 150.)

> This movement is lengthening our days. They increase a thousandth of a second every century. Forty-seven of our present days will someday make up a month. We might eventually lose the moon altogether. Such great planetary movement rightly concerns astronomers, but it need not worry us. It will take 50 million years.

Enliven such writing—and make the main ideas stand out—by expressing the less important information in subordinate clauses and phrases. In the revision below, underlining indicates subordinate structures that used to be main clauses:

> Revised The moon is now drifting away from the earth <u>about one inch a year</u>. <u>At a thousandth of a second every century</u>, this movement is lengthening our days. Forty-seven of our present days will someday make up a month, <u>if we don't eventually lose the moon altogether</u>. Such great planetary movement rightly concerns astronomers, <u>but</u> it need not worry us. It will take 50 million years.

2 Sentence combining

var

13b

As the preceding example shows, subordinating to achieve variety often involves combining short, choppy sentences into longer units that link related information and stress main ideas. Here is another unvaried passage:

> Monotonous Astronomy may seem a remote science. It may seem to have little to do with people's daily lives. Many astronomers find otherwise. They see their science as soothing. It gives perspective to everyday routines and problems.

Combining five sentences into one, the revision is both clearer and easier to read. Underlining highlights the many changes:

> Revised Astronomy may seem a remote science <u>having</u> little to do with people's daily lives, <u>but</u> many astronomers <u>find their science soothing</u> <u>because</u> it gives perspective to everyday routines and problems.

KEY TERMS

SUBORDINATE CLAUSE A word group that contains a subject and verb, begins with a subordinating word such as *because* or *who,* and is not a question: *Tourism is an industry that brings in over $2 billion a year.* (See p. 151.)

PHRASE A word group that lacks a subject or verb or both: *Tourism is an industry valued at over $2 billion a year.* (See p. 148.)

3 Varied sentence beginnings

An English sentence often begins with its subject, which generally captures old information from a preceding sentence (see p. 101):

> The defendant's <u>lawyer</u> was determined to break the prosecution's witness. <u>He</u> relentlessly cross-examined the stubborn witness for a week.

However, an unbroken sequence of sentences beginning with the subject quickly becomes monotonous:

Monotonous   The defendant's lawyer was determined to break the prosecution's witness. He relentlessly cross-examined the witness for a week. The witness had expected to be dismissed within an hour and was visibly irritated. She did not cooperate. She was reprimanded by the judge.

Beginning some of these sentences with other expressions improves readability and clarity:

Revised   The defendant's lawyer was determined to break the prosecution's witness. <u>For a week</u> he relentlessly cross-examined the witness. <u>Expecting to be dismissed within an hour</u>, the witness was visibly irritated. She did not cooperate. <u>Indeed</u>, she was reprimanded by the judge.

var
13b

The underlined expressions represent the most common choices for varying sentence beginnings:

- Adverb modifiers, such as *For a week* (modifies the verb *cross-examined*).
- Adjective modifiers, such as *Expecting to be dismissed within an hour* (modifies *witness*).
- Transitional expressions, such as *Indeed.* (See p. 42 for a list.)

ESL   Placing certain adverb modifiers at the beginning of a sentence requires you to change the normal subject-verb order as well. The most common of these modifiers are negatives, including *seldom, rarely, in no case, not since,* and *not until.*

KEY TERMS

ADVERB   A word or word group that describes a verb, an adjective, another adverb, or a whole sentence: *dressed <u>sharply</u>, <u>clearly</u> unhappy, soaring <u>from the mountain</u>.* (See p. 142.)

ADJECTIVE   A word or word group that describes a noun or pronoun: *<u>sweet</u> smile, <u>certain</u> someone.* (See p. 142.)

	adverb noun verb phrase
Faulty	Seldom a witness has held the stand so long.

	helping adverb verb subject main verb
Revised	Seldom has a witness held the stand so long.

4 Varied word order

Occasionally, you can vary a sentence and emphasize it at the same time by inverting the usual order of parts:

A dozen witnesses testified for the prosecution, and the defense attorney barely questioned eleven of them. The twelfth, however, he grilled. [Normal word order: *He grilled the twelfth, however.*]

Inverted sentences used without need are artificial. Use them only when emphasis demands.

13c Adding details

Relevant details such as facts and examples create the texture and life that keep readers awake and help them grasp your meaning. For instance:

Flat	Constructed after World War II, Levittown, New York, consisted of thousands of houses in two basic styles. Over the decades, residents have altered the houses so dramatically that the original styles are often unrecognizable.
Detailed	Constructed on potato fields after World War II, Levittown, New York, consisted of more than seventeen thousand houses in Cape Cod and ranch styles. Over the decades, residents have added expansive front porches, punched dormer windows through roofs, converted garages to sun porches, and otherwise altered the houses so dramatically that the original styles are often unrecognizable.

14 Appropriate and Exact Words

http://www.uottawa.ca/academic/arts/writcent/hypergrammar/ diction.html   Advice on word choice, from the University of Ottawa.

http://www.unc.edu/depts/wcweb/handouts/style.html Advice on word choice, from the University of North Carolina.

http://webster.commnet.edu/HP/pages/darling/grammar/unbiased.htm Advice on using unbiased language, from the Guide to Grammar and Writing.

http://owl.english.purdue.edu/Files/26.html Advice on avoiding sexist language, from the Purdue Online Writing Lab.

http://www.uottawa.ca/academic/arts/writcent/hypergrammar/ conndeno.html Information on denotation and connotation, from the University of Ottawa.

http://members.home.net/kayem/idioms/idioms.html Information and exercises on idioms, from English-Zone.Com.

The clarity and effectiveness of your writing will depend greatly on the use of words that are appropriate for your writing situation (below) and that express your meaning exactly (p. 121).

14a Choosing the appropriate word

Appropriate words suit your writing situation—your subject, purpose, and audience. In most college and career writing you should rely on what's called STANDARD ENGLISH, the written English normally expected and used in schools, businesses, government, and other places where people of diverse backgrounds must communicate with one another. Standard English is "standard" not because it is better than other forms of English but because it is accepted as the common language, much as dimes and quarters are accepted as the common currency.

The vocabulary of standard English is huge, allowing expression of an infinite range of ideas and feelings; but it does exclude words that only some groups of people use, understand, or find inoffensive. Some of these more limited vocabularies should be avoided altogether; others should be used cautiously and in relevant situations, as when aiming for a special effect with an audience you know will appreciate it. Whenever you doubt a word's status, consult a dictionary (see p. 121).

Note Many computerized grammar and style checkers can be set to flag potentially inappropriate words, such as nonstandard language, slang, colloquialisms, and gender-specific terms (*man-made, mailman*). However, the checker can flag only words listed in its dictionary. And you'll need to determine whether a flagged word is or is not appropriate for your writing situation, as explained on the following pages.

1 Dialect and nonstandard language

Like many countries, the United States includes scores of regional, social, or ethnic groups with their own distinct DIALECTS, or versions of English. Standard English is one of those dialects, and so are Black English, Appalachian English, Creole, and the English of coastal Maine. All the dialects of English share many features, but each also has its own vocabulary, pronunciation, and grammar.

If you speak a dialect of English besides standard English, you need to be careful about using your dialect in situations where standard English is the norm, such as in academic or business writing. Otherwise, your readers may not understand your meaning, or they may perceive your usage as incorrect. (Dialects are not wrong in themselves, but forms imported from one dialect into another may still be perceived as wrong.)

Your participation in the community of standard English does not require you to abandon your own dialect. Of course, you will want to use it with others who speak it. You may want to quote it in an academic paper (as when analyzing or reporting conversation in dialect). And you may want to use it in writing you do for yourself, such as journals, notes, and drafts, which should be composed as freely as possible. But edit your papers carefully to eliminate dialect expressions, especially those which dictionaries label "nonstandard," such as *hisn, hern, hisself, theirselves, them books, them courses, this here school, that there building, knowed, throwed, hadn't ought, could of, didn't never,* and *haven't no.*

appr

14a

2 Slang

SLANG is the language used by a group, such as musicians or computer programmers, to reflect common experiences and to make technical references efficient. The following example is from an essay on the slang of "skaters" (skateboarders):

> Curtis slashed ultra-punk crunchers on his longboard, while the Rube-man flailed his usual Gumbyness on tweaked frontsides and lofty fakie ollies.   —MILES ORKIN, "Mucho Slingage by the Pool"

Among those who understand it, slang may be vivid and forceful. It often occurs in dialogue, and an occasional slang expression can enliven an informal essay. But most slang is too flippant and imprecise for effective communication, and it is generally inappropriate for college or business writing. Notice the gain in seriousness and precision achieved in the following revision:

Slang	Many students start out <u>pretty together</u> but then <u>get weird</u>.
Revised	Many students start out <u>with clear goals</u> but then <u>lose their direction</u>.

3 Colloquial language

COLLOQUIAL LANGUAGE is the everyday spoken language, including expressions such as *get together, go crazy, do the dirty work,* and *get along.*

When you write informally, colloquial language may be appropriate to achieve the casual, relaxed effect of conversation. An occasional colloquial word dropped into otherwise more formal writing can also help you achieve a desired emphasis. But most colloquial language is not precise enough for college or career writing. In such writing you should generally avoid any words and expressions labeled "informal" or "colloquial" in your dictionary.

> **Colloquial** According to a Native American myth, the Great Creator had a dog hanging around with him when he created the earth.
>
> **Revised** According to a Native American myth, the Great Creator was accompanied by a dog when he created the earth.

4 Technical words

All disciplines and professions rely on specialized language that allows the members to communicate precisely and efficiently with each other. Chemists, for instance, have their *phosphatides,* and literary critics have their *motifs* and *subtexts.* Without explanation technical words are meaningless to nonspecialists. When you are writing for nonspecialists, avoid unnecessary technical terms and carefully define terms you must use.

appr

14a

5 Indirect and pretentious writing

Small, plain, and direct words are almost always preferable to big, showy, or evasive words. Take special care to avoid euphemisms, double-talk, and pretentious writing.

A EUPHEMISM is a presumably inoffensive word that a writer or speaker substitutes for a word deemed potentially offensive or too blunt, such as *passed away* for *died* or *misspeak* for *lie.* Use euphemisms only when you know that blunt, truthful words would needlessly hurt or offend members of your audience.

A kind of euphemism that deliberately evades the truth is DOUBLE-TALK (also called DOUBLESPEAK or WEASEL WORDS): language intended to confuse or to be misunderstood. Today double-talk is unfortunately common in politics and advertising—the *revenue enhancement* that is really a tax, the *peace-keeping function* that is really war making, the *biodegradable* bags that last decades. Double-talk has no place in honest writing.

Euphemism and sometimes double-talk seem to keep company with PRETENTIOUS WRITING, fancy language that is more elaborate than its subject requires. Choose your words for their exactness and economy. The big, ornate word may be tempting, but pass it up. Your readers will be grateful.

> **Pretentious**   To perpetuate our endeavor of providing funds for our elderly citizens as we do at the present moment, we will face the exigency of enhanced contributions from all our citizens.
>
> **Revised**   We cannot continue to fund Social Security and Medicare for the elderly unless we raise taxes.

6   Sexist and other biased language

Even when we do not mean it to, our language can reflect and perpetuate hurtful prejudices toward groups of people. Such biased language can be obvious—words such as *nigger, honky, mick, kike, fag, dyke,* or *broad.* But it can also be subtle, generalizing about groups in ways that may be familiar but that are also inaccurate or unfair.

Biased language reflects poorly on the user, not on the person or persons whom it mischaracterizes or insults. Unbiased language does not submit to false generalizations. It treats people respectfully as individuals and labels groups as they wish to be labeled.

appr

14a

Stereotypes of race, ethnicity, religion, age, and other characteristics

A STEREOTYPE is a generalization based on poor evidence, a kind of formula for understanding and judging people simply because of their membership in a group:

Men are uncommunicative.
Women are emotional.
Liberals want to raise taxes.
Conservatives are affluent.

At best, stereotypes betray a noncritical writer, one who is not thinking beyond notions received from others. In your writing, be alert for statements that characterize whole groups of people:

> **Stereotype**   Elderly drivers should have their licenses limited to daytime driving only. [Asserts that all elderly people are poor night drivers.]
>
> **Revised**   Drivers with impaired night vision should have their licenses limited to daytime driving only.

Some stereotypes have become part of the language, but they are still potentially offensive:

Stereotype   The administrators are too blind to see the need for a new gymnasium.

Revised   The administrators do not understand the need for a new gymnasium.

Sexist language

Among the most subtle and persistent biased language is that expressing narrow ideas about men's and women's roles, position, and value in society. Like other stereotypes, this SEXIST LANGUAGE can wound or irritate readers, and it indicates the writer's thoughtlessness or unfairness. The following box suggests some ways of eliminating sexist language:

Eliminating sexist language

- Avoid demeaning and patronizing language:

  Sexist   Dr. Keith Kim and Lydia Hawkins coauthored the article.

  Revised   Dr. Keith Kim and Dr. Lydia Hawkins coauthored the article.

  Revised   Keith Kim and Lydia Hawkins coauthored the article.

  Sexist   Ladies are entering almost every occupation formerly filled by men.

  Revised   Women are entering almost every occupation formerly filled by men.

- Avoid occupational or social stereotypes:

  Sexist   The considerate doctor commends a nurse when she provides his patients with good care.

  Revised   The considerate doctor commends a nurse who provides good care for patients.

  Sexist   The grocery shopper should save her coupons.

  Revised   Grocery shoppers should save their coupons.

- Avoid referring needlessly to gender:

  Sexist   Marie Curie, a woman chemist, discovered radium.

  Revised   Marie Curie, a chemist, discovered radium.

  Sexist   The patients were tended by a male nurse.

  Revised   The patients were tended by a nurse.

- Avoid using *man* or words containing *man* to refer to all human beings. Here are a few alternatives:

  businessman   businessperson
  chairman   chair, chairperson

  (continued)

appr

14a

Eliminating sexist language
(continued)

congressman	representative in Congress, legislator
craftsman	craftsperson, artisan
layman	layperson
mankind	humankind, humanity, human beings, humans
manmade	handmade, manufactured, synthetic, artificial
manpower	personnel, human resources
policeman	police officer
salesman	salesperson, sales representative

Sexist   Man has not reached the limits of social justice.

Revised   Humankind [or Humanity] has not reached the limits of social justice.

Sexist   The furniture consists of manmade materials.

Revised   The furniture consists of synthetic materials.

- Avoid the GENERIC *HE*, the male pronoun used to refer to both genders. (See also p. 192.)

Sexist   The newborn child explores his world.

Revised   Newborn children explore their world. [Use the plural for the pronoun and the word it refers to.]

Revised   The newborn child explores the world. [Avoid the pronoun altogether.]

Revised   The newborn child explores his or her world. [Substitute male and female pronouns.]

Use the last option sparingly—only once in a group of sentences and only to stress the singular individual.

appr
14a

Appropriate labels

We often need to label groups: *swimmers, politicians, mothers, Christians, Westerners, students.* But labels can be shorthand stereotypes, slighting the person labeled and ignoring the preferences of the group members themselves. Although sometimes dismissed as "political correctness," showing sensitivity about labels hurts no one and helps gain your readers' trust and respect.

- Be careful to avoid labels that (intentionally or not) disparage the person or group you refer to. A person with emotional problems is not a *mental patient.* A person with cancer is not a *cancer victim.* A person using a wheelchair is not *wheelchair-bound.*
- Use names for racial, ethnic, and other groups that reflect the preferences of each group's members, or at least many of them.

Examples of current preferences include *African American* or *black, latino/latina* (for Americans and American immigrants of Spanish-speaking descent), and *disabled* (rather than *handicapped*). But labels change often. To learn how a group's members wish to be labeled, ask them directly, attend to usage in reputable periodicals, or check a recent dictionary. A helpful reference is Marilyn Schwartz's *Guidelines for Bias-Free Writing* (1995).

14b   Choosing the exact word

To write clearly and effectively, you will want to find the words that fit your meaning exactly and convey your attitude precisely.

Note A computerized grammar and style checker can provide some help with inexact language. For instance, you can set it to flag commonly confused words (such as *continuous/continual*), misused prepositions in idioms (such as *accuse for* instead of *accuse of*), and clichés. But the checker can flag only words stored in its dictionary. It can't help you at all in using words with appropriate connotations, making abstract words concrete, or solving other problems discussed in this section. You'll need to read your work carefully on your own.

exact

14b

1   Word meanings and synonyms

For writing exactly, a dictionary is essential and a thesaurus can be helpful.

Desk dictionaries

A desk dictionary defines about 150,000 to 200,000 words and provides pronunciation, grammatical functions, history, and other information. Here is a sample from *Merriam-Webster's Collegiate Dictionary:*

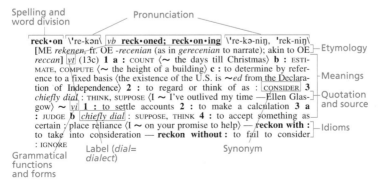

Good desk dictionaries, in addition to *Merriam-Webster's*, include the *American Heritage College Dictionary*, the *Random House Webster's College Dictionary*, and *Webster's New World Dictionary*. Most of these are available in both print and electronic form (CD-ROM or online). In addition, the following Web sites provide online dictionaries or links to online dictionaries:

Colorado State University
http://www.colostate.edu/depts/WritingCenter/resources/
page1.htm
Encyberpedia
http://www.encyberpedia.com/glossary.htm
Internet Public Library
http://www.ipl.org/ref/RR/static/ref2000.html
Research-It
http://www.iTools.com/research-it/research-it.html

ESL If English is not your first language, you probably should have a dictionary prepared especially for ESL students, containing special information on prepositions, count versus noncount nouns, and many other matters. Reliable ESL dictionaries include *COBUILD English Language Dictionary*, *Longman Dictionary of Contemporary English*, and *Oxford Advanced Learner's Dictionary*.

exact

14b

Thesauruses

To find a word with the exact shade of meaning you intend, you may want to consult a thesaurus, or book of SYNONYMS—words with approximately the same meaning. A thesaurus such as *Roget's International Thesaurus* lists most imaginable synonyms for thousands of words. The word *news*, for instance, has half a page of synonyms in *Roget's International*, including *tidings*, *dispatch*, *gossip*, and *journalism*.

Since a thesaurus aims to open up possibilities, its lists of synonyms include approximate as well as precise matches. The thesaurus does not define synonyms or distinguish among them, however, so you need a dictionary to discover exact meanings. In general, don't use a word from a thesaurus—even one you like the sound of—until you are sure of its appropriateness for your meaning.

Note The Web sites given above for online dictionaries contain links to thesauruses as well. Your word processor may also include a thesaurus, making it easy to look up synonyms and insert the chosen word into your text. But still you should consult a dictionary unless you are certain of the word's meaning.

2 The right word for your meaning

All words have one or more basic meanings (called DENOTATIONS)—the meanings listed in the dictionary, without reference to emotional associations. If readers are to understand you, you must use words according to their established meanings.

- Consult a dictionary whenever you are unsure of a word's meaning.
- Distinguish between similar-sounding words that have widely different denotations:

Inexact   Older people often suffer <u>infirmaries</u> [places for the sick].

Exact   Older people often suffer <u>infirmities</u> [disabilities].

Some words, called HOMONYMS, sound exactly alike but differ in meaning: for example, *principal/principle* or *rain/reign/rein.* (See pp. 261–262 for a list of commonly confused homonyms.)

- Distinguish between words with related but distinct meanings:

Inexact   Television commercials <u>continuously</u> [unceasingly] interrupt programming.

Exact   Television commercials <u>continually</u> [regularly] interrupt programming.

In addition to their emotion-free meanings, many words also carry associations with specific feelings. These CONNOTATIONS can shape readers' responses and are thus a powerful tool for writers. The following word pairs have related denotations but very different connotations:

pride: sense of self-worth
vanity: excessive regard for oneself

firm: steady, unchanging, unyielding
stubborn: unreasonable, bullheaded

lasting: long-lived, enduring
endless: without limit, eternal

enthusiasm: excitement
mania: excessive interest or desire

A dictionary can help you track down words with the exact connotations you want. Besides providing meanings, your dictionary may also list and distinguish synonyms to guide your choices. A thesaurus can also help if you use it carefully, as discussed on the facing page.

3 Concrete and specific words

Clear, exact writing balances abstract and general words, which outline ideas and objects, with concrete and specific words, which sharpen and solidify.

- ABSTRACT WORDS name qualities and ideas: *beauty, inflation, management, culture, liberal.* CONCRETE WORDS name things we

exact

14b

can know by our five senses of sight, hearing, touch, taste, and smell: *sleek, humming, brick, bitter, musty.*

- GENERAL WORDS name classes or groups of things, such as *buildings, weather,* or *birds,* and include all the varieties of the class. SPECIFIC WORDS limit a general class, such as *buildings,* by naming one of its varieties, such as *skyscraper, Victorian courthouse,* or *hut.*

Abstract and general words are useful in the broad statements that set the course for your writing.

> The wild horse in America has a <u>romantic</u> history.

> <u>Relations</u> between the sexes today are more <u>relaxed</u> than they were in the past.

But such statements need development with concrete and specific detail. Detail can turn a vague sentence into an exact one:

Vague	The size of his hands made his smallness real. [How big were his hands? How small was he?]
Exact	Not until I saw his delicate, doll-like hands did I realize that he stood a full head shorter than most other men.

If you write on a computer, you can use its Find function to help you find and revise abstract and general words that you tend to overuse. Examples of such words include *nice, interesting, things, very, good, a lot, a little,* and *some.*

exact
14b

4   Idioms

IDIOMS are expressions in any language that do not fit the rules for meaning or grammar—for instance, *put up with, plug away at, make off with.*

Idiomatic combinations of verbs or adjectives and prepositions can be confusing for both native and nonnative speakers of English. A number of these pairings are listed opposite. (More appear on pp. 165–166.)

ESL Those learning English as a second language are justified in stumbling over its prepositions because their meanings can shift depending on context and because they have so many idiomatic uses. In mastering English prepositions, you probably can't avoid memorization. But you can help yourself by memorizing related groups, such as those below:

- *At/in/on* in expressions of time: Use *at* before actual clock time: <u>*at*</u> *8:30.* Use *in* before a month, year, century, or period: <u>*in*</u> *April,* <u>*in*</u> *1985,* <u>*in*</u> *the twenty-first century,* <u>*in*</u> *the next month.* Use *on* before a day or date: <u>*on*</u> *Tuesday,* <u>*on*</u> *August 31.*

Idioms with prepositions

abide by a rule
abide in a place or state

according to
accords with

accuse of a crime

accustomed to

adapt from a source
adapt to a situation

afraid of

agree on a plan
agree to a proposal
agree with a person

angry with

aware of

based on

capable of

certain of

charge for a purchase
charge with a crime

concur in an opinion
concur with a person

contend for a principle
contend with a person

dependent on

differ about or over a question
differ from in some quality
differ with a person

disappointed by or in a person
disappointed in or with a thing

familiar with

identical with or to

impatient at her conduct
impatient of restraint
impatient for a raise
impatient with a person

independent of

infer from

inferior to

involved in a task
involved with a person

oblivious of or to one's
  surroundings
oblivious of something
  forgotten

occupied by a person
occupied in study
occupied with a thing

opposed to

part from a person
part with a possession

prior to

proud of

related to

rewarded by the judge
rewarded for something done
rewarded with a gift

similar to

superior to

wait at a place
wait for a train, a person
wait in a room
wait on a customer

- *At/in/on* in expressions of place: Use *at* before a specific place or address: *at the school, at 511 Iris Street*. Use *in* before a place with limits or before a city, state, country, or continent: *in the house, in a box, in Oklahoma City, in China*. Use *on* to mean "supported by" or "touching the surface of": *on the table, on Iris Street, on page 150*.

- *For/since* in expressions of time: Use *for* before a period of time: <u>for</u> *an hour,* <u>for</u> *two years.* Use *since* before a specific point in time: <u>since</u> *1995,* <u>since</u> *yesterday.*

An ESL dictionary is the best source for the meanings of prepositions; see the recommendations on page 138. In addition, some references focus on prepositions. One is *Oxford Dictionary of Current Idiomatic English,* volume 1: *Verbs with Prepositions and Particles.*

5 Figurative language

FIGURATIVE LANGUAGE (or a FIGURE OF SPEECH) departs from the literal meanings of words, usually by comparing very different ideas or objects:

Literal	As I try to write, I can think of nothing to say.
Figurative	As I try to write, <u>my mind is a slab of black slate</u>.

Imaginatively and carefully used, figurative language can capture meaning more precisely and feelingly than literal language. Here is a figure of speech at work in technical writing (paraphrasing the physicist Edward Andrade):

> The molecules in a liquid move continuously like couples on an overcrowded dance floor, jostling each other.

The two most common figures of speech are the simile and the metaphor. Both compare two things of different classes, often one abstract and the other concrete. A SIMILE makes the comparison explicit and usually begins with *like* or *as:*

> Whenever we grow, we tend to feel it, <u>as</u> a young seed must feel the weight and inertia of the earth when it seeks to break out of its shell on its way to becoming a plant.   —ALICE WALKER

A METAPHOR claims that the two things are identical, omitting such words as *like* and *as:*

> A school is a hopper into which children are heaved while they are young and tender; therein they are pressed into certain standard shapes and covered from head to heels with official rubber stamps.
> —H. L. MENCKEN

To be successful, figurative language must be fresh and unstrained, calling attention not to itself but to the writer's meaning. Be especially wary of mixed metaphors, which combine two or more incompatible figures:

Mixed	Various thorny problems that we try to sweep under the rug continue to bob up all the same.

Improved   Various thorny problems that we try to weed out continue to thrive all the same.

6   Trite expressions

TRITE EXPRESSIONS, or CLICHÉS, are phrases so old and so often repeated that they have become stale. They include the following:

add insult to injury	a needle in a haystack
better late than never	point with pride
cool, calm, and collected	pride and joy
crushing blow	ripe old age
easier said than done	rude awakening
face the music	sadder but wiser
few and far between	shoulder the burden
green with envy	shoulder to cry on
hard as a rock	sneaking suspicion
heavy as lead	stand in awe
hit the nail on the head	strong as an ox
hour of need	thin as a rail
ladder of success	tried and true
moving experience	wise as an owl

Clichés may slide into your drafts while you are trying to find the words for your meaning. To edit clichés, listen to your writing for any expressions that you have heard or used before. You can also supplement your efforts with a computerized style checker, which may include a cliché detector. No such program can flag all possible clichés, though, so you'll have to rely on your own editing as well. When you find a cliché, substitute fresh words of your own or restate the idea in plain language.

15

15 Completeness

Two helpful pages from the Guide to Grammar and Writing:

http://webster.commnet.edu/HP/pages/darling/grammar/composition/ parallelism.htm   Including essential words in compound constructions.

http://webster.commnet.edu/HP/pages/darling/grammar/composition/ editing.htm   Editing and proofreading tips.

The most serious kind of incomplete sentence is the grammatical fragment (see Chapter 31). But sentences are also incomplete when they omit one or more words needed for clarity.

Note Computerized grammar and style checkers will not flag most kinds of incomplete sentences discussed in this section. Only your own careful proofreading can ensure that sentences are complete.

15a   Writing complete compounds

You may omit words from a compound construction when the omission will not confuse readers:

> Environmentalists have hopes for alternative fuels and [for] public transportation.
>
> Some cars will run on electricity and some [will run] on methane.

Such omissions are possible only when the words omitted are common to all the parts of a compound construction. When the parts differ in any way, all words must be included in all parts.

> One new car <u>gets</u> eighty miles per gallon; some old cars <u>get</u> as little as five miles per gallon. [One verb is singular, the other plural.]
>
> Environmentalists believe <u>in</u> and work <u>for</u> fuel conservation. [Idiom requires different prepositions with *believe* and *work*.]

inc

15b

15b   Adding needed words

In haste or carelessness, do not omit small words that are needed for clarity:

Incomplete	Regular payroll deductions are a type painless savings. You hardly notice missing amounts, and after period of years the contributions can add a large total.
Revised	Regular payroll deductions are a type <u>of</u> painless savings. You hardly notice <u>the</u> missing amounts, and after <u>a</u> period of years the contributions can add <u>up to</u> a large total.

Attentive proofreading is the only insurance against this kind of omission. *Proofread all your papers carefully.* See pages 47–48 for tips.

ESL If your native language is not English, you may have difficulty knowing when to use the English articles *a, an,* and *the.* For guidelines on using articles, see pages 202–204.

┌─ KEY TERM ────────────────────────────────

COMPOUND CONSTRUCTION Two or more elements (words, phrases, clauses) that are equal in importance and that function as a unit: *Rain fell; streams overflowed* (clauses); *dogs and cats* (words).

16 Conciseness

Advice on writing concisely:

http://webster.commnet.edu/HP/pages/darling/grammar/concise.htm
From the Guide to Grammar and Writing.

http://leo.stcloudstate.edu/style/wordiness.html From St. Cloud State
University.

http://www.acusysinc.com/English/Wordiness.htm From the Reference Guide to Grammar.

http://owl.english.purdue.edu/Files/127.html From the Purdue Online
Writing Lab.

Concise writing makes every word count. Conciseness is not
the same as mere brevity: detail and originality should not be cut
with needless words. Rather, the length of an expression should be
appropriate to the thought.

You may find yourself writing wordily when you are unsure of
your subject or when your thoughts are tangled. It's fine, even necessary, to stumble and grope while drafting. But you should
straighten out your ideas and eliminate wordiness during revision
and editing.

 Note Any computerized grammar and style checker will identify at least some wordy structures, such as repeated words, weak
verbs, passive voice, and *there is* and *it is* constructions. No checker
can identify all these structures, however, nor can it tell you
whether the structure is appropriate for your ideas. In short, a
checker can't substitute for your own careful reading and editing.

ESL As you'll see in the examples that follow, wordiness is not a
problem of incorrect grammar. A sentence may be perfectly grammatical but still contain unneeded words that interfere with the clarity
and force of your idea.

16a Focusing on the subject and verb

Using the subjects and verbs of your sentences for the key actors and actions will reduce words and emphasize important ideas.
(See pp. 99–101 for more on this topic.)

Wordy The <u>reason</u> why most of the country shifts to daylight savings <u>time is</u> that winter days are much shorter than summer days.

con
16a

129

Ways to achieve conciseness

Wordy (87 words)

The highly pressured <u>nature</u> of critical-care nursing is <u>due to the fact that</u> the patients have life-threatening illnesses. Critical-care nurses must have possession of steady nerves to care for patients who are critically ill and very sick. The nurses must also have possession of interpersonal skills. They must also have medical skills. It is considered by most health-care professionals that these nurses are essential if there is to be improvement of patients who are now in critical care from that status to the status of intermediate care.

- Focus on subject and verb (p. 129), and cut or shorten empty words and phrases (p. 131).
- Avoid nouns made from verbs (p. 129).
- Cut unneeded repetition (p. 132).
- Combine sentences (p. 133).
- Change passive voice to active voice (p. 131).
- Eliminate *there is* constructions (p. 133).
- Cut unneeded repetition (p. 132), and reduce clauses and phrases (p. 132).

con
16a

Concise (37 words)

Critical-care nursing is highly pressured because the patients have life-threatening illnesses. Critical-care nurses must possess steady nerves and interpersonal and medical skills. Most health-care professionals consider these nurses essential if patients are to improve to intermediate care.

Concise   Most of the <u>country</u> <u>shifts</u> to daylight savings time because winter days are much shorter than summer days.

Focusing on subjects and verbs will also help you avoid several other causes of wordiness discussed further on pages 100–101:

Nouns made from verbs

Wordy   The <u>occurrence</u> of the winter solstice, the shortest day of the year, <u>is</u> an event occurring about December 22.

Concise   The winter <u>solstice</u>, the shortest day of the year, <u>occurs</u> about December 22.

Weak verbs

Wordy   The earth's axis <u>has</u> a tilt as the planet <u>is</u> in orbit around the sun so that the northern and southern hemispheres <u>are</u> alternately in alignment toward the sun.

Concise   The earth's axis <u>tilts</u> as the planet <u>orbits</u> around the sun so that the northern and southern hemispheres alternately <u>align</u> toward the sun.

Passive voice

Wordy   During its winter the northern hemisphere <u>is tilted</u> far-
thest away from the sun, so the nights <u>are made</u> longer
and the days <u>are made</u> shorter.

Concise   During its winter the northern hemisphere <u>tilts</u> away
from the sun, <u>making</u> the nights longer and the days
shorter.

See also pages 176–177 on changing the passive voice to the
active voice, as in the example above.

16b   Cutting empty words

Empty words walk in place, gaining little or nothing in meaning. Many can be cut entirely. The following are just a few examples:

all things considered   in a manner of speaking
as far as I'm concerned   in my opinion
for all intents and purposes   last but not least
for the most part   more or less

Other empty words can also be cut, usually along with some of the
words around them:

area	element	kind	situation
aspect	factor	manner	thing
case	field	nature	type

Still others can be reduced from several words to a single word:

For	Substitute
at all times	always
at the present time	now, yet
because of the fact that	because
by virtue of the fact that	because
due to the fact that	because
for the purpose of	for
in order to	to
in the event that	if
in the final analysis	finally

Cutting or reducing such words and phrases will make your
writing move faster and work harder:

con

16b

KEY TERMS

PASSIVE VOICE   The verb form when the subject names the *receiver* of
the verb's action: *The house <u>was destroyed</u> by the tornado.* (See p.
176.)

ACTIVE VOICE   The verb form when the subject names the *performer*
of the verb's action: *The tornado <u>destroyed</u> the house.* (See p. 176.)

Wordy As far as I am concerned, because of the fact that a situation of discrimination continues to exist in the field of medicine, women have not at the present time achieved equality with men.

Concise Because of continuing discrimination in medicine, women have not yet achieved equality with men.

16c Cutting unneeded repetition

Unnecessary repetition weakens sentences:

Wordy Many unskilled workers without training in a particular job are unemployed and do not have any work.

Concise Many unskilled workers are unemployed.

Be especially alert to phrases that say the same thing twice. In the examples below, the unneeded words are underlined:

circle around
consensus of opinion
continue on
cooperate together
final completion
frank and honest exchange
the future to come

important [basic] essentials
puzzling in nature
repeat again
return again
revert back
square [round] in shape
surrounding circumstances

ESL The preceding phrases are redundant because the main word already implies the underlined word or words. A dictionary will tell you what meanings a word implies. *Assassinate,* for instance, means "murder someone well known," so the following sentence is redundant: *Julius Caesar was assassinated and killed.*

16d Reducing clauses and phrases

Modifiers—subordinate clauses, phrases, and single words—can be expanded or contracted depending on the emphasis you want to achieve. (Generally, the longer a construction, the more emphasis it has.) When editing your sentences, consider whether any modifiers can be reduced without loss of emphasis or clarity:

Wordy The Channel Tunnel, which runs between Britain and France, bores through a bed of solid chalk that is twenty-three miles across.

Concise The Channel Tunnel between Britain and France bores through twenty-three miles of solid chalk.

16e   Cutting *there is* or *it is*

You can postpone the sentence subject with the words *there is* (*there are, there was, there were*) and *it is* (*it was*): <u>*There is*</u> reason for voting. <u>*It is*</u> *your vote that counts.* These EXPLETIVE CONSTRUCTIONS can be useful to emphasize the subject (as when introducing it for the first time) or to indicate a change in direction. But often they just add words and create limp substitutes for more vigorous sentences:

Wordy   <u>There were delays and cost overruns that</u> plagued the tunnel's builders. <u>It was a fear of investors that</u> they would not earn profits once the tunnel opened.

Concise   <u>Delays and cost overruns</u> plagued the tunnel's builders. <u>Investors feared</u> that they would not earn profits once the tunnel opened.

ESL   When you must use an expletive construction, be careful to include *there* or *it.* Only commands and some questions can begin with verbs.

16f   Combining sentences

con

16f

Often the information in two or more sentences can be combined into one tight sentence:

Wordy   So far, business has been disappointing. Fewer travelers than were expected have boarded the tunnel train. The train runs between London and Paris.

Concise   So far, business has been disappointing, with fewer travelers than expected boarding the tunnel train that runs between London and Paris.

(See also p. 112 on combining sentences to achieve variety.)

KEY TERMS

MODIFIER   A word or word group that limits or qualifies another word: *slippery road.*

SUBORDINATE CLAUSE   A word group that contains a subject and a verb, begins with a subordinating word such as *because* or *who,* and is not a question. Most subordinate clauses serve as modifiers: *Two accidents occurred on the road, <u>which was unusually slippery</u>.* (See p. 151.)

PHRASE   A word group that lacks a subject or a verb or both. Many phrases serve as modifiers: *road <u>with a slippery surface</u>.* (See p. 148.)

16g   Rewriting jargon

JARGON can refer to the special vocabulary of any discipline or profession (see p. 117). But it has also come to describe vague, inflated language that is overcomplicated, even incomprehensible. When it comes from government or business, we call it *bureaucratese*. It sounds almost as if the writer deliberately ignored every suggestion for clear, concise writing:

Jargon   The necessity for individuals to become separate entities in their own right may impel children to engage in open rebelliousness against parental authority or against sibling influence, with resultant confusion of those being rebelled against.

Translation   Children's natural desire to become themselves may make them rebel against bewildered parents or siblings.

IV

Sentence Parts and Patterns

IV

Sentence Parts and Patterns

PRONOUNS *184*

MODIFIERS *197*

SENTENCE FAULTS *212*

http://webster.commnet.edu/HP/pages/darling/original.htm
Comprehensive grammar information and exercises, from the Guide to Grammar and Writing.

http://www.english.uiuc.edu/cws/wworkshop/grammarmenu.htm
Extensive coverage of the elements of grammar, from the University of Illinois at Urbana-Champaign.

http://www.aitech.ac.jp/~iteslj/quizzes/grammar.html   Online grammar exercises for ESL writers, from the *Internet TESL Journal.*

http://www.clta.on.ca/grammmar.htm   Resources and grammar exercises for ESL writers, from the Centre for Language Training and Assessment.

Grammar describes how language works, and understanding it can help you create clear and accurate sentences. This section explains the kinds of words in sentences (Chapter 17) and how to build basic sentences (18), expand them (19), and classify them (20).

Note   Computerized grammar and style checkers can both offer assistance and cause problems as you compose correct sentences. Look for the cautions and tips for using such checkers in this and the next part of this book. For more information about style and grammar checkers, see page 59.

17 Parts of Speech

All English words fall into eight groups, called PARTS OF SPEECH: nouns, pronouns, verbs, adjectives, adverbs, prepositions, conjunctions, and interjections.

Note   In different sentences a word may serve as different parts of speech. For example:

The government sent <u>aid</u> to the city. [*Aid* is a noun.]
Governments <u>aid</u> citizens. [*Aid* is a verb.]

The *function* of a word in a sentence always determines its part of speech in that sentence.

gr
17a

17a   Recognizing nouns

Nouns name. They may name a person (*Rosie O'Donnell, Jesse Jackson, astronaut*), a thing (*chair, book, Mt. Rainier*), a quality (*pain, mystery, simplicity*), a place (*city, Washington, ocean, Red Sea*), or an idea (*reality, peace, success*).

The forms of nouns depend partly on where they fit in certain groups. As the examples indicate, the same noun may appear in more than one group.

- COMMON NOUNS name general classes of things and do not begin with capital letters: *earthquake, citizen, earth, fortitude, army.*
- PROPER NOUNS name specific people, places, and things and begin with capital letters: *Helen Hunt, Washington Monument, El Paso, US Congress.*
- COUNT NOUNS name things considered countable in English. Most add *-s* or *-es* to distinguish between singular (one) and plural (more than one): *citizen, citizens; city, cities.* Some count nouns form irregular plurals: *woman, women; child, children.*
- NONCOUNT NOUNS name things that aren't considered countable in English (*earth, sugar*), or they name qualities (*chaos, fortitude*). Noncount nouns do not form plurals.
- COLLECTIVE NOUNS are singular in form but name groups: *army, family, herd, US Congress.*

In addition, most nouns form the POSSESSIVE by adding *-'s* to show ownership (*Nadia's books, citizen's rights*), source (*Auden's poems*), and some other relationships.

17b Recognizing pronouns

Most PRONOUNS substitute for nouns and function in sentences as nouns do: *Susanne Ling enlisted in the Air Force when she graduated.*

Pronouns fall into several subclasses depending on their form or function:

- PERSONAL PRONOUNS refer to a specific individual or to individuals: *I, you, he, she, it, we,* and *they.*
- INDEFINITE PRONOUNS, such as *everybody* and *some,* do not substitute for any specific nouns, though they function as nouns (*Everybody speaks*).
- RELATIVE PRONOUNS—*who, whoever, which, that*—relate groups of words to nouns or other pronouns (*The book that won is a novel*).
- INTERROGATIVE PRONOUNS, such as *who, which,* and *what,* introduce questions (*Who will contribute?*).
- DEMONSTRATIVE PRONOUNS, including *this, that,* and *such,* identify or point to nouns (*This is the problem*).

gr
17b

- INTENSIVE PRONOUNS—a personal pronoun plus *-self* or *-selves* (*himself, ourselves*)—emphasize a noun or other pronoun (*He himself asked that question*).
- REFLEXIVE PRONOUNS have the same form as intensive pronouns but indicate that the sentence subject also receives the action of the verb (*They injured themselves*).

The personal pronouns *I, he, she, we,* and *they* and the relative pronouns *who* and *whoever* change form depending on their function in the sentence. (See Chapter 26.)

17c   Recognizing verbs

Verbs express an action (*bring, change, grow, consider*), an occurrence (*become, happen, occur*), or a state of being (*be, seem, remain*).

1   Forms of verbs

Verbs have five distinctive forms. If the form can change as described here, the word is a verb:

- The PLAIN FORM is the dictionary form of the verb. When the subject is a plural noun or the pronoun *I, we, you,* or *they,* the plain form indicates action that occurs in the present, occurs habitually, or is generally true.

  A few artists <u>live</u> in town today.
  They <u>hold</u> classes downtown.

- The *-s* FORM ends in *-s* or *-es*. When the subject is a singular noun, a pronoun such as *everyone,* or the personal pronoun *he, she,* or *it,* the *-s* form indicates action that occurs in the present, occurs habitually, or is generally true.

  The artist <u>lives</u> in town today.
  She <u>holds</u> classes downtown.

- The PAST-TENSE FORM indicates that the action of the verb occurred before now. It usually adds *-d* or *-ed* to the plain form, although most irregular verbs create it in different ways (see pp. 154–56).

  Many artists <u>lived</u> in town before this year.
  They <u>held</u> classes downtown. [Irregular verb.]

- The PAST PARTICIPLE is usually the same as the past-tense form, except in most irregular verbs. It combines with forms of *have* or *be* (*has climbed, was created*), or by itself it modifies nouns and pronouns (*the sliced apples*).

Artists have lived in town for decades.
They have held classes downtown. [Irregular verb.]

- The PRESENT PARTICIPLE adds *-ing* to the verb's plain form. It combines with forms of *be* (*is buying*), modifies nouns and pronouns (*the boiling water*), or functions as a noun (*Running exhausts me*).

A few artists are living in town today.
They are holding classes downtown.

The verb *be* has eight forms rather than the five forms of most other verbs:

Plain form	be
Present participle	being
Past participle	been

	I	*he, she, it*	*we, you, they*
Present tense	am	is	are
Past tense	was	was	were

2 Helping verbs

Some verb forms combine with HELPING VERBS to indicate time, possibility, obligation, necessity, and other kinds of meaning: *can run, was sleeping, had been working*. In these VERB PHRASES *run, sleeping,* and *working* are MAIN VERBS—they carry the principal meaning.

Verb phrase

Helping   Main

Artists can train others to draw.
The techniques have changed little.

gr

17c

These are the most common helping verbs:

be able to	had better	must	used to
be supposed to	have to	ought to	will
can	may	shall	would
could	might	should	

Forms of *be:* be, am, is, are, was, were, been, being
Forms of *have:* have, has, had, having
Forms of *do:* do, does, did

See pages 158-163 for more on helping verbs.

17d Recognizing adjectives and adverbs

ADJECTIVES describe or modify nouns and pronouns. They specify which one, what quality, or how many.

old city
adjective noun

generous one
adjective pronoun

two pears
adjective noun

ADVERBS describe or modify verbs, adjectives, other adverbs, and whole groups of words. They specify when, where, how, and to what extent.

nearly destroyed
adverb verb

too quickly
adverb adverb

very generous
adverb adjective

Unfortunately, taxes will rise.
adverb word group

An *-ly* ending often signals an adverb, but not always: *friendly* is an adjective; *never, not,* and *always* are adverbs. The only way to tell whether a word is an adjective or an adverb is to determine what it modifies.

Adjectives and adverbs appear in three forms: POSITIVE (*green, angrily*), COMPARATIVE (*greener, more angrily*), and SUPERLATIVE (*greenest, most angrily*).

See Chapter 29 for more on adjectives and adverbs.

17e Recognizing connecting words: Prepositions and conjunctions

Connecting words are mostly small words that link parts of sentences. They never change form.

1 Prepositions

PREPOSITIONS form nouns or pronouns (plus any modifiers) into word groups called PREPOSITIONAL PHRASES: *about* love, *down the stairs*. These phrases usually serve as modifiers in sentences, as in *The plants trailed down the stairs*. (See p. 148 for more on prepositional phrases.)

ESL The meanings and uses of English prepositions can be difficult to master. See pages 124–26 for a discussion of prepositions in idioms. See pages 165–66 for uses of prepositions in two-word verbs such as *look after* or *look up*.

Common prepositions

about	before	except for	of	throughout
above	behind	excepting	off	till
according to	below	for	on	to
across	beneath	from	onto	toward
after	beside	in	on top of	under
against	between	in addition to	out	underneath
along	beyond	inside	out of	unlike
along with	by	inside of	outside	until
among	concerning	in spite of	over	up
around	despite	instead of	past	upon
as	down	into	regarding	up to
aside from	due to	like	round	with
at	during	near	since	within
because of	except	next to	through	without

2 Subordinating conjunctions

SUBORDINATING CONJUNCTIONS form sentences into word groups called SUBORDINATE CLAUSES, such as *when the meeting ended*. These clauses serve as parts of sentences: *Everyone was relieved when the meeting ended*. (See p. 150 for more on subordinate clauses.)

Common subordinating conjunctions

after	even if	rather than	until
although	even though	since	when
as	if	so that	whenever
as if	if only	than	where
as long as	in order that	that	whereas
as though	now that	though	wherever
because	once	till	whether
before	provided	unless	while

gr
17e

ESL Subordinating conjunctions convey meaning without help from other function words, such as the coordinating conjunctions *and, but, for,* or *so:*

Faulty <u>Even though</u> the parents are illiterate, <u>but</u> their children may read well. [*Even though* and *but* have the same meaning, so both are not needed.]

Revised <u>Even though</u> the parents are illiterate, their children may read well.

3 Coordinating and correlative conjunctions

Coordinating and correlative conjunctions connect words or word groups of the same kind, such as nouns, adjectives, or sentences.

COORDINATING CONJUNCTIONS consist of a single word:

Coordinating conjunctions

and	nor	for	yet
but	or	so	

Biofeedback or simple relaxation can relieve headaches.
Relaxation works well, and it is inexpensive.

CORRELATIVE CONJUNCTIONS are combinations of coordinating conjunctions and other words:

Common correlative conjunctions

both . . . and	neither . . . nor
not only . . . but also	whether . . . or
not . . . but	as . . . as
either . . . or	

Both biofeedback and relaxation can relieve headaches.
The headache sufferer learns not only to recognize the causes of headaches but also to control those causes.

gr
17f

17f Recognizing interjections

INTERJECTIONS express feeling or command attention. They are rarely used in academic or business writing.

Oh, the meeting went fine.
They won seven thousand dollars! Wow!

18 The Sentence

http://webster.commnet.edu/hp/pages/darling/grammar/diagrams/
diagrams.html-ssi   Examples of basic sentence patterns, from the
Guide to Grammar and Writing.

The SENTENCE is the basic unit of expression. It is grammatically complete and independent: it does not serve as an adjective, adverb, or other single part of speech.

18a   Recognizing subjects and predicates

Most sentences make statements. First the SUBJECT names something; then the PREDICATE makes an assertion about the subject or describes an action by the subject.

Subject	Predicate
Art	thrives.

The SIMPLE SUBJECT consists of one or more nouns or pronouns, whereas the COMPLETE SUBJECT also includes any modifiers. The SIMPLE PREDICATE consists of one or more verbs, whereas the COMPLETE PREDICATE adds any words needed to complete the meaning of the verb plus any modifiers.

Sometimes, as in the short example *Art thrives,* the simple and complete subject and predicate are the same. More often, they are different:

Subject	Predicate

```
          ┌────complete────┐     ┌────complete────┐
                 simple      simple
          Some contemporary art   stirs controversy.
```

```
          ┌──────complete──────┐   ┌──────complete──────┐
            ┌── simple ──┐        ┌── simple ──┐
          Congress and the media   discuss and dispute its value.
```

gr
18a

In the second example, the simple subject and simple predicate are both COMPOUND: in each, two words joined by a coordinating conjunction (*and*) serve the same function.

ESL   The subject of an English sentence may be a noun (*art*) or a pronoun that refers to the noun (*it*), but not both. (See p. 222.)

Faulty	Some art it stirs controversy.
Revised	Some art stirs controversy.

18b Recognizing predicate patterns

All English sentences are based on five patterns, each differing in the complete predicate (the verb and any words following it).

ESL The word order in English sentences may not correspond to word order in the sentences of your native language. English, for instance, strongly prefers subject first, then verb, then any other words, whereas some other languages prefer the verb first.

Pattern 1: The earth trembled.

In the simplest pattern the predicate consists only of an INTRANSITIVE VERB, a verb that does not require a following word to complete its meaning.

Subject	Predicate
	Intransitive verb
The earth	trembled.
The hospital	may close.

Pattern 2: The earthquake destroyed the city.

In pattern 2 the verb is followed by a DIRECT OBJECT, a noun or pronoun that identifies who or what receives the action of the verb. A verb that requires a direct object to complete its meaning is called TRANSITIVE.

Subject	Predicate	
	Transitive verb	*Direct object*
The earthquake	destroyed	the city.
Education	opens	doors.

ESL Only transitive verbs can be used in the passive voice: *The city was destroyed.* Your dictionary will indicate whether a verb is transitive or intransitive. For some verbs (*begin, learn, read, write,* and others), it will indicate both uses.

Pattern 3: The result was chaos.

In pattern 3 the verb is followed by a SUBJECT COMPLEMENT, a word that renames or describes the subject. A verb in this pattern is called a LINKING VERB because it links its subject to the description

gr
18b

KEY TERM

PASSIVE VOICE The verb form when the subject names the receiver of the verb's action: *Bad weather was predicted.* (See pp. 175–177.)

following. The linking verbs include *be, seem, appear, become, grow, remain, stay, prove, feel, look, smell, sound,* and *taste.* Subject complements are usually nouns or adjectives.

Subject	Predicate	
	Linking verb	*Subject complement*
The result	was	chaos.
The man	became	an accountant.

Pattern 4: The government sent the city aid.

In pattern 4 the verb is followed by a direct object and an IN-DIRECT OBJECT, a word identifying to or for whom the action of the verb is performed. The direct object and indirect object refer to different things, people, or places.

Subject	Predicate		
	Transitive verb	*Indirect object*	*Direct object*
The government	sent	the city	aid.
One company	offered	its employees	bonuses.

A number of verbs can take indirect objects, including those above and *allow, bring, buy, deny, find, get, give, leave, make, pay, read, sell, show, teach,* and *write.*

ESL Some verbs are never followed by an indirect object—*admit, announce, demonstrate, explain, introduce, mention, prove, recommend, say,* and some others. However, the direct objects of these verbs may be followed by *to* or *for* and a noun or pronoun that specifies to or for whom the action was done: *The manual explains the new procedure to workers. A video demonstrates the procedure for us.*

Pattern 5: The citizens considered the earthquake a disaster.

In pattern 5 the verb is followed by a direct object and an OB-JECT COMPLEMENT, a word that renames or describes the direct object. Object complements may be nouns or adjectives.

Subject	Predicate		
	Transitive verb	*Direct object*	*Object complement*
The citizens	considered	the earthquake	a disaster.
Success	makes	some people	nervous.

gr
18b

19 Phrases and Subordinate Clauses

http://webster.commnet.edu/HP/pages/darling/grammar/ prepositions.htm   Discussion and examples of prepositions and prepositional phrases, from the Guide to Grammar and Writing.

http://owl.english.purdue.edu/Files/5.html   Information and exercises on verbals, from the Purdue Online Writing Lab.

http://webster.commnet.edu/HP/pages/darling/grammar/clauses.htm Information on clauses, from the Guide to Grammar and Writing.

http://www.uottawa.ca/academic/arts/writcent/hypergrammar/ bldcls.html#clause   Information on clauses, from the University of Ottawa.

Most sentences contain word groups that serve as adjectives, adverbs, or nouns and thus cannot stand alone as sentences.

- A PHRASE lacks either a subject or a predicate or both: *fearing an accident; in a panic.*
- A SUBORDINATE CLAUSE contains a subject and a predicate (like a sentence) but begins with a subordinating word: *when prices rise; whoever laughs.*

19a   Recognizing phrases

1   Prepositional phrases

A PREPOSITIONAL PHRASE consists of a preposition plus a noun, a pronoun, or a word group serving as a noun, called the OBJECT OF THE PREPOSITION. A list of prepositions appears on page 143.

Preposition	Object
of	spaghetti
on	the surface
with	great satisfaction
upon	entering the room
from	where you are standing

Prepositional phrases usually function as adjectives or adverbs.

Life on a raft was an opportunity for adventure.
 adjective phrase   adjective phrase

Huck Finn rode the raft by choice.
                                adverb phrase

With his companion, Jim, Huck met many types of people.
 adverb phrase   adjective phrase

gr
19a

148

2 Verbal phrases

Certain forms of verbs, called VERBALS, can serve as modifiers or nouns. Often these verbals appear with their own modifiers and objects in VERBAL PHRASES.

Note Verbals cannot serve as verbs in sentences. *The sun rises over the dump* is a sentence; *The sun rising over the dump* is a sentence fragment. (See p. 213.)

Participial phrases

Phrases made from present participles (ending in *-ing*) or past participles (usually ending in *-d* or *-ed*) serve as adjectives.

Strolling shoppers fill the malls.
adjective

They make selections determined by personal taste.
adjective phrase

Note With irregular verbs, the past participle may have a different ending—for instance, *hidden funds*. (See p. 154.)

ESL For verbs expressing feeling, the present and past participles have different meanings: *It was a boring lecture. The bored students slept.* (See p. 201.)

Gerund phrases

A GERUND is the *-ing* form of a verb when it serves as a noun. Gerunds and gerund phrases can do whatever nouns can do.

sentence
subject
Shopping satisfies personal needs.
noun

object of preposition
Malls are good at creating such needs.
noun phrase

Infinitive phrases

An INFINITIVE is the plain form of a verb plus *to: to hide*. Infinitives and infinitive phrases serve as adjectives, adverbs, or nouns.

sentence
subject   subject complement
To design a mall is to create an artificial environment.
noun phrase   noun phrase

Malls are designed to make shoppers feel safe.
adverb phrase

The environment supports the impulse to shop.
adjective

gr
19a

ESL Infinitives and gerunds may follow some verbs and not others and may differ in meaning after a verb: *The singer stopped to sing. The singer stopped singing.* (See pp. 163–165.)

3   Absolute phrases

An ABSOLUTE PHRASE consists of a noun or pronoun and a participle, plus any modifiers. It modifies the entire rest of the sentence it appears in.

————absolute phrase————

Their own place established, many ethnic groups are making way for new arrivals.

Unlike a participial phrase (previous page), an absolute phrase always contains a noun that serves as a subject.

participial
——phrase——

Learning English, many immigrants discover American culture.

————absolute phrase————

Immigrants having learned English, their opportunities widen.

4   Appositive phrases

An APPOSITIVE is usually a noun that renames another noun. An appositive phrase includes modifiers as well.

—— appositive phrase

Bizen ware, a dark stoneware, is produced in Japan.

Appositives and appositive phrases sometimes begin with *that is, such as, for example,* or *in other words.*

┌appositive phrase

Bizen ware is used in the Japanese tea ceremony, that is, the Zen

Buddhist observance that links meditation and art.

gr
19b

19b   Recognizing subordinate clauses

A CLAUSE is any group of words that contains both a subject and a predicate. There are two kinds of clauses, and the distinction between them is important.

- A MAIN CLAUSE makes a complete statement and can stand alone as a sentence: *The sky darkened.*

- A SUBORDINATE CLAUSE is just like a main clause *except* that it begins with a subordinating word: <u>*when*</u> *the sky darkened;* <u>*whoever calls*</u>. The subordinating word reduces the clause from a complete statement to a single part of speech: an adjective, adverb, or noun.

Note A subordinate clause punctuated as a sentence is a sentence fragment. (See pp. 214–215.)

Adjective clauses

An ADJECTIVE CLAUSE modifies a noun or pronoun. It usually begins with the relative pronoun *who, whom, whose, which,* or *that.* The relative pronoun is the subject or object of the clause it begins. The clause ordinarily falls immediately after the word it modifies.

—adjective clause
Parents <u>who are illiterate</u> may have bad memories of school.

—adjective clause—
One school, <u>which is open year-round</u>, helps parents learn to read.

Adverb clauses

An ADVERB CLAUSE modifies a verb, an adjective, another adverb, or a whole word group. It always begins with a subordinating conjunction, such as *although, because, if,* or *when* (see p. 143 for a list).

— adverb clause—
The school began teaching parents <u>when adult illiteracy gained national attention</u>.

— adverb clause—   —main clause
<u>Because it was directed at people who could not read</u>, advertising had to be inventive.

Noun clauses

A NOUN CLAUSE replaces a noun in a sentence and serves as a subject, object, or complement. It begins with *that, what, whatever, who, whom, whoever, whomever, when, where, whether, why,* or *how.*

sentence subject
<u>Whether the program would succeed</u> depended on door-to-door
noun clause
advertising.

direct object
Teachers explained in person <u>how the program would work</u>.
noun clause

gr
19b

20 Sentence Types

http://www.uottawa.ca/academic/arts/writcent/hypergrammar/
bldsent.html   Discussion of forms and classes of sentences, from the
University of Ottawa.

The four basic sentence structures vary in the number of main
and coordinate clauses.

20a   Recognizing simple sentences

A SIMPLE SENTENCE consists of a single main clause and no subordinate clause:

<pre>
┌─────────── main clause ───────────┐
Last summer was unusually hot.
</pre>

<pre>
┌────────────────────── main clause ──────────────────────┐
The summer made many farmers leave the area for good or
└─
reduced them to bare existence.
</pre>

20b   Recognizing compound sentences

A COMPOUND SENTENCE consists of two or more main clauses and
no subordinate clause:

<pre>
┌─── main clause ───┐   ┌──── main clause ────┐
Last July was hot, but August was even hotter.
</pre>

<pre>
┌────────── main clause ──────────┐   ┌──────── main clause ────────┐
The hot sun scorched the earth, and the lack of rain killed many
└─
crops.
</pre>

20c   Recognizing complex sentences

A COMPLEX SENTENCE consists of one main clause and one or
more subordinate clauses:

<pre>
┌─── main clause ───┐ ┌──────── subordinate clause ────────┐
Rain finally came, although many had left the area by then.
</pre>

<pre>
┌────────────── main clause ──────────────┐ ┌─ subordinate clause ─┐
Those who remained were able to start anew because the govern-
└─┘ subordinate clause └─
       subordinate clause
ment came to their aid.
</pre>

gr
20c

152

20d Recognizing compound-complex sentences

A COMPOUND-COMPLEX SENTENCE has the characteristics of both the compound sentence (two or more main clauses) and the complex sentence (at least one subordinate clause):

```
       _____ subordinate clause _____    _____ main clause ___
Even  though  government  aid  finally  came,  many  people  had
_____    _____ main clause _____
already  been  reduced  to  poverty,  and  others  had  been  forced  to
____
move.
```

VERBS express actions, conditions, and states of being. The basic uses and forms of verbs are described on pages 140–141. This section explains and solves the most common problems with verbs' forms (Chapter 21), tenses (22), mood (23), and voice (24) and shows how to make verbs match their subjects (25).

21 Verb Forms

http://webster.commnet.edu/HP/pages/darling/grammar/verbs.htm Help with verbs, from the Guide to Grammar and Writing.

http://www.uottawa.ca/academic/arts/writcent/hypergrammar/useverb.html Help with verbs, from the University of Ottawa.

http://webster.commnet.edu/HP/pages/darling/grammar/verbs.htm#irregular Discussion, quizzes, and links on irregular verbs, from the Guide to Grammar and Writing.

http://www.uottawa.ca/academic/arts/writcent/hypergrammar/auxvb.html Information on helping verbs, from the University of Ottawa.

21a Use the correct forms of *sing/sang/sung* and other irregular verbs.

Most verbs are REGULAR: they form their past tense and past participle by adding *-d* or *-ed* to the plain form.

Plain form	Past tense	Past participle
live	lived	lived
act	acted	acted

About two hundred English verbs are IRREGULAR: they form their past tense and past participle in some irregular way. Check a

vb
21a

KEY TERMS

PLAIN FORM The dictionary form of the verb: *I walk. You forget.* (See p. 140.)

PAST-TENSE FORM The verb form indicating action that occurred in the past: *I walked. You forgot.* (See p. 140.)

PAST PARTICIPLE The verb form used with *have, has,* or *had: I have walked.* It may also serve as a modifier: *This is a forgotten book.* (See p. 149.)

Common irregular verbs

Plain form	Past tense	Past participle
arise	arose	arisen
become	became	become
begin	began	begun
bid	bid	bid
bite	bit	bitten, bit
blow	blew	blown
break	broke	broken
bring	brought	brought
burst	burst	burst
buy	bought	bought
catch	caught	caught
choose	chose	chosen
come	came	come
cut	cut	cut
dive	dived, dove	dived
do	did	done
draw	drew	drawn
dream	dreamed, dreamt	dreamed, dreamt
drink	drank	drunk
drive	drove	driven
eat	ate	eaten
fall	fell	fallen
find	found	found
flee	fled	fled
fly	flew	flown
forget	forgot	forgotten, forgot
freeze	froze	frozen
get	got	got, gotten
give	gave	given
go	went	gone
grow	grew	grown
hang (suspend)	hung	hung
hang (execute)	hanged	hanged
hear	heard	heard
hide	hid	hidden
hold	held	held
keep	kept	kept
know	knew	known
lay	laid	laid
lead	led	led
leave	left	left
lend	lent	lent
let	let	let
lie	lay	lain

(continued)

vb
21a

Common irregular verbs
(continued)

Plain form	Past tense	Past participle
lose	lost	lost
pay	paid	paid
prove	proved	proved, proven
ride	rode	ridden
ring	rang	rung
rise	rose	risen
run	ran	run
say	said	said
see	saw	seen
set	set	set
shake	shook	shaken
shrink	shrank, shrunk	shrunk, shrunken
sing	sang, sung	sung
sink	sank, sunk	sunk
sit	sat	sat
sleep	slept	slept
slide	slid	slid
speak	spoke	spoken
spring	sprang, sprung	sprung
stand	stood	stood
steal	stole	stolen
swim	swam	swum
swing	swung	swung
take	took	taken
tear	tore	torn
throw	threw	thrown
wear	wore	worn
write	wrote	written

vb

21a

dictionary under the verb's plain form if you have any doubt about its other forms. If the verb is irregular, the dictionary will list the plain form, the past tense, and the past participle in that order (*go, went, gone*). If the dictionary gives only two forms (as in *think, thought*), then the past tense and the past participle are the same.

The list on the previous page and above includes the most common irregular verbs. (When two forms are possible, as in *dove* and *dived,* both are included.)

Note A computerized grammar and style checker may flag incorrect forms of irregular verbs, but it may also fail to do so. When in doubt about the forms of irregular verbs, refer to the list above, consult a dictionary, or consult the additional lists at the third Web site given on page 154.

21b Distinguish between *sit* and *set, lie* and *lay,* and *rise* and *raise.*

The forms of *sit* and *set, lie* and *lay,* and *rise* and *raise* are easy to confuse.

Plain form	Past tense	Past participle
sit	sat	sat
set	set	set
lie	lay	lain
lay	laid	laid
rise	rose	risen
raise	raised	raised

In each of these confusing pairs, one verb is intransitive (it does not take an object) and one is transitive (it does take an object). (See p. 146 for more on this distinction.)

Intransitive

The patients <u>lie</u> in their beds. [*Lie* means "recline" and takes no object.]

Visitors <u>sit</u> with them. [*Sit* means "be seated" or "be located" and takes no object.]

Patients' temperatures <u>rise</u>. [*Rise* means "increase" or "get up" and takes no object.]

Transitive

Orderlies <u>lay</u> the dinner trays on tables. [*Lay* means "place" and takes an object, here *trays.*]

Orderlies <u>set</u> the trays down. [*Set* means "place" and takes an object, here *trays.*]

Nursing aides <u>raise</u> the shades. [*Raise* means "lift" or "bring up" and takes an object, here *shades.*]

vb
21c

21c Use the *-s* and *-ed* forms of the verb when they are required.

Speakers of some English dialects and nonnative speakers of English sometimes omit verb endings required by standard English. One is the *-s* form of a verb, which is required when *both* of these situations hold:

- The subject is a singular noun (*boy*), an indefinite pronoun (*everyone*), or *he, she,* or *it.*
- The verb's action occurs in the present.

The letter <u>asks</u> [not <u>ask</u>] for a quick response.
Delay <u>is</u> [not <u>be</u>] costly.

Watch especially for the -s forms *has, does,* and *doesn't* (for *does not*).

The company <u>has</u> [not <u>have</u>] delayed responding.
It <u>doesn't</u> [not <u>don't</u>] have the needed data.
The contract <u>does</u> [not <u>do</u>] depend on the response.

Another ending sometimes omitted is -*d* or -*ed,* as in *we bagged* or *used cars.* The ending is particularly easy to omit if it isn't pronounced clearly in speech, as in *asked, discussed, fixed, mixed, supposed, walked,* and *used.* Use the ending for a regular verb in *any* of these situations:

- The verb's action occurred in the past:

  The company <u>asked</u> [not <u>ask</u>] for more time.

- The verb form functions as a modifier:

  The data <u>concerned</u> [not <u>concern</u>] should be retrievable.

- The verb form combines with a form of *be* or *have:*

  The company is <u>supposed</u> [not <u>suppose</u>] to be the best.
  It has <u>developed</u> [not <u>develop</u>] an excellent reputation.

 Note A computerized grammar and style checker will flag many omitted -*s* and -*ed* endings from verbs, such as in *he ask* or *was ask.* But it will miss many omissions, too. You'll need to proofread your papers carefully on your own to catch missing endings.
   ESL Some languages do not require endings equivalent to the -*s* or -*ed* in English. If English is not your native language and you find you omit one or both of these endings, you may need to edit your drafts just for them.

vb

21d

21d Use helping verbs with main verbs appropriately.

Helping verbs combine with main verbs in verb phrases: *The line <u>should have been cut</u>. Who <u>was calling</u>?*
   Note Computerized grammar and style checkers often spot omitted helping verbs and incorrect main verbs with helping verbs, but sometimes they do not. A checker flagged *Many been fortunate, She working,* and *Her ideas are grow more complex* but overlooked other examples on the following pages, such as *The conference will be occurred.* Careful proofreading is the only insurance against missing helping verbs and incorrect main verbs.

1 Required helping verbs

Some English dialects omit helping verbs required by standard English. In the sentences below, the underlined helping verbs are essential:

> Archaeologists <u>are</u> conducting fieldwork all over the world. [Not *Archaeologists conducting.* . . .]
> Many <u>have</u> been fortunate in their discoveries. [Not *Many been.* . . .]
> Some <u>could</u> be real-life Indiana Joneses. [Not *Some be.* . . .]

The omission of a helping verb may create an incomplete sentence, or SENTENCE FRAGMENT, because a present participle (*conducting*), an irregular past participle (*been*), or the infinitive *be* cannot stand alone as the only verb in a sentence (see pp. 212–213). To work as sentence verbs, these verb forms need helping verbs.

2 Combination of helping verb + main verb ESL

Helping verbs and main verbs combine into verb phrases in specific ways.

Note The main verb in a verb phrase (the one carrying the main meaning) does not change to show a change in subject or time: *she has <u>sung</u>, you had <u>sung</u>.* Only the helping verb may change, as in these examples.

Form of *be* + present participle

The PROGRESSIVE TENSES indicate action in progress. Create them with *be, am, is, are, was, were,* or *been* followed by the main verb's present participle, as in the following example.

┌─ KEY TERMS ──

HELPING VERB A verb such as *can, may, be, have,* or *do* that forms a verb phrase with another verb to show time, permission, and other meanings. (See p. 141.)

MAIN VERB The verb that carries the principal meaning in a verb phrase: *has <u>walked</u>, could be <u>happening</u>.* (See p. 141.)

VERB PHRASE A helping verb plus a main verb: *will be singing, would speak.* (See p. 141.)

PRESENT PARTICIPLE The *-ing* form of the verb: *flying, writing.* (See p. 141.)

PROGRESSIVE TENSES Verb tenses expressing action in progress—for instance, *I am flying* (present progressive), *I was flying* (past progressive), *I will be flying* (future progressive). (See p. 169.)

vb

21d

She <u>is working</u> on a new book.

Be and *been* require additional helping verbs to form progressive tenses:

can	might	should ⎫		have ⎫	
could	must	will ⎬ <u>be</u> working		has ⎬ <u>been</u> working	
may	shall	would ⎭		had ⎭	

When forming the progressive tenses, be sure to use the *-ing* form of the main verb:

Faulty   Her ideas are <u>grow</u> more complex. She is <u>developed</u> a new approach to ethics.

Revised   Her ideas are <u>growing</u> more complex. She is <u>developing</u> a new approach to ethics.

Form of *be* + past participle

The PASSIVE VOICE of the verb indicates that the subject *receives* the action of the verb. Create the passive voice with *be, am, is, are, was, were, being,* or *been* followed by the main verb's past participle:

Her latest book <u>was completed</u> in four months.

Be, being, and *been* require additional helping verbs to form the passive voice:

have ⎫		am	was ⎫	
has ⎬ <u>been</u> completed		is	were ⎬ <u>being</u> completed	
had ⎭		are	⎭	

will <u>be</u> completed

Be sure to use the main verb's past participle for the passive voice:

Faulty   Her next book will be <u>publish</u> soon.

Revised   Her next book will be <u>published</u> soon.

vb
21d

┌─ KEY TERMS ───

PAST PARTICIPLE   The *-d* or *-ed* form of a regular verb: *hedged, walked.* Most irregular verbs have distinctive past participles: *eaten, swum.* (See p. 140.)

PASSIVE VOICE   The verb form when the subject names the receiver of the verb's action: *An essay <u>was written</u> by every student.* (See p. 176.)

TRANSITIVE VERB   A verb that requires an object to complete its meaning: *Every student <u>completed</u> an essay* (*essay* is the object of *completed*). (See p. 146.)

Note Use only transitive verbs to form the passive voice:

Faulty   A philosophy conference <u>will be occurred</u> in the same week. [*Occur* is not a transitive verb.]

Revised   A philosophy conference <u>will occur</u> in the same week.

See pages 176–177 for advice on when to use and when to avoid the passive voice.

Forms of *have*

Four forms of *have* serve as helping verbs: *have, has, had, having*. One of these forms plus the main verb's past participle creates one of the perfect tenses, those expressing action completed before another specific time or action:

Some students <u>have complained</u> about the laboratory.
Others <u>had complained</u> before.

Will and other helping verbs sometimes accompany forms of *have* in the perfect tenses:

Several more students <u>will have complained</u> by the end of the week.

Forms of *do*

Do, does, and *did* have three uses as helping verbs, always with the plain form of the main verb:

- To pose a question: *How <u>did</u> the trial <u>end</u>?*
- To emphasize the main verb: *It <u>did end</u> eventually.*
- To negate the main verb, along with *not* or *never: The judge <u>did not withdraw</u>.*

Be sure to use the main verb's plain form with any form of *do:*

Faulty   The judge did <u>remained</u> in court.

Revised   The judge did <u>remain</u> in court.

Modals

The modal helping verbs include *can, could, may,* and *might,* along with several two- and three-word combinations, such as *have to* and *be able to.* (See p. 141 for a list of modals.)

vb

21d

┌─ KEY TERM ───

PERFECT TENSES   Verb tenses expressing an action completed before another specific time or action: *We have eaten* (present perfect), *We had eaten* (past perfect), *We will have eaten* (future perfect). (See p. 169.)

Modals convey various meanings, with these being most common:

- Ability: *can, could, be able to*

  The equipment <u>can detect</u> small vibrations. [Present.]
  The equipment <u>could detect</u> small vibrations. [Past.]
  The equipment <u>is able to detect</u> small vibrations. [Present. Past: *was able to.* Future: *will be able to.*]

- Possibility: *could, may, might, could/may/might have* + past participle

  The equipment <u>could fail</u>. [Present.]
  The equipment <u>may fail</u>. [Present and future.]
  The equipment <u>might fail</u>. [Present and future.]
  The equipment <u>may have failed</u>. [Past.]

- Necessity or obligation: *must, have to, be supposed to*

  The lab <u>must purchase</u> a backup. [Present or future.]
  The lab <u>has to purchase</u> a backup. [Present or future. Past: *had to.*]
  The lab <u>will have to purchase</u> a backup. [Future.]
  The lab <u>is supposed to purchase</u> a backup. [Present. Past: *was supposed to.*]

- Permission: *may, can, could*

  The lab <u>may spend</u> the money. [Present or future.]
  The lab <u>can spend</u> the money. [Present or future.]
  The lab <u>could spend</u> the money. [Present or future, more tentative.]
  The school then announced that the lab <u>could spend</u> the money. [Past.]

- Intention: *will, shall, would*

  The lab <u>will spend</u> the money. [Future.]
  <u>Shall</u> we <u>offer</u> advice? [Future. Use *shall* for questions requesting opinion or consent.]
  We knew we <u>would offer</u> advice. [Past.]

- Request: *could, can, would*

  <u>Could</u> [or <u>can</u> or <u>would</u>] you please <u>obtain</u> a bid? [Present or future.]

- Advisability: *should, had better, ought to, should have* + past participle

  You <u>should obtain</u> three bids. [Present or future.]
  You <u>had better obtain</u> three bids. [Present or future.]
  You <u>ought to obtain</u> three bids. [Present or future.]
  You <u>should have obtained</u> three bids. [Past.]

vb

21d

- Past habit: *would, used to*

In years past we would obtain five bids.
We used to obtain five bids.

The following conventions govern the combination of modals and main verbs shown in the examples:

- One-word modals do not change form to show a change in subject: *I could run, she could run.* Most two- and three-word modals do change form, like other helping verbs: *I have to run, she has to run.*
- Modals can sometimes indicate past, present, or future time, occasionally with a word change (*can* to *could*, for instance), with a form change in a two- or three-word modal (such as *is/was able to*), or with *have* before the past participle of the main verb (*might have driven*).
- Don't use *to* between a one-word modal and the main verb: *can drive*, not *can to drive*. (Most of the two- and three-word modals do include *to: ought to drive.*)
- Don't use two one-word modals together: *I will be able to drive*, not *I will can drive*.

21e   Use a gerund or an infinitive after a verb as appropriate. ESL

Gerunds and infinitives may follow certain verbs but not others. And sometimes the use of a gerund or infinitive with the same verb changes the meaning of the verb.

 Note A computerized grammar and style checker will spot some but not all errors in matching gerunds or infinitives with verbs. Use the lists given here and an ESL dictionary (see p. 122) to determine whether an infinitive or a gerund is appropriate.

1   Either gerund or infinitive

A gerund or an infinitive may come after the following verbs with no significant difference in meaning.

KEY TERMS

GERUND   The *-ing* form of the verb used as a noun: *Smoking is unhealthful.* (See p. 149.)

INFINITIVE   The plain form of the verb usually preceded by *to: to smoke.* An infinitive may serve as an adjective, adverb, or noun. (See p. 149.)

---

vb

21e

begin	continue	intend	prefer
can't bear	hate	like	start
can't stand	hesitate	love	

The pump began <u>working</u>. The pump began <u>to work</u>.

2 Meaning change with gerund or infinitive

With four verbs, a gerund has quite a different meaning from an infinitive:

| forget | stop |
| remember | try |

The engineer stopped <u>eating</u>. [He no longer ate.]
The engineer stopped <u>to eat</u>. [He stopped in order to eat.]

3 Gerund, not infinitive

Do not use an infinitive after these verbs:

admit	discuss	mind	recollect
adore	dislike	miss	resent
appreciate	enjoy	postpone	resist
avoid	escape	practice	risk
consider	finish	put off	suggest
deny	imagine	quit	tolerate
detest	keep	recall	understand

Faulty He finished <u>to eat</u> lunch.

Revised He finished <u>eating</u> lunch.

4 Infinitive, not gerund

Do not use a gerund after these verbs:

agree	claim	manage	promise
appear	consent	mean	refuse
arrange	decide	offer	say
ask	expect	plan	wait
assent	have	prepare	want
beg	hope	pretend	wish

Faulty He decided <u>checking</u> the pump.

Revised He decided <u>to check</u> the pump.

5 Noun or pronoun + infinitive

Some verbs may be followed by an infinitive alone or by a noun or pronoun and an infinitive. The presence of a noun or pronoun changes the meaning.

ask	dare	need	wish
beg	expect	promise	would like
choose	help	want	

He expected to watch.
He expected his workers to watch.

Some verbs *must* be followed by a noun or pronoun before an infinitive:

admonish	encourage	oblige	require
advise	forbid	order	teach
allow	force	permit	tell
cause	hire	persuade	train
challenge	instruct	remind	urge
command	invite	request	warn
convince			

He instructed his workers to watch.

Do not use *to* before the infinitive when it follows one of these verbs and a noun or pronoun:

feel	make ("force")
have	see
hear	watch
let	

He let his workers learn by observation.

21f   Use the appropriate particles with two-word verbs. **ESL**

Some verbs consist of two words: the verb itself and a PARTICLE, a preposition or adverb that affects the meaning of the verb. For example:

Look up the answer. [Research the answer.]
Look over the answer. [Examine the answer.]

The meanings of these two-word verbs are often quite different

vb

21f

┌─ KEY TERMS ─────────────────────────────────────

PREPOSITION   A word such as *about, for,* or *to* that takes a noun or pronoun as its object: *at the house, in the woods.* (See p. 143 for a list of prepositions.)

ADVERB   A word that modifies a verb (*went down*), adjective (*very pretty*), another adverb (*too sweetly*), or a whole word group (*Eventually, the fire died*). (See p. 142.)

└──

from the meanings of the individual words that make them up. (There are some three-word verbs, too, such as *put up with* and *run out of.*) An ESL dictionary, such as one of those mentioned on page 122, will define two-word verbs for you. It will also tell you whether the verbs may be separated in a sentence, as explained below. A computerized grammar and style checker will recognize few if any misuses of two-word verbs. You'll need to proofread on your own to catch and correct errors.

Note Many two-word verbs are more common in speech than in more formal academic or business writing. For formal writing, consider using *research* instead of *look up, examine* or *inspect* instead of *look over.*

1 Inseparable two-word verbs

Verbs and particles that may not be separated by any other words include the following:

catch on	go over	play around	stay away
come across	grow up	run into	stay up
get along	keep on	run out of	take care of
give in	look into	speak up	turn up at

Faulty Children <u>grow</u> quickly <u>up</u>.
Revised Children <u>grow up</u> quickly.

2 Separable two-word verbs

Most two-word verbs that take direct objects may be separated by the object.

Parents <u>help out</u> their children.
Parents <u>help</u> their children <u>out</u>.

If the direct object is a pronoun, the pronoun *must* separate the verb from the particle.

Faulty Parents <u>help out</u> them.
Revised Parents <u>help</u> them <u>out</u>.

The separable two-word verbs include the following:

bring up	give back	make up	throw out
call off	hand in	point out	try on
call up	hand out	put away	try out
drop off	help out	put back	turn down
fill out	leave out	put off	turn on
fill up	look over	take out	turn up
give away	look up	take over	wrap up

22 Verb Tenses

Information and exercises on verb tenses:

http://owl.english.purdue.edu/Files/72.html   From the Purdue Online
Writing Lab.

http://webster.commnet.edu/HP/pages/darling/grammar/verbs.htm#tense
From the Guide to Grammar and Writing.

http://www.hut.fi/u/rvilmi/LangHelp/Grammar/verbs.html   For ESL
writers, from the Grammar Help page.

TENSE shows the time of a verb's action. The table on the next page illustrates the tense forms for a regular verb. (Irregular verbs have different past-tense and past-participle forms. See pp. 153–155.)

Note Computerized grammar and style checkers can provide little help with incorrect verb tenses and tense sequences because correctness is usually dependent on meaning. Proofread carefully yourself to catch errors in tense or tense sequence.

22a Observe the special uses of the present tense (*sing*).

Most academic and business writing uses the past tense (*the rebellion occurred*), but the present tense has several distinctive uses.

Action occurring now
She <u>understands</u> the problem.
We <u>define</u> the problem differently.

Habitual or recurring action
Banks regularly <u>undergo</u> audits.
The audits <u>monitor</u> the banks' activities.

A general truth
The mills of the gods <u>grind</u> slowly.
The earth <u>is</u> round.

Discussion of literature, film, and so on
Huckleberry Finn <u>has</u> adventures we all envy.
In that article the author <u>examines</u> several causes of crime.

Future time
Next week we <u>draft</u> a new budget.
Funding <u>ends</u> in less than a year.

(Future time is really indicated here by *Next week* and *in less than a year.*)

t
22a

167

Tenses of a regular verb (active voice)

Present Action that is occurring now, occurs habitually, or is generally true

Simple present Plain form or -s form

I walk.
You/we/they walk.
He/she/it walks.

Present progressive *Am, is,* or *are* plus *-ing* form

I am walking.
You/we/they are walking.
He/she/it is walking.

Past Action that occurred before now

Simple past Past-tense form (-*d* or -*ed*)

I/he/she/it walked.
You/we/they walked.

Past progressive *Was* or *were* plus *-ing* form

I/he/she/it was walking.
You/we/they were walking.

Future Action that will occur in the future

Simple future Plain form plus *will*

I/you/he/she/it/we/they will walk.

Future progressive *Will be* plus *-ing* form

I/you/he/she/it/we/they will be walking.

Present perfect Action that began in the past and is linked to the present

Present perfect *Have* or *has* plus past participle (-*d* or -*ed*)

I/you/we/they have walked.
He/she/it has walked.

Present perfect progressive *Have been* or *has been* plus *-ing* form

I/you/we/they have been walking.
He/she/it has been walking.

Past perfect Action that was completed before another past action

Past perfect *Had* plus past participle (-*d* or -*ed*)

I/you/he/she/it/we/they had walked.

Past perfect progressive *Had been* plus *-ing* form

I/you/he/she/it/we/they had been walking.

Future perfect Action that will be completed before another future action

Future perfect *Will have* plus past participle (-*d* or -*ed*)

I/you/he/she/it/we/they will have walked.

Future perfect progressive *Will have been* plus *-ing* form

I/you/he/she/it/we/they will have been walking.

t
22a

22b Observe the uses of the perfect tenses (*have/had/will have sung*).

The perfect tenses consist of a form of *have* plus the verb's past participle (*closed, hidden*). They indicate an action completed before another specific time or action. The present perfect tense also indicates action begun in the past and continued into the present.

present perfect
The dancer <u>has performed</u> here only once. [The action is completed at the time of the statement.]

present perfect
Critics <u>have written</u> about the performance ever since. [The action began in the past and continues now.]

past perfect
The dancer <u>had trained</u> in Asia before his performance. [The action was completed before another past action.]

future perfect
He <u>will have performed</u> here again by next month. [The action begins now or in the future and will be completed by a specified time in the future.]

ESL With the present perfect tense, the words *since* and *for* are followed by different information. After *since,* give a specific point in time: *The United States has been a member of the United Nations <u>since 1945</u>.* After *for,* give a span of time: *The United States has been a member of the United Nations <u>for half a century</u>.*

22c Observe the uses of the progressive tenses (*is/was/will be singing*). **ESL**

The progressive tenses indicate continuing (therefore progressive) action. They consist of a form of *be* plus the verb's *-ing* form (present participle). (The words *be* and *been* must be combined with other helping verbs. See p. 160.)

present progressive
The economy <u>is improving</u>.

past progressive
Last year the economy <u>was stagnating</u>.

future progressive
Economists <u>will be watching</u> for signs of growth.

present perfect progressive
The government <u>has been expecting</u> an upturn.

t
22c

past perfect progressive
Various indicators <u>had been suggesting</u> improvement.

future perfect progressive
By the end of this year, investors <u>will have been watching</u> interest rates nervously for nearly a decade.

Note Verbs that express unchanging states (especially mental states) rather than physical actions do not usually appear in the progressive tenses. These verbs include *adore, appear, believe, belong, care, hate, have, hear, know, like, love, mean, need, own, prefer, remember, see, sound, taste, think, understand,* and *want.*

Faulty	She <u>is wanting</u> to study ethics.
Revised	She <u>wants</u> to study ethics.

22d Keep tenses consistent.

Within a sentence, the tenses of verbs and verb forms need not be identical as long as they reflect actual changes in time: *Ramon will graduate from college thirty years after his father arrived in America.* But needless shifts in tense will confuse or distract readers:

Inconsistent	Immediately after Booth <u>shot</u> Lincoln, Major Rathbone <u>threw</u> himself upon the assassin. But Booth <u>pulls</u> a knife and <u>plunges</u> it into the major's arm.
Revised	Immediately after Booth <u>shot</u> Lincoln, Major Rathbone <u>threw</u> himself upon the assassin. But Booth <u>pulled</u> a knife and <u>plunged</u> it into the major's arm.
Inconsistent	The main character in the novel <u>suffers</u> psychologically because he <u>has</u> a clubfoot, but he eventually <u>triumphed</u> over his disability.
Revised	The main character in the novel <u>suffers</u> psychologically because he <u>has</u> a clubfoot, but he eventually <u>triumphs</u> over his disability. [Use the present tense when discussing the content of literature, film, and so on.]

t seq
22e

22e Use the appropriate sequence of verb tenses.

The SEQUENCE OF TENSES is the relation between the verb tense in a main clause and the verb tense in a subordinate clause. The tenses are often different, as in the following sentence:

Ramon's father <u>arrived</u> in the United States thirty years ago, after he <u>had married</u>, and now Ramon <u>has decided</u> that he <u>will return</u> to his father's homeland.

English tense sequence can be tricky for native speakers and especially challenging for nonnative speakers. The main difficulties are discussed below.

1 Past or past perfect tense in main clause

When the verb in the main clause is in the past or past perfect tense, the verb in the subordinate clause must also be past or past perfect:

main clause: subordinate clause:
past   past

The researchers <u>discovered</u> that people <u>varied</u> widely in their knowledge of public events.

main clause: subordinate clause:
past   past perfect

The variation <u>occurred</u> because respondents <u>had been born</u> in different decades.

main clause: subordinate clause:
past perfect   past

None of them <u>had been born</u> when Dwight Eisenhower <u>was</u> President.

Exception Always use the present tense for a general truth, such as *The earth is round:*

main clause: subordinate clause:
past   present

Most <u>understood</u> that popular Presidents <u>are</u> not necessarily good Presidents.

2 Conditional sentences ESL

A CONDITIONAL SENTENCE states a factual relation between cause and effect, makes a prediction, or speculates about what might happen. Such a sentence usually consists of a subordinate clause beginning with *if, when,* or *unless* and a main clause stating the result. The three kinds of conditional sentences use distinctive verbs.

t seq

22e

┌─ KEY TERMS ───

MAIN CLAUSE   A word group that contains a subject and a verb and does not begin with a subordinating word: *Books are valuable.* (See p. 150.)

SUBORDINATE CLAUSE   A word group that contains a subject and a verb, begins with a subordinating word such as *because* or *who,* and is not a question: *Books are valuable <u>when they enlighten</u>.* (See p. 151.)

Factual relation

For statements asserting that something always or usually happens whenever something else happens, use the present tense in both clauses:

subordinate clause: main clause:
present   present

When a voter <u>casts</u> a ballot, he or she <u>has</u> complete privacy.

If the linked events occurred in the past, use the past tense in both clauses:

subordinate clause: main clause:
past   past

When voters <u>registered</u> in some states, they <u>had</u> to pay a poll tax.

Prediction

For a prediction, generally use the present tense in the subordinate clause and the future tense in the main clause:

subordinate clause: main clause:
present   future

Unless citizens <u>regain</u> faith in politics, they <u>will</u> not <u>vote</u>.

Sometimes the verb in the main clause consists of *may, can, should,* or *might* plus the verb's plain form: *If citizens <u>regain</u> faith, they <u>may vote</u>.*

Speculation

Speculations are mainly of two kinds, each with its own verb pattern. For events that are possible in the present but unlikely, use the past tense in the subordinate clause and *would, could,* or *might* plus the verb's plain form in the main clause:

subordinate clause: main clause:
past   *would* + verb

If voters <u>had</u> more confidence, they <u>would vote</u> more often.

Use *were* instead of *was* when the subject is *I, he, she, it,* or a singular noun. (See p. 175 for more on this distinctive verb form.)

subordinate clause: main clause:
past   *would* + verb

If the voter <u>were</u> more confident, he or she <u>would vote</u> more often.

For events that are impossible now, that are contrary to fact, use the same forms as above (including the distinctive *were* when applicable):

subordinate clause: main clause:
past   *might* + verb

If Lincoln <u>were</u> alive, he <u>might inspire</u> confidence.

For events that were impossible in the past, use the past perfect tense in the subordinate clause and *would, could,* or *might* plus the present perfect tense in the main clause:

t seq

22e

subordinate clause: main clause:
past perfect   *might* + present perfect

If Lincoln <u>had lived</u> past the Civil War, he <u>might have helped</u> stabilize the country.

3 Indirect quotations ESL

An INDIRECT QUOTATION reports what someone said or wrote but not in the exact words and not in quotation marks: *Lincoln said <u>that events had controlled him</u>* (quotation: "Events have controlled me"). An indirect quotation generally appears in a subordinate clause (underlined above), with certain conventions governing verb tense in most cases:

- When the verb in the main clause is in the present tense, the verb in the indirect quotation (subordinate clause) is in the same tense as the original quotation:

  main clause: subordinate clause:
  present   present

  Haworth <u>says</u> that Lincoln <u>is</u> our noblest national hero. [Quotation: "Lincoln <u>is</u> our noblest national hero."]

  main clause: subordinate clause:
  present   past

  He <u>says</u> that Lincoln <u>was</u> a complicated person. [Quotation: "Lincoln <u>was</u> a complicated person."]

- When the verb in the main clause is in the past tense, the verb in the indirect quotation usually changes tense from the original quotation. Present tense changes to past tense:

  main clause: subordinate clause:
  past   past

  An assistant to Lincoln <u>said</u> that the President <u>was</u> always generous. [Quotation: "The President <u>is</u> always generous."]

  Past tense and present perfect tense change to past perfect tense. (Past perfect tense does not change.)

  main clause: subordinate clause:
  past   past perfect

  Lincoln <u>said</u> that events <u>had controlled</u> him. [Quotation: "Events <u>have controlled</u> me."]

- When the direct quotation states a general truth or reports a situation that is still true, use the present tense in the indirect quotation regardless of the verb in the main clause:

  main clause: subordinate clause:
  past   present

  Lincoln <u>said</u> that right <u>makes</u> might. [Quotation: "Right <u>makes</u> might."]

t seq

22e

Note As several of the examples show, an indirect quotation differs in at least two additional ways from the original quotation: (1) the indirect quotation is usually preceded by *that*, and (2) the indirect quotation changes pronouns, especially from forms of *I* or *we* to forms of *he, she,* or *they*.

23 Verb Mood

Information on verb mood:

http://webster.commnet.edu/HP/pages/darling/grammar/ verbs.htm#mood   From the Guide to Grammar and Writing.

http://www.uottawa.ca/academic/arts/writcent/hypergrammar/ moods.html   From the University of Ottawa.

Mood in grammar is a verb form that indicates the writer's or speaker's attitude toward what he or she is saying. The INDICATIVE MOOD states a fact or opinion or asks a question: *The theater <u>needs</u> help.* The IMPERATIVE MOOD expresses a command or gives a direction. It omits the subject of the sentence, *you: <u>Help</u> the theater.*

The SUBJUNCTIVE MOOD is trickier and requires distinctive verb forms described below.

Note A computerized grammar and style checker may spot some errors in the subjunctive mood, but it may miss others. Instead of relying on the checker to find and correct problems, proofread your work looking for appropriate uses of subjunctive verbs.

vb

23a

23a   Use the subjunctive verb forms appropriately, as in *I wish I were*.

The subjunctive mood expresses a suggestion, requirement, or desire, or it states a condition that is contrary to fact (that is, imaginary or hypothetical).

- Verbs such as *ask, insist, urge, require, recommend,* and *suggest* indicate request or requirement. They often precede a subordinate clause beginning with *that* and containing the substance of the request or requirement. For all subjects, the verb in the *that* clause is the plain form:

plain
form
Rules require that every donation <u>be</u> mailed.

- Contrary-to-fact clauses state imaginary or hypothetical conditions and usually begin with *if* or *unless* or follow *wish*. For present contrary-to-fact clauses, use the verb's past-tense form (for *be*, use the past-tense form *were*):

past   past
If the theater <u>were</u> in better shape and <u>had</u> more money, its future would be assured.

past
I wish I <u>were</u> able to donate money.

For past contrary-to-fact clauses, use the verb's past perfect form (*had* + past participle):

past perfect
The theater would be better funded if it <u>had been</u> better managed.

Note Do not use the helping verb *would* or *could* in a contrary-to-fact clause beginning with *if:*

Not	Many people would have helped if they <u>would have</u> known.
But	Many people would have helped if they <u>had</u> known.

See also page 172 for more on verb tenses in sentences like these.

23b Keep mood consistent.

Shifts in mood within a sentence or among related sentences can be confusing. Such shifts occur most frequently in directions.

Inconsistent	Cook the mixture slowly, and <u>you should stir</u> it until the sugar is dissolved. [Mood shifts from imperative to indicative.]
Revised	<u>Cook</u> the mixture slowly, and <u>stir</u> it until the sugar is dissolved. [Consistently imperative.]

pass

24

24 Verb Voice

Information on passive and active voice:

*http://webster.commnet.edu/HP/pages/darling/grammar/
verbs.htm#passive*   From the Guide to Grammar and Writing.

http://lc.byuh.edu/cnn_n/Prev_gram.html#Actives   For ESL students, from Brigham Young University in Hawaii.

The VOICE of a verb tells whether the subject of the sentence performs the action (ACTIVE) or is acted upon (PASSIVE).

Active and passive voice

Active voice   The subject acts.

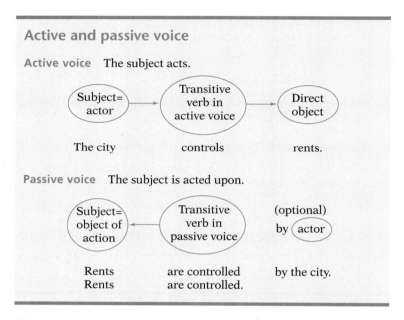

The city   controls   rents.

Passive voice   The subject is acted upon.

Rents   are controlled   by the city.
Rents   are controlled.

The actor in a passive sentence may be named in a prepositional phrase (as in the first passive example above), or the actor may be omitted (as in the second passive example).

ESL   A passive verb always consists of a form of *be* plus the past participle of the main verb: *rents are controlled, people were inspired.* Other helping verbs must also be used with the words *be, being,* and *been: rents have been controlled, people would have been inspired.* Only a transitive verb (one that takes an object) may be used in the passive voice. (See p. 146.)

pass

24a

24a   Generally, prefer the active voice. Use the passive voice when the actor is unknown or unimportant.

The active voice is usually clearer, more concise, and more forthright than the passive voice.

| Weak passive | The Internet is used for research by many schol-ars, and its expansion to the general public has been criticized by some. |
| Strong active | Many scholars use the Internet for research, and some have criticized its expansion to the general public. |

The passive voice is useful in two situations: when the actor is unknown and when the actor is unimportant or less important than the object of the action.

> The Internet was established in 1969 by the US Department of Defense. The network has now been extended internationally to governments, universities, foundations, corporations, and private individuals. [In the first sentence the writer wishes to stress the Internet rather than the Department of Defense. In the second sentence the actor is unknown or too complicated to name.]
>
> After the solution had been cooled to 10°C, the acid was added. [The person who cooled and added, perhaps the writer, is less important than the facts that the solution was cooled and acid was added. Passive sentences are common in scientific writing.]

 Note Most computerized grammar and style checkers can be set to spot the passive voice. But they will then flag every instance, both appropriate (such as when the actor is unknown) and ineffective. And they will flag as passive some unobjectionable phrases that are actually a form of *be* plus a verb form serving as an adjective, such as the underlined words in this sentence: *We were delighted*. You'll need to decide for yourself whether flagged phrases really are passive and whether they are appropriate.

24b Keep voice consistent.

Shifts in voice that involve shifts in subject are usually unnecessary and confusing.

| Inconsistent | Internet newsgroups cover an enormous range of topics for discussion. Forums for meeting people with like interests are provided in these groups. |
| Revised | Internet newsgroups cover an enormous range of topics for discussion and provide forums for meeting people with like interests. |

A shift in voice is appropriate when it helps focus the reader's attention on a single subject, as in *The candidate campaigned vigorously and was nominated on the first ballot.*

25 Agreement of Subject and Verb

Information on subject-verb agreement:

http://webster.commnet.edu/HP/pages/darling/grammar/sv_agr.htm
From the Guide to Grammar and Writing.

http://owl.english.purdue.edu/Files/73.html From the Purdue Online Writing Lab.

http://www.wisc.edu/writetest/Handbook/SubjectVerb.html From the University of Wisconsin at Madison.

A subject and its verb should agree in number and person.

More Japanese Americans live in Hawaii and California than elsewhere. ⏜ subject   verb

Daniel Inouye was the first Japanese American in Congress. ⏜ subject   verb

Most problems of subject-verb agreement arise when endings are omitted from subjects or verbs or when the relation between sentence parts is uncertain.

Note A computerized grammar and style checker will look for problems with subject-verb agreement. Most checkers also allow you to customize settings so that you can turn off other options and look just for agreement problems (see p. 80). However, a checker may mistakenly flag correct agreement and may then suggest "corrections" that are wrong. In addition, a checker may fail to spot actual errors. Do not automatically accept a checker's pointers, and proofread your work carefully on your own.

| vb agr |
| 25a |

25a The -s and -es endings work differently for nouns and verbs.

An *-s* or *-es* ending does opposite things to nouns and verbs: it usually makes a noun *plural,* but it always makes a present-tense

┌─ KEY TERMS ──────────────────────────────

	NUMBER	
PERSON	SINGULAR	PLURAL
First	I eat.	We eat.
Second	You eat.	You eat.
Third	He/she/it eats.	They eat.
	The bird eats.	Birds eat.

178

verb *singular*. Thus if the subject noun is plural, it will end in -*s* or
-*es* and the verb will not. If the subject is singular, it will not end in
-*s* and the verb will.

Singular	Plural
The boy plays.	The boys play.
The bird soars.	The birds soar.

The only exceptions to these rules involve the nouns that form
irregular plurals, such as *child/children, woman/women.* The irregular plural still requires a plural verb: *The children play. The women
read.*

  ESL Most noncount nouns—those that do not form plurals—
take singular verbs: *That information is helpful.* (See p. 181 on collective nouns.)

**25b Subject and verb should agree even when other
words come between them.**

The catalog of course requirements often baffles [not baffle] students.

The requirements stated in the catalog are [not is] unclear.

  Note Phrases beginning with *as well as, together with, along
with,* and *in addition to* do not change the number of the subject:

The president, as well as the deans, has [not have] agreed to revise
the catalog.

25c Subjects joined by *and* usually take plural verbs.

Frost and Roethke were contemporaries.

  Exceptions When the parts of the subject form a single idea or
refer to a single person or thing, they take a singular verb:

Avocado and bean sprouts is a California sandwich.

When a compound subject is preceded by the adjective *each* or
every, the verb is usually singular:

Each man, woman, and child has a right to be heard.

25d   When parts of a subject are joined by *or* or *nor,* the verb agrees with the nearer part.

Either the painter or the carpenter knows the cost.

The cabinets or the bookcases are too costly.

When one part of the subject is singular and the other plural, avoid awkwardness by placing the plural part closer to the verb so that the verb is plural:

Awkward   Neither the owners nor the contractor agrees.

Revised   Neither the contractor nor the owners agree.

25e   With *everyone* and other indefinite pronouns, use a singular or plural verb as appropriate.

Most indefinite pronouns are singular in meaning (they refer to a single unspecified person or thing), and they take a singular verb:

Something smells.   Neither is right.

The plural indefinite pronouns refer to more than one unspecified thing, and they take a plural verb:

Both are correct.   Several were invited.

vb agr
25e

KEY TERM

INDEFINITE PRONOUN   A pronoun that does not refer to a specific person or thing:

Singular			Singular or plural	Plural
anybody	everyone	no one	all	both
anyone	everything	nothing	any	few
anything	much	one	more	many
each	neither	somebody	most	several
either	nobody	someone	some	
everybody	none	something		

The other indefinite pronouns take a singular or a plural verb depending on whether the word they refer to is singular or plural:

All of the money is reserved for emergencies.

All of the funds are reserved for emergencies.

ESL See page 205 for the distinction between *few* ("not many") and *a few* ("some").

25f   Collective nouns such as *team* take singular or plural verbs depending on meaning.

Use a singular verb with a collective noun when the group acts as a unit:

The group agrees that action is necessary.

But when the group's members act separately, not together, use a plural verb:

The old group have gone their separate ways.

The collective noun *number* may be singular or plural. Preceded by *a,* it is plural; preceded by *the,* it is singular:

A number of people are in debt.

The number of people in debt is very large.

ESL Some noncount nouns (nouns that don't form plurals) are collective nouns because they name groups: for instance, *furniture, clothing, mail.* These noncount nouns usually take singular verbs: *Mail arrives daily.* But some of these nouns take plural verbs, including *clergy, military, people, police,* and any collective noun that comes from an adjective, such as *the poor, the rich, the young, the elderly.* If you mean one representative of the group, use a singular noun such as *police officer* or *poor person.*

vb agr

25f

┌─ KEY TERM ──
COLLECTIVE NOUN   A noun with singular form that names a group of individuals or things—for instance, *army, audience, committee, crowd, family, group, team.*
──

25g   *Who, which,* and *that* take verbs that agree with their antecedents.

When used as subjects, *who, which,* and *that* refer to another word in the sentence, called the ANTECEDENT. The verb agrees with the antecedent.

Mayor Garber ought to listen to the people who work for her.

Bardini is the only aide who has her ear.

Agreement problems often occur with relative pronouns when the sentence includes *one of the* or *the only one of the:*

Bardini is one of the aides who work unpaid. [Of the aides who work unpaid, Bardini is one.]

Bardini is the only one of the aides who knows the community. [Of the aides, only one, Bardini, knows the community.]

ESL   In phrases like those above beginning with *one of the,* be sure the noun is plural: *Bardini is one of the aides* [not *aide*] *who work unpaid.*

25h   *News* and other singular nouns ending in *-s* take singular verbs.

Singular nouns ending in *-s* include *athletics, economics, linguistics, mathematics, measles, mumps, news, physics, politics,* and *statistics,* as well as place names such as *Athens, Wales,* and *United States.*

After so long a wait, the news has to be good.

Statistics is required of psychology majors.

A few of these words also take plural verbs, but only when they describe individual items rather than whole bodies of activity or knowledge: *The statistics prove him wrong.*

Measurements and figures ending in *-s* may also be singular when the quantity they refer to is a unit.

Three years is a long time to wait.

Three-fourths of the library consists of reference books.

25i The verb agrees with the subject even when the normal word order is inverted.

Inverted subject-verb order occurs mainly in questions and in constructions beginning with *there* or *it* and a form of *be*.

Is voting a right or a privilege?

Are a right and a privilege the same thing?

There are differences between them.

25j *Is, are,* and other linking verbs agree with their subjects, not subject complements.

Make a linking verb agree with its subject, usually the first element in the sentence, not with the noun or pronoun serving as a subject complement.

The child's sole support is her court-appointed guardians.

Her court-appointed guardians are the child's sole support.

25k Use singular verbs with titles and with words being described or defined.

Hakada Associates is a new firm.

Dream Days remains a favorite book.

Folks is a down-home word for *people*.

vb agr

25k

---KEY TERMS----------

LINKING VERB   A verb that connects or equates the subject and subject complement: for example, *seem, become,* and forms of *be*. (See pp. 146–147.)

SUBJECT COMPLEMENT   A word that describes or renames the subject: *They became chemists.* (See pp. 146–147.)

PRONOUNS—words such as *she* and *who* that refer to nouns—merit special care because all their meaning comes from the other words they refer to. This section discusses pronoun case (Chapter 26), matching pronouns and the words they refer to (27), and making sure pronouns refer to the right nouns (28).

26 Pronoun Case

 Information on pronoun case:

http://www.english.uiuc.edu/cws/wworkshop/grammar/case.htm   From the University of Illinois at Urbana-Champaign.

http://owl.english.purdue.edu/Files/80.html   From the Purdue Online Writing Lab.

http://www.clta.on.ca/gram06.htm   For ESL writers, from the Centre for Language Training and Assessment.

http://www.hut.fi/u/rvilmi/LangHelp/Grammar/nouns.html   For ESL writers, from the Grammar Help page.

CASE is the form of a noun or pronoun that shows the reader how it functions in a sentence.

- The SUBJECTIVE CASE indicates that the word is a subject or subject complement.
- The OBJECTIVE CASE indicates that the word is an object of a verb or preposition.

case
26

---KEY TERMS---

SUBJECT   Who or what a sentence is about: *Biologists often study animals. They often work in laboratories.* (See p. 145.)

SUBJECT COMPLEMENT   A word that renames or describes the sentence subject: *Biologists are scientists. The best biologists are she and Scoggins.* (See p. 146.)

OBJECT OF VERB   The receiver of the verb's action (DIRECT OBJECT): *Many biologists study animals. The animals teach them.* Or the person or thing the action is performed for (INDIRECT OBJECT): *Some biologists give animals homes. The animals give them pleasure.* (See pp. 146–147.)

OBJECT OF PREPOSITION   The word linked by *with, for,* or another preposition to the rest of the sentence: *Many biologists work in a laboratory. For them the lab often provides a second home.* (See p. 148.)

- The POSSESSIVE CASE indicates that the word owns or is the source of a noun in the sentence.

Nouns change form only to show possession: *teacher's* (see pp. 244–246). The following pronouns change much more frequently:

Subjective	Objective	Possessive
I	me	my, mine
you	you	your, yours
he	him	his
she	her	her, hers
it	it	its
we	us	our, ours
you	you	your, yours
they	them	their, theirs
who	whom	whose
whoever	whomever	—

 Note Computerized grammar and style checkers have difficulty with pronoun cases: they may flag as incorrect many appropriate uses of pronouns and yet miss others that are incorrect. Carefully consider any flagged pronoun and review your sentences on your own as well, deciding for yourself which are correct.

26a Distinguish between compound subjects and compound objects: *she and I* vs. *her and me.*

Compound subjects or objects—those consisting of two or more nouns or pronouns—have the same case forms as they would if one noun or pronoun stood alone:

compound
subject
She and Novick discussed the proposal.

compound
object
The proposal disappointed her and him.

case

26a

If you are in doubt about the correct form, try the test below:

A test for case forms in compound constructions

- Identify a compound construction (one connected by *and, but, or, nor*):

[He, Him] and [I, me] won the prize.
The prize went to [he, him] and [I, me].

(continued)

> ## A test for case forms in compound constructions
> *(continued)*
>
> * Write a separate sentence for each part of the compound:
>
>   [He, Him] won the prize. [I, Me] won the prize.
>   The prize went to [he, him]. The prize went to [I, me].
>
> * Choose the pronouns that sound correct:
>
>   He won the prize. I won the prize. [Subjective.]
>   The prize went to him. The prize went to me. [Objective.]
>
> * Put the separate sentences back together:
>
>   He and I won the prize.
>   The prize went to him and me.

26b   Use the subjective case for subject complements: *It was she.*

After a linking verb, a pronoun renaming the subject (a subject complement) should be in the subjective case:

subject
complement
The ones who care most are she and Novick.

subject
complement
It was they whom the mayor appointed.

If this construction sounds stilted to you, use the more natural order: *She and Novick are the ones who care most. The mayor appointed them.*

26c   The use of *who* vs. *whom* depends on the pronoun's function in its clause.

1   Questions

At the beginning of a question use *who* for a subject and *whom* for an object:

subject
Who wrote the policy?

object
Whom does it affect?

┌─ KEY TERM ──

LINKING VERB   A verb, such as a form of *be*, that connects a subject and a word that renames or describes the subject (subject complement): *They are biologists.* (See pp. 147–148.)

└──

To find the correct case of *who* in a question, follow the steps below.

- Pose the question:

  [Who, Whom] makes that decision?
  [Who, Whom] does one ask?

- Answer the question, using a personal pronoun. Choose the pronoun that sounds correct, and note its case:

  [She, Her] makes that decision. She makes that decision. [Subjective.]
  One asks [she, her]. One asks her. [Objective.]

- Use the same case (*who* or *whom*) in the question:

  Who makes that decision? [Subjective.]
  Whom does one ask? [Objective.]

2 Subordinate clauses

In subordinate clauses use *who* and *whoever* for all subjects, *whom* and *whomever* for all objects.

subject⟶
Give old clothes to whoever needs them.

object⟵
I don't know whom the mayor appointed.

To determine which form to use, try the test below:

- Locate the subordinate clause:

  Few people know [who, whom] they should ask.
  They are unsure [who, whom] makes the decision.

- Rewrite the subordinate clause as a separate sentence, substituting a personal pronoun for *who, whom*. Choose the pronoun that sounds correct, and note its case:

  They should ask [she, her]. They should ask her. [Objective.]
  [She, her] usually makes the decision. She usually makes the decision. [Subjective.]

- Use the same case (*who* or *whom*) in the subordinate clause:

  Few people know whom they should ask. [Objective.]
  They are unsure who makes the decision. [Subjective.]

case

26c

┌─ KEY TERM ──────────────────────────────
SUBORDINATE CLAUSE   A word group that contains a subject and a verb and also begins with a subordinating word, such as *who, whom,* or *because.* (See p. 151.)
└───

Note Don't let expressions such as *I think* and *she says* mislead you into using *whom* rather than *who* for the subject of a clause.

subject ⟶

He is the one who I think is best qualified.

To choose between *who* and *whom* in such constructions, delete the interrupting phrase so that you can see the true relation between parts: *He is the one who is best qualified.*

26d   Use the appropriate case in other constructions.

1 *We* or *us* with a noun

The choice of *we* or *us* before a noun depends on the use of the noun:

object of preposition ⟶

Freezing weather is welcomed by us skaters.

subject ⟶

We skaters welcome freezing weather.

2 Pronoun in an appositive

In an appositive the case of a pronoun depends on the function of the word the appositive describes or identifies:

appositive identifies object

The class elected two representatives, DeShawn and me.

appositive identifies subject

Two representatives, DeShawn and I, were elected.

3 Pronoun after *than* or *as*

When a pronoun follows *than* or *as* in a comparison, the case of the pronoun indicates what words may have been omitted. A subjective pronoun must be the subject of the omitted verb:

subject

Some critics like Glass more than he [does].

An objective pronoun must be the object of the omitted verb:

object

Some critics like Glass more than [they like] him.

┌─ KEY TERM ───

APPOSITIVE   A noun or noun substitute that renames another noun immediately before it. (See p. 150.)

---

case

26d

4   Subject and object of infinitive

Both the object *and* the subject of an infinitive are in the objective case:

subject
of infinitive

The school asked <u>him</u> to speak.

object
of infinitive

Students chose to invite <u>him</u>.

5   Case before a gerund

Ordinarily, use the possessive form of a pronoun or noun immediately before a gerund:

The coach disapproved of <u>their</u> lifting weights.

The <u>coach's</u> disapproving was a surprise.

---

27 Agreement of Pronoun and Antecedent

Information on pronoun-antecedent agreement:

http://webster.commnet.edu/HP/pages/darling/grammar/pronouns.htm
From the Guide to Grammar and Writing.

http://owl.english.purdue.edu/Files/79.html   From the Purdue Online Writing Lab.

The ANTECEDENT of a pronoun is the noun or other pronoun to which the pronoun refers:

<u>Homeowners</u> fret over <u>their</u> tax bills.
antecedent   pronoun

<u>Its</u> constant increases make the tax <u>bill</u> a dreaded document.
pronoun   antecedent

For clarity, a pronoun should agree with its antecedent in person, number, and gender.

pn agr

27

> ─KEY TERMS───────────────
>
> INFINITIVE   The plain form of the verb plus *to: to run.* (See p. 149.)
> GERUND   The *-ing* form of a verb used as a noun: *Running is fun.* (See p. 149.)

Note A computerized grammar and style checker cannot help you with agreement between pronoun and antecedent. You'll need to check for errors on your own.

ESL The gender of a pronoun should match its antecedent, not a noun that the pronoun may modify: *Sara Young invited her* [not *his*] *son to join the company's staff.* Also, nouns in English have only neuter gender unless they specifically refer to males or females. Thus nouns such as *book, table, sun,* and *earth* take the pronoun *it.*

27a Antecedents joined by *and* usually take plural pronouns.

Mr. Bartos and I cannot settle our dispute.

The dean and my adviser have offered their help.

Exceptions When the compound antecedent refers to a single idea, person, or thing, then the pronoun is singular.

My friend and adviser offered her help.

When the compound antecedent follows *each* or *every,* the pronoun is singular.

Every girl and woman took her seat.

27b When parts of an antecedent are joined by *or* or *nor,* the pronoun agrees with the nearer part.

Tenants or owners must present their grievances.

Either the tenant or the owner will have her way.

┌─ KEY TERMS ─────────────────────────────────

	NUMBER	
PERSON	SINGULAR	PLURAL
FIRST	*I*	*we*
SECOND	*you*	*you*
THIRD	*he, she, it,*	*they,*
	indefinite pronouns,	plural nouns
	singular nouns	
GENDER		
MASCULINE	*he,* nouns naming males	
FEMININE	*she,* nouns naming females	
NEUTER	*it,* all other nouns	

When one subject is plural and the other singular, the sentence will be awkward unless you put the plural subject second.

Awkward	Neither the tenants nor the owner has yet made her case.
Revised	Neither the owner nor the tenants have yet made their case.

27c With *everyone, person,* and other indefinite words, use a singular or plural pronoun as appropriate.

Indefinite words—indefinite pronouns and generic nouns—do not refer to any specific person or thing. Most indefinite pronouns and all generic nouns are singular in meaning. When they serve as antecedents of pronouns, the pronouns should be singular:

Everyone on the women's team now has her own locker.
indefinite
pronoun

Every person on the women's team now has her own locker.
generic
noun

Five indefinite pronouns—*all, any, more, most, some*—may be singular or plural in meaning depending on what they refer to:

Few women athletes had changing spaces, so most had to change

in their rooms.

── KEY TERMS ──────────────────────

pn agr
27c

INDEFINITE PRONOUN   A pronoun that does not refer to a specific person or thing:

Singular			*Singular or plural*	*Plural*
anybody	everyone	no one	all	both
anyone	everything	nothing	any	few
anything	much	one	more	many
each	neither	somebody	most	several
either	nobody	someone	some	
everybody	none	something		

GENERIC NOUN   A singular noun such as *person, individual,* and *student* when it refers a typical member of a group, not to a particular individual: *The individual has rights.*

Most of the changing space was dismal, its color a drab olive green.

Four indefinite pronouns—*both, few, many, several*—are always plural in meaning:

Few realize how their athletic facilities have changed.

Most agreement problems arise with the singular indefinite words. We often use these words to mean something like "many" or "all" rather than "one" and then refer to them with plural pronouns, as in *Everyone has their own locker* or *A person can padlock their locker.* Often, too, we mean indefinite words to include both masculine and feminine genders and thus resort to *they* instead of the GENERIC *HE*—the masculine pronoun referring to both genders, as in *Everyone has his own locker.* (For more on the generic *he*, which many readers view as sexist, see p. 120.) To achieve agreement in such cases, you have several options:

- Change the indefinite word to a plural, and use a plural pronoun to match:

   Athletes deserve their privacy.

   All athletes are entitled to their own lockers. [Notice that *locker* also changes to *lockers*.]

- Rewrite the sentence to omit the pronoun:

   The athlete deserves privacy.
   Everyone is entitled to a locker.

- Use *he or she* (*him or her, his or her*) to refer to the indefinite word:

   The athlete deserves his or her privacy.

pn agr
27d

However, used more than once in several sentences, *he or she* quickly becomes awkward. (Many readers do not accept the alternative *he/she.*) In most cases, using the plural or rewriting the sentence will not only correct an agreement problem but create a more readable sentence.

27d   Collective nouns such as *team* take singular or plural pronouns depending on meaning.

Use a singular pronoun with a collective noun when referring to the group as a unit:

The committee voted to disband itself.

When referring to the individual members of the group, use a plural pronoun:

The old group have gone their separate ways.

ESL Collective nouns that are noncount nouns (they don't form plurals) usually take singular pronouns: *The mail sits in its own basket.* A few noncount nouns take plural pronouns, including *clergy, military, police, the rich,* and *the poor: The police support their unions.*

28 Reference of Pronoun to Antecedent

Information on pronoun reference:

http://www.uottawa.ca/academic/arts/writcent/hypergrammar/ pronref.html.   From the University of Ottawa.

http://webster.commnet.edu/HP/pages/darling/grammar/pronouns.htm From the Guide to Grammar and Writing.

A pronoun should refer clearly to its ANTECEDENT, the noun it substitutes for. Otherwise, readers will have difficulty grasping the pronoun's meaning.

Note Computerized grammar and style checkers are not sophisticated enough to recognize unclear pronoun reference. For instance, a checker did not flag any of the confusing examples on the next page. You must proofread your work to spot unclear pronoun reference.

ESL A pronoun needs a clear antecedent nearby, but don't use both a pronoun and its antecedent as the subject of the same clause: *Jim* [not *Jim he*] *told Mark to go alone.* (See also p. 222.)

ref

28a

28a   Make a pronoun refer clearly to one antecedent.

When either of two nouns can be a pronoun's antecedent, the reference will not be clear.

> ┌─KEY TERM─────────────────────────────────────
> COLLECTIVE NOUN   A noun with singular form that names a group of individuals or things—for instance, *army, audience, committee, crowd, family, group, team.*

Confusing   Emily Dickinson is sometimes compared with Jane Austen, but she was quite different.

Revise such a sentence in one of two ways:

- Replace the pronoun with the appropriate noun.

   Clear   Emily Dickinson is sometimes compared with Jane Austen, but Dickinson [or Austen] was quite different.

- Avoid repetition by rewriting the sentence. If you use the pronoun, make sure it has only one possible antecedent.

   Clear   Despite occasional comparison, Emily Dickinson and Jane Austen were quite different.

   Clear   Though sometimes compared with her, Emily Dickinson was quite different from Jane Austen.

28b   Place a pronoun close enough to its antecedent to ensure clarity.

A clause beginning with *who, which,* or *that* should generally fall immediately after the word to which it refers:

Confusing   Jody found a dress in the attic that her aunt had worn.

Clear   In the attic Jody found a dress that her aunt had worn.

28c   Make a pronoun refer to a specific antecedent, not an implied one.

ref
28c

A pronoun should refer to a specific noun or other pronoun. A reader can only guess at the meaning of a pronoun when its antecedent is implied by the context, not stated outright.

1   Vague *this, that, which,* or *it*

This, that, which, or *it* should refer to a specific noun, not to a whole word group expressing an idea or situation.

Confusing   The faculty agreed on changing the requirements, but it took time.

Clear   The faculty agreed on changing the requirements, but the agreement took time.

Clear	The faculty agreed on changing the requirements, but the change took time.

Confusing	The British knew little of the American countryside, and they had no experience with the colonists' guerrilla tactics. This gave the colonists an advantage.

Clear	The British knew little of the American countryside, and they had no experience with the colonists' guerrilla tactics. This ignorance and inexperience gave the colonists an advantage.

2 Implied nouns

A noun may be implied in some other word or phrase, such as an adjective (*happiness* implied in *happy*), a verb (*driver* implied in *drive*), or a possessive (*mother* implied in *mother's*). But a pronoun cannot refer clearly to an implied noun, only to a specific, stated one.

Confusing	Cohen's report brought her a lawsuit.

Clear	Cohen was sued over her report.

Confusing	Her reports on psychological development generally go unnoticed outside it.

Clear	Her reports on psychological development generally go unnoticed outside the field.

3 Indefinite *it, they,* or *you*

It, they, and *you* should have definite antecedents—nouns for *it* and *they,* an actual reader being addressed for *you.* Rewrite the sentence if the antecedent is missing.

Confusing	In Chapter 4 of this book it describes the early flights of the Wright brothers.

Clear	Chapter 4 of this book describes the early flights of the Wright brothers.

Confusing	In the average television drama they present a false picture of life.

Clear	The average television drama presents a false picture of life.

In all but very formal writing, *you* is acceptable when the meaning is clearly "you, the reader." But the context must be appropriate for such a meaning.

ref

28c

| Inappropriate | In the fourteenth century <u>you</u> had to struggle simply to survive. |
| Revised | In the fourteenth century <u>one</u> [or <u>a person</u> or <u>people</u>] had to struggle simply to survive. |

28d   Keep pronouns consistent.

Within a sentence or a group of related sentences, pronouns should be consistent. Partly, consistency comes from making pronouns and their antecedents agree (see Chapter 27). In addition, the pronouns within a passage should match each other.

| Inconsistent | <u>One</u> finds when reading that <u>your</u> concentration improves with practice, so that <u>I</u> now comprehend more in less time. |
| Revised | <u>I</u> find when reading that <u>my</u> concentration improves with practice, so that <u>I</u> now comprehend more in less time. |

MODIFIERS describe or limit other words in a sentence. They are adjectives, adverbs, or word groups serving as adjectives or adverbs. This section shows you how to identify and solve problems in the forms of modifiers (Chapter 29) and in their relation to the rest of the sentence (30).

29 Adjectives and Adverbs

http://www.english.uiuc.edu/cws/wworkshop/grammar/adjectivedef.htm
Information on adjectives, from the University of Illinois at Urbana-Champaign.

http://webster.commnet.edu/HP/pages/darling/grammar/adjectives.htm
Information and quizzes on adjectives, from the Guide to Grammar and Writing.

http://webster.commnet.edu/HP/pages/darling/grammar/adverbs.htm
Information and quizzes on adverbs, from the Guide to Grammar and Writing.

http://webster.commnet.edu/HP/pages/darling/grammar/determiners/ determiners.htm Information and quizzes on articles and other determiners, from the Guide to Grammar and Writing.

ADJECTIVES modify nouns (*happy child*) and pronouns (*special someone*). ADVERBS modify verbs (*almost* see), adjectives (*very happy*), other adverbs (*not very*), and whole word groups (*Otherwise, the room was empty*). The only way to tell whether a modifier should be an adjective or an adverb is to determine its function in the sentence.

Note Computerized grammar and style checkers will spot some but not all problems with misused adjectives and adverbs. For instance, a checker flagged *Some children suffer bad* and *Chang was the most wisest person in town* and *Jenny did not feel nothing*. But it did not flag *Educating children good is everyone's focus* or *He was the most unique teacher we had.* You'll need to proofread your work on your own to be sure you've used adjectives and adverbs appropriately.

ESL In English an adjective does not change along with the noun it modifies to show plural number: *white* [not *whites*] *shoes*, *square* [not *squares*] *spaces*, *better* [not *betters*] *chances*. Only nouns form plurals.

ad
29

29a   Use adjectives only to modify nouns and pronouns.

Using adjectives instead of adverbs to modify verbs, adverbs, or other adjectives is nonstandard:

Nonstandard   Educating children <u>good</u> is everyone's focus.

Standard   Educating children <u>well</u> is everyone's focus.

Nonstandard   Some children suffer <u>bad</u>.

Standard   Some children suffer <u>badly</u>.

ESL   To negate a verb or an adjective, use the adverb *not:*

They are <u>not</u> learning. They are <u>not</u> stupid.

To negate a noun, use the adjective *no:*

<u>No</u> child should fail to read.

29b   Use an adjective after a linking verb to modify the subject. Use an adverb to modify a verb.

Some verbs may or may not be linking verbs, depending on their meaning in the sentence. When the word after the verb modifies the subject, the verb is linking and the word should be an adjective: *He looked <u>happy</u>.* When the word modifies the verb, however, it should be an adverb: *He looked <u>carefully</u>.*

Two word pairs are especially tricky. One is *bad* and *badly:*

The weather grew <u>bad</u>.   She felt <u>bad</u>.
        linking adjective   linking adjective
        verb   verb

Flowers grow <u>badly</u> in such soil.
       verb adverb

The other is *good* and *well*. *Good* serves only as an adjective. *Well* may serve as an adverb with a host of meanings or as an adjective meaning only "fit" or "healthy."

> ┌─ KEY TERM ───────────────────────────────
> LINKING VERB   A verb that connects a subject and a word that describes the subject: *They <u>are</u> golfers.* Linking verbs are forms of *be,* the verbs of our five senses (*look, sound, smell, feel, taste*), and *appear, seem, become, grow, turn, prove, remain, stay.* (See pp. 146–147.)

ad
29b

Decker trained <u>well</u>.
verb   adverb

She felt <u>well</u>.
linking adjective
verb

Her health was <u>good</u>.
linking adjective
verb

29c Use the comparative and superlative forms of adjectives and adverbs appropriately.

Adjectives and adverbs can show degrees of quality or amount with the endings *-er* and *-est* or with the words *more* and *most* or *less* and *least*. Most modifiers have three forms:

	Adjectives	Adverbs
Positive The basic form listed in the dictionary	red awful	soon quickly
Comparative A greater or lesser degree of the quality named	redder more/less awful	sooner more/less quickly
Superlative The greatest or least degree of the quality named	reddest most/least awful	soonest most/least quickly

If sound alone does not tell you whether to use *-er/-est* or *more/most*, consult a dictionary. If the endings can be used, the dictionary will list them. Otherwise, use *more* or *most*.

1 Irregular adjectives and adverbs

The irregular modifiers change the spelling of their positive form to show comparative and superlative degrees.

Positive	Comparative	Superlative
Adjectives		
good	better	best
bad	worse	worst
little	littler, less	littlest, least
many ⎫ some ⎬ much ⎭	more	most
Adverbs		
well	better	best
badly	worse	worst

2 Double comparisons

A double comparative or double superlative combines the *-er* or *-est* ending with the word *more* or *most*. It is redundant.

Chang was the wisest [not most wisest] person in town.
He was smarter [not more smarter] than anyone else.

3   Logical comparisons

Absolute modifiers

Some adjectives and adverbs cannot logically be compared—for instance, *perfect, unique, dead, impossible, infinite.* These absolute words can be preceded by adverbs like *nearly* or *almost* that mean "approaching," but they cannot logically be modified by *more* or *most* (as in *most perfect*).

| Not | He was the <u>most unique</u> teacher we had. |
| But | He was a <u>unique</u> teacher. |

Completeness

To be logical, a comparison must also be complete in the following ways:

- The comparison must state a relation fully enough for clarity.

Unclear	Carmakers worry about their industry more than environmentalists.
Clear	Carmakers worry about their industry more than environmentalists <u>do</u>.
Clear	Carmakers worry about their industry more than <u>they worry about</u> environmentalists.

- The items being compared should in fact be comparable.

| Illogical | The cost of an electric car is greater than a gasoline-powered car. [Illogically compares a cost and a car.] |
| Revised | The cost of an electric car is greater than <u>the cost of</u> [or <u>that of</u>] a gasoline-powered car. |

See also pages 109–110 on parallelism with comparisons.

Any versus *any other*

Use *any other* when comparing something with others in the same group. Use *any* when comparing something with others in a different group.

Illogical	Los Angeles is larger than <u>any</u> city in California. [Since Los Angeles is itself a city in California, the sentence seems to say that Los Angeles is larger than itself.]
Revised	Los Angeles is larger than <u>any other</u> city in California.
Illogical	Los Angeles is larger than <u>any other</u> city in Canada. [The cities in Canada constitute a group to which Los Angeles does not belong.]
Revised	Los Angeles is larger than <u>any</u> city in Canada.

29d   Watch for double negatives.

A DOUBLE NEGATIVE is a nonstandard construction in which two negative words such as *no, none, neither, barely, hardly,* or *scarcely* cancel each other out. Some double negatives are intentional: for instance, *She was not unhappy* indicates with understatement that she was indeed happy. But most double negatives say the opposite of what is intended: *Jenny did not feel nothing* asserts that Jenny felt other than nothing, or something. For the opposite meaning, one of the negatives must be eliminated (*She felt nothing*) or one of them must be changed to a positive (*She did not feel anything*).

Faulty	The IRS cannot hardly audit all tax returns. None of its audits never touch many cheaters.
Revised	The IRS cannot audit all tax returns. Its audits never touch many cheaters.

29e   Distinguish between present and past participles as adjectives. ESL

Both present participles and past participles may serve as adjectives: *a burning building, a burned building.* As in the examples, the two participles usually differ in the time they indicate.

But some present and past participles—those derived from verbs expressing feeling—can have altogether different meanings. The present participle refers to something that causes the feeling: *That was a frightening storm.* The past participle refers to something that experiences the feeling: *They quieted the frightened horses.*

The following participles are among those likely to be confused:

amazing/amazed	embarrassing/embarrassed
amusing/amused	exciting/excited
annoying/annoyed	exhausting/exhausted
astonishing/astonished	fascinating/fascinated
boring/bored	frightening/frightened
confusing/confused	frustrating/frustrated
depressing/depressed	interesting/interested

ad

29e

--- KEY TERMS ---

PRESENT PARTICIPLE   The *-ing* form of a verb: *flying, writing.* (See p. 141.)

PAST PARTICIPLE   The *-d* or *-ed* form of a regular verb: *slipped, walked.* Most irregular verbs have distinctive past participles, such as *eaten* or *swum.* (See pp. 140–141.)

pleasing/pleased	surprising/surprised
satisfying/satisfied	tiring/tired
shocking/shocked	worrying/worried

29f   Use *a, an, the,* and other determiners appropriately.   ESL

DETERMINERS are special kinds of adjectives that mark nouns because they always precede nouns. Some common determiners are *a, an,* and *the* (called ARTICLES) and *my, their, whose, this, these, those, one, some,* and *any.*

Native speakers of English can rely on their intuition when using determiners, but nonnative speakers often have difficulty with them because many other languages use them quite differently or not at all. In English the use of determiners depends on the context they appear in and the kind of nouns they precede:

- A PROPER NOUN names a particular person, place, or thing and begins with a capital letter: *February, Joe Allen, Red River.* Most proper nouns are not preceded by determiners.
- A COUNT NOUN names something that is countable in English and can form a plural: *girl/girls, apple/apples, child/children.* A singular count noun is always preceded by a determiner; a plural count noun sometimes is.
- A NONCOUNT NOUN names something not usually considered countable in English, and so it does not form a plural. A noncount noun is sometimes preceded by a determiner. Here is a sample of noncount nouns, sorted into groups by meaning:

Abstractions: confidence, democracy, education, equality, evidence, health, information, intelligence, knowledge, luxury, peace, pollution, research, success, supervision, truth, wealth, work

Food and drink: bread, candy, cereal, flour, meat, milk, salt, water, wine

Emotions: anger, courage, happiness, hate, joy, love, respect, satisfaction

Natural events and substances: air, blood, dirt, gasoline, gold, hair, heat, ice, oil, oxygen, rain, silver, smoke, weather, wood

Groups: clergy, clothing, equipment, furniture, garbage, jewelry, junk, legislation, machinery, mail, military, money, police, vocabulary

Fields of study: accounting, architecture, biology, business, chemistry, engineering, literature, psychology, science

An ESL dictionary will tell you whether a noun is a count noun, a noncount noun, or both. (See p. 122 for recommended dictionaries.)

det
29f

Note Many nouns are sometimes count nouns and sometimes noncount nouns:

> The library has <u>a room</u> for readers. [*Room* is a count noun meaning "walled area."]
> The library has <u>room</u> for reading. [*Room* is a noncount noun meaning "space."]

 Partly because the same noun may fall into different groups, computerized grammar and style checkers are unreliable guides to missing or misused articles and other determiners. For instance, a checker flagged the omitted *a* before *Scientist* in *Scientist developed new processes;* it did not flag the omitted *a* before *new* in *A scientist developed new process;* and it mistakenly flagged the correctly omitted article *the* before *Vegetation* in *Vegetation suffers from drought.* To correct omitted or misused articles, you'll need to proofread carefully on your own.

1 *A, an,* and *the*

With singular count nouns

A or *an* precedes a singular count noun when the reader does not already know its identity, usually because you have not mentioned it before:

> <u>A</u> scientist in our chemistry department developed <u>a</u> process to strengthen metals. [*Scientist* and *process* are being introduced for the first time.]

The precedes a singular count noun that has a specific identity for the reader, usually because (1) you have mentioned it before, (2) you identify it immediately before or after you state it, (3) it is unique (the only one in existence), or (4) it refers to an institution or facility that is shared by a community:

> A scientist in our chemistry department developed a process to strengthen metals. <u>The</u> scientist patented <u>the</u> process. [*Scientist* and *process* were identified in the preceding sentence.]
> <u>The</u> most productive laboratory is <u>the</u> research center in <u>the</u> chemistry department. [*Most productive* identifies *laboratory. In the chemistry department* identifies *research center.* And *chemistry department* is a shared facility.]
> <u>The</u> sun rises in <u>the</u> east. [*Sun* and *east* are unique.]
> Many men and women aspire to <u>the</u> presidency. [*Presidency* is a shared institution.]
> <u>The</u> fax machine has changed business communication. [*Fax machine* is a shared facility.]

The is not used before a singular noun that names a general category:

Wordsworth's poetry shows his love of <u>nature</u> [not <u>the nature</u>].

General Sherman said that <u>war</u> is hell. [*War* names a general category.]

<u>The</u> war in Croatia left many dead. [*War* names a specific war.]

With plural count nouns

A or *an* never precedes a plural noun. *The* does not precede a plural noun that names a general category. *The* does precede a plural noun that names specific representatives of a category.

<u>Men</u> and <u>women</u> are different. [*Men* and *women* name general categories.]

<u>The</u> women formed a team. [*Women* refers to specific people.]

With noncount nouns

A or *an* never precedes a noncount noun. *The* does precede a noncount noun that names specific representatives of a general category.

<u>Vegetation</u> suffers from drought. [*Vegetation* names a general category.]

<u>The</u> vegetation in the park withered or died. [*Vegetation* refers to specific plants.]

With proper nouns

A or *an* never precedes a proper noun. *The* generally does not precede proper nouns.

<u>Garcia</u> lives in <u>Boulder</u>.

There are exceptions, however. For instance, we generally use *the* before plural proper nouns (<u>*the*</u> *Murphys,* <u>*the*</u> *Boston Celtics*) and before the names of groups and organizations (<u>*the*</u> *Department of Justice,* <u>*the*</u> *Sierra Club*), ships (<u>*the*</u> *Lusitania*), oceans (<u>*the*</u> *Pacific*), mountain ranges (<u>*the*</u> *Alps*), regions (<u>*the*</u> *Middle East*), rivers (<u>*the*</u> *Mississippi*), and some countries (<u>*the*</u> *United States,* <u>*the*</u> *Netherlands*).

det

29f

2   Other determiners

The uses of English determiners besides articles also depend on context and kind of noun. The following determiners may be used as indicated with singular count nouns, plural count nouns, or noncount nouns.

With any kind of noun (singular count, plural count, noncount)

my, our, your, his, her, its, their, possessive nouns (*boy's, boys'*)
whose, which(ever), what(ever)

some, any, the other
no

Their account is overdrawn. [Singular count.]
Their funds are low. [Plural count.]
Their money is running out. [Noncount.]

Only with singular nouns (count and noncount)

this, that

This account has some money. [Count.]
That information may help. [Noncount.]

Only with noncount nouns and plural count nouns

most, enough, other, such, all, all of the, a lot of

Most funds are committed. [Plural count.]
Most money is needed elsewhere. [Noncount.]

Only with singular count nouns

one, every, each, either, neither, another

One car must be sold. [Singular count.]

Only with plural count nouns

these, those
both, many, few, a few, fewer, fewest, several
two, three, and so forth

Two cars are unnecessary. [Plural count.]

Note *Few* means "not many" or "not enough." *A few* means "some" or "a small but sufficient quantity."

Few committee members came to the meeting.
A few members can keep the committee going.

Do not use *much* with a plural count noun.

Many [not much] members want to help.

Only with noncount nouns

much, more, little, a little, less, least, a large amount of

Less luxury is in order. [Noncount.]

Note *Little* means "not many" or "not enough." *A little* means "some" or "a small but sufficient quantity."

Little time remains before the conference.
The members need a little help from their colleagues.

Do not use *many* with a noncount noun.

Much [not many] work remains.

det

29f

30 Misplaced and Dangling Modifiers

http://webster.commnet.edu/HP/pages/darling/grammar/modifiers.htm
Information on modifiers, from the Guide to Grammar and Writing.

http://www.uottawa.ca/academic/arts/writcent/hypergrammar/ modifier.html   Information on modifiers, from the University of Ottawa.

http://members.home.net/englishzone/grammar/grammar.html
Information on adverb and adjective order, from English-Zone.Com.

http://owl.english.purdue.edu/Files/24.html   Information on dangling modifiers, from the Purdue Online Writing Lab.

The arrangement of words in a sentence is an important clue to their relationships. Modifiers will be unclear if readers can't connect them to the words they modify.

Note Computerized grammar and style checkers do not recognize many problems with modifiers. For instance, a checker failed to flag the misplaced modifiers in *Gasoline high prices affect usually car sales* or the dangling modifier in *The vandalism was visible passing the building.* Proofread your work on your own to find and correct problems with modifiers.

30a   Reposition misplaced modifiers.

A MISPLACED MODIFIER falls in the wrong place in a sentence. It is usually awkward or confusing. It may even be unintentionally funny.

1   Clear placement

Readers tend to link a modifier to the nearest word it could modify. Any other placement can link the modifier to the wrong word.

Confusing   He served steak to the men on paper plates.

Clear   He served the men steak on paper plates.

Confusing   According to the police, many dogs are killed by automobiles and trucks roaming unleashed.

Clear   According to the police, many dogs roaming unleashed are killed by automobiles and trucks.

mm
30a

206

2   *Only* and other limiting modifiers

LIMITING MODIFIERS include *almost, even, exactly, hardly, just, merely, nearly, only, scarcely,* and *simply.* For clarity place such a modifier immediately before the word or word group you intend it to limit.

Unclear	The archaeologist <u>only</u> found the skull on her last dig.
Clear	The archaeologist found <u>only</u> the skull on her last dig.
Clear	The archaeologist found the skull <u>only</u> on her last dig.

3   Adverbs with grammatical units

Adverbs can often move around in sentences, but some will be awkward if they interrupt certain grammatical units:

- A single-word adverb can interrupt subject and verb: *Bo <u>gladly</u> accepted.* But a longer adverb stops the flow of the sentence:

Awkward	subject ┌────adverb────┐ verb Kuwait, after the Gulf War ended in 1991, began returning to normal.
Revised	┌────adverb────┐ subject verb After the Gulf War ended in 1991, Kuwait began returning to normal.

- Any adverb is awkward between a verb and its direct object:

Awkward	┌─verb─┐ adverb object The war had damaged <u>badly</u> many of Kuwait's oil fields.
Revised	┌─verb─┐ object The war had <u>badly</u> damaged many of Kuwait's oil fields. adverb

- A SPLIT INFINITIVE—an adverb placed between *to* and the verb—annoys many readers:

Awkward	┌infinitive┐ The weather service expected temperatures <u>to</u> not <u>rise</u>.

mm

30a

┌ KEY TERMS ────

ADVERB   A word or word group that describes a verb, adjective, other adverb, or whole word group, specifying how, when, where, or to what extent: *quickly see, solid like a boulder.*

DIRECT OBJECT   The receiver of the verb's action: *The car hit a tree.* (See p. 146.)

INFINITIVE   A verb form consisting of *to* plus the verb's plain (or dictionary) form: *to produce, to enjoy.* (See p. 149.)

infinitive
Revised   The weather service expected temperatures not <u>to rise</u>.

A split infinitive may sometimes be natural and preferable, though it may still bother some readers.

―infinitive―
Several US industries expect <u>to</u> more than <u>triple</u> their use of robots.

Here the split infinitive is more economical than the alternatives, such as *Several US industries expect to increase their use of robots by more than three times.*

- A single-word adverb may interrupt a verb phrase after the first helping verb: *Scientists have lately been using spacecraft to study the sun.* But a longer adverb is usually awkward inside a verb phrase:

helping
verb   adverb
Awkward   The spacecraft *Ulysses* will <u>after traveling near the sun</u>
main verb
report on the sun's energy fields.

adverb
Revised   <u>After traveling near the sun</u>, the spacecraft *Ulysses*
verb phrase
will report on the sun's energy fields.

ESL   In a question, place a one-word adverb after the first helping verb and subject:

helping   rest of
verb   subject   adverb   verb phrase
Will spacecraft <u>ever</u> be able to leave the solar system?

4   Other adverb positions **ESL**

A few adverbs are subject to special conventions for placement:

- Adverbs of frequency include *always, never, often, rarely, seldom, sometimes,* and *usually.* They generally appear at the beginning of a sentence, before a one-word verb, or after the helping verb in a verb phrase:

helping   main
verb   adverb   verb
Robots have <u>sometimes</u> put humans out of work.

adverb   verb phrase
<u>Sometimes</u> robots have put humans out of work.

┌─KEY TERM────────────────────────────────

VERB PHRASE   A verb consisting of a helping verb and a main verb that carries the principal meaning: *will have begun, can see.* (See p. 141.)

Adverbs of frequency always follow the verb *be*.

verb adverb
Robots are <u>often</u> helpful to workers.

- Adverbs of degree include *absolutely, almost, certainly, completely, definitely, especially, extremely, hardly,* and *only.* They fall just before the word modified (an adjective, another adverb, sometimes a verb):

adverb   adjective
Robots have been <u>especially</u> useful in making cars.

- Adverbs of manner include *badly, beautifully, openly, sweetly, tightly, well,* and others that describe how something is done. They usually fall after the verb:

verb adverb
Robots work <u>smoothly</u> on assembly lines.

- The position of the adverb *not* depends on what it modifies. When it modifies a verb, place it after the helping verb (or the first helping verb if more than one):

helping   main
verb   verb
Robots do <u>not</u> think.

When *not* modifies another adverb or an adjective, place it before the other modifier:

adjective
Robots are <u>not</u> sleek machines.

5 Order of adjectives **ESL**

English follows distinctive rules for arranging two or three adjectives before a noun. (A string of more than three adjectives before a noun is rare.) The adjectives follow this order:

Determiner	Opinion	Size or shape	Age	Color	Origin	Material	Noun used as adjective	Noun
many			new				state	laws
	lovely			green	Thai			birds
a		square				wooden		table
all			recent				business	reports
the				blue		litmus		paper

mm
30a

KEY TERM

ADJECTIVE A word that describes a noun or pronoun, specifying which one, what quality, or how many: <u>*good*</u> one, <u>*three*</u> cars. (See p. 142.)

See page 234 on punctuating adjectives before a noun.

30b   Connect dangling modifiers to their sentences.

A DANGLING MODIFIER does not sensibly modify anything in its sentence.

Dangling   Passing the building, the vandalism became visible. [The modifying phrase seems to describe *vandalism,* but vandalism does not pass buildings. Who was passing the building? Who saw the vandalism?]

Dangling modifiers usually introduce sentences, contain a verb form, and imply but do not name a subject: in the example above, the implied subject is the someone or something passing the building. Readers assume that this implied subject is the same as the subject of the sentence (*vandalism* in the example). When it is not, the modifier "dangles" unconnected to the rest of the sentence. Here is another example:

Dangling   Although intact, graffiti covered every inch of the walls and windows. [The walls and windows, not the graffiti, were intact.]

To revise a dangling modifier, you have to recast the sentence it appears in. (Revising just by moving the modifier will leave it dangling: *The vandalism became visible passing the building.*) Choose a revision method depending on what you want to emphasize in the sentence.

Identifying and revising dangling modifiers

- If the modifier lacks a subject of its own (e.g., *when in diapers*), identify what it describes.
- Verify that what the modifier describes is in fact the subject of the main clause. If it is not, the modifier is probably dangling:

  ┌─── modifier ───┐   subject
  Dangling   When in diapers, my mother remarried.

- Revise a dangling modifier (*a*) by recasting it with a subject of its own or (*b*) by changing the subject of the main clause:

  Revision *a*   When I was in diapers, my mother remarried.
  Revision *b*   When in diapers, I attended my mother's second wedding.

- Rewrite the dangling modifier as a complete clause with its own stated subject and verb. Readers can accept that the new subject and the sentence subject are different.

Dangling Passing the building, the vandalism became visible.

Revised As we passed the building, the vandalism became visible.

- Change the subject of the sentence to a word the modifier properly describes.

Dangling Trying to understand the clauses, vandalism has been extensively studied.

Revised Trying to understand the causes, researchers have extensively studied vandalism.

dm

30b

SENTENCE FAULTS

A word group punctuated as a sentence will confuse or annoy readers if it lacks needed parts, has too many parts, or has parts that don't fit together.

31 Sentence Fragments

Information and exercises on sentence fragments:

http://webster.commnet.edu/HP/pages/darling/grammar/fragments.htm From the Guide to Grammar and Writing.

http://owl.english.purdue.edu/Files/67.html From the Purdue Online Writing Lab.

http://www.english.uiuc.edu/cws/wworkshop/grammar/fragments.htm From the University of Illinois at Urbana-Champaign.

http://www.clearcf.uvic.ca/writersguide/Pages/SentFrags.html From the University of Victoria.

http://webnz.com/checkers/GramSentFrag.html For ESL writers, from Superteach.

A SENTENCE FRAGMENT is part of a sentence that is set off as if it were a whole sentence by an initial capital letter and a final period or other end punctuation. Although writers occasionally use fragments deliberately and effectively (see 31c), readers perceive most fragments as serious errors.

Note Computerized grammar and style checkers can spot many but not all sentence fragments. For instance, a checker flagged *The network growing* as a fragment but failed to flag *Thou-*

---

frag

31

Complete sentence versus sentence fragment

A complete sentence or main clause
1. contains a subject and a verb (*The wind blows*)
2. and is not a subordinate clause (beginning with a word such as *because* or *who*).

A sentence fragment
1. lacks a verb (*The wind blowing*),
2. or lacks a subject (*And blows*),
3. or is a subordinate clause not attached to a complete sentence (*Because the wind blows*).

sands of new sites on the Web. Repair any fragments that your checker does find, but proofread your work yourself to ensure that it's fragment-free.

31a Test your sentences for completeness.

A word group punctuated as a sentence should pass *all three* of the following tests. If it does not, it is a fragment and needs to be revised.

Test 1: Find the verb.

Look for a verb in the group of words:

Fragment	Thousands of new sites on the World Wide Web. [Compare a complete sentence: *Thousands of new sites have appeared on the World Wide Web.*]

Any verb form you find must be a FINITE VERB, one that changes form as indicated below. A verbal does not change; it cannot serve as a sentence verb without the aid of a helping verb.

	Finite verbs in complete sentences	Verbals in sentence fragments
Singular	The network grows.	The network growing.
Plural	Networks grow.	Networks growing.
Present	The network grows.	
Past	The network grew.	The network growing.
Future	The network will grow.	

ESL Some languages allow forms of *be* to be omitted as helping verbs or linking verbs. But English requires stating forms of *be:*

Fragments	The network growing. It already larger than its developers anticipated. [Compare complete sentences: *The network is growing. It is already larger than its developers anticipated.*]

frag

31a

KEY TERMS ─────────

VERB   The part of a sentence that asserts something about the subject: *Ducks swim.* Also called PREDICATE. (See p. 145.)

VERBAL   A verb form that can serve as a noun, a modifier, or a part of a sentence verb, but not alone as the only verb of a sentence: *drawing, to draw, drawn.* (See p. 149.)

HELPING VERB   A verb such as *is, were, have, might,* and *could* that combines with various verb forms to indicate time and other kinds of meaning: for instance, *were drawing, might draw.* (See p. 141.)

Test 2: Find the subject.

The subject of the sentence will usually come before the verb. If there is no subject, the word group is probably a fragment:

> **Fragment**   And has enormous popular appeal. [Compare a complete sentence: *And the Web has enormous popular appeal.*]

In one kind of complete sentence, a command, the subject *you* is understood: *[You] Experiment with the Web.*

ESL Some languages allow the omission of the sentence subject, especially when it is a pronoun. But in English, except in commands, the subject is always stated:

> **Fragment**   Web commerce is expanding dramatically. Is threatening traditional stores. [Compare a complete sentence: *It is threatening traditional stores.*]

Test 3: Make sure the clause is not subordinate.

A subordinate clause usually begins with a subordinating word, such as one of the following:

Subordinating conjunctions			Relative pronouns	
after	once	until	that	who/whom
although	since	when	which	whoever/whomever
as	than	where		
because	that	whereas		
if	unless	while		

Subordinate clauses serve as parts of sentences (nouns or modifiers), not as whole sentences:

> **Fragment**   When the government devised the Internet. [Compare a complete sentence: *The government devised the Internet.* Or: *When the government devised the Internet, no expansive computer network existed.*]
>
> **Fragment**   The reason that the government devised the Internet. [This fragment is a noun (*reason*) plus its modifier (*that . . . Internet*). Compare a complete sentence: *The*

---

frag

31a

┌─ KEY TERMS ──

SUBJECT   The part of a sentence that names who or what performs the action or makes the assertion of the verb: *Ducks swim.* (See p. 145.)

SUBORDINATE CLAUSE   A word group that contains a subject and a verb, begins with a subordinating word such as *because* or *who*, and is not a question: *Ducks can swim when they are young.* A subordinate clause may serve as a modifier or as a noun. (See p. 151.)

└──

reason that the government devised the Internet <u>was to provide secure links among departments and defense contractors</u>.)

Note Questions beginning with *how, what, when, where, which, who, whom, whose,* and *why* are not sentence fragments: *Who was responsible? When did it happen?*

31b   Revise sentence fragments.

Correct sentence fragments in one of two ways depending on the importance of the information in the fragment and thus how much you want to stress it:

- Rewrite the fragment as a complete sentence. The information in the fragment will then have the same importance as that in other complete sentences.

Fragment	A recent addition to the Internet is the World Wide Web. <u>Which allows users to move easily between sites.</u>
Revised	A recent addition to the Internet is the World Wide Web. <u>It</u> allows users to move easily between sites.
Fragment	The Internet and now the Web are a boon to researchers. <u>A vast and accessible library</u>.
Revised	The Internet and now the Web are a boon to researchers. <u>They form</u> a vast and accessible library.

- Combine the fragment with the appropriate main clause. The information in the fragment will then be subordinated to that in the main clause.

Fragment	The Web is easy to use. <u>Loaded with links and graphics.</u>
Revised	The Web_, loaded with links and graphics_, is easy to use.
Fragment	With the links, users can move to other Web sites. <u>That they want to consult</u>.
Revised	With the links, users can move to other Web sites_, that they want to consult.

frag

31c

31c   Be aware of the acceptable uses of incomplete sentences.

A few word groups lacking the usual subject-predicate combination are incomplete sentences, but they are not fragments because they conform to the expectations of most readers. They include exclamations (*Oh no!*); questions and answers (*Where next? To Kansas.*); and commands (*Move along. Shut the window.*).

Experienced writers sometimes use sentence fragments when they want to achieve a special effect. Such fragments appear more in informal than in formal writing. Unless you are experienced and thoroughly secure in your own writing, you should avoid all fragments and concentrate on writing clear, well-formed sentences.

32 Comma Splices and Fused Sentences

 Information on comma splices and fused sentences:

http://webster.commnet.edu/HP/pages/darling/grammar/runons.htm
From the Guide to Grammar and Writing.

http://www.english.uiuc.edu/cws/wworkshop/grammar/runons.htm
From the University of Illinois at Urbana-Champaign.

http://www.odu.edu/~wts/csplice.htm From Old Dominion University.

When a sentence contains two main clauses in a row, readers need a signal that one main clause is ending and another beginning. The usual signal is a comma with coordinating conjunction (*The ship was huge, and its mast stood eighty feet high*) or a semicolon (*The ship was huge; its mast stood eighty feet high*).

Two problems in punctuating main clauses deprive readers of this signal. One is the COMMA SPLICE, in which the clauses are joined (or spliced) *only* with a comma:

> **Comma splice** The ship was huge, its mast stood eighty feet high.

The other is the FUSED SENTENCE (or RUN-ON SENTENCE), in which no punctuation or conjunction appears between the clauses.

> **Fused sentence** The ship was huge its mast stood eighty feet high.

cs/fs

32

┌─ KEY TERMS ─────────────────────────────────

MAIN CLAUSE   A word group that contains a subject and a verb and does not begin with a subordinating word: *A dictionary is essential.*

COORDINATING CONJUNCTION   *And, but, or, nor, for, so, yet.* (See p. 144.)

Note Computerized grammar and style checkers can detect many comma splices, but they will not recognize every fused sentence and may flag errors in sentences that are complex but actually correct. Verify that revision is actually needed on any flagged sentence, and read your work carefully on your own to be sure it is correct.

ESL An English sentence may not include more than one main clause unless the clauses are separated by a comma and a coordinating conjunction or by a semicolon. If your native language does not have such a rule or has accustomed you to writing long sentences, you may need to edit your English writing especially for comma splices and fused sentences.

32a   Separate main clauses not joined by *and, but,* or another coordinating conjunction.

If your readers point out comma splices or fused sentences in your writing, you're not creating enough separation between main clauses in your sentences. The following guidelines can help you repair the problem:

Revision of comma splices and fused sentences

1. Underline the main clauses in your draft.
2. When two main clauses fall in the same sentence, check the connection between them.
3. If nothing falls between the clauses or only a comma does, revise in one of the following ways, depending on the relation you want to establish between the clauses. (See the text discussion for examples.)

   Make the clauses into separate sentences.
   Insert a comma followed by *and, but,* or another coordinating conjunction. Or, if the comma is already present, insert just the coordinating conjunction.
   Insert a semicolon between clauses.
   Subordinate one clause to the other.

cs/fs

32a

Separate sentences

Make the clauses into separate sentences when the ideas expressed are only loosely related:

Comma splice   Chemistry has contributed much to our understanding of foods, many foods such as wheat and beans can be produced in the laboratory.

Revised   Chemistry has contributed much to our under-
               standing of foods. Many foods such as wheat and
               beans can be produced in the laboratory.

ESL   Making separate sentences may be the best option if you
are used to writing very long sentences in your native language but
often write comma splices in English.

Coordinating conjunction

Insert a coordinating conjunction in a comma splice when the
ideas in the main clauses are closely related and equally important:

Comma splice   Some laboratory-grown foods taste good, they are
               nutritious.
Revised   Some laboratory-grown foods taste good, <u>and</u> they
               are nutritious.

In a fused sentence insert a comma and a coordinating conjunction:

Fused   Chemists have made much progress they still have
               a way to go.
Revised   Chemists have made much progress, <u>but</u> they still
               have a way to go.

Semicolon

Insert a semicolon between clauses if the relation between the
ideas is very close and obvious without a conjunction:

Comma splice   Good taste is rare in laboratory-grown vegetables,
               they are usually bland.
Revised   Good taste is rare in laboratory-grown vegetables;
               they are usually bland.

Subordination

Subordinate one clause to the other when one idea is less important than the other:

Comma splice   The vitamins are adequate, the flavor is deficient.
Revised   <u>Even though</u> the vitamins are adequate, the flavor
               is deficient.

32b   Separate main clauses related by *however,* *for example,* and so on.

Two groups of words that are not conjunctions describe how
one main clause relates to another: CONJUNCTIVE ADVERBS and other
TRANSITIONAL EXPRESSIONS.

Common conjunctive adverbs and transitional expressions

accordingly	for instance	in the meantime	otherwise
anyway	further	in the past	similarly
as a result	furthermore	likewise	so far
at last	hence	meanwhile	still
at length	however	moreover	that is
besides	incidentally	namely	then
certainly	in contrast	nevertheless	thereafter
consequently	indeed	nonetheless	therefore
even so	in fact	now	thus
finally	in other words	of course	to this end
for all that	in short	on the contrary	undoubtedly
for example	instead	on the whole	until now

(See pp. 41–42 for a longer list of transitional expressions.)

When two clauses are related by a conjunctive adverb or another transitional expression, they must be separated by a period or by a semicolon. The adverb or expression is also generally set off by a comma or commas.

Comma splice   Most Americans refuse to give up unhealthful habits, consequently our medical costs are higher than those of many other countries.

Revised   Most Americans refuse to give up unhealthful habits. Consequently, our medical costs are higher than those of many other countries.

Revised   Most Americans refuse to give up unhealthful habits; consequently, our medical costs are higher than those of many other countries.

Conjunctive adverbs and transitional expressions are different from coordinating conjunctions (*and, but,* and so on) and subordinating conjunctions (*although, because,* and so on):

cs/fs

32b

- Unlike conjunctions, conjunctive adverbs and transitional expressions do not join two clauses into a grammatical unit but merely describe the way two clauses relate in meaning.
- Thus, unlike conjunctions, conjunctive adverbs and transitional expressions can be moved from one place to another in a clause. No matter where in the clause an adverb or expression falls, though, the clause must be separated from another main clause by a period or semicolon:

Most Americans refuse to give up unhealthful habits; our medical costs, consequently, are higher than those of many other countries.

33 Mixed Sentences

 http://webster.commnet.edu/HP/pages/darling/grammar/confusion.htm
Information on mixed sentences, from the Guide to Grammar and
Writing.

A MIXED SENTENCE contains parts that do not fit together. The
misfit may be in grammar or in meaning.

 Note Computerized grammar and style checkers are not
sophisticated enough to recognize most mixed sentences. Proofread
your own work carefully to locate and revise problem sentences.

33a Match subjects and predicates in meaning.

In a sentence with mixed meaning, the subject is said to do or
be something illogical. Such a mixture is sometimes called FAULTY
PREDICATION because the predicate conflicts with the subject.

1 Illogical equation with *be*

When a form of *be* connects a subject and a word that describes
the subject (a complement), the subject and complement must be
logically related:

> **Mixed** A compromise between the city and the country would
> be the ideal place to live.

> **Revised** A community that offered the best qualities of both city
> and country would be the ideal place to live.

2 *Is when, is where*

Definitions require nouns on both sides of *be*. Clauses that
define and begin with *when* or *where* are common in speech but
should be avoided in writing:

> **Mixed** An examination is when you are tested on what you know.

> **Revised** An examination is a test of what you know.

┌─ KEY TERMS ──

SUBJECT The part of a sentence that names who or what performs
the action or makes the assertion of the verb: *Geese fly*. (See p. 145.)

PREDICATE The part of a sentence containing the verb and asserting
something about the subject: *Geese fly*. (See p. 145.)

mixed
33a

3 Reason is because

The commonly heard construction *reason is because* is redundant since *because* means "for the reason that":

Mixed   The <u>reason</u> the temple requests donations <u>is because</u> the school needs expansion.

Revised   The <u>reason</u> the temple requests donations <u>is that</u> the school needs expansion.

Revised   The temple requests donations <u>because</u> the school needs expansion.

4 Other mixed meanings

Faulty predications are not confined to sentences with *be:*

Mixed   The <u>use</u> of emission controls <u>was created</u> to reduce air pollution.

Revised   Emission <u>controls</u> <u>were created</u> to reduce air pollution.

33b Untangle sentences that are mixed in grammar.

Many mixed sentences start with one grammatical plan or construction but end with a different one:

                   modifier (prepositional phrase)   verb

Mixed   By paying more attention to impressions than facts leads us to misjudge others.

This mixed sentence makes a prepositional phrase work as the subject of *leads,* but prepositional phrases function as modifiers, not as nouns, and thus not as sentence subjects.

                  modifier (prepositional phrase)

Revised   By paying more attention to impressions than facts, subject + verb
we misjudge others.

 Mixed sentences are especially likely on a word processor when you connect parts of two sentences or rewrite half a sentence but not the other half. Mixed sentences may also occur when you don't make the subject and verb of a sentence carry the principal meaning. (See p. 99.) Here is another example:

          subject   modifier (prepositional phrase)

Mixed   The fact that someone may be considered guilty just for

associating with someone guilty.

          subject + verb

Revised   The <u>fact is</u> that someone may be considered guilty just for associating with someone guilty.

33c   State parts of sentences, such as subjects, only once. ESL

In some languages other than English, certain parts of sentences may be repeated. These include the subject in any kind of clause or an object or adverb in an adjective clause. In English, however, these parts are stated only once in a clause.

1   Repetition of subject

You may be tempted to restate a subject as a pronoun before the verb. But the subject needs stating only once in its clause:

Faulty	The <u>liquid it</u> reached a temperature of 180°F.
Revised	The <u>liquid</u> reached a temperature of 180°F.

Faulty	<u>Gases</u> in the liquid <u>they</u> escaped.
Revised	<u>Gases</u> in the liquid escaped.

2   Repetition in an adjective clause

ADJECTIVE CLAUSES begin with *who, whom, whose, which, that, where,* and *when* (see also p. 151). The beginning word replaces another word: the subject (*He is the person <u>who</u> called*), an object of a verb or preposition (*He is the person <u>whom</u> I mentioned*), or a preposition and pronoun (*He knows the office <u>where</u> [<u>in which</u>] the conference will occur*).

Do not state the word being replaced in an adjective clause:

Faulty	The technician <u>whom</u> the test depended on <u>her</u> was burned. [*Whom* should replace *her.*]
Revised	The technician <u>whom</u> the test depended on was burned.

Adjective clauses beginning with *where* or *when* do not need an adverb such as *there* or *then:*

Faulty	Gases escaped at a moment <u>when</u> the technician was unprepared <u>then.</u>
Revised	Gases escaped at a moment <u>when</u> the technician was unprepared.

Note *Whom, which,* and similar words are sometimes omitted but are still understood by the reader. Thus the word being replaced should not be stated.

Faulty	Accidents rarely happen to technicians the lab has trained *them.* [*Whom* is understood: . . . *technicians <u>whom</u> the lab has trained.*]
Revised	Accidents rarely happen to technicians the lab has trained.

mixed

33c

V

Punctuation

V

Punctuation

34 End Punctuation

Advice on periods, question marks, and exclamation points:
http://www.uottawa.ca/academic/arts/writcent/hypergrammar/endpunct.html From the University of Ottawa.
http://webster.commnet.edu/HP/pages/darling/grammar/marks.htm
From the Guide to Grammar and Writing.

End a sentence with one of three punctuation marks: a period (.), a question mark (?), or an exclamation point (!).

Note Do not rely on a computerized grammar and spelling checker to identify missing or misused end punctuation. Although a checker may flag missing question marks after direct questions or incorrect combinations of marks (such as a question mark and a period at the end of a sentence), it cannot do much else.

34a Use a period after most sentences and in many abbreviations.

1 Statements, mild commands, and indirect questions

Statement
The airline went bankrupt. It no longer flies.

Mild command
Think of the possibilities. Please consider others.

Indirect question

An INDIRECT QUESTION reports what someone asked but not in the exact form or words of the original question:

The judge asked why I had been driving with my lights off.
No one asked how we got home.

ESL Unlike a direct question, an indirect question uses the wording and subject-verb order of a statement: *The reporter asked why the negotiations failed* [not *why did the negotiations fail*].

2 Abbreviations

Use periods with most abbreviations involving small letters:

p.	Mrs.	e.g.	Minn.
Dr.	Mr.	i.e.	Feb.
Ph.D.	Ms.	a.m., p.m.	ft.

Note When an abbreviation falls at the end of a sentence, use only one period: *The school offers a Ph.D.*

. ? !
34a

225

Many abbreviations of two or more words using all-capital letters may be written with or without periods. Just be consistent.

BA or B.A.   US or U.S.   BC or B.C.   AM or A.M.

Omit periods from these abbreviations:

- The initials of a well-known person: *FDR, JFK.*
- The initials of an organization, corporation, or government agency: *IBM, USMC.*
- A postal abbreviation: *NY, AVE.*
- An ACRONYM, a pronounceable word formed from initials: *UNESCO, VISTA.*

34b Use a question mark after a direct question and sometimes to indicate doubt.

1 Direct questions

Who will follow her**?**
What is the difference between these two people**?**

After indirect questions, use a period: *We wondered who would follow her.* (See the preceding page.)
Questions in a series are each followed by a question mark:

The officer asked how many times the suspect had been arrested. Three times**?** Four times**?** More than that**?**

2 Doubt

A question mark within parentheses can indicate doubt about a number or date.

The Greek philosopher Socrates was born in 470 (**?**) BC and died in 399 BC from drinking poison. [Socrates's birthdate is not known for sure.]

Use sentence structure and words, not a question mark, to express sarcasm or irony.

Not   Stern's friendliness (?) bothered Crane.
But   Stern's <u>insincerity</u> bothered Crane.

34c Use an exclamation point after an emphatic statement, interjection, or command.

No**!** We must not lose this election**!**
Come here immediately**!**

. ? !

34c

Follow mild interjections and commands with commas or periods, as appropriate: *Oh, call whenever you can.*

Note Use exclamation points sparingly, even in informal writing. Overused, they'll fail to impress readers, and they may make you sound overemphatic.

35 The Comma

Information, sometimes with exercises, on using the comma:
http://webster.commnet.edu/HP/pages/darling/grammar/commas.htm
From the Guide to Grammar and Writing.
http://owl.english.purdue.edu/Files/3.html   From the Purdue Online Writing Lab.
http://www.esc.edu/htmlpages/writer/pandg/comma.htm   From the State University of New York.
http://www.uottawa.ca/academic/arts/writcent/hypergrammar/comma.html   From the University of Ottawa.

The comma (,) is the most common punctuation mark inside sentences. Its main uses are shown in the box on the next page.

Note Computerized grammar and style checkers will recognize only some comma errors, ignoring others. Revise any errors that your checker points out, but you'll have to proofread your work on your own to find and correct most errors.

35a   Use a comma before *and, but,* or another coordinating conjunction linking main clauses.

When a coordinating conjunction links words or phrases, do not use a comma: *Dugain plays and sings Irish and English folk songs.* However, *do* use a comma when a coordinating conjunction joins main clauses, as in the next examples.

┌─ KEY TERMS ───

INTERJECTION   A word that expresses feeling or commands attention, either alone or within a sentence: *Oh! Hey! Wow!* (See p. 144.)

COORDINATING CONJUNCTIONS   *And, but, or, nor,* and sometimes *for, so, yet.* (See p. 144.)

MAIN CLAUSE   A word group that contains a subject and a verb and does not begin with a subordinating word: *Water freezes at temperatures below 32°F.* (See p. 150.)

˄
,
35a

Main uses of the comma

- To separate main clauses linked by a coordinating conjunction (opposite).

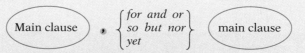

The building is finished, **but** it has no tenants.

- To set off most introductory elements (opposite).

<u>Unfortunately</u>, the only tenant pulled out.

- To set off nonessential elements (p. 230).

The empty building symbolizes a weak local economy, <u>which affects everyone</u>.

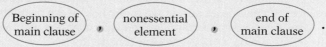

The primary cause, <u>the decline of local industry</u>, is not news.

- To separate items in a series (p. 234).

... item 1 , item 2 , { and / or } item 3 ...

The city needs <u>healthier businesses, new schools,</u> and improved <u>housing</u>.

- To separate coordinate adjectives (p. 234).

... (first adjective) , (second adjective) (word modified) ...

A <u>tall, sleek</u> skyscraper is not needed.

Other uses of the comma:
> To separate parts of dates, addresses, long numbers (p. 235).
> To separate quotations and signal phrases (p. 236).

See also page 237 for when *not* to use the comma.

Caffeine can keep coffee drinkers alert, and it may elevate their mood.

Caffeine was once thought to be safe, but now researchers warn of harmful effects.

Coffee drinkers may suffer sleeplessness, for the drug acts as a stimulant to the nervous system.

Note The comma goes *before,* not after, the coordinating conjunction: *Caffeine increases heart rate, and it* [not *and, it*] *constricts blood vessels.*

Exception Some writers omit the comma between main clauses that are very short and closely related in meaning: *Caffeine helps but it also hurts.* If you are in doubt about whether to use the comma in such a sentence, use it. It will always be correct.

35b Use a comma to set off most introductory elements.

An INTRODUCTORY ELEMENT begins a sentence and modifies a word or words in the main clause that follows. It is usually followed by a comma.

Subordinate clause

Even when identical twins are raised apart, they grow up very like each other.

Verbal or verbal phrase

Explaining the similarity, some researchers claim that one's genes are one's destiny.

Concerned, other researchers deny the claim.

Prepositional phrase

In a debate that has lasted centuries, scientists use identical twins to argue for or against genetic destiny.

┌─ KEY TERMS ───

SUBORDINATE CLAUSE   A word group that contains a subject and a verb, begins with a subordinating word such as *because* or *who,* and is not a question: *When water freezes, crystals form.* (See p. 151.)

VERBAL   A verb form used as an adjective, adverb, or noun. A verbal plus any object or modifier is a VERBAL PHRASE: *frozen water, ready to freeze, rapid freezing.* (See p. 149.)

PREPOSITIONAL PHRASE   A word group consisting of a preposition, such as *for* or *in,* followed by a noun or pronoun plus any modifiers: *in a jar, with a spoon.* (See. p. 148.)

^
,
35b

Transitional expression

Of course, scientists can now look directly at the genes themselves to answer questions.

You may omit the comma after a short subordinate clause or prepositional phrase if its omission does not create confusion: *When snow falls, the city collapses*. *By the year 2000, the world population had topped 6 billion*. But the comma is never wrong.

Note Take care to distinguish *-ing* words used as modifiers from *-ing* words used as subjects. The former almost always take a comma; the latter never do.

```
 ┌────────── modifier ──────────┐    subject    verb
```
Studying identical twins, geneticists learn about inheritance.

```
 ┌────────── subject ──────────┐   verb
```
Studying identical twins helps geneticists learn about inheritance.

35c Use a comma or commas to set off nonessential elements.

Commas around part of a sentence often signal that the element is not essential to the meaning. This NONESSENTIAL ELEMENT may modify or rename the word it refers to, but it does not limit the word to a particular individual or group. The meaning of the word would still be clear if the element were deleted:

Nonessential element

The company, which is located in Oklahoma, has an excellent reputation.

(Because it does not restrict meaning, a nonessential element is also called a NONRESTRICTIVE ELEMENT.)

In contrast, an ESSENTIAL (or RESTRICTIVE) ELEMENT *does* limit the word it refers to: the element cannot be omitted without leaving the meaning too general. Because it is essential, such an element is *not* set off with commas.

Essential element

The company rewards employees who work hard.

┌─ KEY TERM ──────────────────────────────────

TRANSITIONAL EXPRESSION   A word or phrase that shows the relationship between sentences: *for example, however, in fact, of course.* (See p. 41–42.)

└──

∧
¦
35c

A test for nonessential and essential elements

1. Identify the element:

   Hai Nguyen <u>who emigrated from Vietnam</u> lives in Denver.
   Those <u>who emigrated with him</u> live elsewhere.

2. Remove the element. Does the fundamental meaning of the sentence change?

   Hai Nguyen lives in Denver. No.
   Those live elsewhere. YES. [Who are *Those?*]

3. If NO, the element is *nonessential* and *should* be set off with punctuation:

   Hai Nguyen, <u>who emigrated from Vietnam</u>, lives in Denver.

   If YES, the element is *essential* and should *not* be set off with punctuation:

   Those <u>who emigrated with him</u> live elsewhere.

Omitting the underlined words would distort the meaning: the company doesn't necessarily reward *all* employees, only the hardworking ones.

The same element in the same sentence may be essential or nonessential depending on your intended meaning and the context in which the sentence appears.

Essential

Not all the bands were equally well received, however. The band <u>playing old music</u> held the audience's attention. The other groups created much less excitement. [*Playing old music* identifies a particular band.]

Nonessential

A new band called Fats made its debut on Saturday night. The band, <u>playing old music</u>, held the audience's attention. If this performance is typical, the group has a bright future. [*Playing old music* adds information about a band already named.]

Note When a nonessential element falls in the middle of a sentence, be sure to set it off with a pair of commas, one *before* and one *after* the element.

1 Nonessential phrases and clauses

Most nonessential phrases and subordinate clauses function as adjectives to modify nouns or pronouns. In each of the following examples, the underlined words could be omitted with no loss of clarity:

Elizabeth Blackwell was the first woman to graduate from an American medical school, in 1849. [Phrase.]

She was a medical pioneer, helping to found the first medical college for women. [Phrase.]

She taught at the school, which was affiliated with the New York Infirmary. [Clause.]

Blackwell, who published books and papers on medicine, practiced pediatrics and gynecology. [Clause.]

Note Use *that* only in an essential clause, never in a nonessential clause: . . . *school, which* [not *that*] *was affiliated.* . . . Many writers reserve *which* for nonessential clauses.

2 Nonessential appositives

Appositives may also be essential or nonessential, depending on meaning and context. A nonessential appositive merely adds information about the word it refers to:

Toni Morrison's fifth novel, *Beloved,* won the Pulitzer Prize in 1988. [The word *fifth* identifies the novel, while the title adds a detail.]

In contrast, an essential appositive limits or defines the word it refers to:

Morrison's novel *The Bluest Eye* is about an African American girl who longs for blue eyes. [Morrison has written more than one novel, so the title is essential to identify the intended one.]

3 Other nonessential elements

Like nonessential modifiers or appositives, many other elements contribute to texture, tone, or overall clarity but are not essential to the meaning. Unlike nonessential modifiers or appositives, these other nonessential elements generally do not refer to any specific word in the sentence.

Note Use a pair of commas—one before, one after—when any of these elements falls in the middle of a sentence.

┌─ KEY TERMS ──

PHRASE   A word group lacking a subject or a verb or both: *in Duluth, carrying water.* (See p. 148.)

SUBORDINATE CLAUSE   A word group that contains a subject and a verb, begins with a subordinating word such as *who* or *although*, and is not a question: *Samson, who won a gold medal, coaches in Utah.* (See p. 151.)

APPOSITIVE   A noun that renames another noun immediately before it: *His wife, Kyra Sedgwick, is also an actor.* (See p. 150.)

---

^
,
35c

Absolute phrases

<u>Domestic recycling having succeeded</u>, the city now wants to extend the program to businesses.

Many businesses, <u>their profits already squeezed</u>, resist recycling.

Parenthetical and transitional expressions

Generally, set off parenthetical and transitional expressions with commas:

The world's most celebrated holiday is, <u>perhaps surprisingly</u>, New Year's Day. [Parenthetical expression.]

<u>Interestingly</u>, Americans have relatively few holidays. [Parenthetical expression.]

American workers, <u>for example</u>, receive fewer holidays than European workers do. [Transitional expression.]

(Dashes and parentheses may also set off parenthetical expressions. See pp. 252–254.)

When a transitional expression links main clauses, precede it with a semicolon and follow it with a comma (see p. 240):

European workers often have long paid vacations; <u>indeed</u>, they may receive a full month after just a few years with a company.

Note The conjunctions *and* and *but*, sometimes used as transitional expressions, are not followed by commas (see p. 238). Nor are commas required after some transitional expressions that we read without pauses, such as *also, hence, next, now,* and *thus*. A few transitional expressions, notably *therefore* and *instead*, do not need commas when they fall inside or at the ends of clauses.

American workers <u>thus</u> put in more work days. But the days themselves may be shorter.

Phrases of contrast

The substance, <u>not the style</u>, is important.
Substance, <u>unlike style</u>, cannot be faked.

┌─KEY TERMS──────────────────────────────

ABSOLUTE PHRASE A phrase modifying a whole main clause and consisting of a participle and its subject: *Their homework completed, the children watched TV.* (See p. 150.)

PARENTHETICAL EXPRESSION An explanatory or supplemental word or phrase, such as *all things considered, to be frank,* or a brief example or fact. (See pp. 253–254.)

TRANSITIONAL EXPRESSION A word or phrase that shows the relationship between sentences: *for example, however, in fact, of course.* (See p. 41.)

∧
/
35c

Tag questions

Jones should be allowed to vote<u>, should he not</u>?
They don't stop to consider others<u>, do they</u>?

Yes and *no*

<u>Yes</u>, the editorial did have a point.
<u>No</u>, that can never be.

Words of direct address

<u>Cody</u>, please bring me the newspaper.
With all due respec<u>t, sir</u>, I will not.

Mild interjections

<u>Well</u>, you will never know who did it.
<u>Oh</u>, they forgot all about the baby.

35d Use commas between items in a series.

A SERIES consists of three or more items of equal importance.
The items may be words, phrases, or clauses.

Anna Spingle <u>married at the age of seventeen</u>, <u>had three children</u>
<u>by twenty-one</u>, and <u>divorced at twenty-two</u>.
She worked as <u>a cook</u>, <u>a baby-sitter</u>, and <u>a crossing guard</u>.

Some writers omit the comma before the coordinating conjunction in a series (*Breakfast consisted of coffee, eggs and kippers*).
But the final comma is never wrong, and it always helps the reader
see the last two items as separate.

35e Use commas between two or more adjectives that equally modify the same word.

Adjectives that equally modify the same word—COORDINATE
ADJECTIVES—may be separated either by *and* or by a comma.

Spingle's <u>scratched and dented</u> car is an eyesore, but it gets her to
work.
She has dreams of a <u>sleek</u>, shiny car.

┌─KEY TERMS──────────────────────────────

TAG QUESTION   A question at the end of a statement, consisting of a
pronoun, a helping verb, and sometimes *not*: *It isn't wet, is it?*

INTERJECTION   A word that expresses feeling or commands attention: *Oh, must we?*

∧
'

35e

Tests for commas with adjectives

1. Identify the adjectives:

   She was a <u>faithful sincere</u> friend.
   They are <u>dedicated medical</u> students.

2. Can the adjectives be reversed without changing meaning?

   She was a <u>sincere faithful</u> friend.   YES.
   They are <u>medical dedicated</u> students.   No.

3. Can the word *and* be inserted between the adjectives without changing meaning?

   She was a <u>faithful and sincere</u> friend.   YES.
   They are <u>dedicated and medical</u> students.   No.

4. If YES to both questions, the adjectives *should* be separated by a comma:

   She was a <u>faithful, sincere friend</u>.

5. If NO to both questions, the adjectives should *not* be separated by a comma:

   They are <u>dedicated medical</u> students.

Adjectives are not coordinate—and should not be separated by commas—when the one nearer the noun is more closely related to the noun in meaning.

Spingle's children work at <u>various odd</u> jobs.
They all expect to go to a <u>nearby community</u> college.

35f   Use commas in dates, addresses, place names, and long numbers.

When they appear within sentences, dates, addresses, and place names punctuated with commas are also ended with commas.

Dates
July 4, 1776, was the day the Declaration was signed.
The bombing of Pearl Harbor on Sunday, December 7, 1941, prompted American entry into World War II.

Do not use commas between the parts of a date in inverted order (*15 December 1992*) or in dates consisting of a month or season and a year (*December 1941*).

35f

Addresses and place names

Use the address 220 Cornell Road, Woodside, California 94062, for all correspondence.

Columbus, Ohio, is the location of Ohio State University.

Do not use a comma between a state name and a zip code.

Long numbers

Use the comma to separate the figures in long numbers into groups of three, counting from the right. With numbers of four digits, the comma is optional.

The new assembly plant cost $7,525,000.
A kilometer is 3,281 feet [*or* 3281 feet].

ESL   Usage in American English differs from that in some other languages, which use a period, not a comma, to separate the figures in long numbers.

35g   Use commas with quotations according to standard practice.

The words *she said, he writes,* and so on identify the source of a quotation. These SIGNAL PHRASES should be separated from the quotation by punctuation, usually a comma or commas.

Eleanor Roosevelt said, "You must do the thing you think you cannot do."

"Knowledge is power," wrote Francis Bacon.

"The shore has a dual nature," observes Rachel Carson, "changing with the swing of the tides." [The signal phrase interrupts the quotation at a comma and thus ends with a comma.]

Exceptions   When a signal phrase interrupts a quotation between main clauses, follow the signal phrase with a semicolon or a period. The choice depends on the punctuation of the original.

Not   "That part of my life was over," she wrote, "his words had sealed it shut."

But   "That part of my life was over," she wrote. "His words had sealed it shut." [*She wrote* interrupts the quotation at a period.]

Or   "That part of my life was over," she wrote; "his words had sealed it shut." [*She wrote* interrupts the quotation at a semicolon.]

Do not use a comma when a signal phrase follows a quotation ending in an exclamation point or a question mark:

"Claude!" Mrs. Harrison called.

"Why must I come home**?**" he asked.

Do not use a comma with a quotation that is integrated into your sentence structure, including one introduced by *that:*

> James Baldwin insists that "one must never, in one's life, accept . . . injustices as commonplace."
>
> Baldwin thought that the violence of a riot "had been devised as a corrective" to his own violence.

Do not use a comma with a quoted title unless it is a nonessential appositive (p. 232):

> The Beatles recorded "She Loves Me" in the early 1960s.

35h Delete commas where they are not required.

Commas can make sentences choppy and even confusing if they are used more often than needed or in violation of rules 35a–35g. The most common spots for misused commas are discussed below.

1 Not between subject and verb, verb and object, or preposition and object

> **Not**   The returning <u>soldiers, received</u> a warm welcome. [Separated subject and verb.]
>
> **But**   The returning <u>soldiers received</u> a warm welcome.

> **Not**   They had <u>chosen, to fight</u> for their country <u>despite, the risks</u>. [Separated verb *chosen* and its object; separated preposition *despite* and its object.]
>
> **But**   They had <u>chosen to fight</u> for their country <u>despite the risks</u>.

2 Not in most compound constructions

Compound constructions consisting of two elements almost never require a comma. The only exception is the sentence consisting of two main clauses linked by a coordinating conjunction: *The computer failed, but employees kept working* (see pp. 227–229.)

┌─ KEY TERMS ───

NONESSENTIAL APPOSITIVE   A word or words that rename an immediately preceding noun but do not limit or define the noun: *The author's first story, "Biloxi," won a prize.* (See p. 232.)

COMPOUND CONSTRUCTION   Two or more words, phrases, or clauses connected by a coordinating conjunction, usually *and, but, or, nor:* *man and woman, old or young, leaking oil and spewing steam.*

no ⌃ ,
35h

Not   ┌──────── compound subject ────────┐
       Banks, and other financial institutions have helped older
                        ┌──── compound object of preposition────┐
       people with money management, and investment.

But   Banks● and other financial institutions have helped older
       people with money management● and investment.

Not   ┌──────────── compound predicate ────────────┐
       One bank created special accounts for older people, and held
       ┌compound object of verb┐
       classes, and workshops.

But   One bank created special accounts for older people● and
       held classes● and workshops.

3   Not after a conjunction

Not   Parents of adolescents notice increased conflict at puberty,
       and, they complain of bickering.

But   Parents of adolescents notice increased conflict at puberty,
       and● they complain of bickering.

Not   Although, other primates leave the family at adolescence, hu-
       mans do not.

But   Although● other primates leave the family at adolescence, hu-
       mans do not.

4   Not around essential elements

Not   Hawthorne's work, *The Scarlet Letter,* was the first major
       American novel. [The title is essential to distinguish the novel
       from the rest of Hawthorne's work.]

But   Hawthorne's work● *The Scarlet Letter*● was the first major
       American novel.

Not   The symbols, that Hawthorne used, influenced other novelists.
       [The clause identifies which symbols were influential.]

But   The symbols● that Hawthorne used● influenced other novelists.

5   Not around a series

Commas separate the items *within* a series (p. 234) but do not
separate the series from the rest of the sentence.

┌─Key terms──

Conjunction   A connecting word such as a coordinating conjunction (*and, but, or,* and so on) or a subordinating conjunction (*although, because, when,* and so on). (See pp. 143–144.)

Essential element   Limits the word it refers to and thus can't be
omitted without leaving the meaning too general. (See p. 230.)

no ^,
35h

Not   The skills of, hunting, herding, and agriculture, sustained the
      Native Americans.

But   The skills of hunting, herding, and agriculture sustained the
      Native Americans.

6   **Not before an indirect quotation**

Not   The report concluded, that dieting could be more dangerous
      than overeating.

But   The report concluded that dieting could be more dangerous
      than overeating.

36 The Semicolon

Advice on the semicolon:

http://owl.english.purdue.edu/Files/12.html   From the Purdue Online
Writing Lab.

http://www.wisc.edu/writing/Handbook/Semicolons.html   From the
University of Wisconsin at Madison.

http://www.odu.edu/~wts/semicol.htm   From Old Dominion University.

http://leo.stcloudstate.edu/punct/col-semi.html   From St. Cloud State
University.

The semicolon (;) separates equal and balanced sentence elements—usually main clauses (below) and occasionally items in
series (p. 241).

Note A computerized grammar and style checker can spot few
errors in the use of semicolons and may suggest adding them incorrectly. To find semicolon errors, you'll need to proofread on your own.

**36a   Use a semicolon between main clauses not
joined by *and, but,* or another coordinating
conjunction.**

When no coordinating conjunction links two main clauses, the
clauses should be separated by a semicolon.

┌─ KEY TERMS ───┐

MAIN CLAUSE   A word group that contains a subject and a verb and
does not begin with a subordinating word: *Parks help cities breathe.*

COORDINATING CONJUNCTIONS   *And, but, or, nor,* and sometimes *for,
so, yet.*

└──┘

;
36a

A new ulcer drug arrived on the market with a mixed reputation; doctors find that the drug works but worry about its side effects.

The side effects are not minor; some leave the patient quite uncomfortable or even ill.

Note This rule prevents the errors known as comma splice and fused sentence. (See pp. 216–219.)

36b   Use a semicolon between main clauses related by *however, for example,* and so on.

When a conjunctive adverb or another transitional expression relates two main clauses in a single sentence, the clauses should be separated with a semicolon:

An American immigrant, Levi Strauss, invented blue jeans in the 1860s; eventually, his product clothed working men throughout the West.

The position of the semicolon between main clauses never changes, but the conjunctive adverb or transitional expression may move around within the second clause. Wherever the adverb or expression falls, it is usually set off with a comma or commas. (See p. 233.)

Blue jeans have become fashionable all over the world; however, the American originators still wear more jeans than anyone else.

Blue jeans have become fashionable all over the world; the American originators, however, still wear more jeans than anyone else.

Blue jeans have become fashionable all over the world; the American originators still wear more jeans than anyone else, however.

Note This rule prevents the errors known as comma splice and fused sentence. (See pp. 216–219.)

Key terms

Conjunctive adverb   A modifier that describes the relation of the ideas in two clauses, such as *consequently, hence, however, indeed, instead, nonetheless, otherwise, still, then, therefore, thus.* (See pp. 218–219.)

Transitional expression   A word or phrase that shows the relationship between ideas. Transitional expressions include conjunctive adverbs as well as *for example, in fact, of course,* and many other words and phrases. (See p. 41.)

;
36b

36c   Use semicolons between main clauses or series items containing commas.

Normally, commas separate main clauses linked by coordinating conjunctions (*and, but, or, nor*) and items in a series. But when the clauses or series items contain commas, a semicolon between them makes the sentence easier to read.

> Lewis and Clark led the men of their party with consummate skill, inspiring and encouraging them, doctoring and caring for them; and they kept voluminous journals.   —PAGE SMITH
>
> The custody case involved Amy Dalton, the child; Ellen and Mark Dalton, the parents; and Ruth and Hal Blum, the grandparents.

36d   Delete or replace unneeded semicolons.

Too many semicolons can make writing choppy. And semicolons are often misused in certain constructions that call for other punctuation or no punctuation.

1   Not between a main clause and subordinate clause or phrase

The semicolon does not separate unequal parts, such as main clauses and subordinate clauses or phrases.

> **Not** Pygmies are in danger of extinction; because of encroaching development.
>
> **But** Pygmies are in danger of extinction because of encroaching development.
>
> **Not** According to African authorities; only about 35,000 Pygmies exist today.
>
> **But** According to African authorities, only about 35,000 Pygmies exist today.

2   Not before a series or explanation

Colons and dashes, not semicolons, introduce series, explanations, and so forth. (See pp. 243 and 253.)

> **Not** Teachers have heard all sorts of reasons why students do poorly; psychological problems, family illness, too much work, too little time.
>
> **But** Teachers have heard all sorts of reasons why students do poorly: psychological problems, family illness, too much work, too little time.

;
36d

37 The Colon

 http://www.esc.edu/htmlpages/writer/pandg/colons.htm   Advice and an exercise on the colon, from the State University of New York.

The colon (:) is mainly a mark of introduction: it signals that the words following will explain or amplify (below). The colon also has several conventional uses, such as in expressions of time.

 Note Most computerized grammar and style checkers cannot recognize missing or misused colons. You'll have to check for errors yourself.

37a   Use a colon to introduce a concluding explanation, series, appositive, or long or formal quotation.

As an introducer, a colon is always preceded by a complete main clause. It may or may not be followed by a main clause. This is one way the colon differs from the semicolon, which generally separates main clauses only. (See pp. 239–240.)

Explanation

Soul food has a deceptively simple definition: the ethnic cooking of African Americans.

Sometimes a concluding explanation is preceded by *the following* or *as follows* and a colon:

A more precise definition might be <u>the following:</u> soul food draws on ingredients, cooking methods, and dishes originating in Africa, brought to the New World by slaves, and modified or supplemented in the Caribbean and the American South.

Note A complete sentence *after* a colon may begin with a capital letter or a small letter (as in the example above). Just be consistent throughout a paper.

Series

At least three soul food dishes are familiar to most Americans: <u>fried chicken, barbecued spareribs, and sweet potatoes.</u>

┌─ KEY TERM ───
│ MAIN CLAUSE   A word group that contains a subject and a verb and
│ does not begin with a subordinating word: *Soul food is varied.* (See
│ p. 150.)
└───

:

37a

Appositive
Soul food has one disadvantage: fat.

Namely, that is, and other expressions that introduce apposi-tives *follow* the colon: *Soul food has one disadvantage: namely, fat.*

Long or formal quotation
One soul food chef has a solution: "Soul food doesn't have to be greasy to taste good. Instead of using ham hocks to flavor beans, I use smoked turkey wings. The soulful, smoky taste remains, but without all the fat of pork."

37b   Use a colon after the salutation of a business letter, between a title and subtitle, and between divisions of time.

Salutation of business letter
Dear Ms. Burak:

Title and subtitle
Charles Dickens: An Introduction to His Novels

Time
12:26 AM   6:00 PM

37c   Delete or replace unneeded colons.

Use the colon only at the end of a main clause. Do not use it in these situations:

- Delete a colon after a verb:

  Not   The best-known soul food dish is: fried chicken.
  But   The best-known soul food dish is fried chicken.

- Delete a colon after a preposition:

  Not   Soul food recipes can be found in: mainstream cookbooks as well as specialized references.

KEY TERMS

APPOSITIVE   A noun or noun substitute that renames another noun immediately before it: *my brother, Jack.* (See p. 150.)

PREPOSITION   *In, on, outside,* or another word that takes a noun or pronoun as its object: *in the house.* (See p. 143.)

:
37c

But   Soul food recipes can be found in mainstream cookbooks as well as specialized references.

- Delete a colon after *such as* or *including:*

Not   Many Americans have not tasted delicacies <u>such as:</u> chitlins and black-eyed peas.

But   Many Americans have not tasted delicacies <u>such as</u> chitlins and black-eyed peas.

38 The Apostrophe

Advice on using the apostrophe:

http://www.esc.edu/htmlpages/writer/pandg/apost.htm   From the State University of New York.

http://owl.english.purdue.edu/Files/13.html   From the Purdue Online Writing Center.

http://www.uottawa.ca/academic/arts/writcent/hypergrammar/ apostrph.html   From the University of Ottawa.

http://webster.commnet.edu/HP/pages/darling/grammar/ marks.htm#apostrophe   From the Guide to Grammar and Writing.

The apostrophe (') appears as part of a word to indicate possession (below), the omission of one or more letters (p. 247), or (in a few cases) plural number (p. 247).

Note   Computerized grammar and style checkers have mixed results in recognizing apostrophe errors. For instance, most flag missing apostrophes in contractions (as in *isnt*), but many cannot distinguish between *its* and *it's, their* and *they're, your* and *you're, whose* and *who's.* The checkers can identify some apostrophe errors in possessives but will overlook others and may flag correct plurals. Instead of relying on your checker, try using your word processor's Search or Find function to hunt for all words you have ended in *-s.* Then check them to ensure that they correctly omit or include apostrophes and that needed apostrophes are correctly positioned.

38a   Use the apostrophe and sometimes *-s* to form possessive nouns and indefinite pronouns.

A noun or indefinite pronoun shows possession with an apostrophe and, usually, an *-s: the dog's hair, everyone's hope.*

Uses and misuses of the apostrophe

Uses		Misuses	
Possessives of nouns and indefinite pronouns (p. 244)		Singular, not plural, possessives (p. 246)	
Singular	**Plural**	**Not**	**But**
Ms. Park's	the Parks'	the Kim's car	the Kims' car
everyone's	two weeks'	boy's fathers	boys' fathers
Contractions (p. 247)		Plurals of nouns (p. 246)	
it's a girl	shouldn't	**Not**	**But**
you're	won't	book's are	books are
		the Freed's	the Freeds
Optional: Plurals of abbreviations, dates, and words or characters named as words (p. 247)		Third-person singulars of verbs (p. 247)	
MA's or MAs	C's or Cs	**Not**	**But**
1960's or 1960s	if's or ifs	swim's	swims
		Possessives of personal pronouns (p. 247)	
		Not	**But**
		it's toes	its toes
		your's	yours

Note Apostrophes are easy to misuse. For safety's sake, check your drafts to be sure that all words ending in -*s* neither omit needed apostrophes nor add unneeded ones. Also, remember that the apostrophe or apostrophe-plus-*s* is an *addition*. Before this addition, always spell the name of the owner or owners without dropping or adding letters.

1   **Singular words: Add -'s.**

Bill Boughton's skillful card tricks amaze children.

Anyone's eyes would widen.

Most tricks will pique an adult's curiosity, too.

The -'s ending for singular words pertains also to singular words ending in -*s,* as the next examples show.

KEY TERM

INDEFINITE PRONOUN   A pronoun that does not refer to a specific person or thing, such as *anyone, each, everybody, no one,* or *something.* (See p. 180.)

Henry James's novels reward the patient reader.
The business's customers filed suit.

Exception An apostrophe alone may be added to a singular word ending in -*s* when another *s* would make the word difficult to say: *Moses' mother, Joan Rivers' jokes*. But the added -*s* is never wrong (*Moses's, Rivers's*).

2 **Plural words ending in -*s*: Add -' only.**

Workers' incomes have fallen slightly over the past year.
Many students benefit from several years' work after high school.
The Jameses' talents are extraordinary.

Note the difference in the possessives of singular and plural words ending in -*s*. The singular form usually takes -*s*: *James's*. The plural takes only the apostrophe: *Jameses'*.

3 **Plural words not ending in -*s*: Add -'*s*.**

Children's educations are at stake.
We need to attract the media's attention.

4 **Compound words: Add -'*s* only to the last word.**

The brother-in-law's business failed.
Taxes are always somebody else's fault.

5 **Two or more owners: Add -'*s* depending on possession.**

Individual possession
Zimbale's and Mason's comedy techniques are similar. [Each comedian has his own technique.]

Joint possession
The child recovered despite her mother and father's neglect. [The mother and father were jointly neglectful.]

38b **Delete or replace any apostrophe in a plural noun, a singular verb, or a possessive personal pronoun.**

1 **Plural nouns**

The plurals of nouns are generally formed by adding -*s* or -*es*: *boys, families, Joneses, Murphys*. Don't add an apostrophe to form the plural:

Not The Jones' controlled the firm's until 1999.
But The Joneses controlled the firms until 1999.

2 **Singular verbs**

Verbs ending in -s *never* take an apostrophe:

Not   The subway break's down less often now.
But   The subway breaks down less often now.

3 **Possessives of personal pronouns**

His, hers, its, ours, yours, theirs, and *whose* are possessive forms of *he, she, it, we, you, they,* and *who.* They do not take apostrophes:

Not   The house is her's. It's roof leaks.
But   The house is hers. Its roof leaks.

Don't confuse possessive pronouns with contractions. See below.

38c   Use the apostrophe to form contractions.

A CONTRACTION replaces one or more letters, numbers, or words with an apostrophe, as in the following examples:

it is	it's	cannot	can't
they are	they're	does not	doesn't
you are	you're	were not	weren't
who is	who's	class of 1997	class of '97

Note Don't confuse contractions with personal pronouns:

Contractions	Personal pronouns
It's a book.	Its cover is green.
They're coming.	Their car broke down.
You're right.	Your idea is good.
Who's coming?	Whose party is it?

38d   An apostrophe is often optional in the plurals of abbreviations, dates, and words and characters named as words.

Use the apostrophe with most plural abbreviations that contain periods. With unpunctuated abbreviations and with dates, you can omit the apostrophe. (See p. 255 on using periods with abbreviations.)

Ph.D.'s	CD-ROMs	1990s
B.A.'s	BAs	

We often refer to a word, letter, or number as the word or character itself, rather than use it for its meaning: *The word but starts*

38d

with a b. To make such a word or character plural, add an *-s*. An apostrophe is optional as long as you are consistent.

> The sentence has too many but*s* [or but*'*s].
>
> Two 3*s* [or 3*'*s] and two &*s* [or &*'*s] appeared at the end of each chapter.

Note Letters, numbers, and words named as words are underlined (italicized), but the added *-s* and any apostrophe are not. (See p. 273 on this use of underlining or italics.)

---

39   Quotation Marks

Advice on punctuating quotations:

http://www.esc.edu/htmlpages/writer/pandg/quote.htm   From the State University of New York.

http://leo.stcloudstate.edu/research/puncquotes.html   From St. Cloud State University.

Quotation marks—either double (" ") or single (' ')—mainly enclose direct quotations from speech or writing, enclose certain titles, and highlight words used in a special sense. These are the uses covered in this chapter, along with placing quotation marks outside or inside other punctuation marks. Additional issues with quotations are discussed elsewhere in this book:

- Punctuating *she said* and other signal phrases with quotations (p. 236).
- Altering quotations using the ellipsis mark (p. 254) or brackets (p. 257).
- Quoting sources versus paraphrasing or summarizing them (pp. 325–329).
- Avoiding plagiarism when quoting (pp. 329–333).
- Integrating quotations into your text (pp. 334–337).
- Formatting long prose quotations, dialogue, and poetry quotations in MLA style (p. 380) or in APA style (p. 412).

Note Always use quotation marks in pairs, one at the beginning of a quotation and one at the end. Most computerized grammar and style checkers will help you use quotation marks in pairs by flagging a lone mark, and many will identify where other punctuation falls incorrectly inside or outside quotation marks. However,

" "

39

the checkers cannot recognize other possible errors in punctuating quotations. You'll need to proofread carefully yourself.

39a Use double quotation marks to enclose direct quotations.

A DIRECT QUOTATION reports what someone said or wrote, in the exact words of the original:

> "Life," said the psychoanalyst Karen Horney, "remains a very efficient therapist."

Do not use quotation marks with an INDIRECT QUOTATION, which reports what someone said or wrote but not in the exact words.

> The psychoanalyst Karen Horney claimed that life is a good therapist.

39b Use single quotation marks to enclose a quotation within a quotation.

> "In formulating any philosophy," Woody Allen writes, "the first consideration must always be: What can we know? Descartes hinted at the problem when he wrote, 'My mind can never know my body, although it has become quite friendly with my leg.'"

Notice that two different quotation marks appear at the end of the sentence—one single (to finish the interior quotation) and one double (to finish the main quotation).

39c Put quotation marks around the titles of works that are parts of other works.

Use quotation marks to enclose the titles of works that are published or released within larger works. (See the box on the next page.) Use single quotation marks for a quotation within a quoted title, as in the article title and essay title in the box. And enclose all punctuation in the title within the quotation marks, as in the article title.

Note Some academic disciplines do not require quotation marks for titles within source citations. See pages 397–407 (APA style), 431–436 (CBE style), and 444–448 (Columbia online style for the sciences).

" "
39c

Titles to be enclosed in quotation marks

Other titles should be underlined or italicized. (See pp. 271–272.)

Song
"The Star-Spangled Banner"

Short story
"The Gift of the Magi"

Short poem
"Mending Wall"

Article in a periodical
"Does 'Scaring' Work?"

Essay
"Joey: A 'Mechanical Boy'"

Episode of a television or radio program
"The Mexican Connection" (on Sixty Minutes)

Subdivision of a book
"The Mast Head" (Chapter 35 of Moby-Dick)

39d   Quotation marks may enclose words being used in a special sense.

On movie sets movable "wild walls" make a one-walled room seem four-walled on film.

Note Use underlining or italics for defined words.

39e   Delete quotation marks where they are not required.

Title of your paper

Not   "The Death Wish in One Poem by Robert Frost"

But   The Death Wish in One Poem by Robert Frost

Or   The Death Wish in "Stopping by Woods on a Snowy Evening"

Common nickname

Not   As President, "Jimmy" Carter preferred to use his nickname.

But   As President, Jimmy Carter preferred to use his nickname.

Slang or trite expression

Quotation marks will not excuse slang or a trite expression that is inappropriate to your writing. If slang is appropriate, use it without quotation marks.

Not   We should support the President in his "hour of need" rather than "wimp out on him."

But   We should give the President the support he needs rather than turn away like cowards.

39f Place other punctuation marks inside or outside quotation marks according to standard practice.

1 Commas and periods: Inside quotation marks

Swift uses irony in his essay "A Modest Proposal."

Many first-time readers are shocked to see infants described as "delicious."

"'A Modest Proposal,'" wrote one critic, "is so outrageous that it cannot be believed."

Exception When a parenthetical source citation immediately follows a quotation, place any period or comma *after* the citation.

One critic calls the essay "outrageous" (Olms 26).

Partly because of "the cool calculation of its delivery" (Olms 27), Swift's satire still chills a modern reader.

2 Colons and semicolons: Outside quotation marks

A few years ago the slogan in elementary education was "learning by playing"; now educators are concerned with teaching basic skills.

We all know the meaning of "basic skills": reading, writing, and arithmetic.

3 Dashes, question marks, and exclamation points: Inside quotation marks only if part of the quotation

When a dash, question mark, or exclamation point is part of the quotation, place it *inside* quotation marks. Don't use any other punctuation, such as a period or comma:

"But must you—" Marcia hesitated, afraid of the answer.

"Go away!" I yelled.

Did you say, "Who is she?" [When both your sentence and the quotation would end in a question mark or exclamation point, use only the mark in the quotation.]

When a dash, question mark, or exclamation point applies only to the larger sentence, not to the quotation, place it *outside* quotation marks—again, with no other punctuation:

One evocative line in English poetry—"After many a summer dies the swan"—was written by Alfred, Lord Tennyson.

Who said, "Now cracks a noble heart"?

The woman called me "stupid"!

39f

40 Other Marks

http://www.wisc.edu/writing/Handbook/Dashes.html Advice on using dashes, from the University of Wisconsin at Madison.

http://www.esc.edu/htmlpages/writer/pandg/paren.htm Advice and an exercise on using parentheses, from the State University of New York.

http://www.esc.edu/htmlpages/writer/pandg/ellip.htm Advice on using the ellipsis mark, from the State University of New York.

http://www.esc.edu/htmlpages/writer/pandg/brack.htm Advice on using brackets, from the State University of New York.

http://webster.commnet.edu/HP/pages/darling/grammar/ marks.htm#slash Advice on using the slash, from the Guide to Grammar and Writing.

The other marks of punctuation are the dash (below), parentheses (opposite), the ellipsis mark (p. 254), brackets (p. 257), and the slash (p. 257).

Note Some computerized grammar and style checkers will flag a lone parenthesis or bracket so that you can match it with another parenthesis or bracket. But most checkers cannot recognize other misuses of the marks covered here. You'll need to proofread your papers carefully for errors.

40a Use the dash or dashes to indicate shifts and to set off some sentence elements.

The dash (—) is mainly a mark of interruption: it signals a shift, insertion, or break. In your papers, form a dash with two hyphens (--) or use the character called an em dash on your word processor. Do not add extra space around or between the hyphens or around the em dash.

Note When an interrupting element starting with a dash falls in the middle of a sentence, be sure to add the closing dash to signal the end of the interruption. See the first example below.

1 Shifts in tone or thought

The novel—if one can call it that—appeared in 1994.
If the book had a plot—but a plot would be conventional.

2 Nonessential elements

Dashes may be used instead of commas to set off and emphasize modifiers, parenthetical expressions, and other nonessential elements, especially when these elements are internally punctuated:

—

40a

252

The qualities Monet painted—sunlight, rich shadows, deep colors—abounded near the rivers and gardens he used as subjects.

Though they are close together—separated by only a few blocks—the two neighborhoods could be in different countries.

3 Introductory series and concluding series and explanations

Shortness of breath, skin discoloration or the sudden appearance of moles, persistent indigestion, the presence of small lumps—all these may signify cancer. [Introductory series.]

The patient undergoes a battery of tests—CAT scan, bronchoscopy, perhaps even biopsy. [Concluding series.]

Many patients are disturbed by the CAT scan—by the need to keep still for long periods in an exceedingly small space. [Concluding explanation.]

A colon could be used instead of a dash in the last two examples. The dash is more informal.

4 Overuse

Too many dashes can make writing jumpy or breathy:

Not In all his life—eighty-seven years—my great-grandfather never allowed his picture to be taken—not even once. He claimed the "black box"—the camera—would steal his soul.

But In all his eighty-seven years, my great-grandfather did not allow his picture to be taken even once. He claimed the "black box"—the camera—would steal his soul.

40b Use parentheses to enclose parenthetical expressions and labels for lists within sentences.

Note Parentheses *always* come in pairs, one before and one after the punctuated material.

1 Parenthetical expressions

PARENTHETICAL EXPRESSIONS include explanations, facts, digressions, and examples that may be helpful or interesting but are

---

┌─KEY TERM────────────────────────────────
│ NONESSENTIAL ELEMENT Gives added information but does not
│ limit the word it refers to. (See pp. 230–233.)
└──

( )
40b

not essential to meaning. Parentheses de-emphasize parenthetical expressions. (Commas emphasize them more and dashes still more.)

> The population of Philadelphia (now about 1.5 million) has declined since 1950.

Note Don't put a comma before a parenthetical expression enclosed in parentheses. Punctuation after the parenthetical expression should be placed outside the closing parenthesis.

> **Not**   Philadelphia's population compares with Houston's, (just over 1.6 million.)
>
> **But**   Philadelphia's population compares with Houston's (just over 1.6 million).

When it falls between other complete sentences, a complete sentence enclosed in parentheses begins with a capital letter and ends with a period.

> In general, coaches will tell you that scouts are just guys who can't coach. (But then, so are brain surgeons.)   —ROY BLOUNT

2   Labels for lists within sentences

> Outside the Middle East, the countries with the largest oil reserves are (1) Venezuela (63 billion barrels), (2) Russia (57 billion barrels), and (3) Mexico (51 billion barrels).

When you set a list off from your text, do not enclose such labels in parentheses.

40c   Use the ellipsis mark to indicate omissions from quotations.

The ellipsis mark, consisting of three spaced periods (. . .), generally indicates an omission from a quotation. The academic disciplines use two different styles for ellipsis marks in quotations, both illustrated here. For English, foreign languages, and some other humanities, the latest edition of the *MLA Handbook for Writers of Research Papers* requires brackets around any ellipsis mark you add to indicate omission. However, other disciplines do not call for brackets. The guides for these disciplines include the *Chicago Manual of Style* (history, philosophy, and other humanities), the *Publication Manual of the American Psychological Association* (many social sciences), and *Scientific Style and Format: The CBE Manual for Authors, Editors, and Publishers* (many sciences).

All the following examples quote from this passage about environmentalism:

. . .
40c

Original quotation

"At the heart of the environmentalist world view is the conviction that human physical and spiritual health depends on sustaining the planet in a relatively unaltered state. Earth is our home in the full, genetic sense, where humanity and its ancestors existed for all the millions of years of their evolution. Natural ecosystems—forests, coral reefs, marine blue waters—maintain the world exactly as we would wish it to be maintained. When we debase the global environment and extinguish the variety of life, we are dismantling a support system that is too complex to understand, let alone replace, in the foreseeable future."

—EDWARD O. WILSON, "Is Humanity Suicidal?"

1 MLA style

In MLA style, brackets surround your ellipsis marks to distinguish them from any ellipsis marks the quoted author may have used. Insert one space before the opening bracket. Insert one space after the closing bracket unless it precedes another mark of punctuation. Do not insert space between the brackets themselves and the ellipsis mark.

1. Omission of the middle of a sentence

"Natural ecosystems [. . .] maintain the world exactly as we would wish it to be maintained."

2. Omission of the end of a sentence, without source citation

"Earth is our home [. . .]." [The sentence period immediately follows the closing bracket.]

3. Omission of the end of a sentence, with source citation

"Earth is our home [. . .]" (Wilson 27). [The sentence period follows the source citation.]

4. Omission of the beginning of a sentence

"[. . .] [H]uman physical and spiritual health depends on sustaining the planet in a relatively unaltered state." [The brackets around the *H* indicate a change in capitalization from the original.]

5. Omission of parts of two or more sentences

"At the heart of the environmentalist world view is the conviction that human physical and spiritual health depends on sustaining the planet [. . .] where humanity and its ancestors existed for all the millions of years of their evolution."

6. Omission of one or more sentences

"At the heart of the environmentalist world view is the conviction that human physical and spiritual health depends on sustaining the planet in a relatively unaltered state. [. . .] When we debase the global environment and extinguish the variety of life, we are dis-

. . .

40c

mantling a support system that is too complex to understand, let alone replace, in the foreseeable future."

7. Use of a word or phrase
Wilson describes the earth as "our home." [No ellipsis mark needed.]

Note these features of the examples:

- Use an ellipsis mark when it is not otherwise clear that you have left out material from the source, as when the words you quote form a complete sentence that is different in the original (examples 1–5). You don't need an ellipsis mark at the beginning or end of a word or phrase because it will already be obvious that you omitted something (example 7).
- After a grammatically complete sentence, an ellipsis mark either precedes or follows the sentence period (models 2 and 6, respectively). The exception occurs when a parenthetical source citation follows the quotation (example 3), in which case the sentence period falls after the citation.

If you omit one or more lines of poetry or paragraphs of prose from a quotation, use a separate line of ellipsis marks across the full width of the quotation to show the omission.

> In "Song: Love Armed" from 1676, Aphra Behn contrasts two
>
> lovers' experiences of a romance:
>
> > Love in fantastic triumph sate,
> >
> > Whilst bleeding hearts around him flowed,
> >
> > [..]
> >
> > But my poor heart alone is harmed,
> >
> > Whilst thine the victor is, and free. (lines 1-2, 15-16)

(See p. 380 for the format of displayed quotations like this one.)

2   Other styles

When you are following a style guide other than the *MLA Handbook,* such as APA style, do not include brackets around ellipsis marks. Otherwise, the spacing and use of ellipsis marks for different kinds of omissions resembles the MLA style given previously. For instance:

1. Omission of the middle of a sentence
"Natural ecosystems maintain the world exactly as we would wish it to be maintained."

2. Omission of the end of a sentence, without source citation
"Earth is our home. " [Unlike in MLA style, the sentence period, closed up to the last word, precedes the ellipsis mark.]

3. Omission of the end of a sentence, with source citation

"Earth is our home . . ." (Wilson 27). [The sentence period follows the source citation.]

40d   Use brackets to indicate changes in quotations.

Brackets have specialized uses in mathematical equations, but their main use for all kinds of writing is to indicate that you have altered a quotation to explain, clarify, or correct it.

> "That Texaco station [just outside Chicago] is one of the busiest in the nation," said a company spokesperson.

In the style of the Modern Language Association, brackets also surround ellipsis marks that you add to indicate omissions from quotations. See page 255.

The word *sic* (Latin for "in this manner") in brackets indicates that an error in the quotation appeared in the original and was not made by you. Do not underline or italicize *sic* in brackets.

> According to the newspaper report, "The car slammed thru [sic] the railing and into oncoming traffic."

But don't use *sic* to make fun of a writer or to note errors in a passage that is clearly nonstandard.

40e   Use the slash between options, between lines of poetry run into the text, and in electronic addresses.

Option

Some teachers oppose pass/fail courses.

Poetry

Many readers have sensed a reluctant turn away from death in Frost's lines "The woods are lovely, dark and deep, / But I have promises to keep" (13–14).

When separating lines of poetry in this way, leave a space before and after the slash. (See p. 380 for more on quoting poetry.)

Electronic addresses

http://www.stanford.edu/depts/spc/spc.html

See page 88 for more on electronic addresses.

/
40e

VI

Spelling and Mechanics

VI

Spelling and Mechanics

41 Spelling

Advice on spelling:

http://webster.commnet.edu/HP/pages/darling/grammar/spelling.htm
From the Guide to Grammar and Writing.

http://www.uottawa.ca/academic/arts/writcent/hypergrammar/
spelling.html   From the University of Ottawa.

http://www.cooper.com/alan/homonym_list.html   From All About
Homonyms.

You can train yourself to spell better, and this chapter will tell you how. But you can improve instantly by acquiring three habits:

- Carefully proofread your writing.
- Cultivate a healthy suspicion of your spellings.
- Compulsively check a dictionary whenever you doubt a spelling.

Note A word processor's spelling checker can help you find and track spelling errors in your papers. But its usefulness is limited, mainly because it can't spot the confusion of words with similar spellings, such as *their/they're/there*. A grammar and style checker may flag such words, but only the ones listed in its dictionary. You still must proofread your papers yourself. See pages 60–61 for more on spelling checkers and grammar and style checkers.

41a   Anticipate typical spelling problems.

Certain situations, such as misleading pronunciation, commonly lead to misspelling.

1   Pronunciation

In English, pronunciation of words is an unreliable guide to how they are spelled. Pronunciation is especially misleading with HOMONYMS, words pronounced the same but spelled differently. Some homonyms and near-homonyms appear in the following box.

Words commonly confused

accept (to receive)	allusion (indirect reference)
except (other than)	illusion (erroneous belief or
affect (to have an influence on)	perception)
effect (result)	ascent (a movement up)
all ready (prepared)	assent (agreement)
already (by this time)	*(continued)*

Words commonly confused
(continued)

bare (unclothed)
bear (to carry, or an animal)

board (a plane of wood)
bored (uninterested)

brake (stop)
break (smash)

buy (purchase)
by (next to)

cite (to quote an authority)
sight (the ability to see)
site (a place)

desert (to abandon)
dessert (after-dinner course)

discreet (reserved, respectful)
discrete (individual, distinct)

fair (average, or lovely)
fare (a fee for transportation)

forth (forward)
fourth (after *third*)

hear (to perceive by ear)
here (in this place)

heard (past tense of *hear*)
herd (a group of animals)

hole (an opening)
whole (complete)

its (possessive of *it*)
it's (contraction of *it is*)

know (to be certain)
no (the opposite of *yes*)

meat (flesh)
meet (encounter)

passed (past tense of *pass*)
past (after, or a time gone by)

patience (forbearance)
patients (persons under medical
 care)

peace (the absence of war)
piece (a portion of something)

plain (clear)
plane (a carpenter's tool, or an
 airborne vehicle)

presence (the state of being at
 hand)
presents (gifts)

principal (most important, or
 the head of a school)
principle (a basic truth or law)

rain (precipitation)
reign (to rule)
rein (a strap for an animal)

right (correct)
rite (a religious ceremony)
write (to make letters)

road (a surface for driving)
rode (past tense of *ride*)

scene (where an action occurs)
seen (past participle of *see*)

stationary (unmoving)
stationery (writing paper)

their (possessive of *they*)
there (opposite of *here*)
they're (contraction of *they are*)

to (toward)
too (also)
two (following *one*)

waist (the middle of the body)
waste (discarded material)

weak (not strong)
week (Sunday through Saturday)

weather (climate)
whether (*if,* or introducing a
 choice)

which (one of a group)
witch (a sorcerer)

who's (contraction of *who is*)
whose (possessive of *who*)

your (possessive of *you*)
you're (contraction of *you are*)

2 Different forms of the same word

Often, the noun form and the verb form of the same word are spelled differently: for example, *advice* (noun) and *advise* (verb). Sometimes the noun and the adjective forms of the same word differ: *height* and *high*. Similar changes occur in the parts of some irregular verbs (*know, knew, known*) and the plurals of irregular nouns (*man, men*).

3 American vs. British spellings ESL

If you learned English outside the United States, you may be accustomed to British rather than American spellings. Here are the chief differences:

American	British
color, humor	colour, humour
theater, center	theatre, centre
canceled, traveled	cancelled, travelled
judgment	judgement
realize, civilize	realise, civilise
connection	connexion

Your dictionary may list both spellings, but it will specially mark the British one with *chiefly Brit* or a similar label.

41b Follow spelling rules.

1 *ie* vs. *ei*

To distinguish between *ie* and *ei,* use the familiar jingle:

I before *e,* except after *c,* or when pronounced "ay" as in *neighbor* and *weigh.*

i before *e*	believe	thief	hygiene
ei after *c*	ceiling	conceive	perceive
ei sounded as "ay"	sleigh	eight	beige

Exceptions For some exceptions, remember this sentence:

The weird foreigner neither seizes leisure nor forfeits height.

2 Final *e*

When adding an ending to a word with a final *e,* drop the *e* if the ending begins with a vowel:

advise + able = advisable   surprise + ing = surprising

Keep the *e* if the ending begins with a consonant:

care + ful = careful   like + ly = likely

Exceptions Retain the *e* after a soft *c* or *g*, to keep the sound of the consonant soft rather than hard: *courageous, changeable.* And drop the *e* before a consonant when the *e* is preceded by another vowel: *argue + ment = argument, true + ly = truly.*

3   Final *y*

When adding an ending to a word with a final *y*, change the *y* to *i* if it follows a consonant:

beauty, beauties   worry, worried   supply, supplies

But keep the *y* if it follows a vowel, if it ends a proper name, or if the ending is *-ing:*

day, days   Minsky, Minskys   cry, crying

4   Final consonants

When adding an ending to a one-syllable word ending in a consonant, double the final consonant when it follows a single vowel. Otherwise, don't double the consonant.

slap, slapping   park, parking   pair, paired

In words of more than one syllable, double the final consonant when it follows a single vowel *and* ends a stressed syllable once the new ending is added. Otherwise, don't double the consonant.

refer, referring   refer, reference   relent, relented

5   Prefixes

When adding a prefix, do not drop a letter from or add a letter to the original word:

unnecessary   disappoint   misspell

6   Plurals

Most nouns form plurals by adding *s* to the singular form. Add *es* for the plural of nouns ending in *s, sh, ch,* or *x.*

boy, boys   kiss, kisses   church, churches

Nouns ending in *o* preceded by a vowel usually form the plural with *s.* Those ending in *o* preceded by a consonant usually form the plural with *es.*

ratio, ratios   hero, heroes

Some very common nouns form irregular plurals.

child, children   woman, women   mouse, mice

Some English nouns that were originally Italian, Greek, Latin, or French form the plural according to their original language:

analysis, analyses	criterion, criteria	piano, pianos
basis, bases	datum, data	thesis, theses
crisis, crises	medium, media	

A few such nouns may form irregular *or* regular plurals: for instance, *index, indices, indexes; curriculum, curricula, curriculums*. The regular plural is more contemporary.

With compound nouns, add *s* to the main word of the compound. Sometimes this main word is not the last word.

city-states	fathers-in-law	passersby

ESL Noncount nouns do not form plurals, either regularly (with an added *s*) or irregularly. Examples of noncount nouns include *equipment, intelligence,* and *wealth.* See page 202.

42 The Hyphen

Advice on using hyphens in compound words:

http://owl.english.purdue.edu/Files/18.html   From the Purdue Online Writing Lab.

http://webster.commnet.edu/HP/pages/darling/grammar/compounds.htm From the Guide to Grammar and Writing.

Use a hyphen to form compound words and to divide words at the ends of lines.

42a   Use the hyphen in some compound words.

1   Compound adjectives

When two or more words serve together as a single modifier before a noun, a hyphen forms the modifying words clearly into a unit.

She is a well-known actor.
Some Spanish-speaking students work as translators.

┌─ KEY TERM ───
COMPOUND WORD   A word expressing a combination of ideas, such as *cross-reference* or *crossroads.*
└──

When such a compound adjective follows the noun, the hyphen is unnecessary.

> The actor is well known.
> Many students are Spanish speaking.

The hyphen is also unnecessary in a compound modifier containing an -*ly* adverb, even before the noun: *clearly defined terms.*

When part of a compound adjective appears only once in two or more parallel compound adjectives, hyphens indicate which words the reader should mentally join with the missing part.

> School-age children should have eight- or nine-o'clock bedtimes.

2 Fractions and compound numbers

Hyphens join the numerator and denominator of fractions: *one-half, three-fourths.* Hyphens also join the parts of the whole numbers *twenty-one* to *ninety-nine.*

3 Prefixes and suffixes

Do not use hyphens with prefixes except as follows:

- With the prefixes *self-, all-,* and *ex-: self-control, all-inclusive, ex-student.*
- With a prefix before a capitalized word: *un-American.*
- With a capital letter before a word: *T-shirt.*
- To prevent misreading: *de-emphasize, re-create a story.*

The only suffix that regularly requires a hyphen is -*elect,* as in *president-elect.*

42b Use the hyphen to divide words at the ends of lines.

You can avoid occasional short lines in your documents by dividing some words between the end of one line and the beginning of the next. If you write on a word processor, you can set the program to divide words automatically at appropriate breaks (in the Tools menu, select Language and then Hyphenation). To divide words manually, follow these guidelines:

- Divide words only between syllables—for instance, *win-dows,* not *wi-ndows.* Check a dictionary for correct syllable breaks.
- Never divide a one-syllable word.
- Leave at least two letters on the first line and three on the second line. If a word cannot be divided to follow this rule (for instance, *a-bus-er*), don't divide it.

If you must break an electronic address—for instance, in a source citation—do so only after a slash. Do not hyphenate, because readers may perceive any added hyphen as part of the address.

> **Not**   http://www.library.miami.edu/staff/lmc/soc-
>   race.html
>
> **But**   http://www.library.miami.edu/staff/lmc/
>   socrace.html

43 Capital Letters

Information on using capital letters:

http://www.acusysinc.com/English/Capitalization.htm   From the Reference Guide to Grammar.

http://webster.commnet.edu/HP/pages/darling/grammar/capitals.htm
From the Guide to Grammar and Writing.

The following conventions and a desk dictionary can help you decide whether to capitalize a particular word in most writing. The social, natural, and applied sciences require specialized capitalization for terminology, such as *Conditions A and B* or *Escherichia coli.* Consult one of the style guides listed on page 338 for the requirements of the discipline you are writing in.

    Note A computerized grammar and style checker will flag overused capital letters and missing capitals at the beginnings of sentences. It will also spot missing capitals at the beginnings of proper nouns and adjectives—*if* the nouns and adjectives are in the checker's dictionary. For example, a checker caught *christianity* and *europe* but not *china* (for the country) or *Stephen king.* You'll need to proofread for capital letters on your own as well.

ESL Conventions of capitalization vary from language to language. English, for instance, is the only language to capitalize the first-person singular pronoun (*I*), and its practice of capitalizing proper nouns but not most common nouns also distinguishes it from some other languages.

43a   Capitalize the first word of every sentence.

Every writer should own a good dictionary.

When quoting other writers, you should reproduce the capital letters beginning their sentences or indicate that you have altered the source's capitalization. Whenever possible, integrate the quotation into your own sentence so that its capitalization coincides with yours:

> "Psychotherapists often overlook the benefits of self-deception," the author argues.

> The author argues that "the benefits of self-deception" are not always recognized by psychotherapists.

If you need to alter the capitalization in the source, indicate the change with brackets:

> "[T]he benefits of self-deception" are not always recognized by psychotherapists, the author argues.

> The author argues that "[p]sychotherapists often overlook the benefits of self-deception."

Note Capitalization of questions in a series is optional. Both of the following examples are correct:

> Is the population a hundred? Two hundred? More?
> Is the population a hundred? two hundred? more?

Also optional is capitalization of the first word in a complete sentence after a colon.

43b   Capitalize proper nouns, proper adjectives, and words used as essential parts of proper nouns.

1   Proper nouns and proper adjectives

PROPER NOUNS name specific persons, places, and things: *Shakespeare, California, World War I.* PROPER ADJECTIVES are formed from some proper nouns: *Shakespearean, Californian.* Capitalize all proper nouns and proper adjectives but not the articles (*a, an, the*) that precede them:

Proper nouns and adjectives to be capitalized

Specific persons and things

Stephen King	Boulder Dam
Napoleon Bonaparte	the Empire State Building

Specific places and geographical regions

New York City	the Mediterranean Sea
China	the Northeast, the South

But: northeast of the city, going south

Days of the week, months, holidays

Monday	Yom Kippur
May	Christmas

Historical events, documents, periods, movements

the Vietnam War	the Renaissance
the Constitution	the Romantic Movement

Government offices or departments and institutions

House of Representatives	Polk Municipal Court
Department of Defense	Northeast High School

Political, social, athletic, and other organizations and associations and their members

Democratic Party, Democrats	League of Women Voters
Sierra Club	Boston Celtics
B'nai B'rith	Chicago Symphony Orchestra

Races, nationalities, and their languages

Native American	Germans
African American	Swahili
Caucasian	Italian

But: blacks, whites

Religions, their followers, and terms for the sacred

Christianity, Christians	God
Catholicism, Catholics	Allah
Judaism, Orthodox Jews	the Bible [*but* biblical]
Islam, Muslims	the Koran

2 Common nouns used as essential parts of proper nouns

Capitalize the common nouns *street, avenue, park, river, ocean, lake, company, college, county,* and *memorial* when they are part of proper nouns naming specific places or institutions:

Main Street	Lake Superior
Central Park	Ford Motor Company
Mississippi River	Madison College
Pacific Ocean	George Washington Memorial

43c Capitalize most words in titles and subtitles of works.

Within your text, capitalize all the words in a title *except* the following: articles (*a, an, the*); *to* in infinitives; and connecting words (prepositions and conjunctions) of fewer than five letters. Capitalize even these short words when they are the first or last word in a title or when they fall after a colon or semicolon.

"Courtship Through the Ages" *Management: A New Theory*
A Diamond Is Forever "Once More to the Lake"
"Knowing Whom to Ask" *An End to Live For*
Learning from Las Vegas *File Under Architecture*

Note The style guides of the academic disciplines have their own rules for capitals in titles. For instance, MLA style for English and some other humanities capitalizes all subordinating conjunctions but no prepositions. In addition, APA style for the social sciences, CBE style for the sciences, and Columbia online style for the sciences capitalize only the first word and proper names in book and article titles within source citations (see pp. 397–407 on APA, 431–436 on CBE, and 444–448 on Columbia).

43d Capitalize titles preceding persons' names.

Before a person's name, capitalize his or her title. After or apart from the name, do not capitalize the title.

Professor Otto Osborne Otto Osborne, a professor
Doctor Jane Covington Jane Covington, a doctor
Governor Ella Moore Ella Moore, the governor

Note Many writers capitalize a title denoting very high rank even when it follows a name or is used alone: *Lyndon Johnson, past President of the United States.*

43e Use capitals according to convention in online communication.

Although common in electronic mail and other online communication, passages or whole messages written in all-capital letters or with no capital letters are difficult to read. Further, messages in all-capital letters may be taken as overly insistent, even rude (see also p. 65). Use capital letters according to rules 43a–43d in all your online communication.

44 Underlining or Italics

Information on using underlining or italics:

http://webster.commnet.edu/HP/pages/darling/grammar/italics.htm
From the Guide to Grammar and Writing.

http://www.esc.edu/htmlpages/writer/pandg/italic.htm From the State University of New York.

Underlining and *italic type* indicate the same thing: the word or words are being distinguished or emphasized. If you underline two or more words in a row, underline the space between the words, too: Criminal Statistics: Misuses of Numbers.

Note Computerized grammar and style checkers cannot recognize problems with underlining or italics. Check your work yourself to ensure that you have used highlighting appropriately.

44a Use underlining or italics consistently and appropriately for your writing situation.

Word processors have made italic type possible in papers and other documents, and it is now used almost universally in business and some academic disciplines. Still, other disciplines continue to prefer underlining, especially in source citations. (The *MLA Handbook for Writers of Research Papers* and the *Publication Manual of the American Psychological Association* both call for underlining. See pp. 354 and 398, respectively.) Ask your instructor for his or her own preferences.

Depending on your instructor's preferences, use either italics or underlining consistently throughout a document. For instance, if you are writing an English paper and following MLA style for underlining in source citations, use underlining in the body of your paper as well.

44b Underline or italicize the titles of works that appear independently.

Within your text underline or italicize the titles of works, such as books and periodicals, that are published, released, or produced separately from other works. (See the box on the next page.) Use quotation marks for all other titles, such as songs, essays, short stories, articles in periodicals, and episodes of television series. (See pp. 249–250.)

Titles to be underlined or italicized

Other titles should be placed in quotation marks (see pp. 249–250).

Books
War and Peace
And the Band Played On

Plays
Hamlet
The Phantom of the Opera

Pamphlets
The Truth About Alcoholism

Long musical works
Tchaikovsky's Swan Lake
But: Symphony in C

Television and radio programs
The Shadow
NBC Sports Hour

Long poems
Beowulf
Paradise Lost

Periodicals
Time
Philadelphia Inquirer

Published speeches
Lincoln's Gettysburg Address

Movies and videotapes
Schindler's List
How to Relax

Works of visual art
Michelangelo's David
the Mona Lisa

Exceptions Legal documents, the Bible, the Koran, and their parts are generally not underlined or italicized:

Not   We studied the Book of Revelation in the Bible.
But   We studied the Book of Revelation in the Bible.

44c   Underline or italicize the names of ships, aircraft, spacecraft, and trains.

Challenger   Orient Express   Queen Elizabeth 2
Apollo XI   Montrealer   Spirit of St. Louis

44d   Underline or italicize foreign words that are not part of the English language.

A foreign expression should be underlined or italicized when it has not been absorbed into our language. A dictionary will say whether a word is still considered foreign to English.

The scientific name for the brown trout is <u>Salmo trutta</u>. [The Latin scientific names for plants and animals are always underlined or italicized.]

The Latin <u>De gustibus non est disputandum</u> translates roughly as "There's no accounting for taste."

44e Underline or italicize words or characters named as words.

Use underlining or italics to indicate that you are citing a character or word as a word rather than using it for its meaning. Words you are defining fall under this convention.

The word <u>syzygy</u> refers to a straight line formed by three celestial bodies, as in the alignment of the earth, sun, and moon.

Some people say <u>th</u>, as in <u>thought</u>, with a faint <u>s</u> or <u>f</u> sound.

44f Occasionally, underlining or italics may be used for emphasis.

Underlining or italics can stress an important word or phrase, especially in reporting how someone said something. But use such emphasis very rarely, or your writing may sound immature or hysterical.

44g In online communication, use alternatives for underlining or italics.

 Electronic mail and other forms of online communication often do not allow conventional highlighting such as underlining or italics for the purposes described in this chapter. The program may not be able to produce the highlighting or may reserve it for a special function. (On World Wide Web sites, for instance, underlining indicates a link to another site.)

To distinguish book titles and other elements that usually require underlining or italics, type an underscore before and after the element: *Measurements coincide with those in _Joule's Handbook_.* You can also emphasize words with asterisks before and after: *I *will not* be able to attend.*

Don't use all-capital letters for emphasis; they yell too loudly. (See also p. 270.)

45 Abbreviations

Information on abbreviations:

 http://www.acusysinc.com/English/Abbreviations.htm   From the Reference Guide to Grammar.

http://www.esc.edu/htmlpages/writer/pandg/abbrev.htm   From the State University of New York.

The following guidelines on abbreviations pertain to the text of a nontechnical document. All academic disciplines use abbreviations in source citations, and much technical writing, such as in the sciences and engineering, uses many abbreviations in the document text. Consult one of the style guides listed on page 338 for the in-text requirements of the discipline you are writing in.

Usage varies, but writers increasingly omit periods from abbreviations of two or more words written in all-capital letters: *US, BA, USMC.* See pages 225–226 on punctuating abbreviations.

 Note A computerized grammar and style checker may flag some abbreviations, such as *in.* (for *inch*) and *st.* (for *street*). A spelling checker will flag abbreviations it does not recognize. But neither checker can tell you whether an abbreviation is appropriate for your writing situation or will be clear to your readers.

45a   Use standard abbreviations for titles immediately before and after proper names.

Before the name	After the name
Dr. James Hsu	James Hsu, MD
Mr., Mrs., Ms., Hon.,	DDS, DVM, Ph.D.,
St., Rev., Msgr., Gen.	Ed.D., OSB, SJ, Sr., Jr.

Do not use abbreviations such as *Rev., Hon., Prof., Rep., Sen., Dr.,* and *St.* (for *Saint*) unless they appear before a proper name.

45b   Familiar abbreviations and acronyms are acceptable in most writing.

An ACRONYM is an abbreviation that spells a pronounceable word, such as WHO, NATO, and AIDS. These and other abbreviations using initials are acceptable in most writing as long as they are familiar to readers.

Institutions	LSU, UCLA, TCU
Organizations	CIA, FBI, YMCA, AFL-CIO

Corporations	IBM, CBS, ITT
People	JFK, LBJ, FDR
Countries	US, USA

Note If a name or term (such as *operating room*) appears often in a piece of writing, then its abbreviation (*OR*) can cut down on extra words. Spell out the full term at its first appearance, indicate its abbreviation in parentheses, and then use the abbreviation.

45c Use *BC, AD, AM, PM, no.,* and *$* only with specific dates and numbers.

| 44 BC | 11:26 AM (*or* a.m.) | no. 36 (*or* No. 36) |
| AD 1492 | 8:05 PM (*or* p.m.) | $7.41 |

The abbreviation BC ("before Christ") always follows a date, whereas AD (*anno Domini,* Latin for "in the year of the Lord") precedes a date.

Note BCE ("before the common era") and CE ("common era") are increasingly replacing BC and AD, respectively. Both follow the date: *44 BCE, 1492 CE.*

45d Generally reserve Latin abbreviations for source citations and comments in parentheses.

i.e.	*id est:* that is
cf.	*confer:* compare
e.g.	*exempli gratia:* for example
et al.	*et alii:* and others
etc.	*et cetera:* and so forth
NB	*nota bene:* note well

He said he would be gone a fortnight (i.e., two weeks).
Bloom et al., editors, *Anthology of Light Verse*
Trees, too, are susceptible to disease (e.g., Dutch elm disease).

(Note that these abbreviations are generally not italicized or underlined.)

Some writers avoid these abbreviations in formal writing, even within parentheses.

45e Use *Inc., Bros., Co.,* or *&* (for *and*) only in official names of business firms.

Not The Santini <u>bros.</u> operate a large moving firm in New York City <u>&</u> environs.

But   The Santini <u>brothers</u> operate a large moving firm in New York City <u>and</u> environs.

Or   Santini <u>Bros.</u> is a large moving firm in New York City <u>and</u> environs.

45f Generally spell out units of measurement and names of places, calendar designations, people, and courses.

In most academic, general, and business writing, the types of words listed below should always be spelled out. (In source citations and technical writing, however, these words are more often abbreviated.)

Units of measurement
The dog is thirty <u>inches</u> [not <u>in.</u>] high.

Geographical names
The publisher is in <u>Massachusetts</u> [not <u>Mass.</u> or <u>MA</u>].

Names of days, months, and holidays
The truce was signed on <u>Tuesday</u> [not <u>Tues.</u>], <u>April</u> [not <u>Apr.</u>] 16.

Names of people
<u>Robert</u> [not <u>Robt.</u>] Frost writes accessible poems.

Courses of instruction
I'm majoring in <u>political science</u> [not <u>poli. sci.</u>].

---

46 Numbers

Advice on using numbers:

http://webster.commnet.edu/HP/pages/darling/grammar/numbers.htm
From the Guide to Grammar and Writing.

http://researchpaper.com/writing_center/23.html   From Researchpaper.com.

This chapter addresses the use of numbers (numerals versus words) in the text of a document. All disciplines use many more numerals in source citations.

Note Computerized grammar and style checkers will flag numerals beginning sentences and can be customized to ignore or to look for numerals (see pp. 60–61). But they can't tell you whether numerals or spelled-out numbers are appropriate for your writing situation.

46a Use numerals according to standard practice in the field you are writing in.

Always use numerals for numbers that require more than two words to spell out:

> The leap year has <u>366</u> days.
> The population of <u>Minot</u>, North Dakota, is about <u>32,800</u>.

In nontechnical academic writing, spell out numbers of one or two words:

> <u>Twelve</u> nations signed the treaty.
> The ball game drew <u>forty-two thousand</u> people. [A hyphenated number may be considered one word.]

In much business writing, use numerals for all numbers over ten: *five reasons, 11 participants.* In technical academic and business writing, such as in science and engineering, use numerals for all numbers over ten, and use numerals for zero through nine when they refer to exact measurements: *2 liters, 1 hour.* (Consult one of the style guides listed on p. 338 for more details.)

Note Use a combination of numerals and words for round numbers over a million: *26 million, 2.45 billion.* And use either all numerals or all words when several numbers appear together in a passage, even if convention would require a mixture.

ESL In American English a comma separates the numerals in long numbers (*26,000*), and a period functions as a decimal point (*2.06*).

46b Use numerals according to convention for dates, addresses, and other information.

Days and years

| June 18, 1985 | AD 12 | 456 BC | 1999 |

Pages, chapters, volumes, acts, scenes, lines

Chapter 9, page 123
Hamlet, act 5, scene 3

Decimals, percentages, and fractions

22.5   3½
48% (*or* 48 percent)

Addresses	Scores and statistics
355 Clinton Avenue	21 to 7 a ratio of 8 to 1
Washington, DC 20036	a mean of 26

Exact amounts of money	The time of day
$3.5 million $4.50	9:00 AM 3:45 PM

Exceptions Round dollar or cent amounts of only a few words may be expressed in words: *seventeen dollars; sixty cents.* When the word *o'clock* is used for the time of day, also express the number in words: *two o'clock* (not *2 o'clock*).

46c   Spell out numbers that begin sentences.

For clarity, spell out any number that begins a sentence. If the number requires more than two words, reword the sentence so that the number falls later and can be expressed as a numeral.

Not   <u>3.5 billion</u> people live in Asia.
But   The population of Asia is <u>3.5 billion</u>.

VII

Research and Documentation

VII

Research and Documentation

http://www.criticalthinking.org/K12/k12class/strat/stratall.nclk   An extensive list of strategies for critical thinking and writing, from the Foundation for Critical Thinking.

http://www.colostate.edu/Depts/WritingCenter/references/reading/ critread/page1.htm   Extensive guidance on reading critically, from Colorado State University.

http://www.its-ps.uni.edu:206/reineke/developi.htm   Strategies for critical writing, from the University of Northern Iowa.

http://commhum.mccneb.edu/argument/summary.htm   A tutorial for reading arguments critically, from Metropolitan Community College.

http://www.eslplanet.com/teachertools/argueweb/frntpage.htm   A guide to reading and writing arguments, from the ESL Planet.

http://www.powa.org/argufrms.htm   Extensive guidance on writing arguments, from Paradigm Online Writing Assistant.

Throughout college and beyond, you will be expected to think, read, and write critically. CRITICAL here does not mean "negative" but "skeptical," "exacting," "creative." You already operate critically every day as you figure out why things happen to you or what your experiences mean. Critical thinking is also an important skill in conducting research. This chapter introduces more formal methods for thinking and reading critically.

In college and work, much of your critical thinking will focus on written texts (a short story, a journal article, an Internet posting, a site on the World Wide Web) or on visual objects (a photograph, a chart, a film). Like all subjects worthy of critical consideration, such works operate on at least three levels: (1) what the creator actually says or shows, (2) what the creator does not say or show but builds into the work (intentionally or not), and (3) what you think. Discovering each level of the work, even if it is visual, involves four main steps: previewing the material, reading actively, summarizing, and forming a critical response.

ESL   The idea of reading critically may require you to make some adjustments if readers in your native culture tend to seek understanding or agreement more than engagement from what they read. Readers of English use texts for all kinds of reasons, including pleasure, reinforcement, and information. But they also read skeptically, critically, to see the author's motives, test their own ideas, and arrive at new knowledge.

47a   Previewing the material

When you're reading a work of literature, such as a short story or a poem, it's often best just to plunge right in (see p. 451). But for critical reading of other works, it's worthwhile to form some expectations and even some preliminary questions before you start reading word for word. Your reading will be more informed and fruitful.

Use the following questions as a previewing guide:

- *Length:* Is the material brief enough to read in one sitting, or do you need more time? To gauge the length of an online source such as a Web site, study any menus for an indication of the source's complexity. Then scroll through a couple of pages and follow a couple of links to estimate the overall length.
- *Facts of publication:* Does the date of publication suggest currency or datedness? Does the publisher or publication specialize in a particular kind of material—scholarly articles, say, or popular books? For a Web source, who or what sponsors the site: an individual? a nonprofit organization? an academic institution? a corporation? a government body? (See pp. 68 and 322 on reading electronic addresses.)
- *Content cues:* What do the title, summary or abstract, headings, illustrations, and other features tell you? What questions do they raise in your mind?
- *Author:* What does the biographical information tell you about the author's publications, interests, biases, and reputation in the field? For an online message, which may be posted by an unfamiliar or anonymous author, what can you gather about the author from his or her words? If possible, trace unfamiliar authors to learn more about them. (See p. 322.)
- *Yourself:* Do you anticipate particular difficulties with the content? What biases of your own may influence your response to the text—for instance, anxiety, curiosity, boredom, or an outlook similar or opposed to that of the author?

47b   Reading actively

Reading is itself more than a one-step process. Your primary goal is to understand the first level on which the text operates—what the author actually says.

The first time through new material, read as steadily and smoothly as possible, trying to get the gist of what the author is saying and a sense of his or her tone. Then reread the material *slowly* to grasp its content and how it is constructed. That means stopping to puzzle out a paragraph if you didn't get the point, looking up words in a dictionary, or following links at a Web site.

Use your pen, pencil, or keyboard freely to annotate the text or make separate notes. In the following example, a student annotates the introductory paragraphs of "Student Loans," an essay by the economist and columnist Thomas Sowell:

> The first lesson of economics is scarcity: There is never enough of anything to fully satisfy all those who want it.
>
> The first lesson of politics is to disregard the first lesson of economics. When politicians discover some group that is being vocal about not having as much as they want, the "solution" is to give them more. Where do politicians get this "more"? They rob Peter to pay Paul.
>
> After a while, of course, they discover that Peter doesn't have enough. Bursting with compassion, politicians rush to the rescue. Needless to say, they do not admit that robbing Peter to pay Paul was a dumb idea in the first place. On the contrary, they now rob Tom, Dick, and Harry to help Peter.
>
> The latest chapter in this long-running saga is that politicians have now suddenly discovered that many college students graduate heavily in debt. To politicians it follows, as the night follows the day, that the government should come to their rescue with the taxpayers' money.

Annotations (right margin):
- *Basic contradiction between economics and politics*
- ← *biblical reference?*
- *ironic and dismissive language*
- *politicians= fools? or irresponsible?*

(After this introduction, Sowell discusses several reasons why government student-loan programs should not be expanded: they benefit many who don't need financial help, they make college possible for many who aren't serious about education, and they contribute to rising college tuitions.)

47c Summarizing

A good way to master the content of a text and see its strengths and weaknesses is to SUMMARIZE it: distill it to its main points, in your own words. Here is one procedure for summarizing:

- Look up words or concepts you don't know so that you understand the author's sentences and how they relate to each other.
- Work through the text to identify its sections—single paragraphs or groups of paragraphs focused on a single topic, related pages or links in a Web site. To understand how parts of

a work relate to each other, try drawing a tree diagram or creating an outline (pp. 24–27). Although both tools work well for straight text, the tree diagram may work better for nonlinear material such as a Web site.

- Write a one- or two-sentence summary of each section you identify. Focus on the main point of the section, omitting examples, facts, and other supporting evidence.

The following sentence summarizes the first four paragraphs of Thomas Sowell's "Student Loans," on the previous page:

> As their support of the government's student loan program illustrates, politicians ignore the economic reality that using resources to benefit one group (students in debt) involves taking the resources from another group (taxpayers).

Note When you write a summary, using your own words will ensure that you avoid plagiarism. Even when the summary is in your own words, if you use it in something written for others you must cite the source of the ideas. See pp. 329–333.

47d Forming a critical response

Once you've grasped the content of what you're reading—what the author says—then you can turn to understanding what the author does not say outright but suggests or implies or even lets slip. At this stage you are concerned with the purpose or intention of the author and with how he or she carries it out.

Critical thinking and reading consist of four overlapping operations: analyzing, interpreting, synthesizing, and (often) evaluating.

1 Analyzing

ANALYSIS is the separation of something into its parts or elements, the better to understand it. To see these elements in what you are reading, begin with a question that reflects your purpose in analyzing the text: why you are curious about it or what you're trying to make out of it. This question will serve as a kind of lens that highlights some features and not others.

For an example, look at the screen shot on page 285, showing the home page of a Web site that offers relief from student-loan debt. Analyzing this page, you might ask what kind of organization

┌─KEY TERM──

PLAGIARISM Representing someone else's work as your own or closely adhering to the content or arrangement of work other than your own, without citation. Plagiarism is a serious ethical violation; it is literally stealing someone else's ideas.

the Federated Loan Consolidation Corporation is or what its intentions are. Answering either question, you would examine the address of the site (in the field at the top of the page), the organization's name, the paragraph of text, and the design of the page—its use of type, color, and decorative elements.

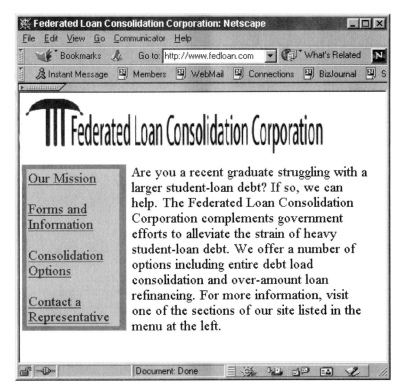

2 Interpreting

Identifying the elements of something is of course only the beginning: you also need to interpret the meaning or significance of the elements and of the whole. Interpretation usually requires you to infer the author's ASSUMPTIONS—that is, opinions or beliefs about what is or what could or should be. (*Infer* means to draw a conclusion based on evidence.)

Assumptions are pervasive: we all adhere to certain values, beliefs, and opinions. But assumptions are not always stated outright. Speakers and writers may judge that their audience already understands and accepts their assumptions; they may not even be aware of their assumptions; or they may deliberately refrain from stating their assumptions for fear that the audience will disagree. That is why your job as a critical thinker is to interpret what the assumptions are.

To discover assumptions of the Federated Loan Consolidation Corporation (previous page), you would look at the address of the Web site, where *com* indicates that the organization is a commercial entity. (See pp. 68 and 322 for more on interpreting electronic addresses.) Yet you might also notice that the page does not resemble those of other corporate sites, which typically have flashier designs incorporating more images, color, and boxes, among other elements. Instead, the page's look is rather plain—the sort of design you might expect from a government site. The prominent *Federated* in the organization's name and *complements government efforts* in the text reinforce the appearance of a government connection. These findings might lead you to infer the following:

> The Federated Loan Consolidation Corporation assumes that its readers (potential customers) will be more willing to explore its refinancing options if they believe that it is a reliable organization somehow affiliated with the government.

3 Synthesizing

If you stopped at analysis and interpretation, critical thinking and reading might leave you with a pile of elements and possible meanings but no vision of the whole. With SYNTHESIS you make connections among parts *or* among wholes. You create a new whole by drawing conclusions about relationships and implications.

The following conclusion draws on elements of the Federated Loan Consolidation Corporation home page and the inference above about the company's understanding of its readers:

> The Federated Loan Consolidation Corporation uses its name, a mention of the government, and a restrained design to appeal to potential customers who may be wary of commercial lending operations.

With synthesis, you create something different from what you started with. To the uncritical reader (perhaps someone burdened with student loans), the home page of the Federated Loan Consolidation Corporation might seem to offer government-backed relief from debt. To you—after analysis, interpretation, and synthesis— the official-looking page is a kind of mask worn by a commercial lender. The difference depends entirely on the critical reading.

4 Evaluating

Much critical reading and writing ends at synthesis: you form and explain your understanding of what the work says and doesn't say. If you are also expected to EVALUATE the work, however, you will go further to judge its quality and significance. You may be evaluating a source you've discovered in research (see pp. 320–324), or you may be completing an assignment to state and defend a judgment, a statement such as *The author does not summon the evidence to support her case* or *On the home page of the Federated Loan Consolidation Corporation, a commercial lender attempts to mislead vulnerable customers by wearing the reassuring costume of government.*

Evaluation takes a certain amount of confidence. You may think that you lack the expertise to cast judgment on another's work, especially if the work is difficult or the author well known. True, the more informed you are, the better a critical reader you are. But conscientious reading and analysis will give you the internal authority to judge a work *as it stands* and *as it seems to you,* against your own unique bundle of experiences, observations, and attitudes.

48

48 Research Strategy

Advice on research writing:

http://webster.commnet.edu/mla.htm   From Capital Community College.

http://www.ipl.org/teen/aplus/stepfirst.htm   From the Internet Public Library.

http://www.wisc.edu/writetest/Handbook/PlanResearchPaper.html From the University of Wisconsin at Madison.

http://karn.ohiolink.edu/~sg-ysu/process.html   From Youngstown State University.

A college research paper, sometimes called a term paper, involves searching through what others have written about a subject, reading critically to understand it, reporting your findings, and synthesizing those findings to come to a conclusion supported by that data. This type of research is called *practical research.* It seeks out published material that may be new to you but that is recorded, public knowledge. Research that establishes knowledge that is new to everyone is called *original* or *primary research.* To distinguish between these two types of research, you may be asked to conduct some original research to supplement your practical research. However, the majority of your college research papers will involve reading the research findings of others.

Even though your research paper uses the works of others, your finished product should be original. Before you begin your research, you will be asked to formulate a research question or a hypothesis. Research writing gives you a chance to apply critical thinking and to work like a detective solving a case. The mystery is the answer to the question you posed. The search for the answer leads you to consider what others think about your subject, but you do more than simply report their views. You build on them to develop and support your own opinion, and ultimately you become an expert in your own right.

Your investigation will be more productive and enjoyable if you take some steps described in this chapter: plan your work (below), keep a research journal (p. 289), find an appropriate topic and research question (p. 289), set goals for your research (p. 291), and keep a working bibliography (p. 295).

48a

48a   Planning your work

Research writing is a *writing* process:

- You work within a particular situation of subject, purpose, audience, and other factors (see Chapter 2).
- You gather ideas and information about your subject (Chapter 3).
- You focus and arrange your ideas (Chapter 4).
- You draft to explore your meaning (Chapter 5).
- You revise and edit to develop, shape, and polish (Chapter 6).

Although the process seems neatly sequential in this list, you know from experience that the stages overlap—that, for instance, you may begin drafting before you've gathered all the information you expect to find, and then while drafting you may discover a source that causes you to rethink your approach. Anticipating the process of research writing can free you to be flexible in your search and open to discoveries.

A thoughtful plan and systematic procedures can help you follow through on the diverse activities of research writing. One step is to make a schedule like the one below that apportions the available time to the necessary work.

Complete
by:
_____   1. Setting a schedule and beginning a research journal (here and below)
_____   2. Finding a researchable topic and question (facing page)
_____   3. Setting research goals (p. 291)

_____ 4. Finding sources, both print and electronic (p. 298), and making a working bibliography (p. 295)

_____ 5. Evaluating and synthesizing sources (pp. 320, 324)
_____ 6. Taking notes using summary, paraphrase, and direct quotation (p. 325) and avoiding plagiarism (p. 329)

_____ 7. Developing a thesis statement and creating a structure (p. 338)
_____ 8. Drafting the paper (p. 339), integrating summaries, paraphrases, and direct quotations into your ideas (p. 334)

_____ 9. Revising and editing the paper (p. 340)
_____ 10. Citing sources in your text (p. 337)
_____ 11. Preparing the list of works cited or references (p. 337)
_____ 12. Preparing the final manuscript (p. 341)
_____ Final paper due

You can estimate that each segment marked off by a horizontal line will occupy _roughly_ one-quarter of the total time—for example, a week in a four-week assignment or two weeks in an eight-week assignment. The most unpredictable segments are the first two, so it's wise to get started early enough to accommodate the unexpected.

48b   Keeping a research journal

While working on a research project, carry index cards or a notebook with you at all times to use as a RESEARCH JOURNAL, a place to record your activities and ideas. (See p. 12 on journal keeping.) In the journal's dated entries, you can write about the sources you consult, the leads you want to pursue, any difficulties you encounter, and, most important, your thoughts about sources, leads, difficulties, new directions, relationships, and anything else that strikes you. The very act of writing in the journal can expand and clarify your thinking.

The research journal is the place for tracking and developing your own ideas. Notes on what your sources actually say should be taken and organized separately, as discussed on pages 325–326.

48c   Finding a researchable topic and question

Before reading this section, you may want to review the suggestions given in Chapter 2 for finding and narrowing a writing subject

48c

(pp. 4–5). Generally, the same procedure applies to writing any kind of research paper. However, selecting and limiting a topic for a research paper can present special opportunities and problems. And before you proceed with your topic, you'll want to transform it into a research question or hypothesis that can guide your search for sources.

1 Appropriate topic

Seek a research subject that interests you and that you care about. (It may be a subject you've already written about without benefit of research.) Starting with your own views will motivate you, and you will be a participant in a dialogue when you begin examining sources.

When you settle on a topic, ask the following questions about it. For each requirement, there are corresponding pitfalls.

- Are ample sources of information available on the topic?

  Avoid very recent topics, such as a newly announced medical discovery or a breaking story in today's newspaper.

- Does the topic encourage research in the kinds and number of sources required by the assignment?

  Avoid (*a*) topics that depend entirely on personal opinion and experience, such as the virtues of your hobby, and (*b*) topics that require research in only one source, such as a straight factual biography.

- Will the topic lead you to an objective assessment of sources and to defensible conclusions?

  Avoid topics that rest entirely on belief or prejudice, such as when human life begins or why women (or men) are superior. Your readers are unlikely to be swayed from their own beliefs.

- Does the topic suit the length of paper assigned and the time given for research and writing?

  Avoid broad topics that have too many sources to survey adequately, such as a major event in history.

2 Research question or hypothesis

Focus your research by constructing a research question or a hypothesis about your topic that can give direction to your research. A research question is similar to a thesis statement in an essay, but it is formed as an objective question you plan to answer by doing the research.

If you already have a strong opinion about the topic or what you think you will find when you conduct the research, you may be better served by formulating a hypothesis instead of a research question. A hypothesis is an assumption or tentative conclusion that is subject to verification or proof through further investigation. When you form a hypothesis, you state what you expect the research will show. Then, you suspend judgment and objectively investigate the published research to see if your hypothesis is correct. To discover your question or hypothesis, consider what about your subject intrigues or perplexes you, what you'd like to know more about. (See below for suggestions on using your own knowledge.)

Try to narrow your research question or hypothesis so that you can answer it in the time and space you have available. On some subjects, you may discover that a great deal has been written, and you may have to narrow your topic to make it manageable. With other subjects, you may have difficulty locating enough information to write your paper, and you must broaden the scope of your research. The question *How will the Internet affect business?* is very broad, encompassing issues as diverse as electronic commerce, information management, and employee training. In contrast, the question *How will Internet commerce benefit consumers?* or *How, if at all, should Internet commerce be taxed?* is much narrower. Each question also requires more than a simple *yes* or *no* answer, so that answering, even tentatively, demands thought about pros and cons, causes and effects.

So, a research paper requires that you do some preliminary research, plan your strategy, and follow a systematic approach to gathering data. (See p. 17 for information regarding how to conduct preliminary research.) As you read and write, your question or hypothesis will probably evolve to reflect your increasing knowledge of the subject.

48d

48d Setting goals for the search

Before you start looking for sources, consider what you already know about your subject and where you are likely to find information on it.

1 Your own knowledge

Discovering what you already know about your topic will guide you in discovering what you don't know. Take some time to spell out facts you have learned, opinions you have heard or read elsewhere, and of course your own opinions. Use one of the discovery techniques discussed in Chapter 3 to explore and develop your ideas: keeping a journal (p. 12 and also p. 289), observing your surroundings (p. 13), freewriting (p. 14), brainstorming (p. 15), clustering (p. 16), asking questions (p. 18), and thinking critically (p. 19).

When you've explored your thoughts, make a list of questions for which you don't have answers, whether factual (*What laws govern taxes in Internet commerce?*) or more open-ended (*Who benefits from a tax-free Internet? Who doesn't benefit?*). These questions will give you clues about the sources you need to look for first.

2 Kinds of sources

For many research projects, you'll want to consult a mix of sources, as described below. You may start by seeking the outlines of your topic—the range and depth of opinions about it—in reference works and articles in popular periodicals or through a search of the World Wide Web. Then, as you refine your views and your research question, you'll move on to more specialized sources, such as scholarly books and periodicals and your own interviews or surveys. (See pp. 298–318 for more on each kind of source.)

Print and online sources

 The sources housed in a traditional library—mainly reference works, periodicals, and books—have two big advantages over most of what you'll find on the Internet: they are cataloged and indexed for easy retrieval; and they are generally reliable, having been screened first by their publishers and then by the library's staff. In contrast, the Internet's retrieval systems are more numerous and can be more difficult to use. Online sources must also be evaluated to verify the reliability of the information. Much of the information posted on the World Wide Web does not pass through any screening before being posted.

Although the University of Phoenix Library Online Collection is accessed via the World Wide Web, most of its resources consist of subscription services to online scholarly journals, reference works, magazines, and newspapers that are published both in print and online. Like all material you gather in your research, the sources in this collection must be read critically. However, the material is screened by the publishers and the owners of the databases that house this information before it is made available on the University of Phoenix Web site. An extensive online library collection such as this provides students with almost unlimited opportunities for research and access to documents published around the world.

Your University of Phoenix instructors may expect you to consider print sources found in traditional libraries, credible sources you locate on the Internet, or online sources you discover on the University of Phoenix Library Online Collection. In some cases, you may be asked to conduct primary, or original, research yourself as part of your assignment. Make sure you understand the types of sources acceptable for your research assignments. For guidelines on evaluating both print and online sources, see pages 320–324.

48d

Primary and secondary sources

As much as possible, you should rely on PRIMARY SOURCES, or firsthand accounts: historical documents (letters, speeches, and so on), eyewitness reports, works of literature, reports on experiments or surveys conducted by the writer, or your own interviews, experiments, observations, or correspondence.

In contrast, SECONDARY SOURCES report and analyze information drawn from other sources, often primary ones: a reporter's summary of a controversial issue, a historian's account of a battle, a critic's reading of a poem, a physicist's evaluation of several studies. Secondary sources may contain helpful summaries and interpretations that direct, support, and extend your own thinking. However, most research-writing assignments expect your own ideas to go beyond those in such sources.

Scholarly and popular sources

The scholarship of acknowledged experts is essential for depth, authority, and specificity. The general-interest views and information of popular sources can help you apply more scholarly approaches to daily life.

- *Check the publisher.* Is it a scholarly journal (such as *Education Forum*) or a publisher of scholarly books (such as Harvard University Press), or is it a popular magazine (such as *Time* or *Newsweek*) or a publisher of popular books (such as Little, Brown)?
- *Check the author.* Have you seen the name elsewhere, which might suggest that the author is an expert?
- *Check the title.* Is it technical, or does it use a general vocabulary?

- *Check the electronic address.* Addresses for Internet sources often include an abbreviation that tells you something about the source: *edu* means the source comes from an educational institution, *gov* from a government body, *org* from a nonprofit organization, *com* from a commercial organization such as a corporation. (See pp. 68 and 322 for more on interpreting electronic addresses.)

Older and newer sources

Check the publication date. For most subjects a combination of older, established sources (such as books) and current sources (such as newspaper articles, interviews, or Web sites) will provide both background and up-to-date information. Only historical subjects or very current subjects require an emphasis on one extreme or another.

Impartial and biased sources

Seek a range of viewpoints. Sources that attempt to be impartial can offer an overview of your subject and trustworthy facts. Sources with clear biases can offer a diversity of opinion. Of course, to discover bias, you may have to read the source carefully (see pp. 321–322); but even a bibliographical listing can be informative.

- *Check the author.* You may have heard of the author as a respected researcher (thus more likely to be objective) or as a leading proponent of a certain view (less likely to be objective).
- *Check the title.* It may reveal something about point of view. (Consider these contrasting titles: "Keep the Internet Tax-Free" and "Taxation of Electronic Commerce: Issues and Questions.")

Note Online sources must be approached with particular care. See pp. 322–324.

Sources with helpful features

Depending on your topic and how far along your research is, you may want to look for sources with features such as illustrations (which can clarify important concepts), bibliographies (which can direct you to other sources), and indexes (which can help you develop keywords for electronic searches; see p. 300).

48d

48e   Keeping a working bibliography

When you begin searching for sources, it may be tempting to pursue each possibility as you come across it. But that approach would prove inefficient and probably ineffective. Instead, you'll want to find out the full range of sources available and then decide on a good number to consult. For a paper of 1800 to 2500 words, try for ten to thirty promising titles as a start.

To keep track of where sources are and what they are, make a WORKING BIBLIOGRAPHY, a file of books, articles, Web sites, and other possibilities. By making a complete list, you'll have a record of all the

48e

Information for a working bibliography

For books

Library call number
Name(s) of author(s), editor(s), translator(s), or others listed
Title and subtitle
Publication data:
  Place of publication
  Publisher's name
  Date of publication
Other important data, such as edition or volume number

For periodical articles

Name(s) of author(s)
Title and subtitle of article
Title of periodical
Publication data:
  Volume number and issue number (if any) in which article appears
  Date of issue
  Page numbers on which article appears

For electronic sources

Name(s) of author(s)
Title and subtitle
Publication data if source is also published in print

Electronic publication data:
  Date of release, online posting, or latest revision
  Name and vendor (or publisher) of a database or name of an online service or network (America Online, Lexis-Nexis, etc.)
  Medium (CD-ROM, online, etc.)
  Format of online source (e-mail, Web page, etc.)
Date you consulted the source
Search terms used to reach the source (for a database)
Complete electronic address

For other sources

Name(s) of author(s), government department, recording artist, or others listed
Title of the work
Format, such as unpublished letter or live performance
Publication or production data:
  Publisher's or producer's name
  Date of publication, release, or production
  Identifying numbers (if any)

information you'll need to find worthwhile sources and, eventually, to acknowledge them in your paper. Some researchers keep their style guides handy and create their working bibliography in proper MLA or APA style. This way, they are assured of having all the data they need for proper citation of their sources. When you have a substantial file, you can decide which sources seem most promising and look them up first or, if necessary, order them through interlibrary loan.

Note Some instructors require that the working bibliography be submitted on note cards (one source to a card), and this system has the advantage of allowing the sources to be shuffled easily. But many researchers have abandoned note cards because computers can print out source information, sort sources, and even transfer data to the user's own disk. (See p. 299.)

1 Source information

When you turn in your paper, you will be expected to attach a list of the sources you have used. So that readers can check or follow up on your sources, your list must include all the information needed to find the sources, in a format readers can understand. (See pp. 337–338.) The box on page 295 shows the information you should record for each type of source so that you will not have to retrace your steps later. (You can download the lists in the box from this book's Web site at *http://www.awlonline.com/littlebrown*. Then copy the appropriate list for each source and fill in the appropriate information.)

2 Bibliographic information for online sources

 Unlike that for printed materials, publication information for online sources can be difficult to find and make sense of. The screen shot on page 297 shows the first page of a Web site. Circled numbers refer to the following numbered explanations.

1. The source's address, or URL, usually appears in the Web browser's Address or Location field near the top of the screen. If the field does not appear, adjust the settings of the browser so that it displays the field.
2. Use as the source title the title of the page you are consulting. This information usually appears as a heading at the top of the page, but if not it may also appear in the bar along the top of the browser window.
3. Important information often appears at or near the bottom of each page. Look here for (*a*) the name of the author or the sponsoring organization, (*b*) an address for reaching the spon-

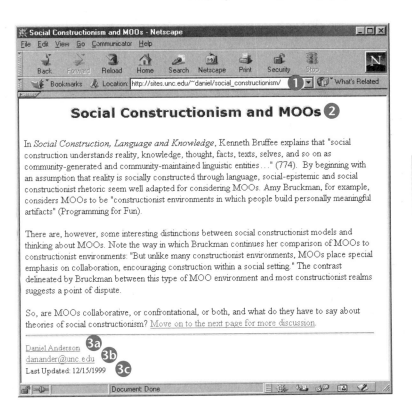

In the screen shot, a Netscape browser window titled "Social Constructionism and MOOs - Netscape" displays the page with the address http://sites.unc.edu/~daniel/social_constructionism/ marked with callout ①, the heading marked with callout ②, and author information marked with callouts ③a, ③b, and ③c.

Social Constructionism and MOOs ②

In *Social Construction, Language and Knowledge*, Kenneth Bruffee explains that "social construction understands reality, knowledge, thought, facts, texts, selves, and so on as community-generated and community-maintained linguistic entities..." (774). By beginning with an assumption that reality is socially constructed through language, social-epistemic and social constructionist rhetoric seem well adapted for considering MOOs. Amy Bruckman, for example, considers MOOs to be "constructionist environments in which people build personally meaningful artifacts" (Programming for Fun).

There are, however, some interesting distinctions between social constructionist models and thinking about MOOs. Note the way in which Bruckman continues her comparison of MOOs to constructionist environments: "But unlike many constructionist environments, MOOs place special emphasis on collaboration, encouraging construction within a social setting." The contrast delineated by Bruckman between this type of MOO environment and most constructionist realms suggests a point of dispute.

So, are MOOs collaborative, or confrontational, or both, and what do they have to say about theories of social constructionism? Move on to the next page for more discussion.

Daniel Anderson ③a
danander@unc.edu ③b
Last Updated: 12/15/1999 ③c

sor or author directly, and (*c*) the publication date or the date of the last revision.

If the page you are reading does not list publication information, look for it on the site's home page. There may be a link to the home page, or you can find it by editing the address in the Address or Location field: working backward, delete the end of the address up to the preceding slash; then hit Enter. (For the address in the screen shot, you would delete *social_constructionism/*.) If that doesn't take you to the home page, delete the end of the remaining address up to the preceding slash and hit Enter. Editing the address in this way, you'll eventually reach the home page.

When scouting a discussion list, Web forum, or newsgroup, save messages that may serve as sources, and keep track of when and where they were posted. You may be able to discover information about the author of a message from the list's archive or from an archive site such as Deja (*http://www.deja.com*). See pages 315–318 for more on these resources.

49 Finding Sources

http://webster.commnet.edu/libroot/workbook/wrkbk.htm A tutorial for information and library skills, from Capital Community College.

http://lcweb.loc/gov/rr Research tools, online bibliographies, subject lists, and indexes to periodicals and abstracts, from the Library of Congress.

http://www.ipl.org/teen/aplus/library.htm Advice on conducting library searches, from the Internet Public Library.

http://www.uwp.edu/info-services/library/teachslf.htm Advice on using the library, from the University of Wisconsin at Parkside.

http://thorplus.lib.purdue.edu/core A tutorial on searching electronically, from Purdue University.

49a

This chapter discusses conducting electronic searches (below) and taking advantage of the range of sources, both print and electronic, that you have access to: reference works (p. 301), books (p. 305), periodicals (p. 306), the World Wide Web (p. 310), other online sources (p. 315), pamphlets and government publications (p. 318), and your own interviews, surveys, and other primary sources (p. 319).

49a Searching electronically

During any research project, you will probably search one or more of the following computerized resources, either at the library or elsewhere, such as from your own computer:

- The library's catalog of holdings is a database allowing you to search for books and other sources. The catalog may include

---

Two tips for researchers

- If you are unsure of how to locate or use your library's resources, make an appointment with a reference librarian. This person is very familiar with all the library's resources and with general and specialized research techniques, and it is his or her job to help you and others with research. Even very experienced researchers often consult reference librarians.
- If sources you need are not available from your library, you may be able to obtain them from another library, usually by mail, often by fax, sometimes electronically. Ask your librarian for help, and plan ahead: interlibrary loans can take a week or longer.

not only your library's holdings but also those of other schools nearby or in your state.

- Databases on CD-ROM, or compact disk, include indexes, bibliographies, and other references and sometimes the entire text of articles.
- Online databases and text archives are stored on computers all over the world and are accessible over the Internet. These resources include many indexes, bibliographies, and other references as well as files of discussion groups and the entire contents of newspapers, magazines, scholarly journals, government reports, and even books. Internet sources found on the World Wide Web vary greatly in reliability and so require special care in evaluation (see pp. 322–324).

49a

1 Your access to sources

Finding answers to the following sets of questions will give you a head start on your electronic research and help smooth your way.

Library resources and their formats

Knowing the library's holdings and their formats will help you plan and carry out your search:

- Which of the library's books are cataloged electronically? Some libraries have all their books listed electronically; others have only recent acquisitions—say, books less than ten years old.

Ways to record information

A pencil and paper aren't necessarily your only tools for recording information.

- Can you print search results in the library? Many libraries provide some printers so that users can print catalog items, periodical listings, and other references located on computer. Some libraries also restrict or charge for printing.

┌─ KEY TERMS ────────────────────────────────

INTERNET A decentralized worldwide network of computer networks that exchange information by using an agreed-upon set of protocols. On the Internet, you can send a message, chat to individuals electronically, participate in a public discussion group, or search for information on almost any subject.

WORLD WIDE WEB The portion of the Internet that allows you to browse linked Web pages, download text files, listen to audio files, view video files, and jump to other documents or Internet sites.

└──

)

- Can you save search results on your own floppy disk? If so, you'll be able to rearrange and supplement source data easily for your working bibliography. But find out what hardware or software you need in order to "read" the search results on your own computer.

2 Keyword searches

Probably the most important element in an electronic search is appropriate KEYWORDS, or DESCRIPTORS, to describe your subject. Most electronic catalogs and databases, as well as Internet search engines, operate by keywords: you type words that define your limited subject (see the box below), and the computer searches for sources using or indexed by those words. On the subject of Internet taxation, keywords might include *Internet AND taxes, electronic commerce AND taxes,* and *Internet AND (sales tax).*

You will probably have to use trial and error in developing your keywords, sometimes running dry (turning up few or no sources)

Ways to refine keywords

You can refine your keywords in ways now standard, with some variations, among most databases and search engines. These devices are called Boolean operators, after the nineteenth century English mathematician George Boole. When in doubt about whether or how to use any of the following devices, consult the Help section of the resource you are using.

- Use the word *NOT* or the symbol – ("minus") to narrow your search by excluding irrelevant words: for instance, *(Internet tax) NOT (access tax).*
- Use the word *AND* or the symbol + to narrow your search by indicating that all the terms should appear in the source or its listing: for example, *Internet AND (sales tax).*
- Use the word *OR* to broaden your search: for example, *Internet AND (sales tax) OR (access tax).*
- Use quotation marks or parentheses (as in the examples above) to indicate that you want to search for the entire phrase, not the separate words.
- To indicate that you will accept different versions of the same word, use a so-called wild card, such as *, in place of the optional letters: for example, *wom*n* includes both *woman* and *women.* (Some systems use ?, :, or + for a wild card instead of *.)
- Be sure to spell your keywords correctly. Some search tools will look for close matches or approximations, but correct spelling gives you the best chance of finding relevant sources.

and sometimes hitting uncontrollable gushers (turning up hundreds or thousands of mostly irrelevant sources). But the process is not busywork—far from it. Besides leading you eventually to worthwhile sources, it can also teach you a great deal about your subject: how you can or should narrow it, how it is and is not described by others, what others consider interesting or debatable about it, what the major arguments are.

See pp. 313–314 for a sample keyword search.

49b   Finding reference works

49b

REFERENCE WORKS, often available on CD-ROM or online, include encyclopedias, dictionaries, digests, bibliographies, indexes, atlases, almanacs, and handbooks. Your research *must* go beyond these sources, but they can help you decide whether you topic really interests you and whether it meets the requirements for a research paper (p. 289). Preliminary research in reference works can also help you develop keywords for computer searches (see p. 300) and can direct you to more detailed sources on your topic.

 Often you can find reference works as well as other resources at Web sites devoted to fields or disciplines. The following lists give general and specific Web references for the humanities, social sciences, and natural and applied sciences:

All disciplines
Internet Public Library
   http://www.ipl.org
Library of Congress
   http://lcweb.loc.gov
LSU Libraries Webliography
   http://www.lib.lsu.edu/weblio.html
World Wide Web Virtual Library
   http://vlib.stanford.edu/overview.html

Humanities
General
EDSITEment
   http://edsitement.neh.fed.us
Voice of the Shuttle
   http://vos.ucsb.edu

Art
Artnet.Com
   http://www.artnet.com
World Wide Arts Resources
   http://wwar.com

Dance

danceonline
http://www.danceonline.com
Sapphire Swan Dance Directory
http://www.SapphireSwan.com/dance

Film

Mining Company's Classic Movies
http://classicfilm.miningco.com/entertainment/classicfilm
Performing Arts Cinema Links
http://www.theatrelibrary.org/links/Cinema.html

History

Gateway to World History
http://www.hartford-hwp.com/gateway
Librarians' Index History Links
http://lii.org/search?title+History&query=History&subsearch=
History&searchtype=subject

Literature

English Server
http://eserver.org
Top Ten Resources for American Literature
http://www.cwrl.utexas.edu/~daniel/amlit/resources.html
Voice of the Shuttle English Literature Page
http://vos.ucsb.edu/shuttle/english.html
Voice of the Shuttle World Literature Page
http://vos.ucsb.edu/shuttle/litother.html

Music

American Music Resource
http://www.uncg.edu/~flmccart/amrhome.html
Web Resources for Study and Research in Music
http://www.ucc.ie/ucc/depts/music/online

Philosophy

Guide to Philosophy on the Internet
http://www.earlham.edu/~peters/philinks.htm
Resources from the American Philosophical Association
http://www.apa.udel.edu/apa/resources

Religion

Internet Resources for the Academic Study of Religion
http://www.academicinfo.net/religindex.html
Virtual Religion Index
http://religion.rutgers.edu/vri

Theater

McCoy's Guide to Theater and Performance Studies
http://www.stetson.edu/departments/csata/thr_guid.html
Theater Connections
http://libweb.uncc.edu/ref-arts/theater

49b

Social sciences

General

Social Sciences Data on the Net
http://odwin.ucsd.edu/idata
World Wide Web Virtual Library's Social Science Resources
http://web.clas.ufl.edu/users/gthursby/socsci

Anthropology

Anthro.Net
http://www.anthro.net
Anthropological Resources on the Internet
http://home.worldnet.fr/clist/Anthro/index.html

Business and economics

Internet Business Library
http://www.bschool.ukans.edu/IntBusLib
Nyenrode Business Information Services
http://www.library.nijenrode.nl

Education

AskERIC
http://ericir.syr.edu
Department of Education
http://www.ed.gov

Ethnic and gender studies

Ethnic Studies at USC
http://www.usc.edu/isd/archives/ethnicstudies
Voice of the Shuttle Gender Studies Page
http://vos.ucsb.edu/shuttle/gender.html

Political science and law

Librarians' Index Law Resources
http://lii.org/search/file/law
Political Science Resources
http://www.psr.keele.ac.uk

Psychology

Mental Health Net
http://mentalhelp.net
University of Houston's Psychology Resources
http://info.lib.uh.edu/indexes/psych.htm

Sociology

Electronic Journals in Sociology
http://www.lib.uwaterloo.ca/discipline/sociology/journals.html
SocioWeb
http://www.socioweb.com/~markbl/socioweb

49b

Natural and applied sciences

General

Librarians' Index Science Resources
http://lii.org/search/file/science
World Wide Web Virtual Library
http://www.vlib.org/Science.html

Biology

BioLinks
http://www.biolinks.com
BioOnline
http://bio.com/resedu

Chemistry

American Chemical Society ChemCenter
http://www.acs.org:80/index.html
University of Houston's Chemistry Resources
http://info.lib.uh.edu/indexes/chem.htm

Computer science

computer.org
http://www.computer.org
Virtual Computer Library
http://www.utexas.edu/computer/vcl

Engineering

Engineering Virtual Library
http://www.eevl.ac.uk
Internet Connections for Engineering
http://www.englib.cornell.edu/ice

Environmental science

EnviroLink
http://www.envirolink.org
World Wide Web Virtual Library Resources
http://earthsystems.org/Environment.shtml

Geology

American Geological Institute
http://www.agiweb.org
USGS Earth Science Resources
http://www.usgs.gov/network/science/earth/earth.html

Health sciences

MedWeb
http://WWW.MedWeb.Emory.Edu/MedWeb
World Health Organization
http://www.who.int

49b

Mathematics

American Mathematical Society
http://www.ams.org
Topics in Mathematics
http://archives.math.utk.edu/topics

Physics and astronomy

NASA Space Science Resources
http://spacescience.nasa.gov
PhysicsWeb
http://www.physicsweb.org

49c   Finding books

Most academic libraries store their book catalogs on computer; however, older volumes—say, those acquired more than ten or fifteen years ago—may still be cataloged in bound volumes or on film.

You can search an electronic catalog for authors' names, titles, or keywords describing your subject. As much as possible, the keywords should match words in *Library of Congress Subject Headings* (*LCSH*), a multivolume work that lists the headings under which the Library of Congress catalogs books. See pages 300–301 for more on keyword searches.

The following screen shot shows the features of a catalog record for a book:

49d Finding periodicals

Most style guides classify printed material into three types: books, periodicals, and other print sources. The term *periodical* is applied to any type of publication that is issued at regular intervals, usually daily, weekly, or monthly. Scholarly journals, magazines, and newspapers are all examples of periodicals. Often, you may be asked to limit your research to scholarly journals, or you may be allowed to use some general interest magazines as well. To distinguish among types of periodicals, the following classifications may be helpful:

Scholarly journals

Researchers or scholars in a given field often write scholarly papers and articles, usually to report on original research. These papers, if considered noteworthy and scientific in their approach, are published in scholarly journals, usually by a professional organization in a particular field or discipline. These journals are issued quarterly, semi-annually, or annually. They are usually read by other scholars, so the publisher assumes the audience understands the terminology, history, and current concerns in the field. Scholarly journals always cite their sources, and they include extensive documentation of previously published research. These periodicals rarely contain any advertising or pictures and consist almost entirely of text. Many journals number each issue separately, but others number their pages consecutively through all the issues in a given year (as an annual volume): *JAMA: The Journal of the American Medical Association, Education Administration Quarterly*, and *Psychological Bulletin*, published by the American Psychological Association, are examples of scholarly journals.

News magazines

The purpose of these periodicals is to report on current events, particularly in the economic or political spectrums. Articles may be written by a member of the editorial staff, a scholar, or a freelance writer. The language of these publications is geared to an educated audience. They are usually published by commercial enterprises or individuals. Generally, these publications indicate the sources of their information, although sometimes the source is kept confidential. *Newsweek, Time,* and *Business Week* are examples of periodicals in this category.

Trade magazines or journals

The main purpose of these periodicals is to report news or to share information in a specific industry, business field, or trade group. They are often published by trade associations or industry groups, and the magazines may draw material from a wide range of sources. Sometimes these sources are cited; other times they are not. Advertisers often use these periodicals to target a specific market, and they are often supported by advertising revenue as well as organization or association dues. *Travel Weekly* and *Computerworld* are examples of periodicals that would fall into this group.

General interest magazines

49d

General interest magazines often take information from scholarly journals and translate it for the general public or a specific lay audience. The articles may be written by a member of the editorial staff, a scholar, or a freelance writer. They may or may not cite their sources. The magazines assume an educated audience, and their purpose is to provide information in a general manner. These periodicals may be very attractive in appearance, although some are in newspaper format. Articles are often heavily illustrated, generally with photographs. They are usually published by commercial enterprises, although some may be published by professional organizations. *Psychology Today* and *National Geographic* are examples of periodicals in this category.

Popular press

These periodicals represent a wide range of formats, seriousness, and credibility. A great deal of advertising usually distinguishes this type of publication, and these magazines are usually highly illustrated and have a glossy, slick appearance. Their primary purpose is to entertain, to sell products, or to promote a particular viewpoint, and they generally target specific groups of individuals who share common characteristics. Articles in these magazines are usually short, written in simple language, and designed to meet a minimal education level. Articles are written by staff members or freelance writers and, often, sources are not cited. *Sports Illustrated*, *Parents*, *Glamour*, and *Better Homes and Gardens* are among specific titles in this category.

Sensational press

These magazines or tabloid newspapers are primarily designed to arouse curiosity or to titillate. They often focus on celebrities or outrageous stories or claims. They rarely cite their sources, and often material is fabricated or exaggerated. Their language is usually very elementary, and they often use "teaser" headlines to attract their readers. *National Enquirer, Globe,* and *Star* are examples of periodicals in this category.

Newspapers

The term "newspaper" is applied to a wide range of publications that range from very authoritative and credible sources to ones with questionable veracity. Newspapers are often published daily or weekly, and they are concerned with views as well as with news. At times, newspapers will conduct investigations, and their reporting constitutes a primary source. At other times, they rely on the reports of others. In addition to substantive news reports, newspapers also contain editorials and often advocate a particular point of view. The *Los Angeles Times*, the *Washington Post*, and the *Boston Globe* are examples of well-known newspapers.

1   Indexes to periodicals

Various indexes to periodicals—most available on **CD-ROM** or online—provide information on the articles in journals, magazines, and newspapers. The following are a few of the most widely used indexes:

- *InfoTrac:* more than fifteen hundred business, government, technical, and general-interest publications.
- *Humanities Index:* journals in language and literature, history, philosophy, and other humanities.
- *MLA International Bibliography of Books and Articles on the Modern Languages and Literatures:* books and periodicals on literature, linguistics, and languages.
- *New York Times Index:* articles in the most comprehensive US newspaper.
- *Social Sciences Index:* journals in economics, psychology, political science, and other social sciences.
- *General Science Index:* journals in biology, chemistry, physics, and other sciences.
- *Readers' Guide to Periodical Literature:* over a hundred popular magazines.

Searching electronic periodical indexes is discussed under electronic searches on pages 298–301. The following record shows the results of an *InfoTrac* search:

```
Subject: INTERNET Subdivision: DEMOGRAPHIC aspects  ]— Subject
                                                        heading and
One Internet, two nations. (Internet usage by ethnic   subheading
groups) (Column) Henry Louis Gates Jr. The New York Times
Oct 31, 1999 s0 pWK15 (N) pWK15 (L) col 2 (20 col in)
```

What price will be paid by those not on the Net? (poor
minorities denied use of the Internet) Pam Belluck. The
New York Times Sept 22, 1999 pD12 (N) pG12 (L) col 1 (50
col in)

UNCF Examines Digital Divide On Campus. (United Negro
College Fund) Ronald Roach. Black Issues in Higher Education August 5, 1999 v16 i11 p32

A Web That Looks Like the World. (Internet demographics)
(Abstract) Business Week March 22, 1999 i3621 pEB46 (1)

Who's on the Internet and why. Dan Johnson. The Futurist
August-Sep 1998 v32 n6 p11 (2)

Continental divide. (differences between Silicon Valley,
CA, and Washington DC) (Special Section: The Backbone of
America) Michael Kinsley. Time, July 7, 1997, v150 n1 p97 (3)

| Periodical title | Date | Volume, issue number, and page number |

49d

The University of Phoenix Library Online Collection utilizes a
number of indexes and databases to provide students, faculty, and
alumni access to periodicals. These indexes and databases include:

- InfoTrac
- ProQuest5000
- EBSCOhost
- Moody's FIS online
- Global Access from Disclosure
- ERIC at Syracuse University
- iTKnowledge

2 Locations of periodicals

Every traditional library lists its complete periodical holdings
either in its main catalog or in a separate catalog. Many periodicals
are available on CD-ROM or online. If a periodical is not available
electronically, recent issues are probably held in the library's periodical room. Back issues are usually stored elsewhere, either in bound
volumes or on film that requires a special machine to read. A librarian will show you how to operate the machine.

3 Abstracts

Many periodical indexes include ABSTRACTS, or summaries, of
articles along with bibliographic information. An abstract can tell
you in advance whether you want to pursue an article further. The
abstract is not the article, however, and should not be used or cited
as if it were. Whenever possible, consult the full article.

49e Finding sources on the World Wide Web

Both for refining your topic and for gathering actual sources, the Web has a number of advantages:

49e

- Since Web publication is faster than print or even CD-ROM publication, you may find more current information on the Web than in a traditional library.
- Many scholarly journals are published online. Some are published *only* online, not in print.
- You can supplement a traditional library's holdings by searching other libraries' catalogs or obtaining documents over the Internet.
- You can get in touch with people who have an interest in your research topic by participating in a discussion group or conducting interviews online.

However, the Web has a number of disadvantages, too:

- It provides limited information on the past. Sources dating from before the 1980s or even more recently probably will not appear on the Web.
- It is not all-inclusive. Most books and many periodicals are available only in a traditional library, not via the Web.
- It changes constantly. No search engine can keep up with the Web's daily additions and deletions, and a source you find today may be different or gone tomorrow.
- Because of the Web's constant change, you must record publication information as you are consulting a source. You may not be able to retrace your steps as you can with print sources. (To track online sources, use the advice and list of elements on pp. 295–297.)
- The Web is a wide-open network. Anyone with the right hardware and software can place information on the Internet, and even a carefully conceived search can turn up sources with widely varying reliability: journal articles, government documents, scholarly data, term papers written by high school students, sales pitches masked as objective reports, wild theories. You must be especially diligent about evaluating Internet sources (see p. 322).

1 Search engines

To find sources on the Web, you use a SEARCH ENGINE that catalogs Web sites in a series of directories and conducts keyword searches (see p. 300). Generally, use a directory when you haven't

Web search engines

The features of search engines change often, and new ones are constantly appearing. For a comprehensive and up-to-date list of the latest search engines, see the links collected by Search Engine Watch at *http://www.searchenginewatch.com/links.*

Directories that review sites

AlphaSearch
 http://www.calvin.edu/library/searreso/internet/as/
BUBL Link
 http://bubl.ac.uk/link
Internet Public Library
 http://www.ipl.org/ref
Librarians' Index to the Internet
 http://www.lii.org
Scout Select
 http://scout.cs.wisc.edu/addserv/toolkit/bookmarks/index.html
WebGEMS
 http://www.fpsol.com/gems/webgems.html

Engines that search multiple engines (meta search engines)

1Blink
 http://www.1blink.com
Dogpile
 http://www.dogpile.com
MetaCrawler
 http://www.metacrawler.com

Engines that provide subject directories and/or keyword searches

AltaVista
 http://www.altavista.com
AskJeeves
 http://www.askjeeves.com
Excite
 http://www.excite.com
Google
 http://www.google.com
HotBot
 http://www.hotbot.lycos.com
Infoseek
 http://www.go.com
Lycos
 http://www.lycos.com
NorthernLight
 http://www.northernlight.com
WebCrawler
 http://www.webcrawler.com
Yahoo!
 http://www.yahoo.com

49e

yet refined your topic or you want a general overview. Use keywords when you have refined your topic and you seek specific information.

Current search engines

The box on page 311 lists the currently most popular search engines. To reach any one of them, enter its address in the Address or Location field of your Web browser.

Note No search engine can catalog the entire Web—indeed, even the most powerful engine may not include half the sites available at any given time, and most engines include only a fifth or less. Thus you should try out more than a single engine, perhaps as many as four or five, to cover a good portion of the Web's offerings.

A sample search engine

The screen shot above, from the HotBot search engine, shows the features common to most engines. The circled numbers are keyed to the following numbered comments.

┌─KEY TERMS──────────────────────────────────

BROWSER A program that allows users to view pages on the World Wide Web. The two most popular browsers are Netscape Communicator and Microsoft Internet Explorer.

1. To search by keywords, type them into the Search field. (See pp. 300–301 on developing keywords.)
2. Customize your search using menus—for instance, select a date range, a language, or a number of results to see.
3. Click on listings for specific kinds of information and sources—for instance, e-mail addresses or postings to discussion groups.
4. Instead of searching by keywords, browse a subject directory to zero in on your general subject and perhaps your specific topic.
5. Click Advanced Search for limiting a search and Help for instructions on searching, formatting keywords, and interpreting search results. Search engines generally list HITS, or sites that match your search criteria, in an order depending on findings such as the number of times your search terms appear within a document; whether the terms appear at the beginning, middle, or end of a document; or whether the terms appear in the title or the address of the document.

49e

Bookmarks and search histories

Your Web browser probably includes functions that allow you to keep track of Web sources and your search:

- BOOKMARKS save site addresses as links. Click Bookmarks or Favorites near the top of the Web browser screen to add a site you want to return to. A bookmark remains on file until you delete it.
- A browser's search history records the sites you visited over a certain period, such as a single online session or a week's sessions. (After that period, the history is deleted.) If you forgot to bookmark a site, you can click History or Go to locate your search history and recover the site.

2 A sample search

The following sample Web search illustrates how the refinement of keywords can narrow a search to maximize the relevant hits and minimize the irrelevant ones. Kisha Alder, a student researching the feasibility of Internet taxes, first used the keywords *taxes AND Internet* on the AltaVista search engine. But, as shown in the screen shot on page 314, the search produced almost 300,000 hits, an unusably large number and a sure sign that Alder's keywords needed revision. A hit is the access of a page on the World Wide Web by a user. Hit also refers to any time a piece of data matches the criteria you set when you use search engines to conduct a Web search.

Alder consulted AltaVista's Advanced Search information for help with revising her keywords. There she discovered that the connector *AND* had located documents that used both *taxes* and *Internet*

AltaVista results with keywords *taxes AND Internet*

but did not necessarily link them, as in *Internet taxes* or *taxes on the Internet*. With the connector *NEAR*, though, Alder could find documents in which her terms fell within ten words of each other, making it more likely that the words would be used together. Indeed, *taxes NEAR Internet* reduced the number of hits to fewer than 18,000, still a too-large number but a fraction of the previous results.

Alder then tried refining her terms, substituting the more specific *sales taxes* for *taxes* and *electronic commerce* for *Internet*. She also used parentheses to instruct AltaVista to search for the exact phrases: *(sales taxes) NEAR (electronic commerce)*. This time, as the screen shot above shows, the search returned a manageable 119 possibilities, including two among the first four that were directly relevant to Alder's topic.

Knowing that no search engine catalogs every Web site, Alder tried her successful keywords at two other engines, Yahoo! and Dogpile. The Yahoo! search was less productive but did turn up one promising source not listed by AltaVista. The Dogpile search, which worked through multiple search engines, returned a long list of 332 items, including many irrelevant ones but also (among the first twenty-five) three more possible sources.

AltaVista results with keywords *(sales taxes) NEAR (electronic commerce)*

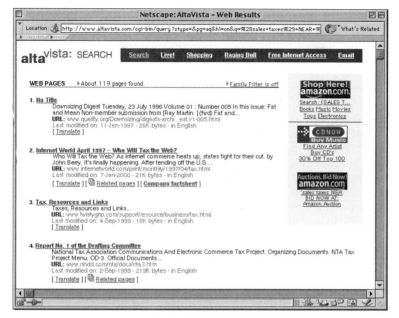

49f Finding other online sources

In addition to the Web, several other online resources can aid your research: electronic mail and discussion lists (pp. 315–317), Web forums and newsgroups (p. 317), and synchronous communication (p. 318).

1 Electronic mail

With electronic mail (e-mail), you can send messages to and receive them from most people who use the Internet, as long as you know their addresses. As a research tool, e-mail allows you to communicate with others who may be interested in your topic. You may, for instance, carry on an e-mail conversation with a teacher at your school or with other students. Or you may interview an expert in another state to follow up on a scholarly article he or she published. (See p. 319 on conducting interviews, and see pp. 63–66 for advice on e-mail format and etiquette.)

2 Discussion lists

A DISCUSSION LIST (sometimes called a LISTSERV) uses e-mail to connect individuals who are interested in a common subject. Subscribers to a list send messages to its electronic address, which are then distributed to the other subscribers' e-mail accounts. (Many college courses use discussion lists for collaboration among students. See p. 67.)

Thousands of discussion lists operate on the Internet, each with a particular purpose and audience. (For indexes of lists, consult *http://tile.net/lists* or *http://www.liszt.com.*) The lists' focus tends to be scholarly or technical: discussions center on building knowledge within the community of subscribers. The discussion on a list may thus be more reliable than that on a Web forum or newsgroup (see the next page). If you find a list relevant to your topic, the discussion might orient you to current issues and debates and might lead you to a particular person who can answer your questions. However, discussion lists are more difficult than other discussion groups to search because you must subscribe to each one, and you may have more difficulty extracting information from a continuing exchange among specialists.

When conducting research on a discussion list, follow the guidelines for e-mail etiquette on pp. 65–66 as well as those following:

- Many lists have explicit purposes and established conventions. Read the first e-mail message that arrives when you join a list to gather information about its priorities and conventions. Save this message, too, because it usually tells you how to cancel your subscription.
- Check for a file of frequently asked questions (FAQs), which will list the topics covered (and *not* covered) by the list and will answer common questions. Many lists also maintain Web archives of past messages that you can read for information or for a sense of a list's conventions.
- Devote some time to reading the list's messages before sending any questions or comments of your own. By reading but not participating (called LURKING), you can get a sense of whether the list is relevant to your research topic (and vice versa) and observe the list's conventions.
- List members are usually glad to help with legitimate questions, but they resent messages that rehash familiar debates or that ask them to do someone else's work. Don't ask for information that you can find elsewhere. Instead, query subscribers about their unique knowledge and experiences.

- Evaluate messages carefully. Many list subscribers are passion-ate experts with fair-minded approaches to their topics, but almost anyone with an Internet connection can post a message to a list. See pages 322–324 on evaluating online sources.

3 Web forums

Many Web sites are devoted to discussions of particular issues. Open to everyone, these FORUMS organize postings into THREADS, or groups of messages and replies on the same topic. You can visit the site and reach the postings through a Web address, or you may be able to subscribe so that all postings come to you automatically by e-mail.

For indexes and links to Web forums, you can consult either *http://www.forumone.com* or *http://www.remarq.com*. Follow the guidelines in the bulleted list above for participating in discussion lists. Although Web forums tend to be less scholarly and focused than discussion lists, the participants still expect newcomers to be familiar with the forum's conventions and its threads before they ask questions or contribute opinions.

Because Web forums are open to anyone, you must be espe-cially diligent in evaluating any messages you consider using as sources. See pages 322–224 on evaluating online sources.

4 Newsgroups

Like Web forums, NEWSGROUPS are open to everyone and offer discussions on an enormous range of topics. You can search rele-vant newsgroups at *http://www.remarq.com* or *http://www.deja.com*. Investigate the options of the sites' archives as well: the sites may sort messages into threads and may allow you to locate information about the author of a given message, which is key in evaluating the message.

Newsgroups are roughly categorized by subject, indicated by the first letters of the address—for instance, *comp* for computers and computer science, *soc* for social issues, *biz* for business. This prefix will give you an idea of whether the group is relevant to your concerns. When you reach a potentially relevant newsgroup, follow the guidelines for participation given in the bulleted list on pages 316–317.

Newsgroup contributions require the same critical evaluation as contributions to discussion lists and Web forums. See pages 322–324 on evaluating online sources.

49f

5 Synchronous communication

With electronic mail, discussion lists, Web forums, and newsgroups, there's a delay between a message you send and any response you receive. But with SYNCHRONOUS (or simultaneous) COMMUNICATION, you and others can correspond in real time, as you might talk on the phone. Synchronous programs include IRC (Internet relay chat), MUDs (multiuser domains), and MOOs (multiuser domains, object-oriented).

Though used mainly for social purposes, such as games and conversations, synchronous programs are also employed in education and research, as for class discussions, collaborative projects, interviews, and academic debates. Your instructors may ask you to use synchronous communication for coursework or research and will provide the software and instructions you need to get started. You can also learn more about synchronous communication at *http://www.du.org/cybercomp.html* or *http://www2.famvid.com/i101/chat.html.*

49g Using pamphlets and government publications

Organizations such as social-service groups, professional societies, and all branches of government publish pamphlets, compilations of data, and other sources that usually cannot be retrieved through a traditional library's book catalog or periodicals listings.

Libraries store pamphlets and other loose materials in file drawers, called VERTICAL FILES. To find out what is available in pamphlet form, consult the *Vertical File Index: A Subject and Title Index to Selected Pamphlet Materials.*

Government publications provide a vast array of data, public records, and other historical and contemporary information. For US government publications, consult the *Monthly Catalog of US Government Publications,* available on computer. Many federal, state, and local government agencies post important publications—legislation, reports, press releases—on their own Web sites. You can find lists of sites for various federal agencies by using the keywords *United States federal government* with a search engine. In addition, several Web sites are useful resources: *http://www.fedstats.gov* (government statistics), *http://www.access.gpo.gov/su_docs* (listings of the Government Printing Office), and *http://infoplease.com/us.html* (links to information on federal, state, and local governments).

49h Generating your own sources

Academic writing will often require you to conduct primary research for information of your own. For instance, you may need to analyze a poem, conduct an experiment, survey a group of people, or interview an expert.

An interview can be especially helpful for a research project because it allows you to ask questions precisely geared to your topic. You can conduct an interview in person, over the telephone, or online using electronic mail (see p. 315) or a form of synchronous communication (see p. 318). A personal interview is preferable if you can arrange it, because you can see the person's expressions and gestures as well as hear his or her tone and words.

Here are a few guidelines for interviews:

49h

- Call or write for an appointment. Tell the person exactly why you are calling, what you want to discuss, and how long you expect the interview to take. Be true to your word on all points.
- Prepare a list of open-ended questions to ask—perhaps ten or twelve for a one-hour interview. Plan on doing some research for these questions to discover background on the issues and your subject's published views on the issues.
- Give your subject time to consider your questions, and listen to your subject's answers so that you can ask appropriate follow-up questions.
- Take care in interpreting answers, especially if you are online and thus can't depend on facial expressions, gestures, and tone of voice to convey the subject's attitudes.
- For in-person and telephone interviews, keep careful notes or, if you have the equipment and your subject agrees, tape-record the interview. For online interviews, save the discussion in a file of its own.
- Before you quote your subject in your paper, check with him or her to ensure that the quotations are accurate.
- Send a thank-you note immediately after the interview. Promise your subject a copy of your finished paper, and send the paper promptly.

http://owl.english.purdue.edu/Files/131.html   Advice on evaluating sources, from the Purdue Online Writing Lab.

http://www2.widener.edu/Wolfgram-Memorial-Library/webeval.htm Guidance for evaluating Web sites, from Widener University.

http://www.users.drew.edu/~sjamieso/Synthesis.htm   Comprehensive advice on synthesizing sources, from Drew University.

http://www.esc.edu/htmlpages/writer/menun.htm   Advice on note taking, paraphrasing, integrating borrowed material, and other work with sources, from the State University of New York.

http://owl.english.purdue.edu/Files/151.htm   Advice on avoiding plagiarism, from the Purdue Online Writing Lab.

50a

Research writing is much more than finding sources and reporting their contents. The challenge and interest come from *interacting* with sources, reading them critically to discover their meanings, judge their quality, and create relationships among them. This chapter shows you how to use the sources you find to extend and support your own ideas, to make your topic your own. The chapter discusses evaluating and synthesizing sources (below and p. 324), taking notes while avoiding plagiarism (pp. 325, 329), integrating sources into your text (p. 334), and documenting sources (p. 337).

ESL Making a topic your own requires thinking critically about sources and developing independent ideas. These goals may at first be uncomfortable for you if your native culture emphasizes understanding and respecting established authority over questioning and enlarging it. The information here will help you work with sources so that you can become an expert in your own right and convincingly convey your expertise to others.

50a Evaluating sources

Before you settle in to take notes, scan your sources to evaluate the kind and extent of ideas and information they offer.

Note   In evaluating sources, you need to consider how they come to you. The print sources you find through the library (including books and articles that are also released electronically) have been previewed for you by their publishers and by the library's staff. They still require your critical reading, but you can have some confidence in the information they contain. With online sources you retrieve direct for the Web, however, you can't assume similar previewing, so your critical reading must be especially rigorous. Special tips for evaluating online sources appear on pages 322–324.

1 Relevance and reliability

Not all the sources you find will prove worthwhile: some may be irrelevant to your topic, and others may be unreliable. Gauging the relevance and reliability of sources is the essential task of evaluating them.

To determine whether sources are relevant, scan the introductions to books and articles and the tables of contents of books. You're looking for opinions and facts that pertain directly to your topic. You're also ensuring that your sources are appropriate in level: you can understand them (if with some effort), and they also expand your knowledge. If you don't see what you need or the source is too high-level or too simple, you can drop it from your list.

Reliability can be more difficult to judge than relevance. If you haven't already done so, study this book's section on critical thinking and argument. When scanning potential sources, look for claims, as-

50a

Guidelines for evaluating sources

For online sources, supplement these guidelines with those opposite.

Determine *relevance:*

- Does the source devote some attention to your topic?
- Where in the source are you likely to find relevant information or ideas?
- Is the source appropriately specialized for your needs? Check the source's treatment of a topic you know something about, to ensure that it is neither too superficial nor too technical.
- How important is the source likely to be for your writing?

Judge *reliability:*

- How up to date is the source? If the publication date is not recent, be sure that other sources will give you more current views.
- Is the author an expert in the field? Look for an author biography, look up the author in a biographical reference, or try to trace the author over the Internet.
- What is the author's bias? Check biographical information or the author's own preface or introduction. Ask a librarian to direct you to book review indexes or citations indexes, which can help you find what others have written about the author or the source.
- Whatever his or her bias, does the author reason soundly, provide adequate evidence, and consider opposing views? (See pp. 481–492.)

sumptions, evidence, tone, fairness, and other features. In addition, look for information about the author's background to satisfy yourself that the author has sufficient expertise in your subject. Then try to determine what his or her bias is. For instance, a book on parapsychology by someone identified as the president of the National Organization of Psychics may contain an authoritative explanation of psychic powers, but the author's view is likely to be biased. It should be balanced by research in other sources whose authors are more skeptical of psychic powers.

This balance or opposition is important. You probably will not find harmony among sources, for reasonable people often disagree in their opinions. Thus you must deal honestly with the gaps and conflicts in sources. Old sources, superficial ones, slanted ones— these should be offset in your research and your writing by sources that are more recent, more thorough, or more objective.

50a

2 Electronic sources

 To a great extent, the same critical reading that serves you with print sources will help you evaluate online sources, too (see the box on p. 321). But online sources can range from scholarly works to corporate promotions, from government-sponsored data to the self-published rantings of crackpots. To evaluate an online source, you'll first need to figure out what it is.

Note For more on reading a Web site critically, see pages 286–287. For advice on gathering source information from a Web site, see pages 295–297.

Check the electronic address.

Look for an abbreviation that tells you where the source originates: *edu* (educational institution), *gov* (government body), *org* (nonprofit organization), *mil* (military), or *com* (commercial organization). With a source coming from *compex.com,* you should assume that the contents reflect the company's commercial purposes (although the information may still be helpful). With a source coming from *harvard.edu,* you can assume that the contents are more scholarly and objective (although you should still evaluate the information yourself).

Determine authorship or sponsorship.

Many sites list the person(s) or group(s) responsible for the site. A Web site may provide links to information about or other work by an author or group. If not, you can refer to a biographical dictionary or conduct a keyword search of the Web (see p. 300). You should also look for mentions of the author or group in your other sources.

Often you will not be able to trace authors or sponsors or even identify them at all. For instance, someone passionate about the rights of adoptees might maintain a Web site devoted to the subject but not identify himself or herself as the author. In such a case, you'll need to evaluate the quality of the information and opinions by comparing them with sources you know to be reliable.

Gauge purpose.

Inferring the purpose of an online source can help you evaluate its reliability. Some sources may seem intent on selling ideas or products. Others may seem to be building knowledge—for instance, by acknowledging opposing views either directly or through links to other sites. Still others may seem determined to scare readers with shocking statistics or anecdotes.

50a

Evaluate a Web site as a whole.

Consider both the design and readability of a Web site and the nature of its links. Is the site thoughtfully designed, or is it cluttered with irrelevant material and graphics? Is it carefully written or difficult to understand? Do the links help clarify the purpose of the site—perhaps leading to scholarly sources or, in contrast, to frivolous or indecent sites?

Weigh the contributions to discussion groups.

You need to read individuals' contributions to discussion groups especially critically because they are unfiltered and unevaluated. Even on a discussion list (pp. 316–317), whose subscribers are likely to be professionals in the field, you may find wrong or misleading data and skewed opinions. With the more accessible Web forums and newsgroups (p. 317), you should view postings with considerable skepticism.

You can try to verify a contribution to a discussion group by looking at other contributions, which may help you confirm or refute the questionable posting, and by communicating directly with the author to ask about his or her background and publications. If you can't verify the information from a discussion group and the author doesn't respond to your direct approach, you should probably ignore the source.

Check for references or links to reliable sources.

An online source may offer as support the titles of sources that you can trace and evaluate—articles in periodicals, other online sources, and so on. A Web site may include links to these other sources.

Be aware, however, that online sources may refer you only to other sources that share the same bias. When evaluating both the original source and its references, look for a fair treatment of opposing views.

Compare online sources with other sources.

Always consider online sources in the context of other sources so that you can distinguish singular, untested views from more mainstream views that have been subject to verification.

50b Synthesizing sources

When you begin to locate the differences and similarities among sources, you move into the most significant part of research writing: forging relationships for your own purpose. This SYNTHESIS is an essential step in reading sources critically and continues through the drafting and revision of a research paper. As you infer connections—say, between one writer's opinions and another's or between two works by the same author—you create new knowledge.

Your synthesis of sources will grow more detailed and sophisticated as you proceed through the research-writing process. Unless you are analyzing primary sources such as the works of a poet, at first read your sources quickly and selectively to obtain an overview of your topic and a sense of how the sources approach it. Don't get bogged down in taking detailed notes, but *do* record your ideas about sources in your research journal (p. 289).

Respond to sources.

Write down what your sources make you think. Do you agree or disagree with the author? Do you find his or her views narrow, or do they open up new approaches for you? Is there anything in the source that you need to research further before you can understand it? Does the source prompt questions that you should keep in mind while reading other sources?

Connect sources.

When you notice a link between sources, jot it down. Do two sources differ in their theories or their interpretations of facts? Does one source illuminate another—perhaps commenting or clarifying or supplying additional data? Do two or more sources report studies that support a theory you've read about or an idea of your own?

Heed your own insights.

Apart from ideas prompted by your sources, you are sure to come up with independent thoughts: a conviction, a point of confusion that suddenly becomes clear, a question you haven't seen anyone else ask. These insights may occur at unexpected times, so it's good practice to keep a notebook handy to record them.

Use sources to support your own ideas.

As your research proceeds, the responses, connections, and insights you form through synthesis will lead you to answer your starting research question with a statement of your thesis (see p. 339). They will also lead you to the main ideas supporting your thesis—conclusions you have drawn from your synthesis of sources, forming the main divisions of your paper. When drafting the paper, make sure each paragraph focuses on an idea of your own, with the support for the idea coming from your sources. In this way, your paper will synthesize others' work into something wholly your own.

50c   Taking notes using summary, paraphrase, and direct quotation

You can accomplish a great deal of synthesis while taking notes from your sources. Note taking is not a mechanical process of copying from books. Rather, as you read and take notes you assess and organize the information in your sources.

Note A common trap in research writing is allowing your sources to control you, rather than vice versa. To avoid this trap, ask how each source illuminates the idea you are building. When you are taking notes, assign each note a heading from an outline (even a rough one) that you have devised to develop your idea.

1   Methods

You can take notes in any or all of four ways: handwriting on note cards, typing on a computer, photocopying, and downloading from online sources. Both handwritten notes and computer notes have disadvantages and advantages: handwriting notes can be tedious, but it is usually convenient; typing notes requires a handy computer, but the notes themselves are easy to incorporate into a draft. Both methods have the distinct advantage of requiring you to interact with sources as you decide what to write or type.

Photocopying and downloading sources might seem the most convenient methods of note taking, and both can reduce the risk of misquoting a source. However, the apparent convenience of these methods is offset by their disadvantages:

- Either method can actually encourage plagiarism by simplifying the process of moving ideas and information from a source into your paper. You must be especially careful to keep clear boundaries between the source material and your own ideas and words.
- The methods can discourage interaction with sources by substituting busy work for thinking. You must read photocopied and downloaded sources as critically as you would any others.

Highlight or annotate the relevant passages of a photocopy with underlining, circles, and marginal notes about their significance for your topic. You can accomplish the same work with a downloaded document by printing it out or by opening the downloaded file into your word-processing program and inserting highlights and comments at relevant passages.

- The methods make it easy to import whole blocks of a source into a draft, especially with downloaded sources that can be excerpted electronically. The guidelines on page 330 for judicious use of quotations apply to sources you photocopy as well as to those you take notes from.

50c

Whatever methods of note taking you use, make sure that each note has all the bibliographic information you'll need to cite the source in your paper if you decide to use the note. (See p. 295 for a list of information.) If you have a working bibliography, the note itself needs only a cross-reference to the full source information and then page numbers or other specifics about the note's location. Also give the note a topic heading that corresponds to a part of your subject, so you can see at a glance where the note fits. (See the samples on the following page.)

2 Summary

When you SUMMARIZE, you condense an extended idea or argument into a sentence or more in your own words. Summary is most useful when you want to record the gist of an author's idea without the background or supporting evidence. The sample computer note on the next page shows a summary of the following passage from a government report on the so-called digital divide between US residents with and without access to the Internet:

Original quotation

The following examples highlight the breadth of the digital divide today:

- Those with a college degree are more than *eight times* as likely to have a computer at home, and nearly *sixteen times* as likely to have home Internet access, as those with an elementary school education.
- A high-income household in an urban area is more than *twenty times* as likely as a rural, low-income household to have Internet access.
- A child in a low-income white family is *three times* as likely to have Internet access as a child in a comparable black family, and *four times* as likely to have access as children in a comparable Hispanic household.

—US Department of Commerce,
Falling Through the Net: Defining the Digital Divide, p. 7

Summary

Digital divide

Dept. of Commerce 7

US residents who are urban, white, college educated, and affluent are <u>much</u> more likely to be connected to the Internet than those who are rural, black or Hispanic, not educated past elementary school, and poor.

50c

3 Paraphrase

When you PARAPHRASE, you capture the author's original ideas, but you still restate them in your own words. Paraphrase is most useful when you want to present or examine an author's line of reasoning but don't feel the original words merit direct quotation. Here is a paraphrase of the quotation from the Department of Commerce report on the previous page:

Paraphrase

Digital divide

Dept. of Commerce 7

Likelihood of being connected to the Internet among US groups:

Home connection, elementary education vs. college education: 1/16 as likely.

Any access, rural setting and low-income household vs. urban setting and affluent household: 1/20 as likely.

Any access, low-income black child vs. low-income white child: 1/3 as likely.

Any access, low-income Hispanic child vs. low-income white child: 1/4 as likely.

Notice that the paraphrase continues the original ideas but uses different words and different sentence structures. In contrast, an unsuccessful paraphrase—one that plagiarizes—copies the author's words or sentence structures or both *without quotation marks.* (See p. 332 for examples.)

ESL If English is your second language, you may have difficulty paraphrasing the ideas in sources because synonyms don't occur to

Paraphrasing a source

- Read the relevant material several times to be sure you understand it.
- Restate the source's ideas in your own words and sentence structures. You need not put down in new words the whole passage or all the details. Select what is relevant to your topic, and restate only that. If complete sentences seem too detailed or cumbersome, use phrases, as in the paraphrase opposite.
- Be careful not to distort meaning. Don't change the source's emphasis or omit connecting words, qualifiers, and other material whose absence will confuse you later or cause you to misrepresent the source.

50c

you or you don't see how to restructure sentences. Before attempting a paraphrase, read the original passage several times. Then, instead of "translating" line by line, try to state the gist of the passage without looking at it. Check your effort against the original to be sure you have captured the source author's meaning and emphasis without using his or her words and sentence structures. If you need a synonym for a word, look it up in a dictionary.

4 Direct quotation

When taking notes, you may be tempted to quote sources rather than bother to summarize or paraphrase them. But this approach has at least two disadvantages:

- Copying quotations does not encourage you to interact with sources, grappling with their meaning, analyzing them, testing them.
- Copying merely postpones the summarizing and paraphrasing until you are drafting your paper. The paper itself must be centered on *your* ideas, not stitched together from quotations.

In a paper analyzing primary sources such as literary works, you will use direct quotation extensively to illustrate and support your analysis. But you should quote from secondary sources only in the circumstances described in the box on the next page.

When taking a quotation from a source, copy the material *carefully*. Take down the author's exact wording, spelling, capitalization, and punctuation. Proofread every direct quotation *at least twice*. If you want to make changes for clarity, use brackets (see p. 257). If you want to omit irrelevant words or sentences, use ellipsis marks, usually three spaced periods (see pp. 254–257). (In MLA style the ellipsis mark is also surrounded by brackets, as illustrated in the note on the next page.)

Tests for direct quotations

- The author's original satisfies one of these requirements:

  The language is unusually vivid, bold, or inventive.

  The quotation cannot be paraphrased without distortion or loss of meaning.

  The words themselves are at issue in your interpretation.

  The quotation represents and emphasizes a body of opinion or the view of an important expert.

  The quotation emphatically reinforces your own idea.

  The quotation is a graph, diagram, or table.

- The quotation is as short as possible.

  It includes only material relevant to your point.

  It is edited to eliminate examples and other unneeded material.

50d

Direct quotation

Digital divide

Dept. of Commerce 7

Digital divide very wide--"Those with a college degree are more than eight times as likely to have a computer at home [. . .] as those with an elementary school education."

50d   Avoiding plagiarism

PLAGIARISM (from a Latin word for "kidnapper") is the presentation of someone else's ideas or words as your own. Whether deliberate or accidental, plagiarism is a serious and often punishable offense.

- *Deliberate* plagiarism:

  Copying or downloading a phrase, a sentence, or a longer passage from a source and passing it off as your own by omitting quotation marks and a source citation.

  Summarizing or paraphrasing someone else's ideas without acknowledging your debt in a source citation.

  Handing in as your own work a paper you have bought, had a friend write, or copied from another student.

- *Accidental* plagiarism:

  Forgetting to place quotation marks around another writer's words.

Checklist for avoiding plagiarism

- What type of source are you using: your own independent material, common knowledge, or someone else's independent material? You must acknowledge every use you make of someone else's material.
- If you are quoting someone else's material, is the quotation exact? Have you inserted quotation marks around quotations run into the text? Have you shown omissions with ellipsis marks and additions with brackets?
- If you are paraphrasing or summarizing someone else's material, have you used your own words and sentence structures? Does your paraphrase or summary employ quotation marks when you resort to the author's exact language? Have you represented the author's meaning without distortion?
- If you are using someone else's material in your own Web site, have you obtained any needed permission for your use? (See p. 333.)
- Have you acknowledged every use of someone else's material in the place where you use it? Are all your source citations complete and accurate? (See p. 337.)
- Does your list of works cited include all the sources you have drawn from in writing your paper? (See p. 337.)

50d

Omitting a source citation from a paraphrase because of carelessness.

Omitting a source citation for another's idea because you are unaware of the need to acknowledge the idea.

ESL   More than in many other cultures, teachers in the United States value students' original thinking and writing. In some other cultures, for instance, students may be encouraged to copy the words of scholars without acknowledgment, in order to demonstrate their mastery of or respect for the scholars' work. But in the United States any use of another's words or ideas without a source citation is plagiarism and is unacceptable. When in doubt about the guidelines in this section, ask your instructor for advice.

1   What you need not acknowledge

Your independent material

Your own observations, thoughts, compilations of facts, or experimental results, expressed in your words and format, do not require acknowledgment. You should describe the basis for your conclusions so that readers can evaluate your thinking, but you need not cite sources for them.

Common knowledge

Common knowledge consists of the standard information on a subject as well as folk literature and commonsense observations.

- Standard information includes the major facts of history, such as the dates of Charlemagne's rule as emperor of Rome (800–14). It does not include interpretations of facts, such as a historian's opinion that Charlemagne was sometimes needlessly cruel in extending his power.
- Folk literature, such as the fairy tale "Snow White," is popularly known and cannot be traced to a particular writer. Literature traceable to a writer is not folk literature, even if it is very familiar.
- A commonsense observation is something most people know, such as that inflation is most troublesome for people with low and fixed incomes. However, an economist's argument about the effects of inflation on Chinese immigrants is not a commonsense observation.

50d

If you do not know a subject well enough to determine whether a piece of information is common knowledge, make a record of the source as you would for any other quotation, paraphrase, or summary. As you read more about the subject, the information may come up repeatedly without acknowledgment, in which case it is probably common knowledge. But if you are still in doubt when you finish your research, always acknowledge the source.

2 What you *must* acknowledge

You must always acknowledge other people's independent material—that is, any facts or ideas that are not common knowledge or your own. The source may be anything, including a book, an article, a movie, an interview, a microfilmed document, a computer program, a newsgroup posting, or an opinion expressed on the radio. You must acknowledge summaries or paraphrases of ideas or facts as well as quotations of the language and format in which ideas or facts appear: wording, sentence structures, arrangement, and special graphics (such as a diagram). You must acknowledge another's material no matter how you use it, how much of it you use, or how often you use it. (See pp. 337–339 for a discussion of how to acknowledge sources.)

Copied language: Quotation marks and a source citation

The following example baldly plagiarizes the original quotation from Jessica Mitford's *Kind and Usual Punishment,* p. 9. Without quotation marks or a source citation, the example matches Mitford's wording (underlined) and closely parallels her sentence structure:

| Original | The character and mentality of the keepers may be of more importance in understanding prisons than the character and mentality of the kept. |
| Plagiarism | But <u>the character</u> of prison officials (<u>the keepers</u>) is more important <u>in understanding prisons than the character</u> of prisoners (<u>the kept</u>). |

To avoid plagiarism, the writer can paraphrase and cite the source (see the last example below) or use Mitford's actual words *in quotation marks* and *with a source citation* (here, in MLA style):

| Revision (quotation) | According to one critic of the penal system, "The character and mentality of the keepers may be of more importance in understanding prisons than the character and mentality of the kept" (Mitford 9). |

50d

Paraphrase or summary: Your own words and sentence structure and a source citation

The example below changes Mitford's sentence structure, but it still uses her words (underlined) without quotation marks and without a source citation:

| Plagiarism | <u>In understanding prisons</u>, we should know more about <u>the character and mentality of the keepers</u> than <u>of the kept</u>. |

To avoid plagiarism, the writer can use quotation marks and cite the source (see above) or *use his or her own words* and still *cite the source* (because the idea is Mitford's, not the writer's):

| Revision (paraphrase) | Mitford holds that we may be able to learn more about prisons from the psychology of the prison officials than from that of the prisoners (9). |

3   Use and acknowledgment of online sources

 Online sources are so accessible and so easy to download into your own documents that it may seem they are freely available, exempting you from the obligation to acknowledge them. They are not. Acknowledging online sources is somewhat trickier than acknowledging print sources, but no less essential. Further, if you are publishing your work online, you need to take account of sources' copyright restrictions as well.

Unpublished projects

When you use material from an online source in a print or online document to be distributed just to your class, your obligation to cite your source can present additional challenges:

- Online sources may change from one day to the next or even be removed entirely. Be sure to record complete source information as noted on page 295 each time you consult the source. Without the source information, you *may not* use the source.
- If you use not only a Web site but also one or more of its linked sites, you must acknowledge the linked sites as well. The fact that one person has used a second person's work does not release you from the responsibility to cite the second work.

Web compositions and copyrights

50d

When you use material from print or online sources in a Web composition that you will publish on the Internet, you must not only acknowledge your sources as discussed above but take the additional precaution of observing copyright restrictions.

The legal convention of *fair use* allows an author to quote a small portion of copyrighted material without obtaining the copyright holder's permission, as long as the author acknowledges the source.

- With print sources, a conservative consensus gives this estimate of fair use: quoting fewer than fifty words from an article or fewer than three hundred words from a book. You'll need the copyright holder's permission to use any longer quotation from an article or book; any quotation at all from a play, poem, or song; and any use of an entire work, such as a photograph, chart, or other illustration.
- Online copyrights and fair-use standards are subjects of intense controversy, and the rules are still evolving. You can play it safe by following the print guidelines above, adding multimedia elements (audio or video clips) to the list of works that require reprint permission.
- You may also need to seek permission to link your site to another one, especially if you rely on the linked site to substantiate your claims or to provide a multimedia element.

Generally, you can find information about a site's copyright on the home page or at the bottoms of other pages: look for a notice using the symbol ©. Most worthwhile sites also provide information for contacting the author or sponsor. (See p. 296 for an illustration.) If you don't find a copyright notice, you *cannot* assume that the work is unprotected by copyright. Only if the site explicitly says it is not copyrighted or is available for free use can you exceed fair use without permission.

Note You can obtain more information on copyright and fair use from either of these Web sites: *http://fairuse.stanford.edu* or *http://www.cetus.org/fairindex.html.*

50e Integrating sources into your text

The evidence of others' information and opinions should back up, not dominate, your own ideas. To synthesize evidence, you need to smooth the transitions between your ideas and words and those of your sources, and you need to give the reader a context for interpreting the borrowed material.

Note The examples in this section use the MLA style of source documentation, discussed in Chapter 52. The source citations not only acknowledge that material is borrowed but also help to indicate where the borrowed material begins or ends. (See p. 351–352.)

1 Introduction of borrowed material

Readers will be distracted from your point if borrowed material does not fit into your sentence. In the passage below, the writer has not meshed the structures of her own and her source's sentences:

> **Awkward** One editor disagrees with this view and "a good reporter does not fail to separate opinions from facts" (Lyman 52).

In the following revision the writer adds words to integrate the quotation into her sentence:

> **Revised** One editor disagrees with this view, <u>maintaining that</u> "a good reporter does not fail to separate opinions from facts" (Lyman 52).

To mesh your own and your source's words, you may sometimes need to make a substitution or addition to the quotation, signaling your change with brackets:

> **Words added** "The tabloids [of England] are a journalistic case study in bad reporting," claims Lyman (52).

Conventions for handling quotations

- For guidelines on when to quote from sources, see p. 329.
- For the punctuation of signal phrases such as *he insists,* see pp. 236–237.
- For guidelines on when to run quotations into your text and when to display them separately from your text, see pp. 380–381 (MLA style) and 412–413 (APA style).
- For the use of brackets around your changes or additions in quotations, see p. 257.
- For the use of the ellipsis mark (. . .) to indicate omissions from quotations, see pp. 254–257.

Verb form changed	A bad reporter, Lyman implies, is one who "[fails] to separate opinions from facts" (52). [The bracketed verb replaces *fail* in the original.]
Capitalization changed	"[T]o separate opinions from facts" is the work of a good reporter (Lyman 52). [In the original, *to* is not capitalized.]
Noun supplied for pronoun	The reliability of a news organization "depends on [reporters'] trustworthiness," says Lyman (52). [The bracketed noun replaces *their* in the original.]

2 Interpretation of borrowed material

Even when it does not conflict with your own sentence structure, borrowed material will be ineffective if you merely dump it in readers' laps without explaining how you intend it to be understood:

| Dumped | Many news editors and reporters maintain that it is impossible to keep personal opinions from influencing the selection and presentation of facts. "True, news reporters, like everyone else, form impressions of what they see and hear. However, a good reporter does not fail to separate opinions from facts" (Lyman 52). |

50e

Reading this passage, we must figure out for ourselves that the writer's sentence and the quotation state opposite points of view. In the following revision, the underlined additions tell us how to interpret the quotation:

| Revised | Many news editors and reporters maintain that it is impossible to keep personal opinions from influencing the selection and presentation of facts. Yet not all authorities agree with this view. One editor grants that "news reporters, like everyone else, form impressions of what they see and hear." But, he insists, "a good reporter does not fail to separate opinions from facts" (Lyman 52). |

Signal phrases

The words *One editor grants* and *he insists* in the revised passage are SIGNAL PHRASES: they tell readers who the source is and what to expect in the quotations that follow. Signal phrases usually contain (1) the source author's name (or a substitute for it, such as *One editor* and *he*) and (2) a verb that indicates the source author's attitude or approach to what he or she says.

Some verbs for signal phrases are in the list on the facing page. Use the present tense of verbs (as in the list) to discuss the writings of others, including literary works, opinions, and reports of conclusions from research. Use the past tense only to describe past events, such as historical occurrences and the procedures used in studies—for example, *In 1993 Holmes stated that he had lied a decade earlier* or *Riley assessed the participants' diets.*

Author is neutral	Author infers or suggests	Author argues	Author is uneasy or disparaging
comments	analyzes	claims	belittles
describes	asks	contends	bemoans
explains	assesses	defends	complains
illustrates	concludes	holds	condemns
notes	considers	insists	deplores
observes	finds	maintains	deprecates
points out	predicts		derides
records	proposes	**Author agrees**	disagrees
relates	reveals		laments
reports	shows	admits	warns
says	speculates	agrees	
sees	suggests	concedes	
thinks	supposes	grants	
writes			

Vary your signal phrases to suit your interpretation of borrowed material and also to keep readers' interest. A signal phrase may precede, interrupt, or follow the borrowed material:

Precedes   Lyman insists that "a good reporter does not fail to separate opinions from facts" (52).

Interrupts   "However," Lyman insists, "a good reporter does not fail to separate opinions from facts" (52).

Follows   "[A] good reporter does not fail to separate opinions from facts," Lyman insists (52).

Background information

You can add information to a quotation to integrate it into your text and inform readers why you are using it. If your readers will recognize it, you can provide the author's name in the text:

Author named   Harold Lyman grants that "news reporters, like everyone else, form impressions of what they see and hear." But, Lyman insists, "a good reporter does not fail to separate opinions from facts" (52).

If the source title contributes information about the author or the context of the quotation, you can provide it in the text:

Title given   Harold Lyman, in his book *The Conscience of the Journalist*, grants that "news reporters, like everyone else, form impressions of what they see and hear." But, Lyman insists, "a good reporter does not fail to separate opinions from facts" (52).

If the quoted author's background and experience reinforce or clarify the quotation, you can provide these credentials in the text:

> **Credentials** Harold Lyman, a newspaper editor for more than
> **given** forty years, grants that "news reporters, like everyone
> else, form impressions of what they see and hear."
> But, Lyman insists, "a good reporter does not fail to
> separate opinions from facts" (52).

You need not name the author, source, or credentials in your text when you are simply establishing facts or weaving together facts and opinions from varied sources. In the following passage, the information is more important than the source, so the name of the source is confined to a parenthetical acknowledgment:

> To end the abuses of the British, many colonists were urging three actions: forming a united front, seceding from Britain, and taking control of their own international relations (Wills 325–36).

50f

50f Documenting sources

Every time you borrow the words, facts, or ideas of others, you must DOCUMENT, or cite, the source—that is, supply a reference (or document) telling readers that you borrowed the material and where you borrowed it from.

Editors and teachers in most academic disciplines require special documentation formats (or styles) in their scholarly journals and in students' papers. All the styles share common features:

- A citation in the text serves two purposes: it signals that material is borrowed, and it refers readers to detailed information about the source so that they can locate both the source and the place in the source where the borrowed material appears.
- Detailed source information, either in footnotes or at the end of the paper, tells readers precisely how to find the source.

Aside from these essential similarities, the disciplines' documentation styles differ markedly in citation form, arrangement of source information, and other particulars. Each discipline's style reflects the needs of its practitioners for certain kinds of information presented in certain ways. For instance, the currency of a source is important in the social sciences, where studies build on and correct each other; thus in-text citations in the social sciences include a source's date of publication. In English, however, currency is less important, so in-text citations do not include date of publication.

The disciplines' documentation formats are described in style guides, including those in the following list. This book presents the styles of the guides that are marked *.

Humanities

The Chicago Manual of Style. 14th ed. 1993. (See pp. 421–429.)

*Gibaldi, Joseph. *MLA Handbook for Writers of Research Papers.* 5th ed. 1999. (See pp. 344–376.)

*Turabian, Kate L. *A Manual for Writers of Term Papers, Theses, and Dissertations.* 6th ed. Rev. John Grossman and Alice Bennett. 1996. (See pp. 421–429.)

Social sciences

American Anthropological Association. "Style Guide and Information for Authors." *American Anthropologist* (1977): 774–79.

American Political Science Association. *Style Manual for Political Science.* Rev. ed. 1993.

*American Psychological Association. *Publication Manual of the American Psychological Association.* 4th ed. 1994. (See pp. 393–407.)

American Sociological Association. "Editorial Guidelines." Inside front cover of each issue of *American Sociological Review.*

Columbia Law Review. *A Uniform System of Citation.* 16th ed. 1996.

Sciences and mathematics

American Chemical Society. *ACS Style Guide: A Manual for Authors and Editors.* 2nd ed. 1997.

American Institute of Physics. *Style Manual for Guidance in the Preparation of Papers.* 4th ed. 1990.

American Mathematical Society. *A Manual for Authors of Mathematical Papers.* Rev. ed. 1990.

American Medical Association. *Manual of Style.* 8th ed. 1989.

Bates, Robert L., Rex Buchanan, and Marla Adkins-Heljeson, eds. *Geowriting: A Guide to Writing, Editing, and Printing in Earth Science.* 5th ed. 1992.

*Council of Biology Editors. *Scientific Style and Format: The CBE Manual for Authors, Editors, and Publishers.* 6th ed. 1994. (See pp. 430–436).

In addition to the starred styles, this book details Columbia style for online sources in the humanities and the sciences, which can supplement any of the other styles. (See pp. 439–448.)

Always ask your instructor which documentation style you should use. If your instructor does not require a particular style, use the one in this book that's most appropriate for the discipline you're writing in. Do follow a single system for citing sources so that you provide all the necessary information in a consistent format.

Note Various computer programs can help you format your source citations in the style of your choice. (BiblioCite and EndNote are two examples.) Such a program will prompt you for needed information (author's name, book title, date of publication, and so on) and will arrange, capitalize, underline, and punctuate the information as required by the style. The program will remove some tedium from documenting sources, but it can't substitute for your own care and attention in giving your sources accurate and complete acknowledgment in the required form. When reviewing the source information created by one of these programs, be sure to check for any inaccuracies or deviations from your approved style guide.

51 Writing the Paper

http://www.esc.edu/htmlpages/writer/menud.htm Guidance on developing a thesis statement, from the State University of New York.
http://www.esc.edu/htmlpages/writer/menub.htm Advice for drafting a research paper, from the State University of New York.
http://www.ipl.org/teen/aplus/linksrevising.htm Links to resources for revising, editing, and proofreading, from the Internet Public Library.

This chapter complements and extends the detailed discussion of the writing situation and the writing process in Chapters 1–6, which also include many tips for using a word processor and more links to helpful Web sites. If you haven't already done so, you may want to read Chapters 1–6 before this one.

51a Focusing and organizing the paper

Before you begin using your source notes in a draft, give some thought to your main idea and your organization.

1 Thesis statement

You began research with a question or a hypothesis about your subject (see p. 289). Though that question or hypothesis may have evolved during research, you should be able to answer it or come to a conclusion once you've consulted most of your sources. Try to state that answer in a THESIS STATEMENT, an assertion that narrows your subject to a single idea. Here, for example, are the research question and thesis statement of Kisha Alder, whose final paper appears on pages 383–389:

Research question
How, if at all, should the Internet be taxed?

Thesis statement
To improve equity between online and traditional stores and between consumers with and without Internet access, tax laws should be revised to allow collection of sales taxes on Internet purchases.

A precise thesis statement will give you a focus as you organize and draft your paper. For more on thesis statements, see pages 20–23.

2 Organization

To structure your paper, you'll need to synthesize, or forge relationships among ideas (see pp. 324–325). Here is one approach:

- Arrange your notes in groups of related ideas and information according to the subject headings you wrote on your notes. Each group should correspond to a main section of your paper: a key idea of your own that supports the thesis.
- Review your research journal for connections between sources and other thoughts that can help you organize your paper.
- Look objectively at your groups of notes. If a group is skimpy, with few notes, consider whether you should drop the category or conduct more research to fill it out. If most of your notes fall into one or two groups, consider whether the categories are too broad and should be divided. (If any of this rethinking affects your thesis statement, revise it accordingly.)
- Within each group, distinguish between the main idea of the group (which should be your own) and the supporting ideas and evidence (which should come from your sources).

See pages 23–28 for more on organizing a paper, including samples of both informal and formal outlines.

51b Drafting, revising, and formatting the paper

1 First draft

In drafting your paper, you do not have to proceed methodically from introduction to conclusion. Instead, draft in sections, beginning with the one you feel most confident about. Each section should center on a principal idea contributing to your thesis, a conclusion you have drawn from reading and responding to sources. Start the section by stating the idea; then support it with information, summaries, paraphrases, and quotations from your notes. Remember to insert source information from your notes as well.

 If you have kept your notes on a computer, you can import them (and source information) directly into your draft and then rewrite and edit them so that they work for your ideas and fit into your sentences.

2 Revision and editing

For a complex project like a research paper, you'll certainly want to revise in at least two stages—first for thesis, structure, and other whole-paper issues, and then for clarity, grammar, and other sentence-level issues. Chapter 6 supports this two-stage approach with checklists for revision (p. 33) and editing (p. 35). The box below provides additional steps to take when revising a research paper:

Checklist for revising a research paper
These steps supplement the revision checklist on p. 33.

51b

- Ensure that your thesis statement accurately describes your topic and your perspective as they emerged during drafting, so that the paper is unified and coherent.
- Be alert for structural problems. (Outlining your draft as suggested on p. 32 can help you see your structure at a glance.)
  Illogical arrangements of ideas.
  Inadequate emphasis of important points and overemphasis of minor points.
  Irrelevant ideas and facts that crept in just because you had notes on them.
- Ensure that *your* ideas, not the ideas of others, drive the paper. Check for places where you neglected to draw conclusions from sources or allowed sources' views to overwhelm your own.
- Look for places where supporting evidence is weak.
- Examine your explanations to be sure your readers will understand them. Define terms and clarify concepts that readers may be unfamiliar with.
- Integrate source material smoothly and clearly into your sentences. (See pp. 334–337.)
- Double-check your source citations for the following:
  A citation for every use of someone else's material, whether in summary, paraphrase, or quotation (see p. 331).
  Quotation marks for quotations; your own words and sentence structures for summaries and paraphrases (see p. 331).
  Accurate and complete source information.
  Correct format for source information, following your instructor's preference for style (see p. 337).

---

3 Format

The final draft of your paper should conform to the document format recommended by your instructor or by the style guide of the discipline in which you are writing (see p. 338). This book details two common formats: Modern Language Association (pp. 376–381) and American Psychological Association (pp. 407–413).

In any discipline you can use a word processor to present your ideas effectively and attractively with readable typefonts, headings, illustrations, and other elements. See pages 72–87 for ideas.

51b

MLA Documentation and Format

MLA Documentation and Format

MLA parenthetical text citations

MLA works-cited models

Books

52 MLA Documentation and Format

The style guide for English, foreign languages, and some other humanities is the *MLA Handbook for Writers of Research Papers*, published by the Modern Language Association. In the documentation system of the *MLA Handbook*, you twice acknowledge the sources of borrowed material:

- In your text, a brief parenthetical citation adjacent to the borrowed material directs readers to a complete list of all the works you cite.
- At the end of your paper, the list of works cited includes complete bibliographical information for every source.

MLA

52a

Every entry in the list of works cited has at least one corresponding citation in the text, and every in-text citation has a corresponding entry in the list of works cited.

This chapter describes MLA documentation: writing text citations (below), placing citations (p. 351), using supplementary notes (p. 353), and preparing the list of works cited (p. 353). A detailed discussion of MLA document format (p. 376) and a sample MLA paper (p. 381) conclude the chapter.

52a   Writing MLA parenthetical text citations

1 Citation formats

In-text citations of sources have two requirements:

- They must include just enough information for the reader to locate the appropriate source in your list of works cited.
- They must include just enough information for the reader to locate the place in the source where the borrowed material appears.

Usually, you can meet both these requirements by providing the author's last name (in the text or in parentheses) and the page(s) in the source on which the borrowed material appears (in parentheses). The reader can find the source in your list of works cited and find the borrowed material in the source itself.

The following models illustrate the basic text-citation forms and also forms for more unusual sources, such as those with no named author or no page numbers. See the tabbed divider at page 348 for an index to all the models.

Note Models 1 and 2 below show the direct relationship between what you include in your text and what you include in a parenthetical citation. If you do *not* name the author in your text, you include the name in parentheses before the page reference (model 1). If you *do* name the author in your text, you do not include the name in parentheses (model 2).

1. Author not named in your text

When you have not already named the author in your sentence, provide the author's last name and the page number(s), with no punctuation between them, in parentheses:

> One researcher concludes that "women impose a distinctive construction on moral problems, seeing moral dilemmas in terms of conflicting responsibilities" (Gilligan 105).

2. Author named in your text

If the author's name is already given in your text, you need not repeat it in the parenthetical citation. The citation gives just the page number(s):

> One researcher, Carol Gilligan, concludes that "women impose a distinctive construction on moral problems, seeing moral dilemmas in terms of conflicting responsibilities" (105).

3. A work with two or three authors

If the source has two or three authors, give all their last names in the text or in the citation. Separate two authors' names with "and":

> As Frieden and Sagalyn observe, "The poor and the minorities were the leading victims of highway and renewal programs" (29).

> According to one study, "The poor and the minorities were the leading victims of highway and renewal programs" (Frieden and Sagalyn 29).

With three authors, add commas and also "and" before the final name:

> The text by Wilcox, Ault, and Agee discusses the "ethical dilemmas in public relations practice" (125).

MLA

52a

One text discusses the "ethical dilemmas in public relations practice" (Wilcox, Ault, and Agee 125).

4. A work with more than three authors

If the source has more than three authors, you may list all their last names or use only the first author's name followed by "et al." (the abbreviation for the Latin "and others"). The choice depends on what you do in your list of works cited (see pp. 355–356).

It took the combined forces of the Americans, Europeans, and Japanese to break the rebel siege of Beijing in 1900 (Lopez et al. 362).

It took the combined forces of the Americans, Europeans, and Japanese to break the rebel siege of Beijing in 1900 (Lopez, Blum, Cameron, and Barnes 362).

5. A work with numbered paragraphs or screens instead of pages

Some electronic sources number each paragraph or screen instead of each page. In citing passages in these sources, give the paragraph or screen number(s) and distinguish them from page numbers: after the author's name, put a comma, a space, and the abbreviation "par." (one paragraph), "pars." (more than one paragraph), "screen," or "screens."

Twins reared apart report similar feelings (Palfrey, pars. 6-7).

6. An entire work or a work with no page or other reference numbers

When you cite an entire work rather than a part of it, the citation will not include any page or paragraph number. Try to work the author's name into your text, in which case you will not need a parenthetical citation. But remember that the source must appear in the list of works cited.

Boyd deals with the need to acknowledge and come to terms with our fear of nuclear technology.

Use the same format when you cite a specific passage from a work that has no page or other reference numbers, such as an online source.

If the author's name does not appear in your text, put it in a parenthetical citation:

Almost 20 percent of commercial banks have been audited for the practice (Friis).

7. A multivolume work

If you consulted only one volume of a multivolume work, your list of works cited will indicate as much (see p. 358), and you can treat the volume as any book.

If you consulted two or more volumes of a multivolume work, your citation must indicate which one you are referring to. In the example the number 5 indicates the volume from which the quotation was taken; the number 438 indicates the page number in that volume.

> After issuing the Emancipation Proclamation, Lincoln said, "What
>
> I did, I did after very full deliberations, and under a very heavy
>
> and solemn sense of responsibility" (5: 438).

8. A work by an author of two or more cited works

If your list of works cited includes two or more works by the same author, then your citation must tell the reader which of the author's works you are referring to. Give the title either in the text or in a parenthetical citation. In a parenthetical citation, give the full title only if it is brief; otherwise, shorten the title to the first one or two main words (excluding *A, An,* or *The*). For the following source, the full title is *The Arts and Human Development:*

> At about age seven, most children begin to use appropriate ges-
>
> tures to reinforce their stories (Gardner, <u>Arts</u> 144-45).

9. An unsigned work

Anonymous works are alphabetized by title in the list of works cited. In the text they are referred to by full or shortened title. This citation refers to an unsigned article titled "The Right to Die." (A page number is unnecessary because the article is no longer than a page.) If you use an abbreviated title, begin with the word by which it is alphabetized in the list of works cited (see p. 353).

> One article notes that a death-row inmate may demand his own
>
> execution to achieve a fleeting notoriety ("Right").

10. A government publication or a work with a corporate author

If the author of the work is listed as a government body or a corporation, cite the work by that organization's name. If the name is long, work it into the text to avoid an intrusive citation.

> A 1998 report by the Hawaii Department of Education predicts an
>
> increase in enrollments (6).

11. An indirect source

When you want to use a quotation that is already in quotation marks—indicating that the author you are reading is quoting someone else—try to find the original source and quote directly from it. If you can't find the original source, then your citation must indicate that your quotation of it is indirect. In the following citation, "qtd. in" ("quoted in") says that Davino was quoted by Boyd:

> George Davino maintains that "even small children have vivid
>
> ideas about nuclear energy" (qtd. in Boyd 22).

The list of works cited then includes only Boyd (the work consulted), not Davino.

12. A literary work

Novels, plays, and poems are often available in many editions, so your instructor may ask you to provide information that will help readers find the passage you cite no matter what edition they consult. For novels, the page number comes first, followed by a semicolon and then information on the appropriate part or chapter of the work.

> Toward the end of James's novel, Maggie suddenly feels "the thick
>
> breath of the definite--which was the intimate, the immediate, the
>
> familiar, as she hadn't had them for so long" (535; pt. 6, ch. 41).

For poems that are not divided into parts, you can omit the page number and supply the line number(s) for the quotation. To prevent confusion with page numbers, precede the number(s) with "line" or "lines" in the first citation; then just use the number(s).

> In Shakespeare's Sonnet 73 the speaker identifies with the trees of
>
> late autumn, "Bare ruined choirs, where late the sweet birds sang"
>
> (line 4). "In me," Shakespeare writes, "thou seest the glowing of
>
> such fire / That on the ashes of his youth doth lie" (9-10).

For verse plays and poems that are divided into parts, omit a page number and cite the appropriate part—act (and scene, if any), canto, book, and so on—plus the line number(s). Use Arabic numerals for parts, including acts and scenes (3.4).

> Later in King Lear Shakespeare has the disguised Edgar say, "The
>
> prince of darkness is a gentleman" (3.4.147).

For prose plays, provide the page number followed by the act and scene, if any (see the reference to *Death of a Salesman* on p. 352).

13. The Bible

When you cite passages of the Bible in parentheses, abbreviate the title of any book longer than four letters—for instance, "Gen." (Genesis), "1 Sam." (1 Samuel), "Ps." (Psalms), "Matt." (Matthew). Then give the chapter and verse(s) in Arabic numerals.

> According to the Bible, at Babel God "did [. . .] confound the language of all the earth" (Gen. 11.9).

14. An electronic source

 Cite an electronic source as you would any other source: usually by author's name or, if there is no author, by title.

> Business forecasts for the fourth quarter tended to be optimistic (White 4).

This example cites a source with page numbers. For a source with paragraph or screen numbers or no numbering, see models 5 and 6 (p. 348).

15. More than one work

If you use a parenthetical citation to refer to more than a single work, separate the references with a semicolon.

> Two recent articles point out that a computer badly used can be less efficient than no computer at all (Gough and Hall 201; Richards 162).

Since long citations in the text can distract the reader, you may choose to cite several or more works in an endnote or footnote rather than in the text. See the next page.

MLA

52a

2 Placement and punctuation of parenthetical citations

Position text citations to accomplish two goals: (1) make it clear exactly where your borrowing begins and ends; (2) keep the citation as unobtrusive as possible. You can accomplish both goals by placing the parenthetical citation at the end of the sentence element containing the borrowed material. This sentence element may be a phrase or a clause, and it may begin, interrupt, or conclude the sentence. Usually, as in the examples below, the element ends with a punctuation mark.

> The inflation rate might climb as high as 30 percent (Kim 164), an increase that could threaten the small nation's stability.

> The inflation rate, which might climb as high as 30 percent (Kim 164), could threaten the small nation's stability.

> The small nation's stability could be threatened by its inflation
> rate, which, one source predicts, might climb as high as 30 per-
> cent (Kim 164).

Notice that in the last example, the addition of *one source predicts*
clarifies that Kim is responsible only for the inflation-rate prediction, not for the statement about stability.

For citations in your running text, generally place the parenthetical citation *before* any punctuation required by your sentence,
as in the examples above. If the borrowed material is a quotation,
place the citation *between* the closing quotation mark and the
punctuation.

> Spelling argues that during the 1970s American automobile man-
> ufacturers met consumer needs "as well as could be expected" (26),
> but not everyone agrees with him.

The exception is a quotation ending in a question mark or exclamation point. Then use the appropriate punctuation inside the closing
quotation mark, and follow the quotation with the text citation and
a period.

> "Of what use is genius," Emerson asks, "if the organ [. . .] cannot
> find a focal distance within the actual horizon of human life?"
> ("Experience" 60). Mad genius is no genius.

When a citation appears after a quotation that ends in a bracketed ellipsis mark, place the citation between the closing quotation
mark and the sentence period (see also p. 255):

> One observer maintains that "American manufacturers must bear
> the blame for their poor sales [. . .]" (Rosenbaum 12).

When a citation appears at the end of a quotation set off from
the text, place it one space *after* the punctuation ending the quotation. No additional punctuation is needed.

> In Arthur Miller's <u>Death of a Salesman</u>, the most poignant defense
> of Willie Loman comes from his wife, Linda:
>
>> He's not the finest character that ever lived. But he's a
>> human being, and a terrible thing is happening to him.
>> So attention must be paid. He's not to be allowed to fall
>> into his grave like an old dog. Attention, attention must
>> finally be paid to such a person. (56; act 1)

(This citation of a play includes the act number as well as the page
number. See p. 350.)

MLA

52a

3 Footnotes or endnotes in special circumstances

Footnotes or endnotes may replace parenthetical citations when you cite several sources at once, when you comment on a source, or when you provide information that does not fit easily in the text. Signal a footnote or endnote in your text with a numeral raised above the appropriate line. Then write a note with the same numeral.

Text   At least five studies have confirmed these results.[1]

Note   [1] Abbott and Winger 266-68; Casner 27; Hoyenga

78-79; Marino 36; Tripp, Tripp, and Walk 179-83.

In a note the raised numeral is indented five spaces and followed by a space. If the note appears as a footnote, place it at the bottom of the page on which the citation appears, set it off from the text with quadruple spacing, and single-space the note itself. If the note appears as an endnote, place it in numerical order with the other endnotes on a page between the text and the list of works cited; double-space all the endnotes.

MLA

52b

52b Preparing the MLA list of works cited

At the end of your paper, a list titled "Works Cited" includes all the sources you quoted, paraphrased, or summarized in your paper. Even though a source may have been used more than once in your paper, it only appears once in the "Works Cited" list. (If your instructor asks you to include sources you examined but did not cite, title the list "Works Consulted.")

The list of works cited always begins a new page, numbered in sequence with the preceding pages. Center the title "Works Cited" at the top margin, one inch from the top of the page. Double-space between the title and the first entry. Format the list as in the sample on page 354. Begin each entry at the left margin. If an entry runs more than one line, indent the second and any subsequent lines one-half inch or five spaces from the left margin. Arrange all your sources in alphabetical order by the last name of the author—or by the last name of the first author if there is more than one. If a source has no named author, alphabetize it by the first main word of the title (excluding *A, An,* or *The*). Use *only* alphabetical order to arrange sources, not another principle such as type of source or date of publication.

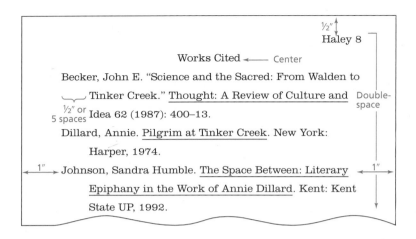

½" ↕

Haley 8

Works Cited ◄——— Center

Becker, John E. "Science and the Sacred: From Walden to

⟋ Tinker Creek." Thought: A Review of Culture and   Double-
space

½" or   Idea 62 (1987): 400–13.
5 spaces

Dillard, Annie. Pilgrim at Tinker Creek. New York:

Harper, 1974.

◄—1"—► Johnson, Sandra Humble. The Space Between: Literary ◄—1"—►

Epiphany in the Work of Annie Dillard. Kent: Kent

State UP, 1992.

An index to all the following models appears at the tabbed divider on pages 344–345. Use your best judgment in adapting the models to your particular sources. If you can't find a model that exactly matches a source you used, locate and follow the closest possible match. You will certainly need to combine formats—for instance, drawing on model 2 ("A book with two or three authors") and model 26 ("An article in a daily newspaper") for a newspaper article with two authors.

Note Computerized bibliography programs can format your list of works cited in MLA style when you provide the source information. However, be cautious in using such programs. See pages 339–340 for more on bibliography programs.

MLA

52b

1   Books

The basic format for a book includes the following elements:

①   ②
Gilligan, Carol. In a Different Voice: Psychological Theory and

③
Women's Development. Cambridge: Harvard UP, 1982.
ⓐ   ⓑ   ⓒ

1. *Author.* Use the author's full name: the last name first, followed by a comma, and then the first name and any middle name or initial. End the name with a period and one space. If only the author's initials are given on the source, use the initials in your citation. Use a suffix that is an essential part of the name, like Jr. or a Roman numeral that appears after a name.

2. *Title.* Give the full title, including any subtitle. Underline the title unless your instructor specifically calls for italics (see p. 271). Capitalize all important words (see pp. 269–270), separate

the main title and the subtitle with a colon and one space, and
end the title with a period and one space.

3. *Publication information.* You can usually find this information
   on the book's title page or on the copyright page immediately
   following.

   a. The city of publication, followed by a colon and one space. If
      several cities are listed, use only the first city shown. For
      cities outside the United States, add an abbreviation of the
      country, or the province for cities in Canada.

   b. The name of the publisher, followed by a comma. Shorten
      most publishers' names—in many cases to a single word. For
      instance, use "Little" for Little, Brown. For university presses,
      use the abbreviations "U" and "P," as in the example.

   c. The date of publication, ending with a period. Use the latest
      copyright date if the publication year does not appear on the
      title page.

When other information is required for a reference, it generally falls
either between the author's name and the title or between the title
and the publication information, as in the following models.

MLA

52b

1. A book with one author

Gilligan, Carol. In a Different Voice: Psychological Theory and

    Women's Development. Cambridge: Harvard UP, 1982.

2. A book with two or three authors

Frieden, Bernard J., and Lynne B. Sagalyn. Downtown, Inc.: How

    America Rebuilds Cities. Cambridge: MIT P, 1989.

Wilcox, Dennis L., Phillip H. Ault, and Warren K. Agee. Public Re-

    lations: Strategies and Tactics. 4th ed. New York: Harper,

    1995.

Give the authors' names in the order provided on the title page.
Reverse the first and last names of the first author *only.* Separate
two authors' names with a comma and "and"; separate three
authors' names with commas and with "and" before the third name.

3. A book with more than three authors

Lopez, Robert S., et al. Civilizations: Western and World. Boston:

    Little, 1975.

You may, but need not, give all authors' names if the work has more
than three authors. If you choose not to give all names, provide the
name of the first author only, and follow the name with a comma

and the abbreviation "et al." (for the Latin *et alii,* meaning "and others").

4. Two or more works by the same author(s)

Gardner, Howard. <u>The Arts and Human Development</u>. New York:
Wiley, 1973.

---. <u>The Quest for Mind: Piaget, Lévi-Strauss, and the Structuralist</u>
<u>Movement</u>. New York: Knopf, 1973.

Give the author's name only in the first entry. For the second and any subsequent works by the same author, substitute three hyphens for the author's name, followed by a period. (If you are citing two or more works by the same editor or translator, follow the hyphens with a comma and "ed." or "trans." as appropriate. See models 5, 6, and 7.) Note that the three hyphens stand for *exactly* the same name or names. If the second source above were by Gardner and somebody else, both names would have to be given in full.

Place an entry or entries using three hyphens immediately after the entry that names the author. Within the set of entries by the same author, arrange the sources alphabetically by the first main word of the title, as in the examples above (<u>Arts</u>, then <u>Quest</u>).

5. A book with an editor

Ruitenbeek, Hendrick, ed. <u>Freud as We Knew Him</u>. Detroit: Wayne
State UP, 1973.

The abbreviation "ed.," separated from the name by a comma, identifies Ruitenbeek as the editor of the work.

6. A book with an author and an editor

Mumford, Lewis. <u>The City in History</u>. Ed. Donald L. Miller. New
York: Pantheon, 1986.

When citing the work of the author, give his or her name first, and give the editor's name after the title, preceded by "Ed." ("Edited by"). When citing the work of the editor, use the form above for a book with an editor, and give the author's name after the title preceded by "By": Miller, Donald L., ed. <u>The City in History</u>. By Lewis Mumford.

7. A translation

Alighieri, Dante. <u>The Inferno</u>. Trans. John Ciardi. New York: NAL,
1971.

When citing the work of the author, give his or her name first, and give the translator's name after the title, preceded by "Trans." ("Translated by"). When citing the work of the translator, give his or her name first, followed by a comma and "trans."; then follow the title with "By" and the author's name: Ciardi, John, trans. The Inferno. By Dante Alighieri.

When a book you cite by author has a translator *and* an editor, give the translator's and editor's names in the order used on the book's title page. For a translated selection from an edited book, see model 18, page 359.

8. A book with a corporate author

Lorenz Research, Inc. Research in Social Studies Teaching. Baltimore: Arrow, 1997.

List the name of the corporation, institution, or other body as author.

9. An anonymous book

The Dorling Kindersley World Reference Atlas. London: Dorling, 1999.

List an anonymous book by its full title. Alphabetize the book by the title's first main word (here "Dorling"), omitting *A, An,* or *The.*

10. The Bible

The Bible. King James Version.

The New English Bible. London: Oxford UP and Cambridge UP, 1970.

When citing a standard version of the Bible (first example), do not underline the title or the name of the version, and you need not provide publication information. For an edition of the Bible (second example), underline the title and give its publication information.

11. A later edition

Bollinger, Dwight L. Aspects of Language. 2nd ed. New York: Harcourt, 1975.

For any edition after the first, place the edition number between the title and the publication information. Use the appropriate designation for editions that are named or dated rather than numbered—for instance, "Rev. ed." for "Revised edition."

12. A republished book

James, Henry. The Golden Bowl. 1904. London: Penguin, 1966.

Place the original date of publication after the title, and then provide the full publication information for the source you are using.

13. A book with a title in its title

Eco, Umberto. Postscript to The Name of the Rose. Trans. William

Weaver. New York: Harcourt, 1983.

When a book's title contains another book title (as here: The Name of the Rose), do not underline the shorter title. When a book's title contains a quotation or the title of a work normally placed in quotation marks, keep the quotation marks and underline both titles: Critical Response to Henry James's "Beast in the Jungle." (Note that the underlining extends under the closing quotation mark.)

14. A work in more than one volume

Lincoln, Abraham. The Collected Works of Abraham Lincoln. Ed.

Roy P. Basler. 8 vols. New Brunswick: Rutgers UP, 1953.

Lincoln, Abraham. The Collected Works of Abraham Lincoln. Ed.

Roy P. Basler. Vol. 5. New Brunswick: Rutgers UP, 1953. 8

vols.

If you use two or more volumes of a multivolume work, give the work's total number of volumes before the publication information ("8 vols." in the first example). Your text citation will indicate which volume you are citing (see p. 349). If you use only one volume, give that volume number before the publication information ("Vol. 5" in the second example). You may add the total number of volumes to the end of the entry ("8 vols." in the second example).

If you cite a multivolume work published over a period of years, give the inclusive years as the publication date: for instance, Cambridge: Harvard UP, 1978-90.

15. A work in a series

Bergman, Ingmar. The Seventh Seal. Mod. Film Scripts Ser. 12.

New York: Simon, 1968.

Place the name of the series (not quoted or underlined) just before the publication information. Abbreviate common words such as *modern* and *series*. Add any series number after the series title.

16. Published proceedings of a conference

<u>Watching Our Language: A Conference Sponsored by the Program</u>

<u>in Architecture and Design Criticism</u>. 6-8 May 1999. New

York: Parsons School of Design, 1999.

Whether in or after the title of the conference, supply information about who sponsored the conference, when it was held, and who published the proceedings. Teat a particular presentation at the conference like a selection from an anthology (model 18).

17. An anthology, compilation, or book collection

Barnet, Sylvan, et al., eds. <u>An Introduction to Literature</u>. 11th ed.

New York: Longman, 1997.

When citing an entire anthology, give the name of the editor or editors (followed by "ed." or "eds.") and then the title of the anthology. This anthology has four editors, so "et al." can replace all but the first editor's name. (See model 3, p. 355.)

18. A selection from an anthology, compilaton, or book collection

Chekhov, Anton. "Misery." Trans. Constance Garnett. <u>An Introduc-</u>

<u>tion to Literature</u>. Ed. Sylvan Barnet et al. 11th ed. New

York: Longman, 1997. 58-61.

When you cite a selection from an anthology or a collection of excerpts from books or articles, you need to add the information about the specific selection you used. The essentials of this listing are these: author of selection; title of selection (in quotation marks); title of anthology (underlined); editors' names preceded by "Ed." ("Edited by"); publication information for the anthology; and inclusive page numbers for the selection (without the abbreviation "pp.").

If the work you cite comes from a collection of works by one author and with no editor, use the following form:

Auden, W. H. "Family Ghosts." <u>The Collected Poetry of W. H.</u>

<u>Auden</u>. New York: Random, 1945. 132-33.

If the work you cite is a scholarly article that was previously printed elsewhere, first provide the complete information for the earlier publication of the piece. Then follow with "Rpt. in" ("Reprinted in") and the information for the source in which you found the scholarly article:

Reekmans, Tony. "Juvenal on Social Change." <u>Ancient Society</u> 2

(1971): 117-61. Rpt. in <u>Private Life in Rome</u>. Ed. Helen West.

Los Angeles: Coronado, 1981. 124-69.

19. Two or more selections from the same anthology

Auden, W. H. "The Unknown Citizen." Barnet et al. 687-88.

Barnet, Sylvan, et al., eds. <u>An Introduction to Literature</u>. 11th ed.

New York: Longman, 1997.

Miller, Arthur. <u>Death of a Salesman</u>. Barnet et al. 1163-231.

When citing more than one selection from the same source, you may avoid repetition by giving the source in full (as in the Barnet et al. entry) and then simply cross-referencing it in entries for the works you used. Thus, instead of full information for the Auden and Miller works, give "Barnet et al." and the appropriate pages in that book. Note that each entry appears in its proper alphabetical place among other works cited.

20. An introduction, preface, foreword, or afterword

Donaldson, Norman. Introduction. <u>The Claverings</u>. By Anthony

Trollope. New York: Dover, 1977. vii-xv.

An introduction, foreword, or afterword is often written by someone other than the book's author. When citing such a piece, give its name without quotation marks or underlining. (But if the work has a title of its own, provide it, in quotation marks, between the name of the author and the name of the piece.) Follow the title of the book with its author's name preceded by "By." Give the inclusive page numbers of the part you cite. (In the example above, the small Roman numerals indicate that the cited work is in the front matter of the book, before page 1.)

When the author of a preface or introduction is the same as the author of the book, give only the last name after the title:

Gould, Stephen Jay. Prologue. <u>The Flamingo's Smile: Reflections in</u>

<u>Natural History</u>. By Gould. New York: Norton, 1985.

13-20.

21. An article in a reference work

Mark, Herman F. "Polymers." <u>The New Encyclopaedia Britannica:</u>

<u>Macropaedia</u>. 15th ed. 1991.

"Reckon." <u>Merriam-Webster's Collegiate Dictionary</u>. 10th ed. 1998.

List an article in a reference work by its title (second example) unless the article is signed (first example). For works with entries arranged alphabetically, you need not include volume or page numbers. For well-known works like those listed above, you may also omit the editors' names and all publication information except any edition number and the year of publication. For works that are not well known, give full publication information.

2 Periodicals: Journals, magazines, and newspapers

The basic format for an article from a periodical includes the following information:

Lever, Janet. "Sex Differences in the Games Children Play."

Social Problems 23 (1976): 478-87.

1. *Author.* Use the author's full name: the last name first, followed by a comma, and then the first name and any middle name or initial. End the name with a period and one space.
2. *Title of the article.* Give the full title, including any subtitle. Place the title in quotation marks, capitalize all important words in the title (see pp. 269–270, and end the title with a period (inside the final quotation mark) and one space.
3. *Publication information.*

   a. The title of the periodical, underlined, followed by a space. Omit any *A, An,* or *The* from the beginning of the title.
   b. The volume and/or issue number (in Arabic numerals), followed by a space. See the note following.
   c. The date of publication, followed by a colon and a space. See the note following.
   d. The inclusive page numbers of the article (without the abbreviation "pp."). For the second number in inclusive page numbers over 100, provide only as many digits as needed for clarity (usually two): 100–01, 398–401, 1026–36. If the article does not run on consecutive pages, provide only the first page number followed by a plus sign: 16+. (See also model 26, next page.)

Note The treatment of volume and issue numbers and publication dates varies depending on the kind of periodical being cited, as the models indicate. For the distinction between journals and magazines, see pages 306–308.

MLA

52b

22. An article in a journal with continuous pagination throughout the annual volume

Lever, Janet. "Sex Differences in the Games Children Play." <u>Social

Problems</u> 23 (1976): 478-87.

Some journals number the pages of issues consecutively throughout a year, so that issue number 3 may begin on page 261. For this kind of journal, give the volume number after the title ("23" in the example above) and place the year of publication in parentheses.

23. An article in a journal that pages issues separately or that numbers only issues, not volumes

Dacey, June. "Management Participation in Corporate Buy-Outs."

<u>Management Perspectives</u> 7.4 (1998): 20-31.

Some journals page each issue separately (starting each issue at page 1). For these journals, give the volume number, a period, and the issue number (as in "7.4" in the entry above). When citing an article in a journal that numbers only issues, not annual volumes, treat the issue number as if it were a volume number, as in model 22.

24. An article in a monthly or bimonthly magazine

Tilin, Andrew. "Selling the Dream." <u>Worth</u> Oct. 1999: 94-100.

Follow the magazine title with the month and the year of publication. (Abbreviate all months except May, June, and July.) Don't place the date in parentheses, and don't provide a volume or issue number.

25. An article in a weekly or biweekly magazine

Stevens, Mark. "Low and Behold." <u>New Republic</u> 24 Dec. 1990:

27-33.

Follow the magazine title with the day, the month (abbreviated), and the year of publication. (Abbreviate all months except May, June, and July.) Don't place the date in parentheses, and don't provide a volume or issue number.

26. An article in a daily newspaper

Lewis, Peter H. "Many Updates Cause Profitable Confusion." <u>New

York Times</u> 21 Jan. 1999, natl. ed.: D1+.

Give the name of the newspaper as it appears on the first page (but without *A*, *An*, or *The*). Then follow model 25, with two differences:

(1) If the newspaper lists an edition at the top of the first page, include that information after the date and a comma. (See "natl. ed." above.) (2) If the newspaper is divided into lettered or numbered sections, provide the section designation before the page number when the newspaper does the same (as in "D1+" above); otherwise, provide the section designation before the colon—for instance, sec. 1: 1+. The plus sign here and with "D1+" in the preceding model indicates that the articles do not run on consecutive pages but start on page 1 or D1 and continue later.

27. An unsigned article

"The Right to Die." Time 11 Oct. 1976: 101.

Begin the entry for an unsigned article with the title of the article. In the list of works cited, alphabetize an anonymous source by the first main word of the title ("Right" in this model).

28. An editorial or letter to the editor

"Bodily Intrusions." Editorial. New York Times 29 Aug. 1990, late
ed.: A20.

Add the word "Editorial" or "Letter"—but without quotation marks—after the title if there is one or after the author's name, as follows:

Dowding, Michael. Letter. Economist 5-11 Jan. 1985: 4.

(The numbers "5-11" in this entry are the publication days of the periodical: the issue spans January 5 through 11.)

29. A review

Dunne, John Gregory. "The Secret of Danny Santiago." Rev. of
Famous All over Town, by Danny Santiago. New York Review
of Books 16 Aug. 1984: 17-27.

"Rev." is an abbreviation for "Review." The name of the author of the work being reviewed follows the title of the work, a comma, and "by." If the review has no title of its own, then "Rev. of . . ." (without quotation marks) immediately follows the name of the reviewer.

30. An abstract of a dissertation or article

Steciw, Steven K. "Alterations to the Pessac Project of Le Cor-
busier." Diss. U of Cambridge, England, 1986. DAI 46 (1986):
565C.

For an abstract appearing in *Dissertation Abstracts* (*DA*) or *Dissertation Abstracts International* (*DAI*), give the author's name and the title, "Diss." (for "Dissertation"), the institution granting the author's degree, the date of the dissertation, and the publication information.

For an abstract of an article, first provide the publication information for the article itself, followed by the information for the abstract:

> Lever, Janet. "Sex Differences in the Games Children Play." Social
>
> Problems 23 (1976): 478-87. Psychological Abstracts 63
>
> (1976): item 1431.

3 Electronic sources

Increasingly, information is being published in electronic form. Since much of the technology being used is new and rapidly changing, standards for citing these sources are still evolving. However, the citation of electronic sources should accomplish the same goal as the citation of printed sources—to enable the reader to locate the source in a subsequent search.

Many authorities classify electronic sources into two types: online sources and other electronic sources. Online sources include World Wide Web sites, reference indexes or databases, online books and periodicals, online postings to listservs or newsgroups, and electronic mail. Other electronic sources include CD-ROMs or diskettes, computer software programs, and synchronous communications such as chat rooms.

Like citations of print sources, citations of online sources require available information such as author, title, and date of publication (date of online posting or last revision for an online source). But online sources also require two special pieces of information:

- Give the date when you consulted the source as well as the date when the source was posted or updated. Online sources can and often do change, so your access date tells readers which version you used. In the works-cited entry, place the posting date first, with other publication information; then place your access date near the end of the entry, just before the electronic address.
- Give the source's exact electronic address, enclosed in angle brackets (< >). Usually, you'll find the address in your Web browser's Location or Address field near the top of the screen as you're viewing the source (see p. 297). Be sure to give the complete address for the specific page you are using, not just for the site's home page.

The complete address includes the protocol (usually *http://*), the Web site's home page address (for example, *www.phoenix. edu*), followed by a slash; and the specific page you accessed on the site (for example, /students/index.html). Sometimes this information is followed by a string of letters and symbols that represent the path the computer took to reach the specific document you accessed. Some of these symbols are computer language and are not relevant to your specific source. You need not cite all these symbols. End the electronic address once you have included all the information mentioned above. Usually, this means copying the exact address until you reach a symbol or an unrecognizable word. Place the address at the end of the entry. If you must break an address from one line to the next, do so *only* after a slash, and do not hyphenate.

Try to locate all the information required in the following models, referring to pages 294–297 for help. However, if you search for and still cannot find some information, then give what you can find.

31. A source on a periodical CD-ROM

A source also published in print:

Lewis, Peter H. "Many Updates Cause Profitable Confusion." New York Times 21 Jan. 1999, natl. ed.: D1+. New York Times Ondisc. CD-ROM. UMI-ProQuest. Mar. 1999.

If you cite a source on CD-ROM that's issued periodically (like a journal or magazine), look for information about a print version of the same source. (The information is usually at the beginning of the source.) If there is such information, provide it as in the model above (1), referring to pages 361–364 as needed. Then provide the following information on the CD-ROM version: the title of the CD-ROM (2), underlined; the medium, "CD-ROM" (3), without quotation marks or underlining; the name of the vendor (or distributor) of the CD-ROM (4); and the date of electronic publication (5).

A periodical CD-ROM without information for a print version:

"Vanguard Forecasts." Business Outlook. CD-ROM. Information Access. Mar. 1999.

If a periodical source appears only on CD-ROM (not also in print), give only the CD-ROM title, the medium, the vendor, and the date.

32. A source on a nonperiodical CD-ROM

Shelley, Mary Wollstonecraft. <u>Frankenstein</u>. <u>Classic Library</u>.

CD-ROM. Alameda: Andromeda, 1993.

If you cite a single-issue CD-ROM, first provide its author (1) and title (2). Underline titles of books or similarly long works; use quotation marks for short works such as stories or parts of books. Then give the underlined title of the entire disk (3), if there is a title; give the medium (4), without quotation marks or underlining; and end with the disk's place of publication, publisher, and date of publication (5).

If the work you cite or the entire disk has a version or edition number, add it at the appropriate place, as shown in the model below:

"Sugar." <u>Concise Columbia Encyclopedia</u>. 3rd ed. <u>Microsoft Book-

shelf</u>. CD-ROM. 1998-99 ed. Redmond: Microsoft, 1998.

This model also shows citation of a part of a work (in quotation marks) with no author.

33. An online book

A book published independently:

James, Henry. <u>The Turn of the Screw</u>. New York: Scribner's,

1908-09. 4 Mar. 1999 <http://www.americanliterature.com/

TS/TSINDX.HTML>.

For an online book published independently, not as part of a scholarly project or other larger site, provide the author's name (1); the underlined title of the book (2); any publication information for the original print version of the book (3); the date you consulted the source (4); and the electronic address in angle brackets (5). If the book was not published in print before, substitute the date of electronic publication for the print publication information. If the book has an editor or translator, include that information as in the following model.

A book within a scholarly project:

Austen, Jane. <u>Emma</u>. Ed. Ronald Blythe. Harmondsworth:

Penguin, 1972. <u>Oxford Text Archive</u>. 1994. Oxford U.

15 Dec. 1997 <ftp://ota.ox.ac.uk/pub/ota/public/english/

Austen/emma.1519>.

For a book published as part of a scholarly project, first list the author and title (1), the name of any editor or translator (2), and any print publication information provided in the source (3). Add the title of the project (4), underlined; the date of electronic publication (5); the name of any sponsoring organization or institution (6); the date of your access (7); and the electronic address (8), which should direct readers to the book rather than to the project as a whole. If the project has an editor, add the name after the project's title (see model 39 on p. 368).

34. An article in an online journal

Palfrey, Andrew. "Choice of Mates in Identical Twins." <u>Modern Psychology</u> 4.1 (1996): 12 pars. 25 Feb. 2000 <http://www.liasu.edu/modpsy/palfrey4(1).htm>.

Follow model 22 or 23 on page 365 for citing a scholarly article (1), but add the date you consulted the source (2) and the electronic address (3). If the journal provides page, paragraph, or other reference numbers, give the inclusive numbers (such as 20-31 for pages, as in model 23 on p. 362) or the total number (such as 12 pars. in the preceding model). Omit reference numbers if the source does not use them.

35. An online abstract

Palfrey, Andrew. "Choice of Mates in Identical Twins." <u>Modern Psychology</u> 4.1 (1996): 12 pars. Abstract. 25 Feb. 2000 <http://www.liasu.edu/modpsy/abstractpalfrey4(1).htm>.

Treat an online abstract like an online journal article (model 34 above), but add "Abstract" (without quotation marks or underlining) between the publication information and the date of your access.

36. An article in an online newspaper

Still, Lucia. "On the Battlefields of Business, Millions of Casualties." <u>New York Times on the Web</u> 3 Mar. 1999. 17 Aug. 1999 <http://www.nytimes.com/specials/downsize/03down1.html>.

For an online newspaper article, provide the author's name (1); the title of the article (2), in quotation marks; the title of the online newspaper (3), underlined; the date of publication (4); the date you consulted the source (5); and the electronic address for the article (6). Provide section, page, or paragraph numbers if the newspaper does, as in model 26 (p. 362).

37. An article in an online magazine

Palevitz, Barry A., and Ricki Lewis. "Death Raises Safety Issues for Primate Handlers." Scientist 2 Mar. 1998: 1+. 27 Mar. 1998 <http://www.the-scientist.library.upenn.edu/ yr1998/mar/palevitz_pl_980302.html>.

Cite an article in an online magazine with the name(s) of the author(s) (1); the title of the article (2), in quotation marks; the title of the periodical (3), underlined; the date of publication (4); any page, paragraph, or other reference numbers (5); the date you consulted the source (6); and the electronic address (7).

MLA

52b

38. An online review

Detwiler, Donald S., and Chu Shao-Kang. Rev. of Important Documents of the Republic of China, ed. Tan Quon Chin. Journal of Military History 56.4 (1992): 669-84. 16 Sept. 1997 <http://www.jstor.org/fcgi-bin/jstor/viewitem.fcg/ 08993718/96p0008x>.

Cite an online review following model 29 on page 366 and the appropriate model on the previous two pages for an online scholarly journal, newspaper, or magazine (1). Include the date you consulted the source (2) and the electronic address (3).

39. An online scholarly project or database

Scots Teaching and Research Network. Ed. John Corbett. 2 Feb. 1998. U of Glasgow. 5 Mar. 1999 <http://www.arts.gla.ac.uk/ www/english/comet/starn/htm>.

When citing an entire project or database, provide the title (1), underlined; the name of any editor (2); the date of publication (3); the name of any organization or institution that sponsors the project or database (4); the date you consulted the source (5); and the electronic address (6). If the project or database has a version number, add it after the editor's name and before the date of publication—for instance, Vers. 3.2.

40. A short work from an online scholarly project or database

Barbour, John. "The Brus." Scots Teaching and Research Network.

Ed. John Corbett. 2 Feb. 1998. U of Glasgow. 5 Mar. 1999

<http://www.arts.gla.ac.uk/www/english/comet/starn/poetry/

brus/contents/htm>.

For a poem, an article, or another short work published as part of a scholarly project or database, start with the author's name (1) and the title of the short work (2), in quotation marks. Then follow the model above for the complete project (3), but give the specific electronic address for the short work (4).

41. A personal or professional online site

Lederman, Leon. Topics in Modern Physics--Lederman. 12 Dec.

1999 <http://www-ed.fnal.gov/samplers/hsphys/people/

lederman.html>.

Cite a personal or professional site with the author's name (1); the title if any (2), underlined; the date you consulted the source (3); and the electronic address (4). If the source has no title, describe it with a label such as "Home page," without quotation marks or underlining. If it has a sponsoring organization or institution, add the name after the title.

42. A work from an online subscription service

Wilkins, Johanna M. "The Myths of the Only Child." Psychology

Update 12 Dec. 1999: 16-20. ProQuest Health and Medical

Complete. ProQuest Direct. Manhattan Community Coll. Lib.,

New York. 20 Dec. 1999 <http://www.umi.com/proquest/>.

Many periodicals are published both in print and online as part of a database. Two common types of online services or databases are those that users subscribe to personally (America Online) and those that organizations or libraries usually subscribe to (Pro-Quest, EBSCOhost, InfoTrac, or Lexis-Nexis). If the service you use gives a specific electronic address for your source, you can generally base your works-cited entry on models 33–41, selecting the one that matches your kind of source. However, if the service does not provide the source's specific address, then you need to follow the model above or the one below. The model above, for a library service, begins with author, title, and publication information as for a magazine article (1). It then adds the name of the database (2), underlined; the name of the service (3), not underlined; the name and location of the subscribing library (4); the date of access (5); and the electronic address of the service's home page (6).

Some subscription services ask users to search with keywords or through a directory (or path) of topics:

> "China--Dragon Kings." The Encyclopedia Mythica. America Online. 6 Jan. 1999. Path: Research and Learn; Encyclopedia; More Encyclopedias; Encyclopedia Mythica.

This model includes the title of the source and the larger work (1), the name of the service (2), the date of access (3), and then "Path:" (without quotation marks or underlining) and the sequence of topics required to reach the source (4), with the topics separated by semicolons.

If you reached the source with a keyword rather than a path, give that information instead—for instance, Keyword: Mythica.

43. Electronic mail

> Millon, Michele. "Re: Grief Therapy." E-mail to the author. 4 May 1997.

For e-mail, give the name of the writer (1); the title, if any, from the e-mail's subject heading (2), in quotation marks; a description of the transmission, including whom it was sent to (3); and the date of posting (4).

44. A posting to a discussion list

The original posting:

> Tourville, Michael. "European Currency Reform." Online posting. 6 Jan. 1999. International Finance Discussion List. 12 Jan. 1999 <finance-dl@weg.isu.edu>.

For a list subscribed to via e-mail, give the author's name (1); the title, if any, from the e-mail's subject heading (2), in quotation marks; the words "Online posting" (3), without quotation marks or underlining; the date of the posting (4); the name of the list (5); the date you consulted the source (6); and the electronic address (7). (See pp. 316–317 for more on discussion lists.)

An archived posting:

> Tourville, Michael. "European Currency Reform." Online posting.
>
> 6 Jan. 1999. International Finance Archive. 2 June 1999
>
> <http://www.weg.isu.edu/finance-dl/46732>.

Whenever possible, cite an archived version of the posting (see p. 316). If the posting has an identifying number, insert it immediately after the list's name—for example, Art Finds Discussion List 22634.

45. A posting to a newsgroup or Web forum

A newsgroup:

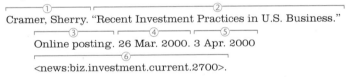

> Cramer, Sherry. "Recent Investment Practices in U.S. Business."
>
> Online posting. 26 Mar. 2000. 3 Apr. 2000
>
> <news:biz.investment.current.2700>.

MLA

52b

A newsgroup is not subscriber-based (see p. 317). For a posting to a newsgroup, give the author's name (1); the title from the subject heading (2), in quotation marks; "Online posting" (3), without quotation marks or underlining; the date of posting (4); the date you consulted the source (5); and, in angle brackets, the group's name preceded by "news:" (6), as in the example.

A Web forum:

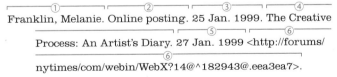

> Franklin, Melanie. Online posting. 25 Jan. 1999. The Creative
>
> Process: An Artist's Diary. 27 Jan. 1999 <http://forums/
>
> nytimes/com/webin/WebX?14@^182943@.eea3ea7>.

Give the author (1); the title, if any, in quotation marks (the example has no title); "Online posting" (2), without quotation marks or underlining; the date of posting (3); the name of the forum (4); the date of access (5); and the electronic address (6).

46. An online graphic, video, or audio file

Hamilton, Calvin J. "Components of Comets." Diagram. Space Art.

1997. 20 Dec. 1999 <wysisiwyg://94/http://spaceart.com/

solar/eng/comet.htm>.

In general, you can base citations of online visual or audio sources on models 52–56 and 60 (pp. 373–376), adding information appropriate for an online source. This example includes the creator's name (1); the title of the source (2); a description of the source (3), without quotation marks or underlining; the title of the larger work in which the source appears (4), underlined; the date of the source (5); the date of access (6); and the electronic address (7).

47. A synchronous communication (MUD, MOO, etc.)

Bruckman, Amy. MediaMOO Symposium: Virtual Worlds for

Business? 20 Jan. 1998. MediaMOO. 26 Feb. 1998

<http://www.cc.gatech.edu/fac/Amy.Bruckman/MediaMOO/

cscw-symposium-98.html>.

MLA
52b

Cite a synchronous communication with the name of the speaker (1); a description of the event (2), without quotation marks or underlining; the date of the event (3); the forum (4); the date you consulted the source (5); and the electronic address (6). Whenever possible, cite an archived version of the communication (see model 44 on p. 370).

48. Computer software

Project Scheduler 8000. Vers. 4.1. Orlando: Scitor, 1999.

For software, provide the title (1), underlined; the version number (2); and the publication information (3), including place of publication, publisher, and date. If you consulted or obtained the software online, replace this publication information with the date of access and the electronic address, as in previous examples.

4 **Other sources**

49. A government publication

Hawaii. Dept. of Education. Kauai District Schools, Profile 1996-

97. Honolulu: Hawaii Dept. of Education, 1998.

Stiller, Ann. <u>Historic Preservation and Tax Incentives</u>. US Dept. of

Interior. Washington: GPO, 1996.

United States. Cong. House. Committee on Ways and Means.

<u>Medicare Payment for Outpatient Occupational Therapy Ser-</u>

<u>vices</u>. 102nd Cong., 1st sess. Washington: GPO, 1991.

If an author is not listed for a government publication, give the appropriate agency as author, as in the first and last examples. Provide information in the order illustrated, separating elements with a period and a space: the name of the government, the name of the agency (which may be abbreviated), and the title and publication information. For a congressional publication (last example), give the house and committee involved before the title, and give the number and session of Congress after the title. In the second and last examples, "GPO" stands for the US Government Printing Office.

50. A pamphlet

<u>Medical Answers About AIDS</u>. New York: Gay Men's Health Crisis,

1998.

Most pamphlets can be treated as books. In the example above, the pamphlet has no listed author, so the title comes first. If the pamphlet has an author, list his or her name first.

51. An unpublished dissertation or thesis

Wilson, Stuart M. "John Stuart Mill as a Literary Critic." Diss. U of

Michigan, 1970.

The title is quoted rather than underlined. "Diss." stands for "Dissertation." "U of Michigan" is the institution that granted the author's degree.

52. A musical composition or work of art

Fauré, Gabriel. Sonata for Violin and Piano no. 1 in A major, op.

15.

Don't underline musical compositions identified only by form, number, and key. Do underline titled operas, ballets, and compositions (<u>Carmen</u>, <u>Sleeping Beauty</u>).

For a work of art, underline the title and include the name and location of the owner. For a work you see only in a photograph, provide the complete publication information, too, as in the following model. Omit such information only if you examined the actual work.

MLA

52b

Sargent, John Singer. <u>Venetian Doorway</u>. Metropolitan Museum of
Art, New York. <u>Sargent Watercolors</u>. By Donelson F. Hoopes.
New York: Watson, 1976. 31.

53. A film or video recording

<u>Schindler's List</u>. Dir. Steven Spielberg. Perf. Liam Neeson and Ben
Kingsley. Universal, 1993.

Start with the title of the work you are citing, unless you are citing
the contribution of a particular individual (see the next model).
Give additional information (writer, lead performers, and so on) as
you judge appropriate. For a film, end with the distributor and date.

For a videocassette, filmstrip, or slide program, include the
original release date (if any) and the medium (without underlining
or quotation marks) before the distributor's name:

George Balanchine, chor. <u>Serenade</u>. Perf. San Francisco Ballet. Dir.
Hilary Bean. 1981. Videocassette. PBS Video, 1987.

54. A television or radio program

Kenyon, Jane, and Donald Hall. "A Life Together." <u>Bill Moyers'
Journal</u>. PBS. WNET, New York. 17 Dec. 1998.

As in model 53, start with a title unless you are citing the work of a
person or persons. The example above begins with the participants'
names, then the episode title (in quotation marks), then the program title (underlined). Finish the entry with the name of the network, the local station and city, and the date.

55. A performance

<u>The English Only Restaurant</u>. By Silvio Martinez Palau. Dir.
Susana Tubert. Puerto Rican Traveling Theater, New York. 27
July 1999.

Ozawa, Seiji, cond. Boston Symphony Orch. Symphony Hall,
Boston. 25 Apr. 1997.

As with films and television programs, place the title first unless
you are citing the work of an individual (second example). Provide
additional information about participants after the title, as well as
the theater, city, and date. Note that the orchestra name in the second example is neither quoted nor underlined.

56. A recording

Siberry, Jane. "Caravan." <u>Maria</u>. Reprise, 1995.

Brahms, Johannes. Concerto no. 2 in B-flat, op. 83. Perf. Artur

Rubinstein. Cond. Eugene Ormandy. Philadelphia Orch. LP.

RCA, 1972.

Begin with the name of the individual whose work you are citing. If you're citing a song, give the title in quotation marks. Then provide the title of the recording, underlining the title (first example) unless it identifies a composition by form, number, and key (second example). After the title, provide the names of any other artists it seems appropriate to mention, the manufacturer of the recording, and the date of release. If the medium is other than compact disk, provide it immediately before the manufacturer's name—for instance, LP (as above) or Audiocassette.

57. A letter

Buttolph, Mrs. Laura E. Letter to Rev. and Mrs. C. C. Jones. 20

June 1857. In <u>The Children of Pride: A True Story of Georgia</u>

<u>and the Civil War</u>. Ed. Robert Manson Myers. New Haven:

Yale UP, 1972. 334-35.

MLA

52b

A published letter is listed under the writer's name. Specify that the source is a letter and to whom it was addressed, and give the date on which it was written. Treat the remaining information like that for a selection from an anthology (model 18, p. 359). (See also p. 363 for the format of a letter to the editor of a periodical.)

For a letter in the collection of a library or archive, specify the writer, recipient, and date, as above, and give the name and location of the archive as well:

James, Jonathan E. Letter to his sister. 16 Apr. 1970. Jonathan E.

James Papers. South Dakota State Archive, Pierre.

For a letter you receive, give the name of the writer, note the fact that the letter was sent to you, and provide the date of the letter:

Packer, Ann E. Letter to the author. 15 June 1999.

Use the form above for personal electronic mail (e-mail) as well, substituting "E-mail" for "Letter": E-mail to the author (see model 43, p. 370).

58. A lecture or address

Carlone, Dennis. "Architecture for the City of the Twenty-First

> Century." Tenth Symposium on Urban Issues. Cambridge City

> Hall, Cambridge. 22 May 2000.

Give the speaker's name, the title (in quotation marks), the title of the meeting, the name of the sponsoring organization, the location of the lecture, and the date. If you do not know the title, replace it with "Lecture," "Address," or another description, but *not* in quotation marks.

59. An interview

Graaf, Vera. Personal interview. 19 Dec. 1999.

Christopher, Warren. Interview. <u>Frontline</u>. PBS. WGBH, Boston. 13

> Feb. 1998.

Begin with the name of the person interviewed. For an interview you conducted, specify "Personal interview" or the medium (such as "Telephone interview," "E-mail interview")—without quotation marks or underlining—and then give the date. For an interview you read, heard, or saw, provide the title if any or "Interview" if not, along with other bibliographic information and the date.

60. A map or other illustration

<u>Women in the Armed Forces</u>. Map. <u>Women in the World: An Inter-

> national Atlas</u>. By Joni Seager and Ann Olson. New York:

> Touchstone, 1999. 44-45.

List the illustration by its title (underlined). Provide a descriptive label ("Map," "Chart," "Table"), without underlining or quotation marks, and the publication information. If the creator of the illustration is credited in the source, put his or her name first in the entry, as with any author.

52c   Formatting a paper in MLA style

The document format recommended by the *MLA Handbook* is fairly simple, with just a few elements. See also pages 72–84 for guidelines on type fonts, headings, lists, and other elements of document design that are not specified in MLA style.

The illustration below shows the formats for the first page and a later page of a paper. For the format of the list of works cited, see page 353.

First page of paper

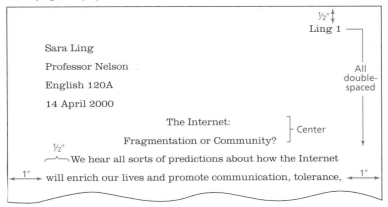

½"↕
Ling 1 ———

Sara Ling

Professor Nelson

English 120A   All
                                                double-
14 April 2000   spaced

                    The Internet:
                                          ⎤ Center
          Fragmentation or Community?   ⎦

½"
        ⌢ We hear all sorts of predictions about how the Internet
←—1"—→ will enrich our lives and promote communication, tolerance, ←—1"—→

A later page of the paper

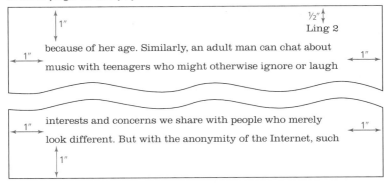

↑
| 1"   ½"↕
↓   Ling 2

←—1"—→ because of her age. Similarly, an adult man can chat about   ←—1"—→
       music with teenagers who might otherwise ignore or laugh

←—1"—→ interests and concerns we share with people who merely   ←—1"—→
       look different. But with the anonymity of the Internet, such

↑
| 1"
↓

1 Paper, type, and margins

Use $8½'' \times 11''$ white bond paper of at least twenty-pound weight, and use the same type of paper throughout a project. Print on only one side of each sheet.

Select a standard, readable serif font such as Courier or Times New Roman (see pp. 76–77). Generally, you can use the same font for any headings, designed and spaced as shown on page 79.

Provide one-inch margins on all sides of the text on each page (see the illustrations above). An uneven right margin is almost always acceptable in academic documents and is preferable as an even (or justified) margin sometimes leaves wide spaces between words.

Checklist for preparing a paper in MLA style

- Have you used sturdy white paper measuring 8½″ × 11″?
- Have you used only one side of each page?
- Is the type readable?
- Is everything double-spaced?
- Do your name, the instructor's name, the course title, and the date appear on the first page?
- Is your paper titled and the title centered?
- Are the margins at least one inch on all sides?
- Are all the pages numbered consecutively in the upper right, starting with page 1 for the first text page? Does your last name appear before each page number?
- If you have used sources, have you cited them in your text and attached a list of works cited that is formatted as shown on p. 357?
- Have you proofread the paper and corrected all errors?
- Are the pages of your paper clipped, stapled, folded, or bound, as requested by your instructor?

MLA

52c

2   Identification and title

MLA style does not require a title page for a paper. Instead, give your name, your instructor's name, the course title, and the date on separate lines in the upper left of the first page—one inch from the top and the left of the paper. (See the sample on the previous page.) Double-space between all lines of this identification.

Double-space also around the title, and center it. If the title runs two lines, center both lines and double-space between them. Use capital and small letters for the title, capitalizing according to the guidelines on pages 269–270. Don't type the title in all-capital letters, underline it, or enclose it in quotation marks. (See the sample on the previous page.)

See page 34 for advice on creating titles.

3   Text

Use a 10-point or 12-point serif typeface for the text. (See page 76 for additional information regarding fonts.) Follow the guidelines below for text format, punctuation, and grammar.

- Indent the first line of every paragraph five spaces and double space throughout your paper, including quotations and the list of works cited.

- Use an ellipsis mark, or spaced periods, to indicate that you have omitted a word, a phrase, a sentence, or more from a quoted passage. Place square brackets around the ellipsis mark that you add. Leave a space before the second and third periods, but no space before the first or after the third. For an ellipsis within a sentence, leave a space before the first bracket and a space after the last bracket. When the ellipsis coincides with the end of your sentence, leave a space before the first bracket, and immediately follow the last bracket with the sentence period and the closing quotation mark. (See p. 254–256 for additional information about using ellipses.)
- Do not hyphenate a word at the end of a typewritten line. You may have to turn off the hyphenation feature on your word processor program to prevent this end-of-line hyphenation.
- Do not break a two-hyphen dash or a three-dot ellipsis mark from one line to the next.
- Do not start a line with a mark of punctuation other than a dash, an opening parenthesis, an opening quotation mark, an opening bracket, or an ellipsis mark.
- Do not end a line with an opening quotation mark, parenthesis, or bracket. Close these marks up to the word following.
- You must always have at least two lines of a paragraph at the bottom of a page and at least two lines of a paragraph at the top of a page. Do not leave widows or orphans in your paper. A widow is the last line of a paragraph that will not fit at the bottom of a page and carries over to the next page. An orphan is the first line of a new paragraph that begins at the bottom of a page. To avoid widows and orphans, the best option is to rewrite the paragraph. If this method does not work, you may move the bottom margin just a bit. However, use this technique only as a last resort.
- Avoid the use of contractions in your paper. For example, say "do not" instead of "don't."
- Follow the guidelines on pages 78 through 83 for using headings, lists, tables, or images in your paper.

4 Paging

Begin numbering your paper on the first text page, and number consecutively through the end. Use Arabic numerals (1, 2, 3), and

MLA

52c

do not add periods, parentheses, hyphens, or the abbreviation "p." However, place your last name before the page number in case the pages become separated after you submit your paper (see the sample on p. 376). Insert one space between your last name and the page number. Align the page number with the right margin, and position it about half an inch from the top of the page, at least two lines above the first line of text.

5   Quotations

MLA style specifies formats for quotations of poetry and prose. For more on punctuating quotations, see pages 236–237 For guidelines on using quotations, see pages 328–329 and 334–337.

Poetry

When you quote a single line from a poem, song, or verse play, run the line into your text and enclose it in quotation marks:

> Dylan Thomas remembered childhood as an idyllic time: "About the lilting house and happy as the grass was green" ("Fern Hill" line 2).

(The parenthetical information above and in the following examples provides MLA source citations. See pp. 346–352.)

Poetry quotations of two or three lines may be placed in the text or displayed separately. In the text enclose the quotation in quotation marks and separate the lines with a slash surrounded by space:

> An example of Robert Frost's incisiveness is in two lines from "Death of the Hired Man": "Home is the place where, when you have to go there / They have to take you in" (119-20).

Quotations of more than three lines of poetry should always be separated from the text with space and an indention. *Do not add quotation marks.*

> Emily Dickinson stripped ideas to their essence, as in this description of "A narrow Fellow in the Grass," a snake:
>
> > I more than once at Noon
> >
> > Have passed, I thought, a Whip lash
> >
> > Unbraiding in the Sun
> >
> > When stopping to secure it
> >
> > It wrinkled, and was gone – (12-16)

Double-space above, below, and throughout a displayed quotation. Indent the quotation one inch from the left margin of the text.

Prose

Run a prose quotation of four or fewer typed lines into your text, and enclose it in quotation marks.

Separate quotations of five or more typed lines from the body of your paper. (Use such quotations sparingly. See pp. 329–330.) *Do not add quotation marks.*

> In his 1967 study of the lives of unemployed black men, Elliot Liebow observes that "unskilled" construction work requires more experience and skill than is generally assumed.
>
>> A healthy, sturdy, active man of good intelligence requires from two to four weeks to break in on a construction job [. . .]. It frequently happens that his foreman or the craftsman he services is not willing to wait that long for him to get into condition or to learn at a glance the difference in size between a rough 2 x 8 and a finished 2 x 10. (62)

Double-space before, after, and throughout a displayed quotation. Indent the quotation one inch from the left.

MLA

52d

Dialogue

When quoting conversations, begin a new paragraph for each speaker.

> "What shall I call you? Your name?" Andrews whispered rapidly, as with a high squeak the latch of the door rose.
> "Elizabeth," she said. "Elizabeth."
> —GRAHAM GREENE, *The Man Within*

When you quote a single speaker for more than one paragraph, put quotation marks at the beginning of each paragraph but at the end of only the last paragraph.

52d Examining a sample paper in MLA style

The sample paper beginning on page 383 follows the guidelines of the *MLA Handbook* for overall format, parenthetical citations, and the list of works cited. Marginal annotations highlight features of the paper.

Note Because the sample paper addresses a current Internet controversy, many of its sources come from the Internet and do not use page or other reference numbers. Thus, as noted in the annotations, the in-text citations of these sources do not give reference numbers. In a paper relying solely on printed journals, books, and other traditional sources, most if not all in-text citations would include page numbers.

A note on outlines

Some instructors ask students to submit a formal outline of the final paper. Advice on constructing such an outline appears on pages 25–27, along with an example written in phrases (a topic outline). Below is an outline of the sample paper following, written in complete sentences. Note that the thesis statement precedes either a topic or a sentence outline.

Thesis statement

To improve equity between online and traditional stores and between consumers with and without Internet access, tax laws should be revised to allow collection of sales taxes on Internet purchases.

I. A Supreme Court ruling and congressional legislation presently govern Internet taxation.
  A. A 1992 Supreme Court decision frees vendors from collecting sales taxes from customers in states where the vendors have no physical presence.
  B. A 1998 law, extended in 2000, placed a moratorium on Internet taxes.
II. A tax-free Internet is unfair to traditional bricks-and-mortar stores.
  A. Sales taxes can make bricks-and-mortar purchases significantly more expensive than online purchases.
  B. Sales taxes exceed online merchants' shipping charges.
III. A tax-free Internet is unfair to consumers who lack Internet access.
  A. A government report shows a huge "digital divide" among US residents.
    1. The affluent are much more likely to have Internet access than the poor.
    2. Whites who are college educated are much more likely to have Internet access than nonwhites with elementary educations.
  B. The digital divide means the poor must pay sales taxes while the affluent can avoid the taxes by shopping online.
IV. The three main arguments against Internet taxation do not rebut the issue of fairness.
  A. Taxes on Internet commerce would not, as claimed, undermine the freedom of the Internet.
  B. Internet commerce does not, as claimed, deserve special protection and encouragement that is not given to traditional commerce.
  C. The very real complexities of Internet taxation do not, as claimed, justify a permanent ban on taxation.

Alder 1

Kisha Alder

Ms. Savarro

English 101

12 April 2000

Who Pays the Bill for

Internet Shopping?

Going to the mall may soon go out of style. These days more and more people are shopping from home over the Internet. In 1999 electronic commerce (e-commerce) took in approximately $18 billion from shoppers; by 2002 that amount is expected to be $76 billion or more (Clausing C1). These numbers are good news for the online stores and for online shoppers, who can anticipate increasing variety in e-commerce offerings. But because taxes are not collected on Internet sales as they are on purchases in almost all states, online stores compete unfairly with traditional "bricks-and-mortar" stores, and shoppers with Internet access have an unfair advantage over shoppers with no such access. To improve equity between online and traditional stores and between consumers with and without access to the Internet, tax laws should be reformulated to allow sales taxes to be collected on Internet purchases.

Internet commerce is regulated by the same tax laws that govern other commerce. However, in 1992 the Supreme Court ruled that vendors do not have to collect taxes on behalf of states where they do not have a physical presence, because such collection would place an unconstitutional burden on interstate commerce (Quill Corp. v. North Dakota 5-8). Buyers are supposed to send the correct taxes to their state governments voluntarily, but they rarely do and states currently have no way to collect (Zimmerman and Hoover 45). In a decision addressing mail-order sales

Writer's name and page number.

Identification: writer's name, instructor's name, course title, date—all double-spaced.

Title centered.

Double-space throughout.

Introduction: gives background to establish the issue.

Citation form: author not named in the text. "C1" is page number.

MLA

52d

Thesis statement.

Background on Internet taxation (next two paragraphs).

Citation form: law case; case name underlined in the text citation.

Citation form: source with two authors.

Alder 2

but considered applicable to Internet sales, the Court's majority urged Congress to reexamine the tax laws governing interstate commerce:

> The underlying issue is not only one that Congress may be better qualified to resolve, but also one that Congress has the ultimate power to resolve [. . .]. Accordingly, Congress is now free to decide whether, when, and to what extent the States may burden interstate mail-order concerns with a duty to collect use taxes. (Quill Corp. v. North Dakota 18-19)

Congress did take some action in 1998, when e-commerce was blossoming, by placing a temporary moratorium on new Internet taxes and by creating the Advisory Commission on Electronic Commerce to study the taxation issue and recommend solutions. This year a majority of the commission recommended extending the moratorium for another five years, through 2006, so that the taxation issue could be studied further and the state and local taxing authorities could simplify their complex and overlapping tax systems (US Advisory Commission). Congress agreed and voted to extend the moratorium (Internet).

As long as the moratorium is in effect, Internet shopping is essentially tax-free. Yet in almost all states, traditional shopping is subject to sales tax. Bricks-and-mortar stores that are required by law to charge and collect sales taxes are at a distinct disadvantage compared to the online stores with no such burden. The local bookstore, music store, and drugstore must charge sales tax; their competitors Amazon.com, CDNOW.com, and PlanetRx.com do not. And the difference can be significant: for instance, California and New York State charge residents at

MLA
52d

Quotation over four lines set off without quotation marks, indented one inch, and double-spaced.

Ellipsis mark in brackets signals omission from quotation.

Citation form: after displayed quotation, citation follows sentence period and one space.

Source: corporate author. Citation form: corporate author only, because online source has no page or other reference numbers.

Citation form: no named author

Contrast between online and traditional commerce (next two paragraphs).

Alder 3

least 7 percent to shop in their own neighborhoods (Eggert 70).

Some online merchants claim that the shipping costs they charge offset the sales taxes they don't charge (Granfield 57). However, many new online companies offer free shipping and handling as an incentive to online shoppers. And even without such promotions, state and local sales taxes far exceed most shipping costs. As one frequent online consumer said, "If I buy more than three CDs [. . .], the shipping cost is less than the sales tax would have been" (James). On balance, the traditional purchase just costs more.

The Internet's tax-free shopping is also damaging to equality among groups of people. Increasingly, governments, scholars, and businesspeople are expressing concern about a "digital divide" between the affluent who have Internet access and the poor who do not. According to a US Department of Commerce study, Falling Through the Net: Defining the Digital Divide, "Households with incomes of $75,000 and higher are more than seven times more likely to have access to the Internet than those at the lowest income levels [below $15,000]" (26; emphasis added). The same study shows that Internet access is three times more common among whites than among African Americans or Hispanic Americans (73) and twelve times more common among those with college educations than among those with elementary school educations (75). Moreover, these gaps are increasing: the divide between the highest and lowest income groups grew 29 percent in the late 1990s (26).

The digital divide has implications for the relative abilities of people in different groups to function effectively in an increasingly electronic world. But where sales taxes are concerned, it does further harm to the disadvantaged. For the most part, white, edu-

---

Selective use of data, with summary of source acknowledged.

Paragraph integrates evidence from two sources.

Ellipsis mark indicates that omitted material fell before comma.

Primary source: e-mail interview. Citation form: source name only, because interview has no page or other reference numbers.

Contrast between shoppers with and without Internet access (next two paragraphs).

MLA

52d

Source named in the text, so not named in parenthetical citations that follow.

Brackets signal words added to clarify the quotation. Citation form: "emphasis added" (after page number and semicolon) indicates underlining was not in original quotation.

Paragraph draws together and acknowledges paraphrases of data from various places in the source.

Writer's own conclusions from data above.

Alder 4

cated, and affluent consumers can shop tax-free because they can shop on the Internet, whereas non-
white, uneducated, and poor consumers have no
choice but to shop locally and pay the required taxes.

Equity thus requires sales taxes on e-commerce, Statement and rebut there are many who argue strongly against such buttal of three opposing views (next
taxes. The writing about Internet taxation (in articles five paragraphs).
and discussion groups and on Web sites) reveals three
major arguments against it. (A fourth, against any
new taxes of any kind, is not specifically relevant to
Internet commerce.)

The first argument holds that Internet freedom
is sacred and should be protected. "To me," writes one Signal phrase interrupts quotation
discussion participant, "the Internet is [. . .] freedom and is set off by
of thought. We can't have the government meddling in commas.
the ability of its citizens to read, speak, and, yes, con- Citation form: author's name only,
duct free enterprise online" (Angeles). But Internet because online
commerce is commerce, after all. Even if the network source has no page
or other reference
often serves as a site for free thought and communica- numbers.
tion, when it serves as a place of business it should be Rebuttals are
writer's own ideas
subject to the same rules as other businesses. and do not require
source citations.

The second major argument against Internet
taxes, related to the first, is expressed in this statement by US Senator Ron Wyden, a strong supporter of Source's name and
credentials given.
a tax-free Internet: "State and local taxes could do ir- Full-sentence intro-
reparable harm to the Internet, killing the goose that duction of a quotation is followed by
could lay billions of dollars in golden eggs." But this a colon.
argument, like the first one, assumes that Internet Citation form: no
parenthetical cita-
commerce deserves special protection and encourage- tion because author
ment--even at the expense of bricks-and-mortar com- is named in text
and online source
merce. In fact, both kinds of commerce contribute to has no page or
other reference
the health of the economy, and they should be pro- numbers.
tected, or taxed, equally.

Finally, the third major argument against Internet taxes holds that the issue is too complex to be resolved, a "logistical nightmare," in the words of a tax-

MLA
52d

Alder 5

ation opponent (Granfield 57). As outlined by more neutral observers--members of the respected accounting firm of Deloitte & Touche--the main complexities are very real: the existence of more than 3000 state and local taxing authorities in the United States, each with its own regulations and rates; the need to bring these jurisdictions into agreement on how to rationalize and simplify their systems; the concern that any federally imposed solution might violate states' rights; and finally the uncertainty about whether an online vendor conducts taxable business where its office, its server, its customer, or all three are located (67-72).

The complexities do seem nightmarish, as tax opponents claim. But the sheer difficulty of the task of creating an Internet tax structure is no justification for not doing what is fair. Both government and business members of the Advisory Commission on Electronic Commerce have expressed beliefs that the Internet should be taxed and optimism that the complexities can be resolved (Stamas). MCI's John Sidgmore says, "Massive changes are going to be required in the state and local tax frameworks, it is true. But there are ways to get through this to a system that is fair for everyone" (qtd. in Stamas).

The Internet has introduced many improvements in our lives, such as the ability to make purchases with the click of a mouse. But at the same time the tax-free status of Internet commerce allows it to compete unfairly with traditional businesses and gives an unfair financial advantage to those who most likely already have plenty of advantages. Congress and Internet businesses must recognize these inequities and must work with state and local taxing authorities to remedy them.

Citation form: author not named in the text.

Citation form (here and end of paragraph): corporate author named in the text.

Summary reduces six pages in the source to a list of four points.

Position of citation indicates that all preceding information comes from the Deloitte & Touche source.

MLA

52d

Citation form: author's name only, because online source has no page or other reference numbers.

Citation form: indirect source (Sidgmore quoted by Stamas).

Conclusion: summary and a call for action.

Alder 6

Works Cited

Angeles, Lemuel. "Internet Freedom." Online posting.
8 Oct. 1999. ZDNet Talkback. 8 May 2000
<http://www.zdnet.com/tklbck/comment/22/
0,7056.html>.

Clausing, Jeri. "States to Consider New Internet Bills."
New York Times 4 Dec. 1999, late ed.: Cl+. New
York Times Ondisc. CD-ROM. UMI-ProQuest.
Mar. 2000.

Deloitte & Touche. Establishing a Framework to Evaluate E-Commerce Tax Policy Options. Berkeley: U
of California P, 1999.

Eggert, Wayne G. "State and Local Sales/Use Tax Sim-
plification." The Sales Tax in the Twenty-First
Century. Ed. Mathhew N. Murray and William F.
Fox. Westport: Praeger, 1997. 67-80.

Granfield, Anne. "Taxing the Internet." Forbes 17 Dec.
1999: 56-58.

The Internet Tax Freedom Act Home Page. 1 June
2000. 3 June 2000. <http://cox.house.gov/nettax/
frmain.htm>.

James, Nora. E-mail interview. 1 May 2000.

Quill Corp. v. North Dakota. 504 US 298. 1992.

Stamas, Vicky. "Tax-Free Web Goods May Disappear."
ZDNet News 23 Jan. 2000. 13 May 2000 <http://
www.zdnet.com/zdnn/stories/news/0,4586.html>.

United States. Advisory Commission on Electronic
Commerce. Report to Congress. Apr. 2000. 25
May 2000 <http://
www.ecommercecommission.org/report.htm>.

---. Dept. of Commerce. National Telecommunications
and Information Administration. Falling
Through the Net: Defining the Digital Divide.

New page for works cited.

Heading centered.

A posting to a Web forum.

Sources are alpha-betized by authors' last names.

A source on a periodical CD-ROM.

Second and subsequent lines of each source are indented one-half inch.

A report by a corporate author.

A work in an anthology.

MLA
52d

An article in a magazine.

A Web site with no listed author or compiler.

An e-mail interview.

A law case: case name not underlined in list of works cited.

An article in an online magazine.

An online government publication with no named author, so government body given as author.

Second source by author of two or more cited works: three hyphens replace author's name (*United States*).

Alder 7

July 1999. 12 May 2000 <http://
www.ntia.doc.gov/ntiahome/digitaldivide/>.

Wyden, Ron. "Statement on the Internet Tax Freedom
Act." <u>Ron Wyden Online</u>. 13 Mar. 1998. 10 May
2000 <http://www.senate.gov/~wyden/docs/
cybstate.htm>.

Zimmerman, Malai, and Kent Hoover. "Use of Third
Parties to Collect State and Local Taxes on Internet Sales." <u>Pacific Business Journal</u> 26.2 (1999):
45-48.

A Web site.

An article from a
journal that pages
each issue sepa-
rately. A source
with two authors.

MLA

52d

APA Documentation and Format

APA Documentation and Format

APA parenthetical text citations

APA references

53 APA Documentation and Format

http://www.apa.org/journals/acorner.html   Answers to frequently asked questions about APA style, from the American Psychological Association.

http://owl.english.purdue.edu/Files/34.html   Guidance on using APA style, from the Purdue Online Writing Lab.

APA

53

The style guide for psychology and some other social sciences is the *Publication Manual of the American Psychological Association* (4th ed., 1994). In the APA documentation style, you acknowledge each of your sources twice:

- In your text, a brief parenthetical citation adjacent to the borrowed material directs readers to a complete list of all the sources you use.
- At the end of your paper, the list of references includes complete bibliographical information for every source.

Every entry in the reference list has at least one corresponding citation in the text, and every in-text citation has a corresponding entry in the list of references.

This chapter describes APA text citations (below) and references (p. 397), details APA document format (p. 407), and concludes with a sample APA paper (p. 414).

53a Writing APA parenthetical text citations

In the APA documentation style, parenthetical citations within the text refer the reader to a list of sources at the end of the text. See the tabbed divider at page 392 for an index to the models for various kinds of sources.

Note Models 1 and 2 below show the direct relationship between what you include in your text and what you include in a parenthetical citation. The citation always includes a publication date and may include a page number. It also includes the author's name if you do *not* name the author in your text (model 1). It does not include the author's name if you *do* name the author in your text (model 2).

1. Author not named in your text

One critic of Milgram's experiments said that the subjects "should have been fully informed of the possible effects on them" (Baumrind, 1968, p. 34).

When you do not name the author in your text, place in parentheses the author's name and the date of the source. The APA requires page number(s) preceded by "p." or "pp." for direct quotations (as in the example) and recommends them for paraphrases. Separate the elements with commas. Position the reference so that it is clear what material is being documented *and* so that the reference fits as smoothly as possible into your sentence structure. (See pp. 351–352 for guidelines.) The following would also be correct:

In the view of one critic of Milgram's experiments (Baumrind, 1968), the subjects "should have been fully informed of the possible effects on them" (p. 34).

2. Author named in your text

Baumrind (1968) said that the subjects in Milgram's study "should have been fully informed of the possible effects on them" (p. 34).

When you use the author's name in the text, do not repeat it in the reference. Place the date after the author's name and any page reference after the borrowed material. If you cite the same source again in the paragraph, you need not repeat the reference as long as it is clear that you are using the same source.

APA

53a

3. A work with two authors

Pepinsky and DeStefano (1987) demonstrate that a teacher's lan-

guage often reveals hidden biases.

One study (Pepinsky & DeStefano, 1987) demonstrates hidden

biases in teachers' language.

When given in the text, two authors' names are connected by "and." In a parenthetical citation, they are connected by an ampersand, "&."

4. A work with three to five authors

Pepinsky, Dunn, Rentl, and Corson (1993) further demonstrate the

biases evident in gestures.

In the first citation of a work with three to five authors, name all the authors, as in the example above. In the second and subsequent references to the work, generally give only the first author's name, followed by "et al." (Latin for "and others"):

In the work of Pepinsky et al. (1993), the loaded gestures include

head shakes and eye contact.

However, two or more sources published in the same year could shorten to the same form—for instance, two references shortening to Pepinsky et al., 1993. In that case, cite the last names of as many authors as you need to distinguish the sources, and then give "et al.": for instance, Pepinsky, Dunn, et al., 1993 and Pepinsky, Bradley, et al., 1993.

5. A work with six or more authors

One study (Rutter et al., 1996) attempts to explain these geograph-

ical differences in adolescent experience.

For six or more authors, even in the first citation of the work, give only the first author's name, followed by "et al." If two or more sources published in the same year shorten to the same form, follow the instructions for model 4 above.

6. A work with a group author

An earlier prediction was even more somber (Lorenz Research,

1997).

For a work that lists an institution, agency, corporation, or other group as author, treat the name of the group as if it were an individual's name.

APA

53a

7. An anonymous work

> One article ("Right to Die," 1976) noted that a death-row inmate
> may crave notoriety.

For an anonymous or unsigned work, use the first two or three words of the title in place of an author's name, excluding an initial *The, A,* or *An.* Underline book and journal titles. Place quotation marks around article titles. (In the list of references, however, do not use quotation marks for article titles. See p. 398.) Capitalize the significant words in all titles cited in the text. (But in the reference list, treat only journal titles this way. See p. 398.)

8. One of two or more works by the same author(s)

> At about age seven, most children begin to use appropriate ges-
> tures to reinforce their stories (Gardner, 1973a).

If your reference list includes two or more works published by the same author(s) *in the same year,* the works should be lettered in the reference list (see p. 400). Then your parenthetical citation should include the appropriate letter, as in "1973a" in the example.

9. Two or more works by different authors

> Two studies (Herskowitz, 1989; Marconi & Hamblen, 1990) found
> that periodic safety instruction can dramatically reduce employ-
> ees' accidents.

List the sources in alphabetical order by the first author's name. Insert a semicolon between sources.

APA

53a

10. An indirect source

> Supporting data appear in a study by Wong (cited in Marconi &
> Hamblen, 1990).

The phrase "cited in" indicates that the reference to Wong's study was found in Marconi and Hamblen. Only Marconi and Hamblen then appears in the list of references.

11. An electronic source

> Ferguson and Hawkins (1998) did not anticipate the "evident hos-
> tility" of participants (par. 6).

Electronic sources can be cited like printed sources, usually with the author's last name and the publication date. When quoting or paraphrasing electronic sources that number paragraphs instead of pages, provide that information in the text citation, substituting "par." (or "pars.") for "p." (or "pp."). If the source does not have numbering of any kind, provide just the author's name and the date.

53b Preparing the APA reference list

In APA style, the in-text parenthetical citations refer to the list of sources at the end of the text. This list, titled "References," includes full publication information on every source cited in the paper. The list falls at the end of the paper, numbered in sequence with the preceding pages. The sample below shows the elements and their spacing.

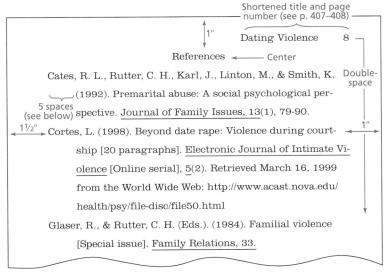

Arrangement

Arrange sources alphabetically by the author's last name or, if there is no author, by the first main word of the title. Do *not* group sources by type (books, journals, and so on).

Spacing

Double-space all entries.

Indention

Use an appropriate indention for each entry. For papers that will be published, the APA recommends indenting the first line of each entry five to seven spaces, like so:

Rodriguez, R. (1982). A hunger of memory: The education of

Richard Rodriguez. Boston: Godine.

APA
53b

When set into type for publication, the initial indentions are then converted into so-called hanging indentions, in which the first line is not indented while the others are. The hanging indention makes it easier for readers to spot authors' names, so the APA recognizes that students who are preparing final copy (not destined for publication) may wish to use the hanging indention for their references, like so:

Rodriguez, R. (1982). <u>A hunger of memory: The education of</u>

<u>Richard Rodriguez.</u> Boston: Godine.

Because it is clearer for readers, the hanging indention is used in the sample on the previous page and in the following models for references, with a five-space indention for the second and subsequent lines of each entry.

Ask your instructor which format he or she prefers.

Punctuation

Separate the parts of the reference (author, date, title, and publication information) with a period and one space. Do not use a final period in references to electronic sources, which conclude with an electronic address (see pp. 403–05).

Authors

List all authors with last name first, separating names and parts of names with commas. Use initials for first and middle names. Use an ampersand (&) before the last author's name.

Publication date

Place the publication date in parentheses after the author's or authors' names, followed by a period. Generally, this date is the year only, though for some sources (such as magazine and newspaper articles) it includes month and sometimes day as well.

Titles

In titles of books and articles, capitalize only the first word of the title, the first word of the subtitle, and proper nouns; all other words begin with small letters. In titles of journals, capitalize all significant words (see pp. 269–270). Unless your instructor specifies italics, underline the titles of books and journals, along with any comma or period following. Do not underline or use quotation marks around the titles of articles.

City of publication

For print sources that are not periodicals (such as books or government publications), give the city of publication. The following US cities do not require state names as well: Baltimore, Boston, Chicago, Los Angeles, New York, Philadelphia, and San Francisco.

Follow their names with a colon. For all other cities, add a comma after the city name and give the two-letter postal abbreviation of the state. Then put a colon after the state.

Publisher's name

For nonperiodical print sources, give the publisher's name after the place of publication and a colon. Use shortened names for many publishers (such as "Morrow" for William Morrow), and omit "Co.," "Inc.," and "Publishers." However, give full names for associations, corporations, and university presses (such as "Harvard University Press"), and do not omit "Books" or "Press" from a publisher's name.

Page numbers

Use the abbreviation "p." or "pp." before page numbers in books and in newspapers, but *not* in other periodicals. For inclusive page numbers, include all figures: "667–668."

Note An index to the following models appears at the tabbed divider on pages 392–93. If you don't see a model listed for the kind of source you used, try to find one that comes close, and provide ample information so that readers can trace the source. Often, you will have to combine models to provide the necessary information on a source—for instance, combining "A book with two or more authors" (2) and "An article in a journal" (11) for a journal article with two or more authors.

1   Books

1. A book with one author

Rodriguez, R. (1982). <u>A hunger of memory: The education of</u>

<u>Richard Rodriguez.</u> Boston: Godine.

The initial "R" appears instead of the author's first name, even though the author's full first name appears on the source. In the title, only the first words of title and subtitle and the proper name are capitalized.

2. A book with two or more authors

Nesselroade, J. R., & Baltes, P. B. (1999). <u>Longitudinal research in</u>

<u>the study of behavioral development.</u> New York: Academic

Press.

An ampersand (&) separates the authors' names.

3. A book with an editor

Dohrenwend, B. S., & Dohrenwend, B. P. (Eds.). (1994). <u>Stressful</u>

<u>life events: Their nature and effects.</u> New York: Wiley.

APA
53b

List the editors' names as if they were authors, but follow the last name with "(Eds.)."—or "(Ed.)." with only one editor. Note the periods inside and outside the final parenthesis.

4. A book with a translator

Trajan, P. D. (1927). <u>Psychology of animals</u> (H. Simone, Trans.).
Washington, DC: Halperin.

The name of the translator appears in parentheses after the title, followed by a comma, "Trans.," a closing parenthesis, and a final period. Note also the absence of periods in "DC."

5. A book with a group author

Lorenz Research (1997). <u>Research in social studies teaching</u>. Baltimore: Arrow Books.

For a work with a group author—such as a research group, government agency, institution, or corporation—begin the entry with the group name. In the references list, alphabetize the work as if the first main word (excluding *The, A,* and *An*) were an author's last name.

6. An anonymous book

<u>Merriam-Webster's collegiate dictionary</u> (10th ed.). (1997). Springfield, MA: Merriam-Webster.

When no author is named, list the work under its title, and alphabetize it by the first main word (excluding *The, A, An*).

7. Two or more works by the same author(s) published in the same year

Gardner, H. (1973a). <u>The arts and human development</u>. New York: Wiley.

Gardner, H. (1973b). <u>The quest for mind: Piaget, Lévi-Strauss, and the structuralist movement</u>. New York: Knopf.

When citing two or more works by exactly the same author(s), published in the same year—as in the examples above—arrange them alphabetically by the first main word of the title (here <u>arts</u>, then <u>quest</u>) and distinguish the sources by adding a letter to the date. Both the date *and* the letter are used in citing the source in the text (see p. 396).

When citing two or more works by exactly the same author(s) but *not* published in the same year, arrange the sources in order of their publication dates, earliest first.

8. A later edition

Bollinger, D. L. (1975). <u>Aspects of language</u> (2nd ed.). New York:
Harcourt Brace Jovanovich.

The edition number in parentheses follows the title and is followed
by a period.

9. A work in more than one volume

Lincoln, A. (1953). <u>The collected works of Abraham Lincoln</u> (R. P.
Basler, Ed.). (Vol. 5). New Brunswick, NJ: Rutgers University
Press.

Lincoln, A. (1953). <u>The collected works of Abraham Lincoln</u> (R. P.
Basler, Ed.). (Vols. 1-8). New Brunswick, NJ: Rutgers University Press.

The first entry cites a single volume (5) in the eight-volume set. The
second cites all eight volumes. In the absence of an editor's name,
the description of volumes would follow the title directly: <u>The collected works of Abraham Lincoln</u> (Vol. 5).

10. An article or chapter in an edited book

Paykel, E. S. (1994). Life stress and psychiatric disorder: Applica-
tions of the clinical approach. In B. S. Dohrenwend & B. P.
Dohrenwend (Eds.), <u>Stressful life events: Their nature and
effects</u> (pp. 239-264). New York: Wiley.

Give the publication date of the collection (1994 above) as the publication date of the article or chapter. After the word "In," provide the
editors' names (in normal order), "(Eds.)" and a comma, the title of
the collection, and the page numbers of the article in parentheses.

APA
53b

2 Periodicals: Journals, magazines, newspapers

11. An article in a journal with continuous pagination throughout the annual volume

Emery, R. E. (1989). Marital turmoil: Interpersonal conflict and
the children of discord and divorce. <u>Psychological Bulletin,
92,</u> 310-330.

Note that you do not place the article title in quotation marks and
that you capitalize only the first words of the title and subtitle. In
contrast, you underline the journal title and capitalize all significant
words. Separate the volume number from the title with a comma,
and underline the number. Do not add "pp." before the page
numbers.

12. An article in a journal that pages issues separately

Dacey, J. (1998). Management participation in corporate buy-outs.

Management Perspectives, 7(4), 20-31.

In this case, place the issue number in parentheses after the volume number without intervening space. Do *not* underline the issue number.

13. An abstract of a journal article

Emery, R. E. (1992). Marital turmoil: Interpersonal conflict and

the children of discord and divorce. Psychological Bulletin,

92, 310-330. (From Psychological Abstracts, 69, Item 1320)

When you cite the abstract of an article, rather than the article itself, give full publication information for the article, followed, in parentheses, by the information for the collection of abstracts, including title, volume number, and either page number or other reference number ("Item 1320" above). If it is not otherwise clear that you are citing an abstract (because the word *abstract* does not appear in the title of the periodical or of the abstracts collection), add "[Abstract]" between the article title and the following period. See model 19, page 404, for an example.

14. An article in a magazine

Van Gelder, L. (1996, December). Countdown to motherhood: When

should you have a baby? Ms., 37-39, 74.

If a magazine has volume and issue numbers, give them as in models 11 and 12. Also give the full date of the issue: year, followed by a comma, month, and day (if any). Give all page numbers even when the article appears on discontinuous pages, without "pp."

15. An article in a newspaper

Lewis, P. H. (1999, January 21). Many updates cause profitable

confusion. The New York Times, pp. D1, D5.

Give month *and* date along with year of publication. Use The in the newspaper name if the paper itself does. For a newspaper (unlike a journal or magazine), precede the page number(s) with "p." or "pp."

16. An unsigned article

The right to die. (1976, October 11). Time, 121, 101.

List and alphabetize the article under its title, as you would an anonymous book (model 6, p. 400).

17. A review

Dinnage, R. (1987, November 29). Against the master and his men
    [Review of the book <u>A mind of her own: The life of Karen</u>
    <u>Horney</u>]. <u>The New York Times Book Review</u>, 10-11.

If the review is not titled, use the bracketed information as the title, keeping the brackets.

3 Electronic sources

The APA *Publication Manual* includes a few models for electronic sources. More recently, the APA Web site (see p. 393) has added new models that extend and in some ways alter those in the *Publication Manual.* The following examples reflect the more recent guidelines when appropriate.

In general, the APA's electronic-source references begin as those for print references do: author(s), date, title. Then you add information on when and how you retrieved the source. For example, an online source might end Retrieved January 8, 1999 from the World Wide Web: http://www.liasu.edu/finance-dl/46732 (in APA style, no period follows an electronic address at the end of the reference). Try to locate all the information required in the following models, referring to pages 295–297 for help. However, if you search for and still cannot find some information, then give what you can find.

Two sources provide more models for electronic sources based on APA style. Each one also differs from APA style, however, so ask your instructor which style you should use.

APA
53b

- Columbia online style for the sciences is discussed in this book's Chapter 56. The differences between APA and Columbia are outlined on page 35.
- Xia Li and Nancy B. Crane's *Electronic Style: A Guide to Citing Electronic Information* (1993) was a source for the APA *Publication Manual.* Li and Crane's formats have since been updated at *http://www.uvm.edu/%7encrane/estyles/apa.html.*

Note Since APA sources do not specify how to break electronic addresses in references, follow MLA style: break only after slashes, and do not hyphenate.

18. A periodical article on CD-ROM

Emory, R. E. (1992). Marital turmoil: Interpersonal conflict and
the children of divorce. Psychological Bulletin, 92, 310-330.
Retrieved from ERIC database (ERIC Document Reproduction
Service, CD-ROM, No. EJ 426 821)

19. An abstract on CD-ROM

Willard, B. L. (1992). Changes in occupational safety standards,
1970-1990 [Abstract]. Retrieved from UMI-ProQuest (Dissertation Abstracts, CD-ROM, Item 7770763)

20. An article in an online journal

Palfrey, A. (1996). Choice of mates in identical twins. Modern Psychology, 4(1). Retrieved February 25, 2000 from the World
Wide Web: http://www.liasu.edu/modpsy/palfrey4(1).htm

21. An article in an online newspaper

Still, L. (1996, March 3). On the battlefields of business, millions of
casualties. The New York Times on the Web. Retrieved August 17, 1999 from the World Wide Web: http://
www.nytimes.com/specials/downsize/03down1.htm

22. A retrievable online posting

Tourville, M. (1999, January 6). European currency reform. International Finance Discussion List. Retrieved February 22,
1999 from the World Wide Web: http://www.liasu.edu/
finance-dl/46732

Include postings to discussion lists and newsgroups in your list of
references only if they are retrievable by others. The source above is
archived and thus retrievable.

23. A nonretrievable online posting

At least one member of the research team has expressed reserva-
tions about the design of the study (L. Kogod, personal communication, February 6, 2000).

Personal electronic mail and other online postings that are not retrievable by others should be cited only in your text, as in the example above.

24. A source from an online database

Wilkins, J. M. (1999, December 12). The myths of the only child.

Psychology Update, 16-20. Retrieved December 20, 1999 from

ProQuest Direct database (ProQuest Health and Medical Com-

plete) on the World Wide Web: http://www.umi.com/proquest/

Many reference works and periodicals are published in online databases to which your library subscribes, such as ProQuest Direct or Lexis-Nexis. When you obtain a source from an online database, your retrieval statement should include your date of access; the online service (here, ProQuest Direct database); the name of the particular database in which you found your source, in parentheses; and the address of the service's home page.

25. Software

Project scheduler 8000 [Computer software]. (1999). Orlando, FL:

Scitor.

4 Other sources

26. A report

Gerald. K. (1958). Medico-moral problems in obstetric care (Report

No. NP-71). St. Louis, MO: Catholic Hospital Association.

Treat the report like a book, but provide any report number in parentheses immediately after the title, with no punctuation between them.

For a report from the Educational Resources Information Center (ERIC), provide the ERIC document number in parentheses at the end of the entry:

Jolson, M. K. (1981). Music education for preschoolers (Report No.

TC-622). New York: Teachers College, Columbia University.

(ERIC Document Reproduction Service No. ED 264 488)

APA
53b

27. A government publication

U.S. House. Committee on Ways and Means. (1991). Medicare payment for outpatient physical and occupational therapy services. 102d Cong., 2d Sess. Washington, DC: U.S. Government Printing Office.

Stiller, A. (1996). Historic preservation and tax incentives. U.S. Department of the Interior. Washington, DC: U.S. Government
Printing Office.

Hawaii. Department of Education. (1998). Kauai district schools,
profile 1998-99. Honolulu, HI: Author.

If no individual is given as the author, list the publication under the
name of the sponsoring agency. When the agency is both the author
and the publisher, use "Author" in place of the publisher's name.

28. An abstract of an unpublished dissertation

Steciw, S. K. (1986). Alterations to the Pessac project of Le Cor-
busier (Doctoral dissertation, University of Cambridge, England, 1986). Dissertation Abstracts International, 46, 565C.

For an abstract of an unpublished doctoral dissertation, give the
university and the year of the dissertation in parentheses after the
title. Then give the source of the abstract, the volume number, and
the page number.

29. An interview

Brisick, W. C. (1988, July 1). [Interview with Ishmael Reed]. Publishers Weekly, 41-42.

List a published interview under the interviewer's name. Provide the
publication information appropriate for the kind of source the
interview appears in (here, a magazine). Immediately after the date,
in brackets, specify that the piece is an interview and, if necessary,
provide other identifying information. If the interview has its own
title, insert it after the date, as with a review (model 17, p. 403).

Note that interviews you conduct yourself are not included in
the list of references. Instead, use an in-text parenthetical citation,
as shown in model 23 (p. 404) for a nonretrievable online posting.

30. A videotape, recording, or other audiovisual source

Spielberg, S. (Director). (1993). Schindler's list [Videotape]. Los
Angeles: Viacom.

Siberry, J. (1995). Caravan. On <u>Maria</u> [CD]. Burbank, CA: Reprise.

For audiovisual sources such as films, videotapes, television or radio programs, or recordings, begin with the name of the person whose work you are citing, followed by his or her function, if appropriate, in parentheses. Immediately after the title, give the medium in brackets. Then give the location and name of the distributor.

53c   Formatting a paper in APA style

The APA *Publication Manual* distinguishes between documents intended for publication (which will be set in type) and those submitted by students (which are the final copy). The guidelines below apply to most undergraduate papers. Check with your instructor for any modifications to this format.

Note See pages 397–99 for the APA format of a reference list. And see pages 72–83 for guidelines on other elements of document design.

1   Paper, type, and margins

Use 8½" x 11" good quality, white paper, and use the same type of paper throughout a paper. Print on only one side of each sheet. The paper must be clean and neatly prepared with the type dark, clear, and readable.

Select a conventional serif or sans serif typeface (such as Arial or Times New Roman) with 12-point type.

Use a 1½-inch margin on the left and 1-inch margins on the other sides. (The wider left margin allows for a binder.) Use the flush-left style, and leave the right margin uneven, or ragged.

APA

53c

2   Title, structure, and format

The title page includes the full title, your name, the course title, the instructor's name, and the date. The title should summarize the main topic of your paper and be a maximum of ten to twelve words. Include a shortened form of the title along with the page number at the top of this and all other pages. Number the title page 1. The APA allows either the centered layout below or the layout shown on page 414, in which all title-page information appears on the top half of the page.

Title page

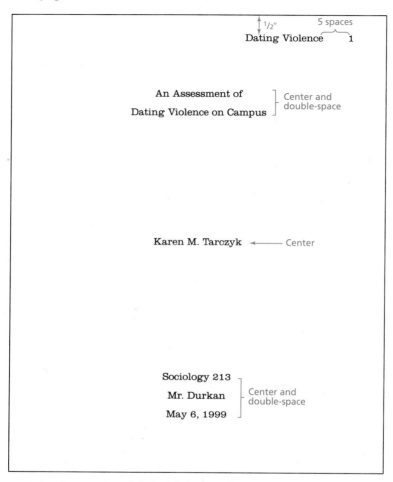

The first section, labeled "Abstract," summarizes (in about 100 words) your subject, research method, findings, and conclusions. Put the abstract on a page by itself. Include an abstract only if your instructor requires one.

Abstract

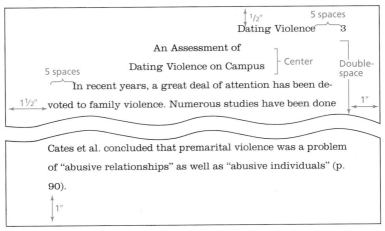

The body of the paper begins with a restatement of the paper's title and then an introduction (not labeled). In a research paper, the introduction concisely presents the problem you researched, your research method, the relevant background (such as related studies), and the purpose of your research.

First page of body

In a research paper, the next section, labeled "Method," provides a detailed discussion of how you conducted your research, including a description of the research subjects, any materials or tools you used (such as questionnaires), and the procedure you followed. In the illustration on the facing page, the label "Method" is a first-level heading, formatted as in the sample. When you need second- and third-level headings in addition, use these formats, always double-spacing:

APA

53c

First-Level Heading

Second-Level Heading

    Third-level heading. Run this heading into the text paragraph.

Later page of body

>   Dating Violence   4
>
>   All the studies indicate a problem that is being neglected. My objective was to gather data on the extent and nature of premarital violence and to discuss possible interpretations.
>
>   Method   Double-space
>
> Sample
>
>   I conducted a survey of 200 students (134 females, 66 males) at a large state university in the northeastern United States. The sample consisted of students enrolled in an intro-

    Research papers usually conclude with a "Results" section and a "Discussion" section. The "Results" section (labeled with a first-level heading) summarizes the data you collected, explains how you analyzed them, and presents them in detail, often in tables, graphs, or charts.

    The "Discussion" section (labeled with a first-level heading) interprets the data and presents your conclusions. (When the discussion is brief, you may combine it with the previous section under the heading "Results and Discussion.")

    The "References" section, beginning a new page, includes all your sources. See pages 397–99 for an explanation and illustration.

3 Text

    Follow the guidelines below for text format, punctuation, and grammar.

- Indent the first line of every paragraph of text five to seven spaces. The default setting on the tab key of most word processors is acceptable.
- The text should be doubled-spaced throughout the paper. However, single-spacing may be used when it would improve readability (e.g., tables or lists). Triple- or quadruple-spacing may be used judiciously if it would improve the appearance and

APA

53c

readability (e.g., after chapter titles, before major subheadings, before footnotes, and before and after tables or lists in the text).

- Do not hyphenate a word at the end of a typewritten line. You may have to turn off the hyphenation feature on your word processor program to prevent this end-of-line hyphenation.

- You must always have at least two lines of a paragraph at the bottom of a page and at least two lines of a paragraph at the top of a page. Do not leave widows or orphans in your paper. A widow is the last line of a paragraph that will not fit at the bottom of a page and carries over to the next page. An orphan is the first line of a new paragraph that begins at the bottom of a page. To avoid widows and orphans, the best option is to rewrite the paragraph. If this method does not work, you may move the bottom margin just a bit. However, use this technique only as a last resort.

- Avoid the use of contractions in your paper. For example, say "do not," instead of "don't."

- Italics may be substituted when underlining in citations, but not if the manuscript is for publication.

- Leave one space between words.

- Leave one space after all punctuation, as follows:

> After commas, colons, and semicolons.
> After punctuation marks at the ends of sentences.
> After periods that separate parts of a reference citation.
> After the period with the initials in personal names.

- Do not space after internal periods in abbreviations or around colons in ratios.

- Hyphens, dashes, and minus signs are each typed differently:

> Hyphens: Use no space before or after a hyphen
> Dashes: Type as two hyphens with no space before or after the dash
> Minus signs: Type as a hyphen with space on both sides
> Negative value: Type as a hyphen with a space before but no space after

- Use an ellipsis mark, or spaced periods, to indicate that you have omitted a word, a phrase, a sentence, or more from a quoted passage. Use three periods with spaces before the second and third periods within a sentence to indicate that you have omitted material from the original source. Use four points to indicate any omission between two sentences. The first point indicates the period at the end of the first sentence quoted, and the three ellipsis points follow. Do not use ellipsis points at the beginning or end of any quotation unless, in order to prevent misinterpretation, you need to emphasize that the quotation begins or ends in midsentence.

- Do not break a two-hyphen dash or ellipsis points from one line to the next.
- Do not start a line with a mark of punctuation other than a dash, an opening parenthesis, an opening quotation mark, an opening bracket, or an ellipsis mark.
- Follow the guidelines on pages 78 through 83 for using lists and tables in your paper.

4 Spacing, page numbers, quotations, and illustrations

Number pages consecutively, starting with the title page. Identify each page (including the title page) with a shortened version of the title as well as a page number, as illustrated in the samples above and opposite.

Run into your text all quotations of forty words or less, and enclose them in quotation marks. For quotations of more than forty words, set them off from your text by indenting all lines five spaces, double-spacing above and below. For student papers, the APA allows single-spacing of displayed quotations:

Echoing the opinions of other Europeans at the time, Freud had a poor view of Americans:

> The Americans are really too bad. . . . Competition is much more pungent with them, not succeeding means civil death to every one, and they have no private resources apart from their profession, no hobby, games, love or other interests of a cultured person. And success means money. (1961, p. 86)

Do not use quotation marks around a quotation displayed in this way.

Present data in tables and figures (graphs or charts), as appropriate. (See the sample on p. 413 for a clear format to follow.) Begin each illustration on a separate page. Number each kind of illustration consecutively and separately from the other (Table 1, Table 2, etc., and Figure 1, Figure 2, etc.). Refer to all illustrations in your text—for instance, "(See Figure 3.)." Generally, place illustrations immediately after the text references to them. (See pp. 79–83 for more discussion of illustrations, along with samples.)

5 Headings, headers, and running heads

These terms have different meanings in the APA style. Definitions and guidelines for use of these elements are provided below.

Heading

Headings are the section titles in your paper, and they establish the importance of each section. All sections of equal importance

APA
53c

should have the same level of heading throughout a manuscript or document. Headings function as a type of outline to reveal the paper's organization. Avoid having only one subsection heading within a section, just as you would in an outline. Use at least two subsection headings within any given section, or use none.

Headings follow a top-down progression in levels. The major section headings are called level one headings. If you subdivide a section heading into subheadings, these subheadings become level two headings. If you subdivide a level two heading, these subheadings become level three headings, and so on. APA allows up to five levels of headings, but most student papers use no more than three levels.

Below are additional guidelines for use of headings:

- Headings should accurately reflect the organization of the paper.
- Headings of the same level should be consistent throughout the paper.

For a short paper, one level of heading may be sufficient. In such cases, use only centered capital letters and small letters in headings. For many papers, two levels of headings meet the requirements. In this instance, use centered capital letters and small letters in headings and flush left, underlined capital letters and small letters in side headings. For some papers, three levels of headings are needed. In this case, use the centered capital letters and small letters in headings; the flush left, underlined capital letters and small letters in side headings; and indented, underlined, small letters in paragraph headings ending with a period.

Header

This term is also referred to as the *manuscript page header*. The header identifies each manuscript page, with the first two or three words from the paper's title. Place the manuscript page header in the upper right-hand corner five spaces to the left of the page number. The manuscript page header is not the same as the running head, which goes only on the title page.

Running Head

The running head is an abbreviated title that is placed on the title page of published documents. Type the running head flush left at the top of the title page (but below the manuscript page header) in all capital letters. Do not exceed fifty characters, including punctuation and spaces between words.

APA
53c

53d   Examining a sample paper in APA style

The following excerpts from a sociology paper illustrate elements of a research paper using the APA style of documentation and format.

[Alternative title page layout (see p. 408).]

Dating Violence   1

Shortened title and page number.

An Assessment of

Dating Violence on Campus

Karen M. Tarczyk

Sociology 213

Mr. Durkan

May 6, 1999

Quadruple-space to title.

Double-space all information: title, name, course title, instructor, date.

[New page.]

Dating Violence   2

Abstract

Little research has examined the patterns of abuse and violence occurring within couples during courtship. With a questionnaire administered to a sample of college students, the extent and nature of such abuse and violence were investigated. The results, interpretations, and implications for further research are discussed.

Abstract: summary of subject, research method, conclusions.

APA

53d

[New page.]

Dating Violence   3

An Assessment of

Dating Violence on Campus

In recent years, a great deal of attention has been devoted to family violence. Numerous studies have been done on spouse and child abuse. However, violent behavior occurs in dating relationships as well, yet the problem of dating violence has been relatively ignored by sociological research. It should be exam-

Double-space throughout.

Title repeated on first text page.

Introduction: presentation of the problem researched by the writer.

Dating Violence   4

ined further since the premarital relationship is one context in which individuals learn and adopt behaviors that surface in marriage.

The sociologist James Makepeace (1989) contends that courtship violence is a "potential mediating link" between violence in one's family of orientation and violence in one's later family of procreation (p. 103). Studying dating behaviors at Bemidji State University in Minnesota, Makepeace reported that one-fifth of the respondents had had at least one encounter with dating violence. He then extended these percentages to students nationwide, suggesting the existence of a major hidden social problem.

More recent research supports Makepeace's. Cates, Rutter, Karl, Linton, and Smith (1997) found that 22.3% of respondents at Oregon State University had been either the victim or the perpetrator of premarital violence. Another study (Cortes, 1998) found that so-called date rape, while much more publicized and discussed, was reported by many fewer woman respondents (2%) than was other violence during courtship (21%).

[The introduction continues.]

All these studies indicate a problem that is being neglected. My objective was to gather data on the extent and nature of premarital violence and to discuss possible interpretations.

Method

Sample

I conducted a survey of 200 students (134 females, 66 males) at a large state university in the northeastern United States. The sample consisted of students enrolled in an introductory sociology course.

[The explanation of method continues.]

Citation form: author named in the text.

Citation form: page number given for quotation.

Citation form: source with three to five authors, named in the text.

Citation form: author not named in the text.

APA
53d

First- and second-level headings.

"Method" section: discussion of how research was conducted.

Dating Violence   5

The Questionnaire

    A questionnaire exploring the personal dynamics of relationships was distributed during regularly scheduled class. Questions were answered anonymously in a 30-minute period. The survey consisted of three sections.

[The explanation of method continues.]

    Section 3 required participants to provide information about their current dating relationships. Levels of stress and frustration, communication between partners, and patterns of decision making were examined. These variables were expected to influence the amount of violence in a relationship. The next part of the survey was adopted from Murray Strauss's Conflict Tactics Scales (1982). These scales contain 19 items designed to measure conflict and the means of conflict resolution, including reasoning, verbal aggression, and actual violence. The final page of the questionnaire contained general questions on the couple's use of alcohol, sexual activity, and overall satisfaction with the relationship.

Results

    The questionnaire revealed significant levels of verbal aggression and threatened and actual violence among dating couples. A high number of students, 50% (62 of 123 subjects), reported that they had been the victim of verbal abuse, either being insulted or sworn at. In addition, almost 14% (17 of 123) of respondents admitted being threatened with some type of violence, and more than 14% (18 of 123) reported being pushed, grabbed, or shoved. (See Table 1.)

[The explanation of results continues.]

APA
53d

"Results" section: summary and presentation of data.

Reference to table.

Dating Violence   6

[Table on a page by itself.]

Table 1

Incidence of Courtship Violence

Table presents data
in clear format.

Type of violence	Number of students reporting	Percentage of sample
Insulted or swore	62	50.4
Threatened to hit or throw something	17	13.8
Threw something	8	6.5
Pushed, grabbed, or shoved	18	14.6
Slapped	8	6.5
Kicked, bit, or hit with fist	7	5.7
Hit or tried to hit with something	2	1.6
Threatened with a knife or gun	1	0.8
Used a knife or gun	1	0.8

Discussion

Violence within premarital relationships has
been relatively ignored. The results of the present
study indicate that abuse and force do occur in dating
relationships. Although the percentages are small, so
was the sample. Extending them to the entire campus
population of 5,000 would mean significant numbers.
For example, if the nearly 6% incidence of being
kicked, bitten, or hit with a fist is typical, then 300
students might have experienced this type of violence.

"Discussion" sec-
tion: interpretation
of data and presen-
tation of conclu-
sions.

APA
53d

[The discussion continues.]

If the courtship period is characterized by abuse
and violence, what accounts for it? The other sections
of the survey examined some variables that appear to

influence the relationship. Level of stress and frustration, both within the relationship and in the respondent's life, was one such variable. The communication level between partners, both the frequency of discussion and the frequency of agreement, was another.

[The discussion continues.]

The method of analyzing the data in this study, utilizing frequency distributions, provided a clear overview. However, more tests of significance and correlation and a closer look at the social and individual variables affecting the relationship are warranted. The courtship period may set the stage for patterns of married life. It merits more attention.

[New page.]

Dating Violence   7

References

Cates, R. L., Rutter, C. H., Karl, J., Linton, M., & Smith, K. (1997). Premarital abuse: A social psychological perspective. Journal of Family Issues, 13(1), 79-90.

Cortes, L. (1998). Beyond date rape: Violence during courtship [20 paragraphs]. Electronic Journal of Intimate Violence. Retrieved March 16, 1999 from the World Wide Web: http://acast.nova.edu/health/psy/file-disc/file50.html

Glaser, R., & Rutter, C. H. (Eds.). (1994). Familial violence [Special issue]. Family Relations, 43.

Makepeace, J. M. (1989). Courtship violence among college students. Family Relations, 28, 97-103.

Strauss, M. L. (1982). Conflict Tactics Scales. New York: Sociological Tests.

New page for reference list.

Heading centered.

An article in a print journal.

Sources are alphabetized by authors' last names.

An article in an on-line journal.

Double-space throughout.

Second and subsequent lines of each source are indented five spaces (see p. 397).

A book. ("Tactics Scales" is part of a proper name.)

APA
53d

Chicago and CBE Documentation

Chicago and CBE Documentation

Chicago note and works-cited models

54 Chicago Documentation

http://www.press.uchicago.edu/Misc/Chicago/cmosfaq.html Answers to frequently asked questions about Chicago style, from the University of Chicago Press.

History, art history, philosophy, and some other humanities use endnotes or footnotes to document sources, following one style recommended by *The Chicago Manual of Style* (14th ed., 1993) and the student guide adapted from it, Kate L. Turabian's *A Manual for Writers of Term Papers, Theses, and Dissertations* (6th ed., revised by John Grossman and Alice Bennett, 1996). The Chicago note style is described below.

54a Distinguishing Chicago notes and works-cited entries

In the Chicago note style, raised numerals in the text refer to footnotes (bottoms of pages) or endnotes (end of paper) that contain complete source information. A separate list of works cited is optional: ask your instructor for his or her preference.

Single-space both footnotes and endnotes. Separate footnotes from the text with a short line:

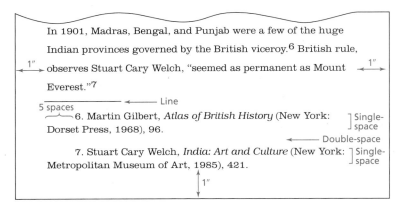

In 1901, Madras, Bengal, and Punjab were a few of the huge Indian provinces governed by the British viceroy.⁶ British rule, observes Stuart Cary Welch, "seemed as permanent as Mount Everest."⁷

6. Martin Gilbert, *Atlas of British History* (New York: Dorset Press, 1968), 96.

7. Stuart Cary Welch, *India: Art and Culture* (New York: Metropolitan Museum of Art, 1985), 421.

With endnotes, use the format below for a list of works cited, substituting the heading "NOTES" and numbered entries as for footnotes.

For the list of sources at the end of the paper, use the format below. Arrange the sources alphabetically by the authors' last names.

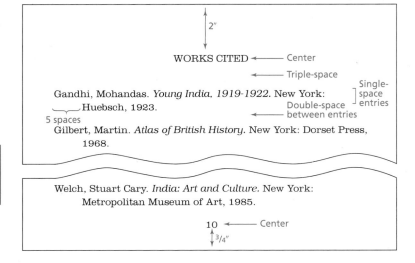

WORKS CITED

Gandhi, Mohandas. *Young India, 1919-1922.* New York: Huebsch, 1923.

Gilbert, Martin. *Atlas of British History.* New York: Dorset Press, 1968.

Welch, Stuart Cary. *India: Art and Culture.* New York: Metropolitan Museum of Art, 1985.

10

The following examples illustrate the essentials of a note and a works-cited entry:

Note

> 6. Martin Gilbert, *Atlas of British History* (New York: Dorset Press, 1968), 96.

Works cited

Gilbert, Martin. *Atlas of British History.* New York: Dorset Press, 1968.

Notes and works-cited entries share certain features:

- Italicize or underline the titles of books and periodicals (ask your instructor for his or her preference).
- Enclose in quotation marks the titles of parts of books or articles in periodicals.
- Do not abbreviate publishers' names, but omit "Inc.," "Co.," and similar abbreviations.
- Do not use "p." or "pp." before page numbers.

Notes and works-cited entries also differ in important ways:

Note	Works-cited entry
Start with a number (typed on the line and followed by a period) that corresponds to the note number in the text.	Do not begin with a number.
Indent the first line five spaces.	Indent the second and subsequent lines five spaces.
Give the author's name in normal order.	Begin with the author's last name.
Use commas between elements.	Use periods between elements.
Enclose publication information in parentheses, with no preceding punctuation.	Precede the publication information with a period, and don't use parentheses.
Include the specific page number(s) you borrowed from, omitting "p." or "pp."	Omit page numbers except for parts of books or articles in periodicals.

 Many computerized word processors will automatically position footnotes at the bottoms of appropriate pages. Some will automatically number notes and even renumber them if you add or delete one or more.

Chic
54b

54b Models of Chicago notes and works-cited entries

In the following models for common sources, notes and works-cited entries appear together for easy reference. (An index to the models appears at the tabbed divider on p. 416.) Be sure to use the numbered note form for notes and the unnumbered works-cited form for works-cited entries.

1   Books

1. A book with one, two, or three authors

1. Carol Gilligan, *In a Different Voice: Psychological Theory and Women's Development* (Cambridge: Harvard University Press, 1982), 27.

Gilligan, Carol. *In a Different Voice: Psychological Theory and Women's Development.* Cambridge: Harvard University Press, 1982.

1. Dennis L. Wilcox, Phillip H. Ault, and Warren K. Agee, *Public Relations: Strategies and Tactics,* 4th ed. (New York: HarperCollins, 1995), 182.

Wilcox, Dennis L., Phillip H. Ault, and Warren K. Agee. *Public Relations: Strategies and Tactics.* 4th ed. New York: HarperCollins, 1995.

2. A book with more than three authors

2. Geraldo Lopez and others, *China and the West* (Boston: Little, Brown, 1990), 461.

Lopez, Geraldo, Judith P. Salt, Anne Ming, and Henry Reisen. *China and the West.* Boston: Little, Brown, 1990.

3. A book with an editor

3. Hendrick Ruitenbeek, ed., *Freud as We Knew Him* (Detroit: Wayne State University Press, 1973), 64.

Ruitenbeek, Hendrick, ed. *Freud as We Knew Him.* Detroit: Wayne State University Press, 1973.

4. A book with an author and an editor

4. Lewis Mumford, *The City in History,* ed. Donald L. Miller (New York: Pantheon, 1986), 216-17.

Mumford, Lewis. *The City in History.* Edited by Donald L. Miller. New York: Pantheon, 1986.

5. A translation

5. Dante Alighieri, *The Inferno,* trans. John Ciardi (New York: New American Library, 1971), 51.

Alighieri, Dante. *The Inferno.* Translated by John Ciardi. New York: New American Library, 1971.

6. An anonymous work

6. *The Dorling Kindersley World Reference Atlas* (London: Dorling Kindersley, 1994), 150-51.

The Dorling Kindersley World Reference Atlas. London: Dorling Kindersley, 1994.

7. A later edition

7. Dwight L. Bollinger, *Aspects of Language,* 2d ed. (New York: Harcourt Brace Jovanovich, 1975), 20.

Bollinger, Dwight L. *Aspects of Language.* 2d ed. New York: Harcourt Brace Jovanovich, 1975.

8. A work in more than one volume

Citation of one volume without a title:

8. Abraham Lincoln, *The Collected Works of Abraham Lincoln,* ed. Roy P. Basler (New Brunswick: Rutgers University Press, 1953), 5:426-28.

Lincoln, Abraham. *The Collected Works of Abraham Lincoln.* Edited by Roy P. Basler. Vol. 5. New Brunswick: Rutgers University Press, 1953.

Citation of one volume with a title:

8. Linda B. Welkin, *The Age of Balanchine,* vol. 3 of *The History of Ballet* (New York: Columbia University Press, 1969), 56.

Welkin, Linda B. *The Age of Balanchine.* Vol. 3 of *The History of Ballet.* New York: Columbia University Press, 1969.

9. A selection from an anthology

9. Rosetta Brooks, "Streetwise," in *The New Urban Landscape,* ed. Richard Martin (New York: Rizzoli, 1990), 38-39.

Brooks, Rosetta. "Streetwise." In *The New Urban Landscape,* ed. Richard Martin, 37-60. New York: Rizzoli, 1990.

10. A work in a series

10. Ingmar Bergman, *The Seventh Seal,* Modern Film Scripts Series, no. 12 (New York: Simon and Schuster, 1968), 27.

Bergman, Ingmar. *The Seventh Seal.* Modern Film Scripts Series, no. 12. New York: Simon and Schuster, 1968.

11. An article in a reference work

The abbreviation "s.v." in the examples stands for the Latin *sub verbo,* "under the word."

11. *Merriam-Webster's Collegiate Dictionary,* 10th ed., s.v. "reckon."

Merriam-Webster's Collegiate Dictionary, 10th ed., s.v. "reckon."

11. Mark F. Herman, "Polymers," in *The New Encyclopaedia Britannica: Macropaedia,* 16th ed.

Herman, Mark F. "Polymers." In *The New Encyclopaedia Britannica: Macropaedia,* 16th ed.

2   Periodicals: Journals, magazines, newspapers

12. An article in a journal with continuous pagination throughout the annual volume

12. Janet Lever, "Sex Differences in the Games Children Play," *Social Problems* 23 (1976): 482.

Lever, Janet. "Sex Differences in the Games Children Play." *Social Problems* 23 (1976): 478-87.

13. An article in a journal that pages issues separately

13. June Dacey, "Management Participation in Corporate Buy-Outs," *Management Perspectives* 7, no. 4 (1998): 22.

Dacey, June. "Management Participation in Corporate Buy-Outs." *Management Perspectives* 7, no. 4 (1998): 20-31.

14. An article in a popular magazine

14. Mark Stevens, "Low and Behold," *New Republic*, 24 December 1990, 28.

Stevens, Mark. "Low and Behold." *New Republic*, 24 December 1990, 27-33.

15. An article in a newspaper

15. Peter H. Lewis, "Many Updates Cause Profitable Confusion," *New York Times*, 21 January 1999, national ed., D5.

Lewis, Peter H. "Many Updates Cause Profitable Confusion." *New York Times*, 21 January 1999, national ed., D1, D5.

16. A review

16. John Gregory Dunne, "The Secret of Danny Santiago," review of *Famous All over Town*, by Danny Santiago, *New York Review of Books*, 16 August 1984, 25.

Dunne, John Gregory. "The Secret of Danny Santiago." Review of *Famous All over Town*, by Danny Santiago. *New York Review of Books*, 16 August 1984, 17-27.

3   Electronic sources

The Chicago Manual offers some models for documenting electronic sources, and *A Manual for Writers* updates these and adds a few more. For other electronic sources and simpler formats, you can use Columbia online style for the humanities, discussed in Chapter 56. Page 451 shows how to adapt Columbia style to Chicago style. There are differences between the two styles, so ask your instructor which style you should use for online sources.

Note Since Chicago style does not specify how to break electronic addresses in notes and works-cited entries, follow MLA style: break only after slashes, and do not hyphenate.

Chic
54b

17. A source on a periodical CD-ROM

A source also published in print:

17. Peter H. Lewis, "Many Updates Cause Profitable Confusion," *New York Times*, 21 January 1999, national ed., D5. *New York Times Ondisc* [CD-ROM], UMI-ProQuest, March 1999.

Lewis, Peter H. "Many Updates Cause Profitable Confusion." *New York Times*, 21 January 1999, national ed., D1, D5. *New York Times Ondisc* [CD-ROM]. UMI-ProQuest, March 1999.

A source not published in print:

17. "Vanguard Forecasts," *Business Outlook* [CD-ROM], Information Access, March 1998.

"Vanguard Forecasts." *Business Outlook* [CD-ROM]. Information Access, March 1998.

18. A source on a nonperiodical CD-ROM

18. Mary Wollstonecraft Shelley, *Frankenstein, Classic Library* [CD-ROM] (Alameda, Calif.: Andromeda, 1993).

Shelley, Mary Wollstonecraft. *Frankenstein. Classic Library* [CD-ROM]. Alameda, Calif.: Andromeda, 1993.

19. An online book

19. Jane Austen, *Emma* [book online], ed. Ronald Blythe (Harmondsworth, Eng.: Penguin, 1972, accessed 15 December 1999), *Oxford Text Archive;* available from ftp://ota.ox.ac.uk/public/english/Austen/emma.1519; Internet.

Austen, Jane. *Emma* [book online]. Edited by Ronald Blythe. Harmondsworth, Eng.: Penguin, 1972. Accessed 15 December 1999. *Oxford Text Archive.* Available from ftp://ota.ox.ac.uk/public/english/Austen/emma.1519; Internet.

20. An article in an online periodical

20. Andrew Palfrey, "Choice of Mates in Identical Twins," *Modern Psychology* 4, no. 1 (1996): par. 10 [journal online]; available from http://www.liasu.edu/modpsy/palfrey4(1).htm; Internet; accessed 25 February 2000.

Palfrey, Andrew. "Choice of Mates in Identical Twins." *Modern Psychology* 4, no. 1 (1996): 12 pars. [journal online]. Available from http://www.liasu.edu/modpsy/palfrey4(1).htm; Internet. Accessed 25 February 2000.

21. An online database

21. *Scots Teaching and Research Network* [database online], ed. John Corbett (Glasgow: University of Glasgow, 2 February 1998, accessed 5 March 1999); available from http://www.arts.gla.ac.uk/www/comet/starn.htm; Internet.

Chic

54b

Scots Teaching and Research Network [database online]. Edited by John Corbett. Glasgow: University of Glasgow, 2 February 1998. Accessed 5 March 1999. Available from http://www.arts.gla.ac.uk/www/comet/starn.htm; Internet.

4 Other sources

22. A government publication

22. House, *Medicare Payment for Outpatient Physical and Occupational Therapy Services*, 102d Cong., 1st sess., 1991, H. Doc. 409, 12-13.

U.S. Congress. House. *Medicare Payment for Outpatient Physical and Occupational Therapy Services*. 102d Cong., 1st sess., 1991. H. Doc. 409.

23. A letter

A published letter:

23. Mrs. Laura E. Buttolph to Rev. and Mrs. C. C. Jones, 20 June 1857, *The Children of Pride: A True Story of Georgia and the Civil War,* ed. Robert Manson Myers (New Haven: Yale University Press, 1972), 334.

Buttolph, Mrs. Laura E. Letter to Rev. and Mrs. C. C. Jones, 20 June 1857. In *The Children of Pride: A True Story of Georgia and the Civil War,* ed. Robert Manson Myers. New Haven: Yale University Press, 1972.

A personal letter:

23. Ann E. Packer, letter to author, 15 June 1998.

Packer, Ann E. Letter to author. 15 June 1998.

24. An interview

24. Warren Christopher, interview by William Lindon, *Frontline,* Public Broadcasting System, 13 February 1998.

Christopher, Warren. Interview by William Lindon. *Frontline.* Public Broadcasting System, 13 February 1998.

25. A work of art

25. John Singer Sargent, *In Switzerland,* watercolor, 1908, Metropolitan Museum of Art, New York.

Sargent, John Singer. *In Switzerland,* watercolor, 1908. Metropolitan Museum of Art, New York.

26. A film or video recording

26. *Serenade,* George Balanchine, San Francisco Ballet, PBS Video, 1985, videocassette.

Serenade. George Balanchine. San Francisco Ballet. PBS Video, 1985. Videocassette.

27. A sound recording

27. Johannes Brahms, Concerto no. 2 in B-flat, Artur Rubinstein, Philadelphia Orchestra, Eugene Ormandy, RCA BRC4-6731, 1992.

Brahms, Johannes. Concerto no. 2 in B-flat. Artur Rubinstein. Philadelphia Orchestra. Eugene Ormandy. RCA BRC4-6731, 1992.

5 Two or more citations of the same source

To minimize clutter and give a quick sense of how often you cite a source, the Chicago style allows a shortened form for subsequent citations of a source you have already cited fully. Your instructor may also allow the shortened form for a first citation of a source if full information appears in a list of works cited.

You may use the Latin abbreviation "ibid." (meaning "in the same place") to refer to the same source cited in the preceding note:

8. Janet Lever, "Sex Differences in the Games Children Play," *Social Problems* 23 (1976): 482.

9. Ibid., 483.

For any source already cited in your notes, not just immediately before, you may use the author's name and (if the author is responsible for more than one cited source) a shortened form of the title.

1. Carol Gilligan, *In a Different Voice: Psychological Theory and Women's Development* (Cambridge: Harvard University Press, 1982), 27.

2. Carol Gilligan, "Moral Development in the College Years," *The Modern American College*, ed. A. Chickering (San Francisco: Jossey-Bass, 1981), 286.

3. Gilligan, *In a Different Voice*, 47.

Omit the title if you are using only one source by the cited author.

The Chicago style recommends in-text parenthetical citations when you cite one or more works repeatedly. This practice allows you to avoid many notes saying "ibid." or giving the same author's name. In the example following, the note number refers to the complete source information in an endnote; the numbers in parentheses are page numbers in the same source.

British rule, observes Stuart Cary Welch, "seemed as permanent as Mount Everest."[7] Most Indians submitted, willingly or not, to British influence in every facet of life (423-24).

55 CBE Documentation

 http://www.wisc.edu/writing/Handbook/DocCBE6.html   Guidance on CBE documentation style, from the University of Wisconsin at Madison.

Writers in the life sciences, physical sciences, and mathematics rely for documentation style on *Scientific Style and Format: The CBE Style Manual for Authors, Editors, and Publishers* (6th ed., 1994). (CBE is the Council of Biology Editors.) This book details two styles of in-text citation: one using author and date and one using numbers. Both types of text citation refer to a list of references at the end of the paper (facing page). Ask your instructor which style you should use.

55a   Writing CBE name-year text citations

In the CBE name-year style, parenthetical text citations provide the last name of the author being cited and the source's year of publication. At the end of the paper, a list of references, arranged alphabetically by authors' last names, provides complete information on each source. (See opposite.)

The CBE name-year style closely resembles the APA name-year style detailed on pages 394–97. You can follow the APA examples for in-text citations, making several notable changes for CBE:

- Do not use a comma to separate the author's name and the date: (Baumrind 1968, p. 34).
- For sources with two authors, separate their names with "and" (not "&"): (Pepinsky and DeStefano 1987).
- For sources with three or more authors, use "and others" (not "et al.") after the first author's name: (Rutter and others 1996).
- For anonymous sources, give the author as "Anonymous" both in the text citation—(Anonymous 1976)—and in the list of references (model 6, p. 434).

CBE

55b

55b   Writing CBE numbered text citations

In the CBE number style, raised numbers in the text refer to a numbered list of references at the end of the paper.

Two standard references[1,2] use this term.

These forms of immunity have been extensively researched.[3]

430

According to one report,[4] research into some forms of viral immunity is almost nonexistent.

Hepburn and Tatin[2] do not discuss this project.

Assignment of numbers

The number for each source is based on the order in which you cite the source in the text: the first cited source is 1, the second is 2, and so on.

Reuse of numbers

When you cite a source you have already cited and numbered, use the original number again (see the last example above, which reuses the number 2 from the first example on the facing page).

This reuse is the key difference between the CBE numbered citations and numbered references to footnotes or endnotes (pp. 421–429). In the CBE style, each source has only one number, determined by the order in which the source is cited. With notes, in contrast, the numbering proceeds in sequence, so that sources have as many numbers as they have citations in the text.

Citation of two or more sources

When you cite two or more sources at once, arrange their numbers in sequence and separate them with a comma and no space, as in the first example on the facing page.

55c Preparing the CBE reference list

For both the name-year and the number styles of in-text citation, provide a list, titled "References," of all sources you have cited. Format the page as shown for APA references on page 397 (but you may omit the shortened title before the page number).

Follow these guidelines for references, noting the important differences in name-year and number styles:

Spacing

Single-space each entry, and double-space between entries.

Arrangement

The two styles differ in their arrangement of entries:

Name-year style
Arrange entries alphabetically by authors' last names.

Number style
Arrange entries in numerical order—that is, in order of their citation in the text.

CBE
55c

Format

In both styles, begin the first line of each entry at the left margin and indent subsequent lines:

Name-year style

> Hepburn PX, Tatin JM. 1995. Human physiology. New York: Columbia Univ Pr. 1026 p.

Number style

> 2. Hepburn PX, Tatin JM. Human physiology. New York: Columbia Univ Pr; 1995. 1026 p.

Authors

List each author's name with the last name first, followed by initials for first and middle names. (See the examples above.) Do not use a comma between an author's last name and initials, and do not use periods or space with the initials. Do use a comma to separate authors' names.

Placement of dates

The two styles differ, as shown in the examples on the facing page.

Name-year style
The date follows the author's or authors' names.

Number style
The date follows the publication information (for a book) or the periodical title (for a journal, magazine, or newspaper).

Journal titles

Do not underline or italicize journal titles. For titles of two or more words, abbreviate words of six or more letters (without periods) and omit most prepositions, articles, and conjunctions. Capitalize each word. For example, *Annals of Medicine* becomes Ann Med, and *Journal of Chemical and Biochemical Studies* becomes J Chem Biochem Stud. See the Rowell examples on the facing page.

Book and article titles

Do not underline, italicize, or use quotation marks around a book or an article title. Capitalize only the first word and any proper nouns. See the Rowell examples and model 2 on the facing page.

Publication information for journal articles

Both the name-year and the number styles give the journal's volume number, a colon, and the inclusive page numbers of the article: 28:329-33 in the Rowell examples following. (If the journal has an issue number, it follows the volume number in parentheses: 62(2):26-40.) However, the styles differ in the punctuation as well as the placement of the date:

Name-year style
The date, after the author's name and a period, is followed by a period:

> Rowell LB. 1996. Blood pressure regulation during exercise. Ann Med 28:329-33.

Number style
The date, after the journal title and a space, is followed by a semicolon:

> 3. Rowell LB. Blood pressure regulation during exercise. Ann Med 1996;28:329-33.

The following examples show both a name-year reference and a number reference for each type of source. An index to the models appears at the tabbed divider on page 421.

1 Books

1. A book with one author

> Gould SJ. 1987. Time's arrow, time's cycle. Cambridge: Harvard Univ Pr. 222 p.
>
> 1. Gould SJ. Time's arrow, time's cycle. Cambridge: Harvard Univ Pr; 1987. 222 p.

2. A book with two to ten authors

> Hepburn PX, Tatin JM. 1995. Human physiology. New York: Columbia Univ Pr. 1026 p.
>
> 2. Hepburn PX, Tatin JM. Human physiology. New York: Columbia Univ Pr; 1995. 1026 p.

3. A book with more than ten authors

> Evans RW, Bowditch L, Dana KL, Drummond A, Wildovitch WP, Young SL, Mills P, Mills RR, Livak SR, Lisi OL, and others. 1998. Organ transplants: ethical issues. Ann Arbor: Univ of Michigan Pr. 498 p.
>
> 3. Evans RW, Bowditch L, Dana KL, Drummond A, Wildovitch WP, Young SL, Mills P, Mills RR, Livak SR, Lisi OL, and others. Organ transplants: ethical issues. Ann Arbor: Univ of Michigan Pr; 1998. 498 p.

4. A book with an editor

> Jonson P, editor. 1997. Anatomy yearbook. Los Angeles: Anatco. 628 p.

4. Jonson P, editor. Anatomy yearbook. Los Angeles: Anatco; 1997. 628 p.

5. A selection from a book

Krigel R, Laubenstein L, Muggia F. 1997. Kaposi's sarcoma. In: Ebbeson P, Biggar RS, Melbye M, editors. AIDS: a basic guide for clinicians. 2nd ed. Philadelphia: WB Saunders. p 100-26.

5. Krigel R, Laubenstein L, Muggia F. Kaposi's sarcoma. In: Ebbeson P, Biggar RS, Melbye M, editors. AIDS: a basic guide for clinicians. 2nd ed. Philadelphia: WB Saunders; 1997. p 100-26.

6. An anonymous work

[Anonymous]. 1992. Health care for multiple sclerosis. New York: US Health Care. 86 p.

6. [Anonymous]. Health care for multiple sclerosis. New York: US Health Care; 1992. 86 p.

7. Two or more cited works by the same author published in the same year

Gardner H. 1973a. The arts and human development. New York: J Wiley. 406 p.

Gardner H. 1973b. The quest for mind: Piaget, Lévi-Strauss, and the structuralist movement. New York: AA Knopf. 492 p.

(The number style does not require such forms.)

2   Periodicals: Journals, magazines, newspapers

8. An article in a journal with continuous pagination throughout the annual volume

Ancino R, Carter KV, Elwin DJ. 1983. Factors contributing to viral immunity: a review of the research. Dev Biol 30:156-9.

8. Ancino R, Carter KV, Elwin DJ. Factors contributing to viral immunity: a review of the research. Dev Biol 1983;30:156-9.

9. An article in a journal that pages issues separately

Kim P. 1986 Feb. Medical decision making for the dying. Milbank Quar 64(2):26-40.

9. Kim P. Medical decision making for the dying. Milbank Quar 1986 Feb;64(2):26-40.

10. An article in a newspaper

Krauthammer C. 1986 June 13. Lifeboat ethics: the case of Baby Jesse. Washington Post;Sect A:33(col 1).

10. Krauthammer C. Lifeboat ethics: the case of Baby Jesse. Washington Post 1986 June 13;Sect A:33(col 1).

11. An article in a magazine

Van Gelder L. 1996 Dec. Countdown to motherhood: when should you have a baby? Ms.:37-9.

11. Van Gelder L. Countdown to motherhood: when should you have a baby? Ms. 1996 Dec:37-9.

3 Electronic sources

 The CBE's *Scientific Style and Format* includes just a few models for electronic sources, and they form the basis of the following examples. For additional models and simpler formats, you can use Columbia online style for the sciences, discussed in Chapter 56. Pages 445–446 show how to adapt Columbia style to the CBE styles (both name-year and number) and details the differences between the styles. Ask your instructor which style you should use.

Note Since the CBE does not specify how to break electronic addresses, follow MLA style: break only after slashes, and do not hyphenate.

12. A source on CD-ROM

Reich WT, editor. 1998. Encyclopedia of bioethics [CD-ROM]. New York: Co-Health.

12. Reich WT, editor. Encyclopedia of bioethics [CD-ROM]. New York: Co-Health; 1998.

13. An online journal article

Grady GF. 1993 May 2. The here and now of hepatitis B immunization. Today's Med [serial online]. Available from: http://www.fmrt.org/todaysmedicine/Grady050293.html. Accessed 1999 Dec 27.

13. Grady GF. The here and now of hepatitis B immunization. Today's Med [serial online] 1993 May 2. Available from: http://www.fmrt.org/todaysmedicine/Grady050293.html. Accessed 1999 Dec 27.

14. An online book

Ruch BJ, Ruch DB. 1999. Homeopathy and medicine: resolving the conflict [book online]. New York: Albert Einstein Coll of Medicine. Available from: http://www.einstein.edu/medicine/books/ruch.html. Accessed 2000 Jan 28.

14. Ruch BJ, Ruch DB. Homeopathy and medicine: resolving the conflict [book online]. New York: Albert Einstein Coll of Medicine; 1999. Available from: http://www.einstein.edu/medicine/books/ruch.html. Accessed 2000 Jan 28.

15. Computer software

Project scheduler 8000 [computer program]. 1999. Version 4.1. Orlando (FL): Scitor. 1 computer disk: 3 1/2 in. Accompanied by: 1 manual. System requirements: IBM PC or fully compatible computer; Windows 95 or higher; 8 MB RAM; hard disk with a minimum of 2 MB of free space.

15. Project scheduler 8000 [computer program]. Version 4.1. Orlando (FL): Scitor; 1999. 1 computer disk: 3 1/2 in. Accompanied by: 1 manual. System requirements: IBM PC or fully compatible computer; Windows 95 or higher; 8 MB RAM; hard disk with a minimum of 2 MB of free space.

4   Other sources

16. A government publication

Committee on Science and Technology, House (US). 1991. Hearing on procurement and allocation of human organs for transplantation. 102nd Cong., 1st Sess. House Doc. nr 409.

16. Committee on Science and Technology, House (US). Hearing on procurement and allocation of human organs for transplantation. 102nd Cong., 1st Sess. House Doc. nr 409; 1991.

17. A nongovernment report

Warnock M. 1992. Report of the Committee on Fertilization and Embryology. Baylor University, Department of Embryology. Waco (TX): Baylor Univ. Report nr BU/DE.4261.

17. Warnock M. Report of the Committee on Fertilization and Embryology. Baylor University, Department of Embryology. Waco (TX): Baylor Univ; 1992. Report nr BU/DE.4261.

18. A sound recording, video recording, or film

Teaching Media. 1993. Cell mitosis [videocassette]. White Plains (NY): Teaching Media. 1 videocassette: 40 min, sound, black and white, 1/2 in.

18. Cell mitosis [videocassette]. White Plains (NY): Teaching Media; 1993. 1 videocassette: 40 min, sound, black and white, 1/2 in.

CBE
55c

Columbia Documentation for Online Sources

Columbia Documentation for Online Sources

Columbia works-cited models for the humanities

Columbia reference models for the sciences

56 Columbia Documentation for Online Sources

 http://www.columbia.edu/cu/cup/cgos   An overview of Columbia online style, with updates, from Columbia University Press.

The style manuals in many disciplines do not yet provide detailed guidelines for citing the many kinds of sources available on the Internet. In response, Janice R. Walker and Todd Taylor wrote *The Columbia Guide to Online Style,* published by Columbia University Press in 1998.

The Columbia Guide offers models for both the humanities and the sciences. The humanities models reflect MLA style (Chapter 52), and the science models reflect APA style (Chapter 53)—although there are differences in both cases. The Columbia models can also be adapted for the other two styles covered in this book: Chicago for the humanities (Chapter 54) and CBE for the sciences (Chapter 55).

56a   Distinguishing the elements of Columbia style

Columbia style adapts MLA and APA styles, but it also stresses the likely and important elements that allow readers to trace online sources. These elements may be the same as those in conventional printed sources, but often they are not.

Author

The author may be identified only by a login name (such as *jqsmith*) or a fictitious name (such as *c_major*). List the source by this name if it's all you can find, but take special care in evaluating and using such a source. (See pp. 322–329 on evaluating online sources.) Cite a source with no identifiable author by its title.

Title

For the title of a complete work, such as a book or periodical, use italics rather than underlining. If your document were posted on the Web, underlining would signal a hypertext link. Also italicize the titles of online sites and the names of information services.

Date of access

Online sources may change often, so always provide the date of your access so that readers know just which version you used. The date falls at the end of the citation, in parentheses, and in the format "day mo. year"—for instance, (31 Aug. 2000). If the source's

Col
56a

439

publication or revision date and your access date are identical, use only the access date.

Electronic address

Always provide an online source's exact and complete electronic address—the complete path for readers to follow in retrieving the source themselves. The address falls just before the access date with no special introduction or additional punctuation—for instance, finance-dl@weg.isu.edu (31 Aug. 1998). Follow MLA style for breaking long addresses: break only after slashes, and do not hyphenate.

58b   Using Columbia online style for the humanities

Columbia online style adapts most elements of MLA documentation (Chapter 51) to provide a thorough system for documenting online sources in the humanities.

- As in MLA style, a citation in the text provides the author's last name and the page or other number where the borrowed material appears—for instance, One researcher disagrees (Johnson 143) or Johnson disagrees (143). (See pp. 347–351 for a variety of examples.) Because many online sources do not use page, paragraph, section, or other numbers, in-text citations of electronic sources may consist only of the author's name.
- Also as in MLA style, a list titled "Works Cited" at the end of your paper arranges your sources alphabetically by the author's last name, or by the first main word of the title if there is no author.

1   Key differences from MLA style

Columbia online style differs from MLA style (pp. 364–372) in several ways:

Columbia online style	MLA style
Titles of complete works (books, journals) are italicized.	Titles of complete works are underlined.
The electronic address precedes the date of access and is not enclosed in angle brackets: finance-dl@weg.isu.edu (23 Feb. 1997).	The electronic address follows the date of access and is enclosed in angle brackets: 23 Feb. 1997 <finance-dl@weg.isu.edu>.
The date of access is enclosed in parentheses.	The date of access is not enclosed in parentheses.
The publication medium is not specially identified.	The publication medium—for instance, "Online posting"—often appears after the title.

Ask your instructor which format you should use for online sources.

2 Chicago style

You can merge Columbia humanities style and Chicago humanities style (Chapter 54) to create citations for online sources that Chicago does not currently cover. The following note and works-cited models show such mergers, drawing on Chicago examples given on page 427.

Footnote or endnote

19. Jane Austen, *Emma*, ed. Ronald Blythe (Harmondsworth, Eng.: Penguin, 1972), *Oxford Text Archive*, ftp://ota.ox.ac.uk/ public/english/Austen/emma.1519 (15 Dec. 1999).

Works-cited entry

Austen, Jane. *Emma*. Edited by Ronald Blythe. Harmondsworth, Eng.: Penguin, 1972. *Oxford Text Archive*. ftp://ota.ox.ac.uk/ public/english/Austen/emma.1519 (15 Dec. 1999).

These Columbia-Chicago mergers differ from the corresponding Chicago models on page 427 in several ways:

Columbia online style	Chicago style
The publication medium is not specially identified.	The publication medium—for instance, "book online"—appears after the title in brackets.
The electronic address precedes the date of your access at the end of the entry, and neither is introduced. See the works-cited entry above.	The positions of the electronic address and the access date vary, and both are introduced. In the Chicago works-cited entry for the Austen book, the access date follows the publication date of 1972—Accessed 15 December 1999—and the address falls at the end of the entry—Available from ftp://ota.ox.ac.uk/public/ english/Austen/emma.1519; Internet.
The date of access is enclosed in parentheses, and the month is abbreviated.	The date of access is not enclosed in parentheses, and the month is spelled out.

Ask your instructor which format you should use for online sources.

3 Models of Columbia humanities style

An index to the following models appears at the tabbed divider on page 438.

Col

56b

1. A site on the World Wide Web

Lederman, Leon. *Topics in Modern Physics--Lederman.* 10 Oct. 1999. http://www-ed.fnal.gov/samplers/hsphys/people/lederman.html (12 Dec. 1999).

2. A revised or modified site

Ruggira, Wendy. "Chiropractic: Past, Present and Future." *Chiromen.com.* Mod. 30 Sept. 1999. http://chiromen.com/chiropractic.htm (4 Feb. 2000).

3. A book

A book previously published in print:

James, Henry. *The Turn of the Screw.* New York: Scribner's, 1908-09. 1998. *American Literary Classics a Chapter a Day.* http://www.americanliterature.com/TS/TSINDX.HTML (4 Mar. 2000).

An original book:

Cooper, Phoebe, ed. *Sam and Daphne Maeglin: Selected Correspondence, 1940-1964.* 1999. http://www.alphabetica.org/maeglin (21 Mar. 2000).

4. An article in a periodical

Palfrey, Andrew. "Choice of Mates in Identical Twins." *Modern Psychology* 4.1 (1996): 12 pars. http://www.liasu.edu/modpsy/palfrey4(l).htm (25 Feb. 2000).

5. A group or organization as author

Exxon Corporation. "Managing Risk." *Environment, Health and Safety Progress Report.* 1999. http://www.exxon.com/exxoncorp/news/publications/safety_report/index.html (6 Apr. 2000).

United States. Dept. of State. Bureau of Public Affairs. *History of the National Security Council, 1947-1997.* Aug. 1998. http://www.whitehouse.gov/WH/EOP/NSC/html/History.html (6 Feb. 1999).

6. A maintained or compiled site

Scots Teaching and Research Network. Maint. John Corbett. 2 Feb. 1998. U of Glasgow. http://www.arts.gla.ac.uk/www/comet/starn.htm (5 Mar. 2000).

7. A graphic, video, or audio file

Hamilton, Calvin J. "Components of Comets." 1997. *Space Art.*
wysisiwyg://94/http://spaceart.com/solar/eng/comet.htm
(20 Dec. 1999).

8. Personal electronic mail

Millon, Michele. "Re: Grief Therapy." Personal e-mail (4 May 1999).

9. A posting to a discussion list

Tourville, Michael. "European Currency Reform." 6 Jan. 1999. *International Finance Discussion List.* finance-dl@weg.isu.edu (8 Jan. 1999).

10. A posting to a newsgroup or forum

Cramer, Sherry. "Recent Investment Practices." 26 Mar. 2000.
news:biz.investment.current.2700 (3 Apr. 2000).

11. An archived posting

Tourville, Michael. "European Currency Reform." 6 Jan. 1999. *International Finance Discussion List.* http://www.weg.isu.edu/finance-dl/46732 (2 Feb. 1999).

12. An encyclopedia

White, Geoffrey. "Ethnopsychology." *The MIT Encyclopedia of Cognitive Sciences.* Ed. Rob Wilson and Frank Keil. Cambridge: MIT P, 1997. http://mitpress.mit.edu/MITECS/work/whiteg_r.html (26 Mar. 1999).

13. A database

United States. Dept. of Health and Human Services. "Depression Is a Treatable Illness: A Patient's Guide." Apr. 1993. *Health Services Technology Assessment Texts.* No. 93-0533. http://text.nlm.nih.gov/ftrs/pick?collect=depp&cd=1&t=930533 (26 Sept. 1999).

14. A gopher or FTP site

Provide directions to a specific source in one of two ways: give the unique address of the file, as in the example above; or give the address of the home page, a space, and the path to the file. In the following example, the space occurs at the end of line 2, after "uk."

Goetsch, Sallie. "And What About Costume?" *Didaskalia: Ancient Theatre Today* 2.2 (1995). gopher://gopher.warwicku.ac.uk Didaskalia/Didaskalia: Ancient Theatre Today/1995/ 03Features/Goetsch (26 May 1999).

15. A telnet site

Johnson, Earl. "My House: Come In." *Houses of Cyberspace.* 7 Aug. 1999. telnet://edwin.ohms.bookso.com.7777 @go #50827, press 10 (11 Aug. 1999).

16. A synchronous communication

Wendy_Librarian_. "Online Integrity (#421)." *Internet Public Library MOO.* telnet://moo.ipl.org.8888 @go #421 (4 Jan. 1999).

17. Software

Project Scheduler 8000. Vers. 4.1. Orlando: Scitor, 1999.

56c   Using Columbia online style for the sciences

Columbia style adapts most elements of APA style (Chapter 53) to provide a thorough system for documenting online sources in the social, natural, and applied sciences.

- As in APA style, a citation in the text provides the author's last name, the date of publication, and the page or other number where specific borrowings appear—for instance, One researcher called the study "deeply flawed" (Johnson, 1998, p. 143) or Johnson (1998) called the study "deeply flawed" (p. 143). (See pp. 394–97 for a variety of examples.) Because many online sources do not use page, paragraph, or other numbers, citations of specific borrowings from electronic sources often consist only of the author's name and the date.
- Also as in APA style, a list titled "References" falls at the end of your paper. In it you arrange your sources alphabetically by the author's last name, or by the first main word of the title if there is no author.

1   Key differences from APA style

Though it includes many more kinds of online sources than APA style currently does, Columbia style does differ from APA style (pp. 403–05) in several significant ways:

Columbia online style

Titles of complete works (books, journals) are italicized.

A full publication date after the author's name is in the format "year, month day": 1999, December 12. All other dates are in the format "day mo. year": 12 Dec. 1999.

The electronic address precedes the date of your access, with the date in parentheses: http://www.thinck.com/insec.html (21 Jan. 1998).

A period ends the entry.

APA style

Titles of complete works are underlined.

A full publication date after the author's name is also in the format "year, month day": 1999, December 12. But all other dates are in the format "month day, year": December 12, 1999.

The electronic address follows the date of your access, and the two are linked in a statement: Retrieved January 21, 1998 from the World Wide Web: http://www.thinck.com/insec.html

A period does not end the entry.

Ask your instructor which format you should use for online sources.

2 CBE style

CBE style (Chapter 55) currently provides few models for citing online sources. By merging Columbia science style and either the CBE name-year style or the CBE number style, you can create citations for kinds of sources not covered by CBE, such as a Web site:

Name-year style

Lederman L. 1999 Oct 10. *Topics in modern physics--Lederman.* http://www.ed.fnal.gov/samplers/hsphys/people/ lederman.html (12 Dec. 1999).

Number style

4. Lederman L. *Topics in modern physics--Lederman.* 1999 Oct 10. http://www.ed.fnal.gov/samplers/hsphys/people/ lederman.html (12 Dec. 1999).

Such mergers of Columbia and CBE styles involve some alterations in the CBE models shown on pages 435–436.

Columbia online style

The publication medium is not specially identified.

The electronic address and the date of your access are not introduced: finance-dl@weg.isu.edu (23 Feb. 1997).

CBE style

The publication medium—for instance, "serial online"—appears in brackets after the title.

Both the electronic address and the date of your access are introduced: Available from: finance-dl@weg.isu.edu. Accessed 1997 Feb 23.

Columbia online style	CBE style
The date of access is enclosed in parentheses and is in the format "day mo. year" (the month abbreviated with a period).	The date of access is not enclosed in parentheses and is in the format "year mo day" (the month abbreviated without a period).

Ask your instructor which format you should use for online sources.

3 Models of Columbia science style

An index to the following models appears at the tabbed divider on page 437.

1. A site on the World Wide Web

Lederman, L. (1999, October 10). *Topics in modern physics--Lederman.* http://www-ed.fnal.gov/samplers/hsphys/people/lederman.html (12 Dec. 1999).

2. A revised or modified site

Ruggira, W. (1998). Chiropractic: Past, present and future (Mod. 30 Sept. 1999). *Chiromen.com.* http://chiromen.com/chiropractic.htm (4 Feb. 2000).

3. A book

A book previously published in print:

James, H. (1998). *The turn of the screw.* New York: Scribner's, 1908-1909. *American literary classics a chapter a day.* http://www.americanliterature.com/TS/TSINDX.HTML (4 Mar. 2000).

An original book:

Cooper, P. (Ed.). (1999). *Sam and Daphne Maeglin: Selected correspondence, 1940-1964.* http://www.alphabetica.org/maeglin (21 Mar. 2000).

4. An article in a periodical

Palfrey, A. (1996). Choice of mates in identical twins. *Modern Psychology, 4*(1). http://www.liasu.edu/modpsy/palfrey4(1).htm (25 Feb. 2000).

5. A group or organization as author

Exxon Corporation. (1999). Managing risk. *Environment, health*

and safety progress report. http://www.exxon.com/
exxoncorp/news/publications/safety_report/index.html
(6 Apr. 2000).

U.S. Department of State. Bureau of Public Affairs. (1998, August). *History of the National Security Council, 1947-1997.*
http://www.whitehouse.gov/WH/EOP/NSC/html/History.html
(6 Feb. 1999).

6. A maintained or compiled site

Scots teaching and research network. (1998, February 2).
(J. Corbett, Maint.). University of Glasgow. http://
www.arts.gla.ac.uk/www/comet/starn.html (5 Mar. 2000).

7. A graphic, video, or audio file

Hamilton, C. J. (1997). Components of comets [graphic file]. *Space art.* wysisiwyg://94/http://spaceart.com/solar/eng/comet/htm
(20 Dec. 1999).

8. Personal electronic mail

Millon, M. Re: Grief therapy [personal e-mail]. (4 May 1999).

Note that APA style calls for citing nonretrievable sources only in your text (see p. 404).

9. A posting to a discussion list

Tourville, M. (1999, January 6). European currency reform. *International finance discussion list.* finance-dl@weg.isu.edu
(8 Jan. 1999).

Note that APA style calls for citing nonretrievable sources only in your text (see p. 404). Model 11 shows the format for an archived posting, which is retrievable.

10. A posting to a newsgroup or forum

Cramer, S. (2000, March 26). Recent investment practices.
news:biz.investment.current.2700 (3 Apr. 2000).

Note that APA style calls for citing nonretrievable sources only in your text (see p. 404). Model 11 shows the format for an archived posting, which is retrievable.

11. An archived posting

Tourville, M. (1999, January 6). European currency reform. *Inter-*

national finance discussion list. http://www.weg.isu.edu/
finance-dl/46732 (2 Feb. 1999).

12. An encyclopedia

White, G. (1997). Ethnopsychology. In R. Wilson & F. Keil (Eds.),
The MIT encyclopedia of cognitive sciences. Cambridge, MA:
MIT Press. http://mitpress.mit.edu/MITECS/work/
whiteg_r.html (26 Mar. 1999).

13. A database

U.S. Department of Health and Human Services. (1993, April). Depression is a treatable illness: A patient's guide. *Health services technology assessment texts* (No. 93-0533). http://
text.nlm.nih.gov/ftrs/pick?collect=depp&cd=1&t=930533
(26 Sept. 1999).

14. A gopher or FTP site

Provide directions to a specific source in one of two ways: give
the unique address of the file, as in the example above; or give the
address of the home page, a space, and the path to the file. In this
example, the space occurs at the end of line 2, after "uk":

Goetsch, S. (1995). And what about costume? *Didaskalia: Ancient
Theatre Today, 2*(2). gopher://gopher.warwicku.ac.uk
Didaskalia/Didaskalia: Ancient Theatre Today/1995/
03Features/Goetsch (26 May 1999).

15. A telnet site

Johnson, E. (1999, August 7). My house: Come in. *Houses of cyberspace.* telnet://edwin.ohms.bookso.com.7777 @go #50827,
press 10 (11 Aug. 1999).

16. A synchronous communication

Wendy_Librarian_. Online integrity (#421). *Internet Public Library
MOO.* telnet://moo.ipl.org.8888 @go #421 (4 Jan. 1999).

17. Software

Project scheduler 8000. (1999). Orlando, FL: Scitor.

VIII

Special Writing Situations

VIII

Special Writing Situations

57 Reading and Writing About Literature

By Sylvan Barnet

Resources for reading and writing about literature:

http://vos.ucsb.edu/shuttle/english.html From Voice of the Shuttle.

http://eserver.org From Carnegie Mellon University.

http://www.brocku.ca/english/jlye/criticalreading.html From Brock University.

http://www.unc.edu/depts/wcweb/handouts/literature.html From the University of North Carolina.

Writers of literature—stories, novels, poems, and plays—are concerned with presenting human experience concretely, with *showing* rather than *telling*, with giving a sense of the feel of life. Reading and writing about literature thus require extremely close attention to the feel of the words. For instance, the word *woods* in Robert Frost's "Stopping by Woods on a Snowy Evening" has a rural, folksy quality that *forest* doesn't have, and many such small distinctions contribute to the poem's effect.

When you read literature, you interpret distinctions like these, forming an idea of the work. When you write about literature, you state your idea as your thesis, and you support the thesis with evidence from the work. (See pp. 20–23 for more on thesis statements.)

Note Writing about literature is not merely summarizing literature. Your thesis is a claim about the meaning or effect of the literary work, not a statement of its plot. And your paper is a demonstration of your thesis, not a retelling of the work's changes or events.

57a Reading literature

Reading literature critically involves interacting with a text, not in order to make negative judgments but in order to understand the work and evaluate its significance or quality. Such interaction is not passive, like scanning a newspaper or watching television. Instead, it is a process of engagement, of diving into the words themselves.

You will become more engaged if you write while you read. If you own the book you're reading, don't hesitate to underline or highlight passages that especially interest you. Don't hesitate to annotate the margins, indicating your pleasures, displeasures, and uncertainties with remarks such as *Nice detail* or *Do we need this long description?* or *Not believable.* If you don't own the book, make these notes on separate sheets or on your computer.

451

57b

An effective way to interact with a text is to keep a READING JOURNAL. A journal is not a diary in which you record your doings but a place in which you develop and store your reflections on what you read, such as an answer to a question you may have posed in the margin of the text or a response to something said in class. You may, for instance, want to reflect on why your opinion is so different from that of another student. You may even make an entry in the form of a letter to the author or from one character to another. (See p. 12 for more on journal keeping.)

57b   Analyzing literature

1   Meaning in literature

In analyzing literature, you face right off the question of *meaning*. Readers disagree all the time over the meanings of works of literature, partly because (as noted earlier) literature *shows* rather than *tells:* it gives concrete images of imagined human experiences, but it usually does not say how we ought to understand the images. Further, readers bring different experiences to their reading and thus understand images differently. In writing about literature, then, we can offer only our *interpretation* of the meaning rather than *the* meaning. Still, most people agree that there are limits to interpretation: it must be supported by evidence that a reasonable person finds at least plausible if not totally convincing.

2   Analytical approaches

One reason interpretations of meaning differ is that readers approach literary works differently, focusing on certain elements and interpreting those elements distinctively. Some of the critical approaches you may encounter in studying literature are these:

- HISTORICAL or CULTURAL CRITICISM focuses on the context in which a literary work was created and how that context affected the work. The critic may examine the author's social, political, and intellectual surroundings or may concentrate on the author's own biography: his or her life experiences or psychological makeup.
- FEMINIST CRITICISM focuses on the representation of gender in literature, particularly in the literary canon—the body of work represented in the standard anthologies, discussed in the schools, and examined in the scholarly journals. Feminist critics are especially concerned with the writings of women and with the responses of women to the depiction of both sexes in literature.

- READER-RESPONSE CRITICISM focuses on the reactions of an audience to a work of literature, asking why readers respond as they do to a text. In this view the meaning of the text lies not just on the page but in how the reader constructs the text.
- DECONSTRUCTIVE CRITICISM regards a work of literature skeptically, resisting the obvious meanings and focusing on the ambiguities in the work, especially the internal contradictions. Perceiving that the relationship of words and their meanings is both arbitrary and forever changing—even within the same work—deconstructive critics emphasize multiple meanings and what a text does not say.
- FORMALIST CRITICISM (also called NEW CRITICISM) focuses primarily on a literary work as a constructed text, as an independent unity understood in itself rather than as an artifact of a particular context or reader response. Beginning with a personal response, the formalist critic tries to account for the response by examining the form of the work (hence *formalism*) and the relations among its elements.

3 Questions for a literary analysis

A formalist approach to literature has certain advantages for inexperienced critics: it engages you immediately in the work of literature itself, without requiring extensive historical or cultural background, and it introduces the conventional elements of literature that all critical approaches discuss, even though they view the elements differently. The list below poses questions for each element that can help you think constructively and imaginatively about what you read.

- PLOT: the relationships and patterns of events. (Even a poem has a plot—for instance, a change in mood from grief to resignation.)

  What actions happen?
  What conflicts occur?
  How do the events connect to each other and to the whole?

- CHARACTERS: the people the author creates (including the narrator of a story or the speaker of a poem).

  Who are the principal people in the work?
  How do they interact?
  What do their actions, words, and thoughts reveal about their personalities and the personalities of others?
  Do the characters stay the same, or do they change? Why?

- POINT OF VIEW: the perspective or attitude of the speaker in a poem or the voice who tells a story. The point of view may be FIRST PERSON (a participant, using *I*) or THIRD PERSON (an

57b

outsider, using *he, she, it, they*). A first-person narrator may be a major or a minor character in the narrative and may be RELI-ABLE or UNRELIABLE (unable to report events wholly or accurately). A third-person narrator may be OMNISCIENT (knows what goes on in all characters' minds), LIMITED (knows what goes on in the mind of only one or two characters), or OBJEC-TIVE (knows only what is external to the characters).

Who is the narrator (or the speaker of a poem)?
How does the narrator's point of view affect the narrative?

- TONE: the narrator's or speaker's attitude, perceived through the words (for instance, joyful, bitter, or confident).

  What tone (or tones) do you hear? If there is a change, how do you account for it?
  Is there an ironic contrast between the narrator's tone (for instance, confidence) and what you take to be the author's attitude (for instance, pity for human overconfidence)?

- IMAGERY: word pictures or visual details involving the senses (sight, sound, touch, smell, taste).

  What images does the writer use? What senses do they draw on?
  What patterns are evident in the images (for instance, religious or commercial images)?
  What is the significance of the imagery?

- SYMBOLISM: concrete things standing for larger and more abstract ideas (for instance, the American flag may symbolize freedom, or a dead flower may symbolize mortality).

  What symbols does the author use? What do they seem to signify?
  How does the symbolism relate to the theme of the work?

- SETTING: the place where the action happens.

  What does the locale contribute to the work?
  Are scene shifts significant?

- FORM: the shape or structure of the work.

  What *is* the form? (For example, a story might divide sharply in the middle, moving from happiness to sorrow.)
  What parts of the work does the form emphasize, and why?

- THEME: the central idea, a conception of human experience suggested by the work as a whole. Theme is neither plot (what happens) nor subject (such as youth or mourning or marriage). Rather it is what the author says with that plot about that subject.

Can you state the theme in a sentence? For instance, you might state the following about Kate Chopin's "The Story of an Hour" (next page): *Happiness depends partly on freedom.*

Do certain words, passages of dialogue or description, or situations seem to represent the theme most clearly?

How do the work's elements combine to develop the theme?

- APPEAL: the degree to which the work pleases you.

What do you especially like or dislike about the work? Why?

Do you think your responses are unique, or would they be common to most readers? Why?

57c   Examining two literary works and sample papers

The following pages reprint two works of literature (a short story and a poem), each followed by a student paper on the work. In each student paper the author develops a thesis about the work, supporting this main idea with quotations, paraphrases, and summaries from the work being discussed, a primary source. In the second paper (p. 460), the author also draws sparingly on secondary sources (other critics' views), which further support his own views.

Note the following features of the students' papers:

- The writers do not merely summarize the literary works they write about. Occasionally, they briefly summarize to make their meaning clear, but their essays consist mostly of their own analysis.

KEY TERMS

QUOTATION   An exact repetition of an author's words, placed in quotation marks. (See also pp. 248–249, 380–381.)

PARAPHRASE   A restatement of an author's words, closely following the author's line of thought but using different words and sentence structures. (See also pp. 327–328.)

SUMMARY   A condensation of an extended passage into a sentence or more. (See also pp. 326–327.)

PRIMARY SOURCE   A firsthand account: for instance, a historical document, a work of literature, or your own observations. (See also p. 293.)

SECONDARY SOURCE   A report on or analysis of other sources, often primary ones: for instance, a historian's account of a battle or a critic's view of a poem. (See also p. 293.)

- Each writer uses many quotations from the literary work to provide evidence for his or her ideas and to let readers hear the voice of the work.
- Both writers integrate quotations smoothly into their own sentences (see pp. 334–337).
- The writers use the present tense of verbs (*Chopin shows*; *Mrs. Mallard dies*) to describe both the author's work and the action in the work.

For the format of a literature paper, consult several other sections of this handbook:

- Use MLA document format for treatment of margins, quotations, and other elements (pp. 376–381).
- Cite sources with MLA parenthetical text citations and a list of works cited (pp. 346–376).
- Use ellipsis marks in brackets ([. . .]) to indicate deletions from quotations (pp. 254–257). Use brackets to indicate additions to quotations (p. 257).

1   A short story and an essay about it

Short story

Kate Chopin
The Story of an Hour

Knowing that Mrs. Mallard was afflicted with a heart trouble, great care was taken to break to her as gently as possible the news of her husband's death.

It was her sister Josephine who told her, in broken sentences, veiled hints that revealed in half concealing. Her husband's friend Richards was there, too, near her. It was he who had been in the newspaper office when intelligence of the railroad disaster was received, with Brently Mallard's name leading the list of "killed." He had only taken the time to assure himself of its truth by a second telegram, and had hastened to forestall any less careful, less tender friend in bearing the sad message.

She did not hear the story as many women have heard the same, with a paralyzed inability to accept its significance. She wept at once with sudden, wild abandonment, in her sister's arms. When the storm of grief had spent itself she went away to her room alone. She would have no one follow her.

There stood, facing the open window, a comfortable, roomy armchair. Into this she sank, pressed down by a physical exhaustion that haunted her body and seemed to reach into her soul.

She could see in the open square before her house the tops of trees that were all aquiver with the new spring life. The delicious breath of rain was in the air. In the street below a peddler was crying his wares. The notes of a distant song which some one was singing reached her faintly, and countless sparrows were twittering in the eaves.

There were patches of blue sky showing here and there through the clouds that had met and piled one above the other in the west facing her window.

She sat with her head thrown back upon the cushion of the chair quite motionless, except when a sob came up into her throat and shook her, as a child who has cried itself to sleep continues to sob in its dreams.

She was young, with a fair, calm face, whose lines bespoke repression and even a certain strength. But now there was a dull stare in her eyes, whose gaze was fixed away off yonder on one of those patches of blue sky. It was not a glance of reflection, but rather indicated a suspension of intelligent thought.

There was something coming to her and she was waiting for it, fearfully. What was it? She did not know; it was too subtle and elusive to name. But she felt it creeping out of the sky, reaching toward her through the sounds, the scents, the color that filled the air.

Now her bosom rose and fell tumultuously. She was beginning to recognize this thing that was approaching to possess her, and she was striving to beat it back with her will—as powerless as her two white slender hands would have been.

When she abandoned herself a little whispered word escaped her slightly parted lips. She said it over and over under her breath: "Free, free, free!" The vacant stare and the look of terror that had followed it went from her eyes. They stayed keen and bright. Her pulses beat fast, and the coursing blood warmed and relaxed every inch of her body.

She did not stop to ask if it were not a monstrous joy that held her. A clear and exalted perception enabled her to dismiss the suggestion as trivial.

She knew that she would weep again when she saw the kind, tender hands folded in death; the face that had never looked save with love upon her, fixed and gray and dead. But she saw beyond that bitter moment a long procession of years to come that would belong to her absolutely. And she opened and spread her arms out to them in welcome.

There would be no one to live for her during those coming years; she would live for herself. There would be no powerful will bending her in the blind persistence with which men and women believe they have a right to impose a private will upon a fellow creature. A kind intention or a cruel intention made the act seem no less a crime as she looked upon it in that brief moment of illumination.

And yet she had loved him—sometimes. Often she had not. What did it matter! What could love, the unsolved mystery, count for in face of this possession of self-assertion which she suddenly recognized as the strongest impulse of her being.

"Free! Body and soul free!" she kept whispering.

Josephine was kneeling before the closed door with her lips to the keyhole, imploring for admission. "Louise, open the door! I beg; open the door—you will make yourself ill. What are you doing, Louise? For heaven's sake open the door."

"Go away. I am not making myself ill." No; she was drinking in the very elixir of life through that open window.

Her fancy was running riot along those days ahead of her. Spring days, and summer days, and all sorts of days that would be her own. She breathed a quick prayer that life might be long. It was only yesterday she had thought with a shudder that life might be long.

She arose at length and opened the door to her sister's importunities. There was a feverish triumph in her eyes, and she carried herself unwittingly like a goddess of Victory. She clasped her sister's waist and together they descended the stairs. Richards stood waiting for them at the bottom.

Some one was opening the front door with a latchkey. It was Brently Mallard who entered, a little travel-stained, composedly carrying his grip-sack and umbrella. He had been far from the scene of accident, and did not even know there had been one. He stood amazed at Josephine's piercing cry; at Richards' quick motion to screen him from the view of his wife.

But Richards was too late.

When the doctors came they said she had died of heart disease—of joy that kills.

An essay on fiction (no secondary sources)

Ironies of Life in Kate Chopin's
"The Story of an Hour"

Kate Chopin's "The Story of an Hour"—which takes only a few minutes to read—has an ironic ending: Mrs. Mallard dies just when she is beginning to live. On first reading, the ending seems almost too ironic for belief. On rereading the story, however, one sees that the ending is believable partly because it is consistent with other ironies in the story.

After we know how the story turns out, if we reread it we find irony at the very start. Because Mrs. Mallard's friends and her sister assume, mistakenly, that she was deeply in love with her husband, Brently Mallard, they take great care to tell her gently of his death. They mean well, and in fact they do well, bringing her an hour of life, an hour of joyous freedom, but it is ironic that they think their news is sad. True, Mrs. Mallard at first expresses grief when she hears the news, but soon (unknown to her friends) she finds joy in it. So Richards's "sad message" (12), though sad in Richards's eyes, is in fact a happy message.

Among the small but significant ironic details is the statement near the end of the story that when Mallard entered the house, Richards tried to conceal him from Mrs. Mallard, but "Richards was too late" (13). Almost at the start of the story, in the second paragraph, Richards "hastened" (12) to bring his sad news. But if Richards had arrived "too late" at the start, Brently Mallard would have arrived at home first, and Mrs. Mallard's life would not have ended an hour later but would simply have gone on as it had been. Yet another irony at the end of the story is the diagnosis of the doctors. They say she died of "heart disease—of joy that kills" (13). In one sense they are right: Mrs. Mallard has for the last hour experienced a great joy. But of course the doctors totally misunderstand the joy that kills her. It is not joy at seeing her husband alive, but her realization that the great joy she experienced during the last hour is over.

All of these ironic details add richness to the story, but the central irony resides not in the well-intentioned but ironic actions of Richards, or in the unconsciously ironic words of the doctors, but in Mrs. Mallard's own life. She "sometimes" (13) loved her husband, but in a way she has been dead, a body subjected to her husband's will. Now, his apparent death brings her new life. Appropriately, this new life comes to her at the season of the year when "the tops of trees [. . .] were all aquiver with the new spring life" (12). But, ironically, her new life will last only an hour. She is "Free, free, free" (12), but only until her husband walks through the doorway. She looks forward to "summer days" (13), but she will not see even the end of this spring day. If her years of marriage were ironic, bringing her a sort of living death instead of joy, her new life is ironic too, not only because it grows out of her moment of grief for her supposedly dead husband, but also because her vision of "a long procession of years" (12) is cut short within an hour on a spring day.

Work Cited

Chopin, Kate. "The Story of an Hour." Literature for Composition. Ed. Sylvan Barnet et al. 5th ed. New York: Longman, 2000. 12-13.

—JANET VONG (student)

2 **A poem and an essay about it**

Poem

Gwendolyn Brooks

The Bean Eaters

They eat beans mostly, this old yellow pair.
Dinner is a casual affair.
Plain chipware on a plain and creaking wood,
Tin flatware.

Two who are Mostly Good.   5
Two who have lived their day,
But keep on putting on their clothes
And putting things away.

And remembering . . .
Remembering, with tinklings and twinges,   10

As they lean over the beans in their rented back room that is
full of beads and receipts and dolls and cloths, tobacco
crumbs, vases and fringes.

An essay on poetry (with secondary sources)

Marking Time Versus Enduring in
Gwendolyn Brooks's "The Bean Eaters"

Gwendolyn Brooks's poem "The Bean Eaters" runs only eleven
lines. It is written in plain language about very plain people. Yet its
meaning is ambiguous. One critic, George E. Kent, says the old
couple who eat beans "have had their day and exist now as time-
markers" (141). However, another reader, D. H. Melhem, perceives
not so much time marking as "endurance" in the old couple (123).
Is this poem a despairing picture of old age or a more positive por-
trait?

"The Bean Eaters" describes an "old yellow pair" who "eat
beans mostly" (line 1) off "Plain chipware" (3) with "Tin flatware"
(4) in "their rented back room" (11). Clearly, they are poor. Their
existence is accompanied not by friends or relatives—children or
grandchildren are not mentioned—but by memories and a few pos-
sessions (9–11). They are "Mostly Good" (5), words Brooks capitalizes at the end of a line, perhaps to stress the old people's adher-
ence to traditional values as well as their lack of saintliness. They
are unexceptional, whatever message they have for readers.

The isolated routine of the couple's life is something Brooks
draws attention to with a separate stanza:

> Two who are Mostly Good.
> Two who have lived their day,
> But keep on putting on their clothes
> And putting things away. (5–8)

Brooks emphasizes how isolated the couple is by repeating "Two
who." Then she emphasizes how routine their life is by repeating
"putting."

A pessimistic reading of this poem seems justified. The critic
Harry B. Shaw reads the lines just quoted as perhaps despairing:
"they are putting things away as if winding down an operation and
readying for withdrawal from activity" (80). However, Shaw
observes, the word *But* also indicates the couple's "determination
to go on living, a refusal to give up and let things go" (80). This dual
meaning is at the heart of Brooks's poem: the old people live a mea-
ger existence, yes, but their will, their self-control, and their connection with another person—their essential humanity—are
unharmed.

The truly positive nature of the poem is revealed in the last
stanza. In Brooks's words, the old couple remember with some
"twinges" perhaps, but also with "tinklings" (10), a cheerful image.
As Melhem says, these people are "strong in mutual affection and
shared memories" (123). And the final line, which is much longer
than all the rest and which catalogs the evidence of the couple's

58

long life together, is almost musically affirmative: "As they lean over the beans in their rented back room that is full of beads and receipts and dolls and cloths, tobacco crumbs, vases and fringes" (11).

What these people have is not much, but it is something.

Works Cited

Brooks, Gwendolyn. "The Bean Eaters." Literature: An Introduction to Fiction, Poetry, and Drama. Ed. X. J. Kennedy and Dana Gioia. 7th ed. New York: Longman, 1999. 732.

Kent, George E. A Life of Gwendolyn Brooks. Lexington: UP of Kentucky, 1990.

Melhem, D. H. Gwendolyn Brooks: Poetry and the Heroic Voice. Lexington: UP of Kentucky, 1987.

Shaw, Harry B. Gwendolyn Brooks. Twayne's United States Authors Ser. 395. Boston: Twayne, 1980.

—KENNETH SCHEFF (student)

58 Writing for Business

http://www.colostate.edu/Depts/WritingCenter/references/documents/bletter/page1.htm   Advice on writing business letters, from Colorado State University.

http://www.quintcareers.com/cover_letters.html   A tutorial and examples for writing job-application letters, from Quintessential Careers.

http://owl.english.purdue.edu/bw/resume/resume.html   A tutorial for résumé writing, from the Purdue Online Writing Lab.

http://www.careermosaic.com/cm/rwc/rwc1.html   Information on résumés, cover letters, thank you letters, and more, from CareerMosaic.

http://www.colostate.edu/Depts/WritingCenter/references/documents/memo/page1.htm   Advice on writing memos, from Colorado State University.

When you write for business, you are addressing busy people who want to see quickly why you are writing and how they should respond to you. Follow these general guidelines:

- State your purpose right at the start.
- Be straightforward, clear, concise, objective, and courteous.
- Observe conventions of grammar and usage, which make your writing clear and impress your reader with your care.

This chapter explains and illustrates some business-writing basics: business letter format (below), job-application letters (p. 464), résumés (p. 465), memos (p. 468), and electronic communication (p. 468). See Chapter 9 on document design for pointers on type fonts, page layout, headings, and other elements of business documents. See page 85 in that chapter for a sample of a business report.

ESL Business writing in your native culture may differ from American business writing. For instance, writers may be expected to begin with polite questions about the addressee or with compliments for the addressee's company. When writing to American businesspeople, get right to the point, even if at first your opening sounds abrupt or even impolite. See the examples opposite and on page 469.

58a Writing business letters and résumés

1 Business letter format

For any business letter, use either unlined white paper measuring $8\frac{1}{2}'' \times 11''$ or what is called letterhead stationery with your address printed at the top of the sheet. Type the letter single-spaced (with double space between elements) on only one side of a sheet.

A common form for business letters is illustrated on the facing page.

- The RETURN-ADDRESS HEADING gives your address (but not your name) and the date. (If you are using stationery with a printed heading, you need only give the date.) Place your heading at least an inch from the top of the page. Align the heading at the left margin.
- The INSIDE ADDRESS shows the name, title, and complete address of the person you are writing to. Place the address at least two lines below the return-address heading.
- The SALUTATION greets the addressee. Position it at the left margin, two lines below the inside address and two lines above the body of the letter. Follow it with a colon. Whenever possible, address your letter to a specific person. (Call the company or department to ask whom to address.) If you can't find a person's name, then use a job title (*Dear Human Resources Manager, Dear Customer Service Manager*) or use a general salutation (*Dear Smythe Shoes*). Use *Ms.* as the title for a woman when she has no other title, when you don't know how she prefers to be addressed, or when you know that she prefers *Ms.*

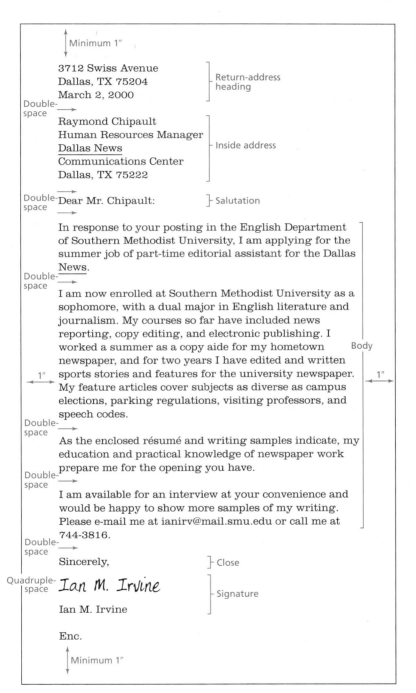

Minimum 1″

3712 Swiss Avenue
Dallas, TX 75204
March 2, 2000

Return-address heading

Double-space

Raymond Chipault
Human Resources Manager
Dallas News
Communications Center
Dallas, TX 75222

Inside address

Double-space

Dear Mr. Chipault:

Salutation

In response to your posting in the English Department of Southern Methodist University, I am applying for the summer job of part-time editorial assistant for the Dallas News.

Double-space

I am now enrolled at Southern Methodist University as a sophomore, with a dual major in English literature and journalism. My courses so far have included news reporting, copy editing, and electronic publishing. I worked a summer as a copy aide for my hometown newspaper, and for two years I have edited and written sports stories and features for the university newspaper. My feature articles cover subjects as diverse as campus elections, parking regulations, visiting professors, and speech codes.

Body

1″

1″

Double-space

As the enclosed résumé and writing samples indicate, my education and practical knowledge of newspaper work prepare me for the opening you have.

Double-space

I am available for an interview at your convenience and would be happy to show more samples of my writing. Please e-mail me at ianirv@mail.smu.edu or call me at 744-3816.

Double-space

Sincerely,

Close

Quadruple-space

Ian M. Irvine

Ian M. Irvine

Signature

Enc.

Minimum 1″

58a

- The BODY of the letter, containing its substance, begins at the left margin. Instead of indenting the first line of each paragraph, insert an extra line of space between paragraphs.
- The letter's CLOSE begins two lines below the last line of the body and aligns at the left margin. The close should reflect the level of formality in the salutation: *Respectfully, Cordially, Yours truly,* and *Sincerely* are more formal closes; *Regards* and *Best wishes* are less formal. Capitalize only the first word, and follow the close with a comma.
- The SIGNATURE falls below the close and has two parts: your name typed four lines below the close, and your handwritten signature in the space between. Give your name as you sign checks and other documents.
- Below the signature at the left margin, you may want to include additional information such as *Enc.* (indicating an enclosure with the letter) or *cc: Margaret Zusky* (indicating that a copy is being sent to the person named).

Use an envelope that will accommodate the letter once it is folded horizontally in thirds. The envelope should show your name and address in the upper left corner and the addressee's name, title, and address in the center. For easy machine reading, the United States Postal Service recommends all capital letters and no punctuation (spaces separate the elements on a line), as in this address:

RAYMOND CHIPAULT
HUMAN RESOURCES MANAGER
DALLAS NEWS
COMMUNICATIONS CENTER
DALLAS TX 75222-0188

2   Job-application letter

The sample on the previous page illustrates the key features of a job-application letter:

- The letter should be an interpretation of your résumé for a particular job, not a detailed account of the entire résumé. Instead of reciting your job history, highlight and reshape only the relevant parts.
- Announce at the outset what job you seek and how you heard about it.
- Include any special reason you have for applying, such as a specific career goal.
- Summarize your qualifications for this particular job, including relevant facts about education and employment history and emphasizing notable accomplishments. Mention that additional information appears in an accompanying résumé.

- At the end of the letter, mention that you are available for an interview at the convenience of the addressee, or specify when you will be available (for instance, when your current job or classes leave your free, or when you could travel to the employer's city).

3 Résumé

For the résumé that accompanies your letter of application, you can use the guidelines below and the samples on the next two pages. (The samples illustrate only one possible organization; another, for instance, arranges employment history not by job but by functions and skills.) For more on résumé writing, see the Web sites given on page 461.

- Provide the following, in table form: your name, postal address, phone number, and e-mail address; career objective; education; employment history; any special skills or awards; and information about how to obtain your references. (See the sample on the next page.)
- Use headings to mark the various sections of the résumé, spacing around them and within sections so that important information stands out.
- Usage varies on capital letters in résumés. Keep in mind that passages with many capitals can be hard to read. Definitely use capitals for proper nouns (pp. 268–269), but consider dropping them for job titles, course names, department names, and the like.
- Limit your résumé to one page so that it can be quickly reviewed. However, if your experience and education are extensive, a two-page résumé is preferable to a single cramped, unreadable page.
- If you are submitting a printed résumé, you may want to use some of the techniques of document design discussed on pages 72–83. On the next two pages, the sample résumé appears both in a traditional format and in a more contemporary design.

Employers often want an electronic version of a résumé so that they can add it to a computerized database of applicants. The employers may scan your printed résumé to convert it to an electronic file, or they may request electronic copy from you in the first place. If you think a potential employer may use an electronic version of your résumé, follow these additional guidelines:

- Keep the design simple so that the résumé can be read accurately by a scanner or transmitted accurately by electronic

(Text continues p. 468)

58a

Ian M. Irvine
3712 Swiss Avenue
Dallas, TX 75204
214-744-3816
ianirv@mail.smu.edu

Position desired
Part-time editorial assistant.

Education
Southern Methodist University, 1998 to present.
Current standing: sophomore.
Major: English literature and journalism.
Journalism courses: news reporting, copy editing,
electronic publishing, communications arts, broadcast
journalism.

Abilene (Texas) Senior High School, 1994-1998.
Graduated with academic, college-preparatory degree.

Employment history
1998 to present. Reporter, Daily Campus, student
newspaper of Southern Methodist University.
Write regular coverage of baseball, track, and soccer
teams. Write feature stories on campus policies and
events. Edit sports news, campus listings, features.

Summer 1999. Copy aide, Abilene Reporter-News.
Routed copy, ran errands, and assisted reporters with
research.

Summer 1998. Painter, Longhorn Painters, Abilene.
Prepared and painted exteriors and interiors of houses.

Special skills
Fluent in Spanish.
Proficient in Internet research and word processing.

References
Available on request:

Placement Office
Southern Methodist University
Dallas, TX 75275

58a

Ian M. Irvine

3712 Swiss Avenue
Dallas, TX 75204
214-744-3816
ianirv@mail.smu.edu

Position
desired   Part-time editorial assistant.

Education   *Southern Methodist University*, 1998 to present.
Current standing: sophomore.
Major: English literature and journalism.
Journalism courses: news reporting, copy editing,
electronic publishing, communications arts, broad-
cast journalism.

Abilene (Texas) Senior High School, 1994-1998.
Graduated with academic, college-preparatory
degree.

Employment   1998 to present. Reporter, *Daily Campus*, student
history   newspaper of Southern Methodist University.
Write regular coverage of baseball, track, and soccer teams. Write feature stories on campus policies
and events. Edit sports news, campus listings,
features.

Summer 1999. Copy aide, *Abilene Reporter-News*.
Routed copy, ran errands, and assisted reporters
with research.

Summer 1998. Painter, Longhorn Painters, Abilene.
Prepared and painted exteriors and interiors of
houses.

Special skills   Fluent in Spanish.
Proficient in Internet research and word processing.

References   Available on request:

Placement Office
Southern Methodist University
Dallas, TX 75275

58c

mail. Avoid images, unusual type, more than one column, vertical or horizontal lines, and highlighting (boldface, italic, or underlining). If its highlighting were removed, the traditionally designed sample on page 466 could probably be scanned or transmitted electronically. The two-column sample on page 467 perhaps could not.

- Use concise, specific words to describe your skills and experience. The employer's computer may use keywords (often nouns) to identify the résumés of suitable job candidates, and you want to ensure that your résumé includes the appropriate keywords. Name your specific skills—for example, the computer programs you can operate—and write concretely with words like *manager* (not *person with responsibility for*) and *reporter* (not *staff member who reports*). Look for likely keywords in the employer's description of the job you seek.

58b Writing business memos

Business memorandums (memos, for short) address people within the same organization. A memo can be quite long, but more often it deals briefly with a specific topic, such as an answer to a question, a progress report, or an evaluation.

Both the form and the structure of a memo are designed to get to the point and dispose of it quickly (see the sample on the facing page). State your reason for writing in the first sentence. Devote the first paragraph to a concise presentation of your answer, conclusion, or evaluation. In the rest of the memo explain your reasoning or evidence. Use headings or lists as appropriate to highlight key information.

Most companies have their own conventions for memo formats. The heading usually consists of the company name, the addressee's name, the writer's name (initialed in handwriting), the date, and a subject description or title. (See the sample.) The body of the memo is usually single-spaced, with double spacing between paragraphs and no paragraph indentions. An indication of who receives copies of the memo can be given two spaces below the last line of the body.

58c Communicating electronically

 Communicating via electronic devices, especially electronic mail and fax machines, speeds up correspondence but also creates new challenges. E-mail now plays such a prominent role in communication of all sorts that it is discussed extensively as part of essen-

58c

Bigelow Wax Company

TO: Aileen Rosen, Director of Sales
FROM: Patricia Phillips, Territory 12 *PP*
DATE: March 17, 2000
SUBJECT: 1999 sales of Quick Wax in Territory 12

Since it was introduced in January of 1999, Quick Wax has been
unsuccessful in Territory 12 and has not affected the sales of our
Easy Shine. Discussions with customers and my own analysis of
Quick Wax suggest three reasons for its failure to compete with our
product.

1. Quick Wax has not received the promotion necessary for a new
    product. Advertising—primarily on radio—has been sporadic
    and has not developed a clear, consistent image for the product.
    In addition, the Quick Wax sales representative in Territory 12 is
    new and inexperienced; he is not known to customers, and his
    sales pitch (which I once overheard) is weak. As far as I can tell,
    his efforts are not supported by phone calls or mailings from his
    home office.

2. When Quick Wax does make it to the store shelves, buyers do
    not choose it over our product. Though priced competitively
    with our product, Quick Wax is poorly packaged. The container
    seems smaller than ours, though in fact it holds the same eight
    ounces. The lettering on the Quick Wax package (red on blue) is
    difficult to read, in contrast to the white-on-green lettering on
    the Easy Shine package.

3. Our special purchase offers and my increased efforts to serve
    existing customers have had the intended effect of keeping
    customers satisfied with our product and reducing their
    inclination to stock something new.

Copies: L. Mendes, Director of Marketing
         L. MacGregor, Customer Service Manager

tial computer skills (see pp. 63–67). Generally, the standards for
business e-mail are the same as for other business correspondence.

Faxes follow closely the formats of print documents, whether
letters (p. 462) or memos (opposite and above). But there are some
key differences:

- Small type, photographs, horizontal lines, and other elements
  that look fine on your copy may not be legible to the addressee.
- Most faxes require a cover sheet with fax-specific information:
  the addressee's name, company, and fax number; the date, time,

59a

and subject; your own name and fax and telephone numbers (the telephone number is important in case something goes wrong with the transmission); and the total number of pages (including the cover sheet) in the fax.

- Because fax transmissions can go astray, it's often wise to advise your addressee to expect a fax. Such advice is essential if the fax is confidential, because the machine is often shared.
- Transmission by fax can imply that the correspondence is urgent. If yours isn't, consider using the mail. (Swamping your correspondents with needless faxes can make you the child who cried wolf when you really have an urgent message to transmit.)

59 Writing Essays

One of the most common types of writing assignments students are given in school is the essay. An essay is a relatively short composition, written in prose style. It expresses personal ideas, opinions, and emotions rather than intellectual or scientific ideas.

Essays can be written for many purposes. They may be expository, where your goal is to explain or give reasons why something occurred. They may employ narration to tell a story. They may also be persuasive and seek to convince the reader of a particular point of view. Or the writer's goal might be a combination of the above.

This chapter is not designed to be a comprehensive guide to writing all types of essays. Rather, it explains and illustrates some of the basics of effective essay development.

59a   Using the basic building blocks of an essay

All good essays share some common characteristics. They have a clear thesis, they are well organized, and they are well developed. The model for essay organization has been called the *five-paragraph essay*. This basic structure is discussed and illustrated below and may help you clarify and organize your ideas. Your essays may be more complex than this, but the basic structure should guide you in structuring your paper. Be sure to review the writing process discussed in Chapters 1–7 and use that process to develop your essays.

59a

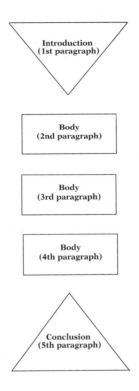

1 Introduction

When you begin your essay, you may have a broad, general idea of your topic. The purpose of the introduction is to narrow the topic and to create a focus for your paper.

An introduction draws readers from their world into your world.

- It focuses readers' attention on the topic and arouses their curiosity about what you have to say.
- It specifies your subject and implies your attitude.
- Often it includes your thesis statement (see p. 20).
- It is concise and sincere.

Start your essay with an attention-getter to introduce readers to the topic and to create interest in it. The following are options for achieving this purpose.

Some strategies for gaining attention

- Ask a question and immediately answer it.
- Ask a question and answer it later in the essay.
- Ask a rhetorical question (one that does not require an answer).
- Use a vivid opening quotation that relates to your topic.
- Present an idea that your thesis refutes.
- Tell a brief story, relate an incident, or provide a short anecdote.
- Create a visual image that represents your subject.
- Offer a surprising statistic or other fact.
- Open with a startling statement.
- State an opinion related to your thesis.
- Make a general statement that narrows to the specific topic.
- Provide background.
- Make a historical comparison or contrast.
- Outline a problem or dilemma.
- Define a word central to your subject.

Next, develop a thesis statement that expresses the main idea of your essay. (See page 20 for more information about constructing a thesis statement.) The rest of your introduction should develop the thesis. Many writers follow the thesis with a brief preview of the main points of the essay to help readers anticipate what lies ahead. This preview often employs signposts, brief words such as *first* or *finally* that signal the reader the key points you plan to make in the essay. Signposts should be presented in the order in which the points appear in the body of the essay.

ESL   These options for an introduction may not be what you are used to if your native language is not English. In other cultures readers may seek familiarity or reassurance from an author's introduction, or they may prefer an indirect approach to the subject. In English, however, writers and readers prefer originality and concise, direct expression.

Effective openings

A very common introduction opens with a statement of the essay's general subject, clarifies or limits the subject in one or more sentences, and then asserts the point of the essay in the thesis statement (underlined in the examples on the next page):

We Americans are a clean people. We bathe or shower regularly and spend billions of dollars each year on soaps and deodorants to wash away or disguise our dirt and odor. Yet cleanliness is a relatively recent habit with us. <u>From the time of the Puritans until the turn of the twentieth century, bathing in the United States was rare and sometimes even illegal.</u>
　　　　　　—AMANDA HARRIS (student), "The Cleaning of America"

Can your home or office computer make you sterile? Can it strike you blind or dumb? The answer is: probably not. Nevertheless, reports of side effects relating to computer use should be examined, especially in the area of birth defects, eye complaints, and postural difficulties. <u>Although little conclusive evidence exists to establish a causal link between computer use and problems of this sort, the circumstantial evidence can be disturbing.</u>
　　　　　　—THOMAS HARTMANN, "How Dangerous Is Your Computer?"

Additional examples of effective introductions appear in complete writing samples on pages 48, 383, 414, 458, 460, 469, and 489.

Introduction *don'ts*

When writing and revising your introduction, avoid some approaches that are likely to bore readers or make them question your sincerity or control:

- Don't reach back too far with vague generalities or truths, such as those beginning "Throughout human history . . ." or "In today's world. . . ." You may have needed a warm-up paragraph to start drafting, but your readers can do without it.
- Don't start with "The purpose of this essay is . . . ," "In this essay I will . . . ," or any similar flat announcement of your intention or topic.
- Don't refer to the title of the essay in the first sentence—for example, "This is my favorite activity" or "This is a big problem."
- Don't start with "According to Webster . . ." or a similar phrase leading to a dictionary definition. A definition can be an effective springboard to an essay, but this kind of lead-in has become dull with overuse.
- Don't apologize for your opinion or for inadequate knowledge with "I'm not sure if I'm right, but I think . . . ," "I don't know much about this, but . . . ," or similar lines.

2 Body

Many essays contain three main points, so the five-paragraph essay is based on this number, although this number certainly is not mandatory. However, an essay should generally contain no more than six main ideas. It is difficult for a reader to follow your train of thought if you are making more than six key points. A basic essay will present each point in a separate paragraph that contains a topic sentence, supporting sentences, and transitions.

The topic sentence may be considered a mini-thesis for each paragraph. It should provide the main point of the paragraph. The rest of a well-developed paragraph consists of supporting sentences that explain or provide concrete details or examples to make that point. Transitions are words or phrases that build bridges between sentences and paragraphs to help an essay flow smoothly. Words such as *on the other hand*, *in addition*, and *consequently* can act as transitions. (See p. 41 for additional information about transitions.)

3 Conclusion

An essay's conclusion should serve several purposes: it should return to the main idea and summarize it. It should also broaden that conclusion by discussing it and by tying the main points together in a meaningful way for the reader. Finally, the writer should reflect on the conclusion and discuss its implications or the relevance or importance of the topic or study. The conclusion is also the place for the reader to motivate readers to take action, if that is one of the essay's purposes. The essay should then end with a bang, not a whimper. Create a memorable final sentence to wrap up the essay.

Usually set off in its own paragraph, the conclusion may consist of a single sentence or a group of sentences. It may take one or more of the following approaches:

Some strategies for conclusions

- Strike a note of hope or despair.
- Give a symbolic or powerful fact or other detail.
- Give an especially compelling example.
- Create a visual image that represents your subject.
- Use a quotation.
- Recommend a course of action.
- Summarize the paper.
- Echo the approach of the introduction.
- Restate your thesis and reflect on its implications.

The following paragraph concludes the essay on bathing habits whose introduction is on page 472–473. The writer both summarizes her essay and echoes her introduction.

> Thus changed attitudes and advances in plumbing finally freed us to bathe whenever we want. Perhaps partly to make up for our ancestors' bad habits, we have transformed that freedom into a national obsession.
> —AMANDA HARRIS (student), "The Cleaning of America"

In the next paragraph the author concludes an essay on environmental protection with a call for action:

> Until we get the answers, I think we had better keep on building power plants and growing food with the help of fertilizers and such insect-controlling chemicals as we now have. The risks are well known, thanks to the environmentalists. If they had not created a widespread public awareness of the ecological crisis, we wouldn't stand a chance. But such awareness by itself is not enough. Flaming manifestos and prophecies of doom are no longer much help, and a search for scapegoats can only make matters worse. The time for sensations and manifestos is about over. Now we need rigorous analysis, united effort and very hard work.
> —PETER F. DRUCKER, "How Best to Protect the Environment"

Conclusions have several pitfalls you'll want to avoid:

- Don't simply restate your introduction—statement of subject, thesis statement, and all. Presumably the paragraphs in the body of your essay have contributed something to the opening statements, and it's that something you want to capture in your conclusion.
- Don't start off in a new direction, with a subject different from or broader than the one your essay has been about.
- Don't conclude more than you reasonably can from the evidence you have presented. If your essay is about your frustrating experience trying to clear a parking ticket, you cannot reasonably conclude that *all* local police forces are too tied up in red tape to be of service to the people.
- Don't apologize for your essay or otherwise cast doubt on it. Don't say, "Even though I'm no expert," or "This may not be convincing, but I believe it's true," or anything similar. Rather, to win your readers' confidence, display confidence.

59b Developing body paragraphs

Some assignments may give you specific guidelines for organizing essay sections, but often, this task is up to you. To develop or shape an essay, one or more of the following patterns may help.

Usually, the pattern you use will be suggested by the material you want to convey to the reader. For example, if your task is to tell a story, narration will probably be the pattern that is most effective. On the other hand, if your purpose is to show similarities or differences between two points of view, comparison and contrast may serve you better. (Pages 37 through 41 provide additional information about constructing effective paragraphs.)

To develop or shape an idea in a paragraph, one or more of the following patterns may help. (These patterns may also be used to develop entire essays. See p. 19.)

1   Narration

Narration retells a significant sequence of events, usually in the order of their occurrence (that is, chronologically). A narrator is concerned not just with the sequence of events but also with their consequence, their importance to the whole.

> Jill's story is typical for "recruits" to religious cults. She was very lonely in college and appreciated the attention of the nice young men and women who lived in a house near campus. They persuaded her to share their meals and then to move in with them. Between intense bombardments of "love," they deprived her of sleep and sometimes threatened to throw her out. Jill became increasingly confused and dependent, losing touch with any reality besides the one in the group. She dropped out of school and refused to see or communicate with her family. Before long she, too, was preying on lonely college students.
> —HILLARY BEGAS (student), "The Love Bombers"

2   Description

Description details the sensory qualities of a person, scene, thing, or feeling, using concrete and specific words to convey a dominant mood, to illustrate an idea, or to achieve some other purpose.

> The sun struck straight upon the house, making the white walls glare between the dark windows. Their panes, woven thickly with green branches, held circles of impenetrable darkness. Sharp-edged wedges of light lay upon the window-sill and showed inside the room plates with blue rings, cups with curved handles, the bulge of a great bowl, the criss-cross pattern in the rug, and the formidable corners and lines of cabinets and bookcases. Behind their conglomeration hung a zone of shadow in which might be a further shape to be disencumbered of shadow or still denser depths of darkness.   —VIRGINIA WOOLF, *The Waves*

3 Illustration or support

An idea may be developed with several specific examples, like those used by Charles Kuralt on page 36, or with a single extended example, as in the next paragraph:

> The language problem that I was attacking loomed larger and larger as I began to learn more. When I would describe in English certain concepts and objects enmeshed in Korean emotion and imagination, I became slowly aware of nuances, of differences between two languages even in simple expression. The remark "Kim entered the house" seems to be simple enough, yet, unless a reader has a clear visual image of a Korean house, his understanding of the sentence is not complete. When a Korean says he is "in the house," he may be in his courtyard, or on his porch, or in his small room! If I wanted to give a specific picture of entering the house in the Western sense, I had to say "room" instead of house—sometimes. I say "sometimes" because many Koreans entertain their guests on their porches and still are considered to be hospitable, and in the Korean sense, going into the "room" may be a more intimate act than it would be in the English sense. Such problems!
>
> —KIM YONG IK, "A Book-Writing Venture"

Sometimes you can develop a paragraph by providing your reasons for stating a general idea. For instance:

> There are three reasons, quite apart from scientific considerations, that mankind needs to travel in space. The first reason is the need for garbage disposal: we need to transfer industrial processes into space, so that the earth may remain a green and pleasant place for our grandchildren to live in. The second reason is the need to escape material impoverishment: the resources of this planet are finite, and we shall not forgo forever the abundant solar energy and minerals and living space that are spread out all around us. The third reason is our spiritual need for an open frontier: the ultimate purpose of space travel is to bring to humanity not only scientific discoveries and an occasional spectacular show on television but a real expansion of our spirit.
>
> —FREEMAN DYSON, "Disturbing the Universe"

4 Definition

Defining a complicated, abstract, or controversial term often requires extended explanation. The following definition of the word *quality* comes from an essay asserting that "quality in product and effort has become a vanishing element of current civilization." Notice how the writer pins down her meaning by offering examples and by setting up contrasts with nonquality.

In the hope of possibly reducing the hail of censure which is certain to greet this essay (I am thinking of going to Alaska or possibly Patagonia in the week it is published), let me say that quality, as I understand it, means investment of the best skill and effort possible to produce the finest and most admirable result possible. Its presence or absence in some degree characterizes every man-made object, service, skilled or unskilled labor—laying bricks, painting a picture, ironing shirts, practicing medicine, shoemaking, scholarship, writing a book. You do it well or you do it half-well. Materials are sound and durable or they are sleazy; method is painstaking or whatever is easiest. Quality is achieving or reaching for the highest standard as against being satisfied with the sloppy or fraudulent. It is honesty of purpose as against catering to cheap or sensational sentiment. It does not allow compromise with the second-rate.   —Barbara Tuchman, "The Decline of Quality"

5 Division or analysis

With division or analysis, you separate something into its elements to understand it better—for instance, you might divide a newspaper into its sections, such as national news, regional news, lifestyle, and so on. As in the paragraph below, you may also interpret the meaning and significance of the elements you identify.

The surface realism of the soap opera conjures up an illusion of "liveness." The domestic settings and easygoing rhythms encourage the viewer to believe that the drama, however ridiculous, is simply an extension of daily life. The conversation is so slow that some have called it "radio with pictures." (Advertisers have always assumed that busy housewives would listen, rather than watch.) Conversation is casual and colloquial, as though one were eavesdropping on neighbors. There is plenty of time to "read" the character's face; close-ups establish intimacy. The sets are comfortably familiar: well-lit interiors of living rooms, restaurants, offices, and hospitals. Daytime soaps have little of the glamour of their prime-time relations. The viewer easily imagines that the conversation is taking place in real time.   —Ruth Rosen, "Search for Yesterday"

Analysis is a key skill in critical reading. See pages 281–283.

6 Classification

When you sort many items into groups, you classify the items to see their relations more clearly. The following paragraph identifies three groups, or classes, of parents:

In my experience, the parents who hire daytime sitters for their school-age children tend to fall into one of three groups. The first group includes parents who work and want someone to be at home when the children return from school. These parents are looking for an extension of themselves, someone who will give the care they would give if they were at home. The second group includes parents who may be home all day themselves but are too disorganized or too frazzled by their children's demands to handle child care alone. They are looking for an organizer and helpmate. The third and final group includes parents who do not want to be bothered by their children, whether they are home all day or not. Unlike the parents in the first two groups, who care for their children however they can, these parents seek a permanent substitute for themselves. —NANCY WHITTLE (student), "Modern Parenting"

7 Comparison and contrast

Comparison and contrast may be used separately or together to develop an idea. The following paragraph illustrates one of two common ways of organizing a comparison and contrast: SUBJECT BY SUBJECT, first one subject and then the other.

Consider the differences also in the behavior of rock and classical music audiences. At a rock concert, the audience members yell, whistle, sing along, and stamp their feet. They may even stand during the entire performance. The better the music, the more active they'll be. At a classical concert, in contrast, the better the performance, the more *still* the audience is. Members of the classical audience are so highly disciplined that they refrain from even clearing their throats or coughing. No matter what effect the powerful music has on their intellects and feelings, they sit on their hands. —TONY NAHM (student), "Rock and Roll Is Here to Stay"

The next paragraph illustrates the other common organization: POINT BY POINT, with the two subjects discussed side by side and matched feature for feature:

The first electronic computer, ENIAC, went into operation just over fifty years ago, yet the differences between it and today's home computer are enormous. ENIAC was enormous itself, consisting of forty panels, each two feet wide and four feet deep. Today's PC or Macintosh, by contrast, can fit on one's desk or even lap. ENIAC had to be configured by hand, with its programmers taking up to two days to reset switches and cables. Today, the average home user can change programs in an instant. And for all its size and inconvenience, ENIAC was also slow. In its time, its operating speed of 100,000 pulses per second seemed amazingly fast. However, today's home machine can operate at 1 billion pulses per second or faster.
—SHIRLEY KAJIWARA (student), "The Computers We Deserve"

59b

8   Cause-and-effect analysis

When you use analysis to explain why something happened or what did or may happen, then you are determining causes or effects. In the following paragraph the author looks at the cause of an effect—Japanese collectivism:

> The *shinkansen* or "bullet train" speeds across the rural areas of Japan giving a quick view of cluster after cluster of farmhouses surrounded by rice paddies. This particular pattern did not develop purely by chance, but as a consequence of the technology peculiar to the growing of rice, the staple of the Japanese diet. The growing of rice requires the construction and maintenance of an irrigation system, something that takes many hands to build. More importantly, the planting and the harvesting of rice can only be done efficiently with the cooperation of twenty or more people. The "bottom line" is that a single family working alone cannot produce enough rice to survive, but a dozen families working together can produce a surplus. Thus the Japanese have had to develop the capacity to work together in harmony, no matter what the forces of disagreement or social disintegration, in order to survive.
> —WILLIAM OUCHI, *Theory Z: How American Business Can Meet the Japanese Challenge*

9   Process analysis

When you analyze how to do something or how something works, you explain a process. The following example identifies the process, describes the equipment needed, and details the steps in the process:

> As a car owner, you waste money when you pay a mechanic to change the engine oil. The job is not difficult, even if you know little about cars. All you need is a wrench to remove the drain plug, a large, flat pan to collect the draining oil, plastic bottles to dispose of the used oil, and fresh oil. First, warm up the car's engine so that the oil will flow more easily. When the engine is warm, shut it off and remove its oil-filler cap (the owner's manual shows where this cap is). Then locate the drain plug under the engine (again consulting the owner's manual for its location) and place the flat pan under the plug. Remove the plug with the wrench, letting the oil flow into the pan. When the oil stops flowing, replace the plug and, at the engine's filler hole, add the amount and kind of fresh oil specified by the owner's manual. Pour the used oil into the plastic bottles and take it to a waste-oil collector, which any garage mechanic can recommend.
> —ANTHONY ANDREAS (student), "Do-It-Yourself Car Care"

60 Argumentative or Persuasive Writing

The operations of critical thinking and reading discussed in Chapter 47—analysis, interpretation, synthesis, evaluation—come into play in critical writing, too, as you form, test, and support your own views. In ARGUMENT, the most common type of critical writing, you further seek to open readers' minds to your opinion, change readers' own opinions, or move readers to action.

An argument has four main elements: topic, claims, evidence, and assumptions. (The last three are adapted from the work of the British philosopher Stephen Toulmin.)

60a Understanding and using the elements of argument

1 The topic

An argument starts with a topic and often with an opinion about the topic as well—that is, an idea that makes you want to write about the topic. (If you don't have a topic or you aren't sure what you think about it, try some of the discovery techniques discussed on pp. 12–20.) Your initial opinion should meet several requirements:

- It can be disputed: reasonable people can disagree over it.
- It *will* be disputed: it is controversial.
- It is narrow enough to research and argue in the space and time available.

On the flip side of these requirements are several kinds of statements or views that will not work as the starting place of argument: indisputable facts, such as the functions of the human liver; personal preferences or beliefs, such as a moral commitment to vegetarianism; and ideas that few would disagree with, such as the virtues of a secure home.

2 Claims

CLAIMS are statements that require support. In an argument you refine your initial opinion into a central claim and assert it outright as the THESIS STATEMENT, or main idea: it is what the argument is about. For instance:

The college needs a new chemistry laboratory to replace the existing outdated lab.

Claims are usually statements of opinion, fact, or belief:

- An OPINION is a judgment that is based on facts and arguable on the basis of facts, such as the example above about a new chemistry lab.
- A FACT is potentially verifiable and thus not arguable—for example, *The cost of medical care is rising.*
- A BELIEF, while seemingly arguable, is not based on facts and so cannot be contested on the basis of facts—for example, *The primary goal of government should be to provide equality of opportunity for all.*

Only an opinion may serve as the thesis statement of an argument. A claim of fact or belief may serve as a secondary claim supporting the thesis but not as the thesis statement itself.

3 Evidence

EVIDENCE demonstrates the validity of your claims. The evidence to support the claim above about the need for a new chemistry lab might include the present lab's age, an inventory of facilities and equipment, and the testimony of chemistry professors.

There are several kinds of evidence:

- FACTS, statements whose truth can be verified: *Poland is slightly smaller than New Mexico.*
- STATISTICS, facts expressed as numbers: *Of those polled, 62 percent prefer a flat tax.*
- EXAMPLES, specific instances of the point being made: *Many groups, such as the elderly and the disabled, would benefit from this policy.*
- EXPERT OPINIONS, the judgments formed by authorities on the basis of their own examination of the facts: *Affirmative action is necessary to right past injustices, a point argued by Howard Glickstein, a past director of the US Commission on Civil Rights.*
- APPEALS to readers' beliefs or needs, statements that ask readers to accept a claim in part because it states something they already accept as true without evidence: *The shabby, antiquated chemistry lab shames the school, making it seem a second-rate institution.*

Evidence must be reliable to be convincing. Ask these questions about your evidence:

- Is it accurate—trustworthy, exact, and undistorted?
- Is it relevant—authoritative, pertinent, and current?

60b

- Is it representative—true to its context, neither under- nor over-representing any element of the sample it's drawn from?
- Is it adequate—plentiful and specific?

4 Assumptions

An ASSUMPTION is an opinion, a principle, or a belief that ties evidence to claims: the assumption explains why a particular piece of evidence is relevant to a particular claim. For instance:

Claim: The college needs a new chemistry laboratory.
Evidence (in part): The testimony of chemistry professors.
Assumption: Chemistry professors are the most capable of evaluating the present lab's quality.

Assumptions are not flaws in arguments but necessities: we all acquire beliefs and opinions that shape our views of the world. Just as interpreting a work's assumptions is a significant part of critical reading (see pp. 281–282), so discovering your own assumptions is a significant part of argumentative critical writing. If your readers do not share your assumptions or perceive that you are not forthright about your biases, they will be less receptive to your argument. (See the following discussion of reasonableness.)

ESL The ways of conceiving and writing arguments described here may be initially uncomfortable to you if your native culture approaches such writing differently. In some cultures, for example, a writer is expected to begin indirectly, to avoid asserting his or her opinion outright, to rely for evidence on appeals to tradition, or to establish a compromise rather than argue a position. Writers of English, however, look or aim for a well-articulated opinion, evidence gathered from many sources, and a direct and concise argument for the opinion.

60b Writing reasonably

Reasonableness is essential if an argument is to establish common ground between you and your readers. Readers expect logical thinking, appropriate appeals, fairness toward the opposition, and, combining all of these, writing that is free of fallacies.

1 Logical thinking

The thesis of your argument is a conclusion you reach by reasoning about evidence. Two processes of reasoning, induction and deduction, are familiar to you even if you aren't familiar with their names.

Induction

When you're about to buy a used car, you consult friends, relatives, and consumer guides before deciding what kind of car to buy. Using INDUCTION, or INDUCTIVE REASONING, you make specific observations about cars (your evidence) and you induce, or infer, a GENERALIZATION that Car X is most reliable. The generalization is a claim supported by your observations.

You might also use inductive reasoning in a term paper on print advertising:

> Analyze advertisements in newspapers and magazines (evidence).
> Read comments by advertisers, publishers, and critics (more evidence).
> Form a conclusion about print advertising (generalization/claim).

Reasoning inductively, you connect your evidence to your generalization by assuming that what is true in one set of circumstances (the ads you look at) is true in a similar set of circumstances (other ads). With induction you create new knowledge out of old.

The more evidence you accumulate, the more probable it is that your generalization is true. Note, however, that absolute certainty is not possible. At some point you must *assume* that your evidence justifies your generalization, for yourself and your readers. Most errors in inductive reasoning involve oversimplifying either the evidence or the generalization. See pages 486–488 on fallacies.

Deduction

You use DEDUCTION, or DEDUCTIVE REASONING, when you proceed from your generalization that Car X is the most reliable used car to your own specific circumstances (you want to buy a used car) to the conclusion that you should buy a Car X. In deduction your assumption is a generalization, principle, or belief that you think is true. It links the evidence (new information) to the claim (the conclusion you draw). With deduction you apply old information to new.

Say that you want the school administration to postpone new room fees for one dormitory. You can base your argument on a deductive SYLLOGISM:

> *Premise:* The administration should not raise fees on dorm rooms in poor condition. [A generalization or belief that you assume to be true.]
> *Premise:* The rooms in Polk Hall are in poor condition. [New information: a specific case of the first premise.]
> *Conclusion:* The administration should not raise fees on the rooms in Polk Hall. [Your claim.]

As long as the premises of a syllogism are true, the conclusion derives logically and certainly from them. Errors in constructing syllogisms lie behind many of the fallacies discussed on pages 486–488.

2   Rational, emotional, and ethical appeals

In most arguments you will combine RATIONAL APPEALS to readers' capacities for logical reasoning with EMOTIONAL APPEALS to readers' beliefs and feelings. The following example illustrates both: the second sentence makes a rational appeal (to the logic of financial gain), and the third sentence makes an emotional appeal (to the sense of fairness and open-mindedness).

> Advertising should show more physically challenged people. The millions of disabled Americans have considerable buying power, yet so far advertisers have made no attempt to tap that power. Further, by keeping the physically challenged out of the mainstream depicted in ads, advertisers encourage widespread prejudice against disability, prejudice that frightens and demeans those who hold it.

For an emotional appeal to be successful, it must be appropriate for the audience and the argument:

- It must not misjudge readers' actual feelings.
- It must not raise emotional issues that are irrelevant to the claims and the evidence. (See opposite for a discussion of specific inappropriate appeals, such as bandwagon and ad hominem.)

A third kind of approach to readers, the ETHICAL APPEAL, is the sense you give of being a competent, fair person who is worth heeding. A rational appeal and an appropriate emotional appeal contribute to your ethical appeal, and so does your acknowledging opposing views (see below). An argument that is concisely written and correct in grammar, spelling, and other matters will underscore your competence. In addition, a sincere and even tone will assure readers that you are a balanced person who wants to reason with them.

A sincere and even tone need not exclude language with emotional appeal—words such as *frightens* and *demeans* at the end of the example about advertising. But avoid certain forms of expression that will mark you as unfair:

- Insulting words such as *idiotic* or *fascist*.
- Biased language such as *fags* or *broads* (see pp. 118–121).
- Sarcasm—for instance, using the sentence *What a brilliant idea* to indicate contempt for the idea and its originator.
- Exclamation points! They'll make you sound shrill!

60b

3   Acknowledgment of opposing views

A good test of your fairness in argument is how you handle possible objections. Assuming your thesis is indeed arguable, then others can marshal their own evidence to support a different view or views. You need to find out what these other views are and what the support is for them. Then, in your argument, you need to take these views on, refute those you can, grant the validity of others, and demonstrate why, despite their validity, the opposing views are less compelling than your own. (See the sample essay on pp. 72–74 for examples.)

Before you draft your paper, list for yourself all the opposing views you can think of. You'll find them in your research, by talking to friends, and by critically thinking about your own ideas. Figure out which opposing views you can refute (do more research if necessary), and prepare to concede those views you can't refute. It's not a mark of weakness or failure to admit that the opposition has a point or two. Indeed, by showing yourself to be honest and fair, you strengthen your ethical appeal and thus your entire argument.

4   Fallacies

FALLACIES—errors in argument—either evade the issue of the argument or treat the argument as if it were much simpler than it is.

Evasions

An effective argument squarely faces the central issue or question it addresses. An ineffective argument may dodge the issue in one of the following ways:

- BEGGING THE QUESTION: treating an opinion that is open to question as if it were already proved or disproved.

  The college library's expenses should be reduced by cutting subscriptions to useless periodicals. [Begged questions: Are some of the library's periodicals useless? Useless to whom?]

- NON SEQUITUR (Latin: "It does not follow"): linking two or more ideas that in fact have no logical connection.

  If high school English were easier, fewer students would have trouble with the college English requirement. [Presumably, if high school English were easier, students would have *more* trouble.]

- RED HERRING: introducing an irrelevant issue intended to distract readers from the relevant issues.

  A campus speech code is essential to protect students, who already have enough problems coping with rising tuition. [Tuition costs and speech codes are different subjects. What protections do students need that a speech code will provide?]

- APPEAL TO READERS' FEAR OR PITY: substituting emotions for reasoning.

  She should not have to pay taxes because she is an aged widow with no friends or relatives. [Appeals to people's pity. Should age and loneliness, rather than income, determine a person's tax obligation?]

- BANDWAGON: inviting readers to accept a claim because everyone else does.

  As everyone knows, marijuana use leads to heroin addiction. [What is the evidence?]

- AD HOMINEM (Latin: "to the man"): attacking the qualities of the people holding an opposing view rather than the substance of the view itself.

  One of the scientists has been treated for emotional problems, so his pessimism about nuclear waste merits no attention. [Do the scientist's previous emotional problems invalidate his current views?]

Oversimplifications

In a vain attempt to create something neatly convincing, an ineffective argument may conceal or ignore complexities in one of the following ways:

- HASTY GENERALIZATION: making a claim on the basis of inadequate evidence.

  It is disturbing that several of the youths who shot up schools were users of violent video games. Obviously, these games can breed violence, and they should be banned. [A few cases do not establish the relation between the games and violent behavior. Most youths who play violent video games do not behave violently.]

- SWEEPING GENERALIZATION: making an insupportable statement. Many sweeping generalizations are ABSOLUTE STATEMENTS involving words such as *all, always, never,* and *no one* that allow no exceptions. Others are STEREOTYPES, conventional and oversimplified characterizations of a group of people:

  People who live in cities are unfriendly.
  Californians are fad-crazy.
  Women are emotional.
  Men can't express their feelings.

  (See also pp. 118–121 on sexist and other biased language.)

- REDUCTIVE FALLACY: oversimplifying (reducing) the relation between causes and effects.

  Poverty causes crime. [If so, then why do people who are not poor commit crimes? And why aren't all poor people criminals?]

- POST HOC FALLACY (from Latin, *post hoc, ergo propter hoc:* "after this, therefore because of this"): assuming that because *A* preceded *B*, then *A* must have caused *B*.

  The town council erred in permitting the adult bookstore to open, for shortly afterward two women were assaulted. [It cannot be assumed without evidence that the women's assailants visited or were influenced by the bookstore.]

- EITHER/OR FALLACY: assuming that a complicated question has only two answers, one good and one bad, both good, or both bad.

  Either we permit mandatory drug testing in the workplace or productivity will continue to decline. [Productivity is not necessarily dependent on drug testing.]

60c   Organizing an argument

All arguments include the same parts:

- The introduction establishes the significance of the subject and provides background. The introduction generally includes the thesis statement. However, if you think your readers may have difficulty accepting your thesis statement before they see at least some support for it, then it may come later in the paper. (See pp. 471–473 for more on introductions.)
- The body states the claims that support the thesis and, in one or more paragraphs, develops each claim with clearly relevant evidence. See below for more on organizing the body.
- The response to opposing views details those views and either demonstrates your argument's greater strengths or concedes the opponents' points. See below for more on organizing this response.
- The conclusion restates the thesis, summarizes the argument, and makes a final appeal to readers. (See pp. 474–475 for more on conclusions.)

The structure of the body and the response to opposing views depend on your subject, purpose, audience, and form of reasoning. Here are several possible arrangements:

The traditional scheme

Claim 1 and evidence
Claim 2 and evidence
Claim X and evidence
Response to opposing views

The problem-solution scheme

The problem: claims and
 evidence
The solution: claims and
 evidence
Response to opposing views

Variations on the traditional scheme

Use a variation if you believe your readers will reject your argument without an early or intermittent response to opposing views.

Response to opposing views
Claim 1 and evidence
Claim 2 and evidence
Claim X and evidence

Claim 1 and evidence
Response to opposing views
Claim 2 and evidence
Response to opposing views
Claim X and evidence
Response to opposing views

60d   Examining a sample argument

The following student essay illustrates the principles discussed in this chapter. As you read the essay, note especially the structure, the relation of claims and supporting evidence, the kinds of appeals the author makes, and the ways he addresses opposing views. (The essay can be downloaded from this book's Web site at *http://www.awlonline.com/littlebrown.*)

Share the Ride

Every year we encounter more bad news about the environment, and a good portion of it is due to the private automobile. Respected scientists warn that carbon dioxide emissions, such as those from cars, may produce disastrous global warming. Soot, sulfur, and other automobile emissions are contributing to reduced air quality almost everywhere. The oil that powers cars comes from rapidly depleting reserves, leading to an unhappy choice between imports of foreign oil and exploration, such as offshore drilling, that threatens the environment.

Introduction: identification of problem

In its own way Beverly Community College contributes to the problem. Campus parking lots are filled with about 1800 cars every weekday, so that means 3600 trips a day are made to and from campus. If just a third of the solo drivers shared rides with one another, the total trips to and from campus would be reduced by at least 600. It is time

60d

for the BCC community to make a difficult move toward an organized car-pooling system that would achieve this modest goal.

Thesis statement: proposal for a solution

The first step in getting car-pools going is to form a task force of administrators, faculty, and students to devise a workable system. School records would be used to connect people who live near each other and would be willing to car-pool. With administration backing, the task force would initiate a school-wide campaign of meetings, rallies, posters, and other public-relations efforts to overcome resistance to car-pooling, answer questions, and win converts. The administration would assign staff to help with records and to keep the system current each term, since schedules and the student population change. As soon as administrators thought it was feasible, they could give a big boost to the system by creating monetary incentives to car-pool. Students who participate in car-pooling could receive a tuition rebate—say, $100 a term for full-time students. Faculty and staff could receive equivalent bonuses. In addition, parking fees could be instituted to discourage driving to school.

Explanation of the proposed solution

The most obvious advantage of this proposal is that it would reduce car trips and thus reduce needless use of oil and pollution of the air. If the average length of a trip to or from BCC is 10 miles (a conservative number) and the average car gets 30 miles to the gallon (a generous number), then it takes only 3 trips to burn a gallon of gasoline. Saving just 600 trips a day would keep 200 gallons of gasoline in the pumps. The effects on air pollution can be seen in the example of carbon dioxide. Burning a single gallon of gasoline produces 20 pounds of carbon dioxide (New York Times 766), so a daily savings of 600 BCC trips would reduce carbon dioxide emissions by 4000 pounds.

Support for the proposal: first advantage

That unused gasoline would also save money for participants. If a full-time student drove half as often as now, the gasoline savings would be about $30 a term, plus the savings in wear and tear on the car. If the school instituted a $100 tuition rebate, the cash savings would rise to $130 a term. If the school instituted a parking fee of, say, $1 a day, the cash savings would rise to more than $160 a term. (All figures assume that car-pools consist of two people who share driving and expenses equally.)

Support for the proposal: second advantage

There are more abstract advantages, too. Individual freedom is a cherished right in our society, but it has no meaning outside the community.

Support for the proposal: third advantage

Like recycling and other environmental efforts, carpooling would ask the individual to make a sacrifice on behalf of the community. Car-poolers would be actively participating in something larger than themselves, instead of just furthering their own self-interest.

Members of the BCC administration may point out that the proposed program asks for sacrifice from the school as well. They may object that rebates or bonuses and the costs of running the program are not feasible given the school's tight budget. True, $100 rebates or bonuses for an estimated 600 participants would cost $60,000 a term, and administrative time would also cost something. But considerable money could be raised by instituting a dollar parking fee, which could produce as much as $1500 a day, nearly $100,000 a term, in revenue. Furthermore, sponsoring a car-pooling system is no more than many corporations do that encourage their employees to take public transportation by contributing to their monthly passes. Businesses, schools, and other institutions that require their people to assemble in one place should help reduce the environmental cost of commuting.

Probable opposing view and response

Of course, it is the cost of commuters' convenience that will probably make or break the program. Students and faculty may have to arrive at school earlier than they want or leave later because of their car-pools. While considerable, this inconvenience could over time be turned to an advantage if carpoolers learned to use their extra on-campus time wisely to prepare for classes (work they would have to do at home anyway). In addition, this inconvenience might seem worthwhile in exchange for helping the environment and the concrete rewards of a rebate or bonus and savings on parking.

Probable opposing view and response

It is no small flaw in the proposal that not all commuters would be able to participate in the program, even if they wanted to. The fact is that many part-time faculty and students have schedules that are too complicated or erratic to permit carpooling. Many teachers and students must make intermediate stops between their homes and BCC, such as for work. These commuters would not have access to the rebates or bonuses and still would be subject to the parking fee.

Probable opposing view

This unfairness is regrettable but, for now, unavoidable; we have to start somewhere. A change away from single-passenger cars to car-pools is like all other significant changes we must make on be-

Response to probable opposing view

Conclusion

60d

half of the environment. The shift in consciousness and responsibility will be halting and prolonged, and the costs and benefits will not always be distributed equally. One thing we can be sure of, however, is that the shift will not occur at all if we don't take the difficult first steps.

Work Cited

The New York Times 1999 Almanac. Ed. John W. Wright. New York: Penguin, 1998.

—LEE MORRISON

Glossary of Usage

Index

Glossary of Usage

Index

Glossary of Usage

This glossary provides notes on words or phrases that often cause problems for writers. The recommendations for standard written English are based on current dictionaries and usage guides. Items labeled NONSTANDARD should be avoided in speech and especially in writing. Those labeled COLLOQUIAL and SLANG occur in speech and in some informal writing but are best avoided in the more formal writing usually expected in college and business. (Words and phrases labeled *colloquial* include those labeled by many dictionaries with the equivalent term *informal*.)

a, an   Use *a* before words beginning with consonant sounds, including those spelled with an initial pronounced *h* and those spelled with vowels that are sounded as consonants: *a historian, a one-o'clock class, a university*. Use *an* before words that begin with vowel sounds, including those spelled with an initial silent *h: an orgy, an L, an honor*.

The article before an abbreviation depends on how the abbreviation is to be read: *She was once an AEC undersecretary* (*AEC* is to be read as three separate letters). *Many Americans opposed a SALT treaty* (*SALT* is to be read as one word, *salt*).

See also pp. 202–204 on the uses of *a/an* versus *the*.

accept, except   *Accept* is a verb meaning "receive." *Except* is usually a preposition or conjunction meaning "but for" or "other than"; when it is used as a verb, it means "leave out." *I can accept all your suggestions except the last one. I'm sorry you excepted my last suggestion from your list.*

advice, advise   *Advice* is a noun, and *advise* is a verb: *Take my advice; do as I advise you.*

affect, effect   Usually *affect* is a verb, meaning "to influence," and *effect* is a noun, meaning "result": *The drug did not affect his driving; in fact, it seemed to have no effect at all.* But *effect* occasionally is used as a verb meaning "to bring about": *Her efforts effected a change.* And *affect* is used in psychology as a noun meaning "feeling or emotion": *One can infer much about affect from behavior.*

agree to, agree with   *Agree to* means "consent to," and *agree with* means "be in accord with": *How can they agree to a treaty when they don't agree with each other about the terms?*

all ready, already   *All ready* means "completely prepared," and *already* means "by now" or "before now": *We were all ready to go to the movie, but it had already started.*

all right   *All right* is always two words. *Alright* is a common misspelling.

all together, altogether   *All together* means "in unison" or "gathered in one place." *Altogether* means "entirely." *It's not altogether true that our family never spends vacations all together.*

495

allusion, illusion   An *allusion* is an indirect reference, and an *illusion* is a deceptive appearance: *Paul's constant allusions to Shakespeare created the illusion that he was an intellectual.*

almost, most   *Almost* means "nearly"; *most* means "the greater number (or part) of." In formal writing, *most* should not be used as a substitute for *almost: We see each other almost [not most] every day.*

a lot   *A lot* is always two words, used informally to mean "many." *Alot* is a common misspelling.

among, between   In general, use *among* for relationships involving more than two people or for comparing one thing to a group to which it belongs. *The four of them agreed among themselves that the choice was between New York and Los Angeles.*

amount, number   Use *amount* with a singular noun that names something not countable (a noncount noun): *The amount of food varies.* Use *number* with a plural noun that names more than one of something countable (a plural count noun): *The number of calories must stay the same.*

and/or   *And/or* indicates three options: one or the other or both (*The decision is made by the mayor and/or the council*). If you mean all three options, *and/or* is appropriate. Otherwise, use *and* if you mean both, *or* if you mean either.

ante-, anti-   The prefix *ante-* means "before" (*antedate, antebellum*); *anti-* means "against" (*antiwar, antinuclear*). Before a capital letter or *i*, *anti-* takes a hyphen: *anti-Freudian, anti-isolationist.*

anxious, eager   *Anxious* means "nervous" or "worried" and is usually followed by *about. Eager* means "looking forward" and is usually followed by *to. I've been anxious about getting blisters. I'm eager [not anxious] to get new running shoes.*

anybody, any body; anyone, any one   *Anybody* and *anyone* are indefinite pronouns; *any body* is a noun modified by *any; any one* is a pronoun or adjective modified by *any. How can anybody communicate with any body of government? Can anyone help Amy? She has more work than any one person can handle.*

any more, anymore   *Any more* means "no more"; *anymore* means "now." Both are used in negative constructions. *He doesn't want any more. She doesn't live here anymore.*

apt, liable, likely   *Apt* and *likely* are interchangeable. Strictly speaking, though, *apt* means "having a tendency to": *Horace is apt to forget his lunch in the morning. Likely* means "probably going to": *Horace is leaving so early today that he's likely to catch the first bus.*

   Liable normally means "in danger of" and should be confined to situations with undesirable consequences: *Horace is liable to trip over that hose.* Strictly, *liable* means "responsible" or "exposed to": *The owner will be liable for Horace's injuries.*

are, is   Use *are* with a plural subject (*books are*), *is* with a singular subject (*book is*).

as   Substituting for *because, since,* or *while, as* may be vague or ambiguous: *As we were stopping to rest, we decided to eat lunch.* (Does *as* mean "while" or "because"?) *As* should never be used as a substitute for *whether* or *who. I'm not sure whether* [not *as*] *we can make it. That's the man who* [not *as*] *gave me directions.*

as, like   In formal speech and writing, *like* should not introduce a full clause (with a subject and a verb) because it is a preposition. The preferred choice is *as* or *as if: The plan succeeded as* [not *like*] *we hoped. It seemed as if* [not *like*] *it might fail. Other plans like it have failed.*

as, than   In comparisons, *as* and *than* precede a subjective-case pronoun when the pronoun is a subject: *I love you more than he* [*loves you*]. *As* and *than* precede an objective-case pronoun when the pronoun is an object: *I love you as much as* [*I love*] *him.* (See also p. 188.)

assure, ensure, insure   *Assure* means "to promise": *He assured us that we would miss the traffic. Ensure* and *insure* often are used interchangeably to mean "make certain," but some reserve *insure* for matters of legal and financial protection and use *ensure* for more general meanings: *We left early to ensure that we would miss the traffic. It's expensive to insure yourself against floods.*

at   The use of *at* after *where* is wordy and should be avoided: *Where are you meeting him?* is preferable to *Where are you meeting him at?*

awful, awfully   Strictly speaking, *awful* means "awe-inspiring." As intensifiers meaning "very" or "extremely" (*He tried awfully hard*), *awful* and *awfully* should be avoided in formal speech or writing.

a while, awhile   *Awhile* is an adverb; *a while* is an article and a noun. *I will be gone awhile* [not *a while*]. *I will be gone for a while* [not *awhile*].

bad, badly   In formal speech and writing, *bad* should be used only as an adjective; the adverb is *badly. He felt bad because his tooth ached badly.* In *He felt bad,* the verb *felt* is a linking verb and the adjective *bad* describes the subject. See also p. 198.

being as, being that   Colloquial for *because,* the preferable word in formal speech or writing: *Because* [not *Being as*] *the world is round, Columbus never did fall off the edge.*

beside, besides   *Beside* is a preposition meaning "next to." *Besides* is a preposition meaning "except" or "in addition to" as well as an adverb meaning "in addition." *Besides, several other people besides you want to sit beside Dr. Christensen.*

better, had better   *Had better* (meaning "ought to") is a verb modified by an adverb. The verb is necessary and should not be omitted: *You had better* [not *better*] *go.*

between, among   See *among, between.*

bring, take   Use *bring* only for movement from a farther place to a nearer one and *take* for any other movement. *First take these books to the library for renewal; then take them to Mr. Daniels. Bring them back to me when he's finished.*

Usage

but, hardly, scarcely These words are negative in their own right; using *not* with any of them produces a double negative (see p. 201). *We have but* [not *haven't got but*] *an hour before our plane leaves. I could hardly* [not *couldn't hardly*] *make out her face.*

but, however, yet Each of these words is adequate to express contrast. Don't combine them. *He said he had finished, yet* [not *but yet*] *he continued.*

can, may Strictly, *can* indicates capacity or ability, and *may* indicates permission: *If I may talk with you a moment, I believe I can solve your problem.*

censor, censure To *censor* is to edit or remove from public view on moral or some other grounds; to *censure* is to give a formal scolding. *The lieutenant was censured by Major Taylor for censoring the letters her soldiers wrote home from boot camp.*

center around *Center on* is more logical than, and preferable to, *center around.*

cite, sight, site *Cite* is a verb usually meaning "quote," "commend," or "acknowledge": *You must cite your sources. Sight* is both a noun meaning "the ability to see" or "a view" and a verb meaning "perceive" or "observe": *What a sight you see when you sight Venus through a strong telescope. Site* is a noun meaning "place" or "location" or a verb meaning "situate": *The builder sited the house on an unlikely site.*

climatic, climactic *Climatic* comes from *climate* and refers to the weather: *Last winter's temperatures may indicate a climatic change. Climactic* comes from *climax* and refers to a dramatic high point: *During the climactic duel between Hamlet and Laertes, Gertrude drinks poisoned wine.*

complement, compliment To *complement* something is to add to, complete, or reinforce it: *Her yellow blouse complemented her black hair.* To *compliment* something is to make a flattering remark about it: *He complimented her on her hair. Complimentary* can also mean "free": *complimentary tickets.*

conscience, conscious *Conscience* is a noun meaning "a sense of right and wrong"; *conscious* is an adjective meaning "aware" or "awake." *Though I was barely conscious, my conscience nagged me.*

contact Often used imprecisely as a verb instead of a more exact word such as *consult, talk with, telephone,* or *write to.*

continual, continuous *Continual* means "constantly recurring": *Most movies on television are continually interrupted by commercials. Continuous* means "unceasing": *Some cable channels present movies continuously without commercials.*

could of See *have, of.*

credible, creditable, credulous *Credible* means "believable": *It's a strange story, but it seems credible to me. Creditable* means "deserving of credit" or "worthy": *Steve gave a creditable performance. Credulous* means "gullible": *The credulous Claire believed Tim's lies.* See also *incredible, incredulous.*

criteria   The plural of *criterion* (meaning "standard for judgment"): *Our criteria are strict. The most important criterion is a sense of humor.*

data   The plural of *datum* (meaning "fact"). Though *data* is often used as a singular noun, most careful writers still treat it as plural: *The data fail* [not *fails*] *to support the hypothesis.*

device, devise   *Device* is the noun, and *devise* is the verb: *Can you devise some device for getting his attention?*

different from, different than   *Different from* is preferred: *His purpose is different from mine.* But *different than* is widely accepted when a construction using *from* would be wordy: *I'm a different person now than I used to be* is preferable to *I'm a different person now from the person I used to be.*

Usage

differ from, differ with   To *differ from* is to be unlike: *The twins differ from each other only in their hairstyles.* To *differ with* is to disagree with: *I have to differ with you on that point.*

discreet, discrete   *Discreet* (noun form *discretion*) means "tactful": *What's a discreet way of telling Maud to be quiet? Discrete* (noun form *discreteness*) means "separate and distinct": *Within a computer's memory are millions of discrete bits of information.*

disinterested, uninterested   *Disinterested* means "impartial": *We chose Pete, as a disinterested third party, to decide who was right. Uninterested* means "bored" or "lacking interest": *Unfortunately, Pete was completely uninterested in the question.*

don't   *Don't* is the contraction for *do not,* not for *does not: I don't care, you don't care,* and *he doesn't* [not *don't*] *care.*

due to the fact that   Wordy for *because.*

eager, anxious   See *anxious, eager.*

effect   See *affect, effect.*

elicit, illicit   *Elicit* is a verb meaning "bring out" or "call forth." *Illicit* is an adjective meaning "unlawful." *The crime elicited an outcry against illicit drugs.*

emigrate, immigrate   *Emigrate* means "to leave one place and move to another": *The Chus emigrated from Korea. Immigrate* means "to move into a place where one was not born": *They immigrated to the United States.*

ensure   See *assure, ensure, insure.*

enthused   Used colloquially as an adjective meaning "showing enthusiasm." The preferred adjective is *enthusiastic: The coach was enthusiastic* [not *enthused*] *about the team's victory.*

et al., etc.   Use *et al.,* the Latin abbreviation for "and other people," only in source citations: *Jones et al.* Avoid *etc.,* the Latin abbreviation for "and other things," in formal writing, and do not use it to refer to people or to substitute for precision, as in *The government provides health care, etc.*

everybody, every body; everyone, every one   *Everybody* and *everyone* are indefinite pronouns: *Everybody* [*everyone*] *knows Tom steals. Every one* is a pronoun modified by *every,* and *every body* a noun modified by *every.* Both refer to each thing or person of a specific group and are typically followed by *of: The game commissioner has stocked every body of fresh water in the state with fish, and now every one of our rivers is a potential trout stream.*

Usage

everyday, every day   *Everyday* is an adjective meaning "used daily" or "common"; *every day* is a noun modified by *every: Everyday problems tend to arise every day.*

everywheres   Nonstandard for *everywhere.*

except   See *accept, except.*

except for the fact that   Wordy for *except that.*

explicit, implicit   *Explicit* means "stated outright": *I left explicit instructions. Implicit* means "implied, unstated": *We had an implicit understanding.*

farther, further   *Farther* refers to additional distance (*How much farther is it to the beach?*), and *further* refers to additional time, amount, or other abstract matters (*I don't want to discuss this any further*).

fewer, less   *Fewer* refers to individual countable items (a plural count noun), *less* to general amounts (a noncount noun, always singular). *Skim milk has fewer calories than whole milk. We have less milk left than I thought.*

flaunt, flout   *Flaunt* means "show off"; *If you have style, flaunt it. Flout* means "scorn" or "defy": *Hester Prynne flouted convention and paid the price.*

flunk   A colloquial substitute for *fail.*

fun   As an adjective, *fun* is colloquial and should be avoided in most writing: *It was a pleasurable* [not *fun*] *evening.*

further   See *farther, further.*

get   This common verb is used in many slang and colloquial expressions: *get lost, that really gets me, getting on. Get* is easy to overuse: watch out for it in expressions such as *it's getting better* (substitute *improving*) and *we got done* (substitute *finished*).

good, well   *Good* is an adjective, and *well* is nearly always an adverb: *Larry's a good dancer. He and Linda dance well together. Well* is properly used as an adjective only to refer to health: *You look well.* (*You look good,* in contrast, means "Your appearance is pleasing.")

good and   Colloquial for "very": *I was very* [not *good and*] *tired.*

had better   See *better, had better.*

had ought The *had* is unnecessary and should be omitted: *He ought* [not *had ought*] *to listen to his mother.*

hanged, hung Though both are past-tense forms of *hang, hanged* is used to refer to executions and *hung* is used for all other meanings: *Tom Dooley was hanged* [not *hung*] *from a white oak tree. I hung* [not *hanged*] *the picture you gave me.*

hardly See *but, hardly, scarcely.*

have, of Use *have,* not *of,* after helping verbs such as *could, should, would, may,* and *might: You should have* [not *should of*] *told me.*

he, she; he/she Convention has allowed the use of *he* to mean "he or she": *After the infant learns to creep, he progresses to crawling.* However, many writers today consider this usage inaccurate and unfair because it seems to exclude females. The construction *he/she,* one substitute for *he,* is awkward and objectionable to most readers. The better choice is to make the pronoun plural, to rephrase, or, sparingly, to use *he or she.* For instance: *After infants learn to creep, they progress to crawling. After learning to creep, the infant progresses to crawling. After the infant learns to creep, he or she progresses to crawling.* See also pp. 120 and 191–192.

Usage

herself, himself See *myself, herself, himself, yourself.*

hisself Nonstandard for *himself.*

hopefully *Hopefully* means "with hope": *Freddy waited hopefully for a glimpse of Eliza.* The use of *hopefully* to mean "it is to be hoped," "I hope," or "let's hope" is now very common; but since many readers continue to object strongly to the usage, try to avoid it. *I hope* [not *Hopefully*] *the law will pass.*

idea, ideal An *idea* is a thought or conception. An *ideal* (noun) is a model of perfection or a goal. *Ideal* should not be used in place of *idea: The idea* [not *ideal*] *of the play is that our ideals often sustain us.*

if, whether For clarity, use *whether* rather than *if* when you are expressing an alternative: *If I laugh hard, people can't tell whether I'm crying.*

illicit See *elicit, illicit.*

illusion See *allusion, illusion.*

immigrate, emigrate See *emigrate, immigrate.*

implicit See *explicit, implicit.*

imply, infer Writers or speakers *imply,* meaning "suggest": *Jim's letter implies he's having a good time.* Readers or listeners *infer,* meaning "conclude": *From Jim's letter I infer he's having a good time.*

incredible, incredulous *Incredible* means "unbelievable"; *incredulous* means "unbelieving": *When Nancy heard Dennis's incredible story, she was frankly incredulous.* See also *credible, creditable, credulous.*

individual, person, party *Individual* should refer to a single human being in contrast to a group or should stress uniqueness: *The US Consti-*

tution places strong emphasis on the rights of the individual. For other meanings *person* is preferable: *What person* [not *individual*] *wouldn't want the security promised in that advertisement? Party* means "group" (*Can you seat a party of four for dinner?*) and should not be used to refer to an individual except in legal documents. See also *people, persons.*

infer   See *imply, infer.*

in regards to   Nonstandard for *in regard to, as regards,* or *regarding.*

inside of, outside of   The *of* is unnecessary when *inside* and *outside* are used as prepositions: *Stay inside* [not *inside of*] *the house. The decision is outside* [not *outside of*] *my authority. Inside of* may refer colloquially to time, though in formal English *within* is preferred: *The law was passed within* [not *inside of*] *a year.*

insure   See *assure, ensure, insure.*

irregardless   Nonstandard for *regardless.*

is, are   See *are, is.*

is because   See *reason is because.*

is when, is where   These are faulty constructions in sentences that define: *Adolescence is a stage* [not *is when a person is*] *between childhood and adulthood. Socialism is a system in which* [not *is where*] *government owns the means of production.* See also p. 220.

its, it's   *Its* is the pronoun *it* in the possessive case: *That plant is losing its leaves. It's* is a contraction for *it is: It's likely to die if you don't water it.* Many people confuse *it's* and *its* because possessives are most often formed with *-'s;* but the possessive *its,* like *his* and *hers,* never takes an apostrophe.

-ize, -wise   The suffix *-ize* changes a noun or adjective into a verb: *revolutionize, immunize.* The suffix *-wise* changes a noun or adjective into an adverb: *clockwise, otherwise, likewise.* Avoid the two suffixes except in established words: *I'm highly sensitive* [not *sensitized*] *to that kind of criticism. Financially* [not *Moneywise*], *it's a good time to buy real estate.*

kind of, sort of, type of   In formal speech and writing, avoid using *kind of* or *sort of* to mean "somewhat": *He was rather* [not *kind of*] *tall.*

   Kind, sort, and *type* are singular and take singular modifiers and verbs: *This kind of dog is easily trained.* Agreement errors often occur when these singular nouns are combined with the plural adjectives *these* and *those: These kinds* [not *kind*] *of dogs are easily trained. Kind, sort,* and *type* should be followed by *of* but not by *a. I don't know what type of* [not *type* or *type of a*] *dog that is.*

   Use *kind of, sort of,* or *type of* only when the word *kind, sort,* or *type* is important: *That was a strange* [not *strange sort of*] *statement.*

lay, lie   *Lay* means "put" or "place" and takes a direct object: *We could lay the tablecloth in the sun.* Its main forms are *lay, laid, laid. Lie* means "recline" or "be situated" and does not take an object: *I lie awake at night. The town lies east of the river.* Its main forms are *lie, lay, lain.* (See also p. 157.)

leave, let *Leave* and *let* are interchangeable only when followed by *alone; leave me alone* is the same as *let me alone.* Otherwise, *leave* means "depart" and *let* means "allow": *Jill would not let Sue leave.*

less See *fewer, less.*

liable See *apt, liable, likely.*

lie, lay See *lay, lie.*

like, as See *as, like.*

like, such as Strictly, *such as* precedes an example that represents a larger subject, whereas *like* indicates that two subjects are comparable. *Steve has recordings of many great saxophonists such as Ben Webster and Lee Konitz. Steve wants to be a great jazz saxophonist like Ben Webster and Lee Konitz.*

Usage

likely See *apt, liable, likely.*

literally This word means "actually" or "just as the words say," and it should not be used to qualify or intensify expressions whose words are not to be taken at face value. The sentence *He was literally climbing the walls* describes a person behaving like an insect, not a person who is restless or anxious. For the latter meaning, *literally* should be omitted.

lose, loose *Lose* means "mislay": *Did you lose a brown glove? Loose* means "unrestrained" or "not tight": *Ann's canary got loose. Loose* also can function as a verb meaning "let loose": *They loose the dogs as soon as they spot the bear.*

lots, lots of Colloquial substitutes for *very many, a great many,* or *much.* Avoid *lots* and *lots of* in college or business writing.

may, can See *can, may.*

may be, maybe *May be* is a verb, and *maybe* is an adverb meaning "perhaps": *Tuesday may be a legal holiday. Maybe we won't have classes.*

may of See *have, of.*

media *Media* is the plural of *medium* and takes a plural verb: *All the news media are increasingly visual.* The singular verb is common, even in the media, but most careful writers still use the plural verb.

might of See *have, of.*

moral, morale As a noun, *moral* means "ethical conclusion" or "lesson": *The moral of the story escapes me. Morale* means "spirit" or "state of mind": *Victory improved the team's morale.*

most, almost See *almost, most.*

must of See *have, of.*

myself, herself, himself, yourself The *-self* pronouns refer to or intensify another word or words: *Paul helped himself; Jill herself said so.* The *-self* pronouns are often used colloquially in place of personal pronouns, but that use should be avoided in formal speech and writing: *No* *one except me* [not *myself*] *saw the accident. Our delegates will be Susan and you* [not *yourself*].

nowheres   Nonstandard for *nowhere*.

number   See *amount, number*.

of, have   See *have, of*.

off of   *Of* is unnecessary. Use *off* or *from* rather than *off of: He jumped off* [or *from*, not *off of*] *the roof*.

OK, O.K., okay   All three spellings are acceptable, but avoid this colloquial term in formal speech and writing.

on account of   Wordy for *because of*.

on the other hand   This transitional expression of contrast should be preceded by its mate, *on the one hand: On the one hand, we hoped for snow. On the other hand, we feared that it would harm the animals.* However, the two combined can be unwieldy, and a simple *but, however, yet,* or *in contrast* often suffices: *We hoped for snow. Yet we feared that it would harm the animals.*

outside of   See *inside of, outside of*.

owing to the fact that   Wordy for *because*.

party   See *individual, person, party*.

people, persons   In formal usage, *people* refers to a general group: *We the people of the United States.... Persons* refers to a collection of individuals: *Will the person or persons who saw the accident please notify....* Except when emphasizing individuals, prefer *people* to *persons*. See also *individual, person, party*.

per   Except in technical writing, an English equivalent is usually preferable to the Latin *per: $10 an* [not *per*] *hour; sent by* [not *per*] *parcel post; requested in* [not *per* or *as per*] *your letter*.

percent (per cent), percentage   Both these terms refer to fractions of one hundred. *Percent* always follows a numeral (*40 percent of the voters*), and the word should be used instead of the symbol (%) in general writing. *Percentage* stands alone (*the percentage of voters*) or follows an adjective (*a high percentage*).

person   See *individual, person, party*.

persons   See *people, persons*.

phenomena   The plural of *phenomenon* (meaning "perceivable fact" or "unusual occurrence"): *Many phenomena are not recorded. One phenomenon is attracting attention*.

plenty   A colloquial substitute for *very: The reaction occurred very* [not *plenty*] *fast*.

plus   *Plus* is standard as a preposition meaning "in addition to": *His income plus mine is sufficient.* But *plus* is colloquial as a conjunctive adverb: *Our organization is larger than theirs; moreover* [not *plus*], *we have more money.*

precede, proceed   The verb *precede* means "come before": *My name precedes yours in the alphabet.* The verb *proceed* means "move on": *We were told to proceed to the waiting room.*

prejudice, prejudiced   *Prejudice* is a noun; *prejudiced* is an adjective. Do not drop the *-d* from *prejudiced: I was fortunate that my parents were not prejudiced* [not *prejudice*].

pretty   Overworked as an adverb meaning "rather" or "somewhat": *He was somewhat* [not *pretty*] *irked at the suggestion.*

previous to, prior to   Wordy for *before.*

Usage

principal, principle   *Principal* is an adjective meaning "foremost" or "major," a noun meaning "chief official," or, in finance, a noun meaning "capital sum." *Principle* is a noun only, meaning "rule" or "axiom." *Her principal reasons for confessing were her principles of right and wrong.*

proceed, precede   See *precede, proceed.*

question of whether, question as to whether   Wordy substitutes for *whether.*

raise, rise   *Raise* means "lift" or "bring up" and takes a direct object: *The Kirks raise cattle.* Its main forms are *raise, raised, raised. Rise* means "get up" and does not take an object: *They must rise at dawn.* Its main forms are *rise, rose, risen.* (See also p. 157.)

real, really   In formal speech and writing, *real* should not be used as an adverb; *really* is the adverb and *real* an adjective. *Popular reaction to the announcement was really* [not *real*] *enthusiastic.*

reason is because   Although colloquially common, this expression should be avoided in formal speech and writing. Use a *that* clause after *reason is: The reason he is absent is that* [not *is because*] *he is sick.* Or: *He is absent because he is sick.* (See also p. 221.)

respectful, respective   *Respectful* means "full of (or showing) respect": *Be respectful of other people. Respective* means "separate": *The French and the Germans occupied their respective trenches.*

rise, raise   See *raise, rise.*

scarcely   See *but, hardly, scarcely.*

sensual, sensuous   *Sensual* suggests sexuality; *sensuous* means "pleasing to the senses." *Stirred by the sensuous scent of meadow grass and flowers, Cheryl and Paul found their thoughts growing increasingly sensual.*

set, sit   *Set* means "put" or "place" and takes a direct object: *He sets the pitcher down.* Its main forms are *set, set, set. Sit* means "be seated" and does not take an object: *She sits on the sofa.* Its main forms are *sit, sat, sat.* (See also p. 157.)

shall, will   *Will* is the future-tense helping verb for all persons: *I will go, you will go, they will go.* The main use of *shall* is for first-person questions requesting an opinion or consent: *Shall I order a pizza? Shall we dance? Shall* can also be used for the first person when a formal effect is desired (*I shall expect you around three*), and it is occasionally used with the second or third person to express the speaker's determination (*You shall do as I say*).

should of   See *have, of.*

sight, site, cite   See *cite, sight, site.*

since   *Since* mainly relates to time: *I've been waiting since noon.* But *since* is also often used to mean "because": *Since you ask, I'll tell you.* Revise sentences in which the word could have either meaning, such as *Since you left, my life is empty.*

sit, set   See *set, sit.*

site, cite, sight   See *cite, sight, site.*

so   Avoid using *so* alone or as a vague intensifier: *He was so late. So* needs to be followed by *that* and a clause that states a result: *He was so late that I left without him.*

somebody, some body; someone, some one   *Somebody* and *someone* are indefinite pronouns; *some body* is a noun modified by *some;* and *some one* is a pronoun or an adjective modified by *some. Somebody ought to invent a shampoo that will give hair some body. Someone told Janine she should choose some one plan and stick with it.*

sometime, sometimes, some time   *Sometime* means "at an indefinite time in the future": *Why don't you come up and see me sometime? Sometimes* means "now and then": *I still see my old friend Joe sometimes. Some time* means "a span of time": *I need some time to make the payments.*

somewheres   Nonstandard for *somewhere.*

sort of, sort of a   See *kind of, sort of, type of.*

such   Avoid using *such* as a vague intensifier: *It was such a cold winter. Such* should be followed by *that* and a clause that states a result: *It was such a cold winter that Napoleon's troops had to turn back.*

such as   See *like, such as.*

supposed to, used to   In both these expressions, the *-d* is essential: *I used to* [not *use to*] *think so. He's supposed to* [not *suppose to*] *meet us.*

sure   Colloquial when used as an adverb meaning *surely: James Madison sure was right about the need for the Bill of Rights.* If you merely want to be emphatic, use *certainly: Madison certainly was right.* If your goal is to convince a possibly reluctant reader, use *surely: Madison surely was right.*

sure and, sure to; try and, try to   *Sure to* and *try to* are the correct forms: *Be sure to* [not *sure and*] *buy milk. Try to* [not *Try and*] *find some decent tomatoes.*

take, bring   See *bring, take.*

than, as   See *as, than.*

than, then   *Than* is a conjunction used in comparisons, *then* an adverb indicating time: *Holmes knew then that Moriarty was wilier than he had thought.*

that, which   *That* introduces an essential clause: *We should use the lettuce that Susan bought* (*that Susan bought* limits the lettuce to a particular lettuce). *Which* can introduce both essential and nonessential clauses, but many writers reserve *which* only for nonessential clauses: *The leftover lettuce, which is in the refrigerator, would make a good salad* (*which is in the refrigerator* simply provides more information about the lettuce we already know of). Essential clauses (with *that* or *which*) are not set off by commas; nonessential clauses (with *which*) are. See also pp. 230–232.

that, which, who   Use *that* for animals, things, and sometimes collective or anonymous people: *The rocket that failed cost millions. Infants that walk need constant tending.* Use *which* only for animals and things: *The river, which flows south, divides two countries.* Use *who* only for people and for animals with names: *Dorothy is the girl who visits Oz. Her dog, Toto, who accompanies her, gives her courage.*

their, there, they're   *Their* is the possessive form of *they: Give them their money. There* indicates place (*I saw her standing there*) or functions as an expletive (*There is a hole behind you*). *They're* is a contraction for *they are: They're going fast.*

theirselves   Nonstandard for *themselves.*

then, than   See *than, then.*

these kind, these sort, these type, those kind   See *kind of, sort of, type of.*

this, these   *This* is singular: *this car* or *This is the reason I left. These* is plural: *these cars* or *These are not valid reasons.*

thru   A colloquial spelling of *through* that should be avoided in all academic and business writing.

to, too, two   *To* is a preposition; *too* is an adverb meaning "also" or "excessively"; and *two* is a number. *I too have been to Europe two times.*

too   Avoid using *too* as an intensifier meaning "very": *Monkeys are too mean.* If you do use *too*, explain the consequences of the excessive quality: *Monkeys are too mean to make good pets.*

toward, towards   Both are acceptable, though *toward* is preferred. Use one or the other consistently.

try and, try to   See *sure and, sure to; try and, try to.*

type of   See *kind of, sort of, type of.* Don't use *type* without *of: It was a family type of* [not *type*] *restaurant.* Or better: *It was a family restaurant.*

uninterested   See *disinterested, uninterested.*

unique   *Unique* means "the only one of its kind" and so cannot sensibly be modified with words such as *very* or *most*: *That was a unique* [not *a very unique* or *the most unique*] *movie.*

usage, use   *Usage* refers to conventions, most often those of a language: *Is "hadn't ought" proper usage? Usage* is often misused in place of the noun *use: Wise use* [not *usage*] *of insulation can save fuel.*

use, utilize   *Utilize* can be used to mean "make good use of": *Many teachers utilize computers for instruction.* But for all other senses of "place in service" or "employ," prefer *use.*

Usage

used to   See *supposed to, used to.*

wait for, wait on   In formal speech and writing, *wait for* means "await" (*I'm waiting for Paul*) and *wait on* means "serve" (*The owner of the store herself waited on us*).

ways   Colloquial as a substitute for *way: We have only a little way* [not *ways*] *to go.*

well   See *good, well.*

whether, if   See *if, whether.*

which, that   See *that, which.*

which, who, that   See *that, which, who.*

who's, whose   *Who's* is the contraction of *who is: Who's at the door? Whose* is the possessive form of *who: Whose book is that?*

will, shall   See *shall, will.*

-wise   See *-ize, -wise.*

would have   Avoid this construction in place of *had* in clauses that begin *if* and state a condition contrary to fact: *If the tree had* [not *would have*] *withstood the fire, it would have been the oldest in town.* See also p. 175.

would of   See *have, of.*

you   In all but very formal writing, *you* is generally appropriate as long as it means "you, the reader." In all writing, avoid indefinite uses of *you,* such as *In one ancient tribe your first loyalty was to your parents.* See also pp. 195–196.

your, you're   *Your* is the possessive form of *you: Your dinner is ready. You're* is the contraction of *you are: You're bound to be late.*

yourself   See *myself, herself, himself, yourself.*

Index

Index

Index

Index

Index

Index

ESL GUIDE

Throughout the handbook the symbol **ESL** signals topics of special interest to writers using English as a second language. This index arranges the topics for easy reference. Because ESL material is thoroughly integrated with the rest of the handbook, you can follow any of the page numbers given to reach a broader discussion of the topic as well.

CONTENTS

EDITING SYMBOLS

Boldface numbers and letters refer to chapters and sections of the handbook.

ab	Faulty abbreviation, **45**
ad	Misuse of adjective or adverb, **29**
agr	Error in agreement, **25, 27**
ap	Apostrophe needed or mis-used, **38**
appr	Inappropriate word, **14a**
arg	Faulty argument, **51**
awk	Awkward construction
cap	Use capital letter, **43**
case	Error in case form, **26**
cit	Missing source citation or error in form of citation, **50**
coh	Coherence lacking, **4, 6**
con	Be more concise, **16**
coord	Coordination needed, **11**
cs	Comma splice, **32**
d	Ineffective diction (word choice), **14**
det	Error in use of determiner, **29f**
dm	Dangling modifier, **30**
emph	Emphasis lacking or faulty, **11**
exact	Inexact word, **14**
frag	Sentence fragment, **31**
fs	Fused sentence, **32**
gr	Error in grammar, **17–20**
hyph	Error in use of hyphen, **42**
inc	Incomplete construction, **15**
ital	Italicize or underline, **44**
k	Awkward construction
lc	Use lowercase letter, **43**
mixed	Mixed construction, **33**
mm	Misplaced modifier, **30**
mng	Meaning unclear
no cap	Unnecessary capital letter, **43**
no ⌃	Comma not needed, **35**
no ¶	No new paragraph needed, **6**
num	Error in use of numbers, **46**
p	Error in punctuation, **34–40**
. ? !	Period, question mark, exclamation point, **34**
⌃	Comma, **35**
;	Semicolon, **36**

:	Colon, **37**
⌄	Apostrophe, **38**
" "	Quotation marks, **39**
— ( ) . . . [ ] /	Dash, parentheses, ellipsis mark, brackets, slash, **40**
par, ¶	Start new paragraph, **6**
¶ coh	Paragraph not coherent, **6**
¶ dev	Paragraph not developed, **6**
¶ un	Paragraph not unified, **6**
pass	Ineffective passive voice, **24**
pn agr	Error in pronoun-antecedent agreement, **27**
ref	Error in pronoun reference, **28**
rep	Unnecessary repetition, **16**
rev	Revise or proofread, **6**
run-on	Run-on (fused) sentence, **32**
shift	Inconsistency, **22, 23, 24, 28**
sp	Misspelled word, **41**
spec	Be more specific, **6, 14**
sub	Subordination needed or faulty, **11**
t	Error in verb tense, **22**
t seq	Error in tense sequence, **22**
trans	Transition needed, **6**
und	Underline (italicize), **44**
usage	See Glossary of Usage, p. 493
var	Vary sentence structure, **13**
vb	Error in verb form, **21**
vb agr	Error in subject-verb agreement, **25**
w	Wordy, **16**
ww	Wrong word, **14**
//	Faulty parallelism, **12**
#	Separate with a space
⌒	Close up the space
⸜	Delete
t⌒e⌒h	Transpose letters or words
x	Obvious error
∧	Something missing, **15**
??	Manuscript illegible or meaning unclear